The Emergence of the Modern American Theater, 1914–1929

The Emergence
of the Modern
American Theater
1914–1929

Ronald H. Wainscott

Yale University Press

New Haven and London

Library of Congress
Cataloging-in-Publication Data

Wainscott, Ronald Harold, 1948–
    The emergence of the modern American theater, 1914–1929 / Ronald H. Wainscott.
        p. cm.
    Includes bibliographical references and index.
    ISBN 0–300–06776—3 (C : alk. paper)
    1. Theater—United States—History—20th century. 2. American drama—20th century—History and criticism.
    I. Title.
    PN2266.3.W35   1997
    792'.0973'09041—dc20   96–31372
                                                              CIP

A catalogue record for this book is available from the British Library.

The paper in this book meets the guidelines for permanence and durability of the Committee on Production Guidelines for Book Longevity of the Council on Library Resources.

10 9 8 7 6 5 4 3 2 1

For Jeremy Fletcher Wainscott

Contents

Illustrations follow page　　　　　　　118

Preface　　　　　　　　　　　　　　　ix

1 Introduction　　　　　　　　　　　　1

2 Drama in the Trenches from *War Brides*
to *What Price Glory*　　　　　　　　7

3 The American Theater Versus the Congress
of the United States　　　　　　　　37

4 She Would Be Erotic: The Virtuous Role
of the Postwar Sex Farceuse　　　　　53

5 Popular Culture at the Crossroads:
Wooing Censorship with *The Demi-Virgin*　　75

6 The Vogue of Expressionism in Postwar America   91

7 The Calvin Coolidge Grand Tour   141

8 *Red Dawn* to *Red Rust:*
The Russian Revolution and Visions of Shifting
Political Power in Postwar Drama   164

Afterword   188

Appendix: The Sex Farces That Appeared
Between 1915 and 1921   191

Notes   193

Bibliography   223

Index   253

Preface

The preparation of this book began with the research for my last one, *Staging O'Neill: The Experimental Years, 1920–1934* (1988). As I searched newspapers for material about the initial productions of Eugene O'Neill, I encountered mysterious references to a major conflict between the U.S. Congress and theatrical producers in New York soon after World War I. I was intrigued and surprised that I had never read anything about a showdown between the professional theater and the federal government. But my exploration of this event had to wait until the O'Neill book was completed. Further along the way in the O'Neill book, censorship struggles over sex farces and the impact of World War I on the American theater battled for my attention, but I assumed that each of these topics would comprise a separate project, not realizing until later that these and other events and developments of the postwar, pre-Depression era were interrelated and could best be explored under the same critical and historical umbrella in a second book. As my new work proceeded, it became increasingly clear that I needed to include the war years themselves for analysis of the theater in the 1920s.

As a result, the essential historical boundaries of my study are 1914 to 1929, with occasional forays to 1911 or 1912, and sometimes earlier. Key early years, however, are 1915 (which marked the crystallization of the New Stagecraft in design), 1917 (when the United States officially entered the Great War), and 1919 (the first full year after the Armistice, the time of the congressional-theatrical conflict, the actors' strike, the Red Scare, and the launching of a new era of dramatic activity).

The chapters do not proceed in a linear march, although each chapter is basically chronological in its presentation of events. Each chapter returns to the beginning of my period to elucidate the rather complex skein of activity. Just as living through events can be confusing and unfocused, so can a parade of historical retracing if it fails to be refocused for the reader. I have endeavored to do this to emphasize historical themes and developments that have gone unnoticed, especially in histories of theater and the development of drama in the United States. Although I have separated dramatic practice and themes into categories like the praise or censure of the big-business ethic and the paranoid reaction to Communism, I have at the same time tried to link them to each other, as well as to the other themes examined within the book.

I draw on many contemporary reviews, not because their criticism is always incisive (although this is often the case) but because if we are to understand the significance of the artistic experiences both when they occurred and today, we must understand the critical responses to the plays and productions when they were new. Even reactionary and misinterpretive reviews are helpful; sometimes they are more representative of popular responses to difficult and challenging events than more insightful articles. It is easy in retrospect to ridicule "wrong-headed" criticism, and I hope I have avoided this trap, although occasionally the unintentional humor of a review is difficult to resist.

As is typical in endeavors like this, my acknowledgments are legion, and I trust I have included all who have made positive contributions to the text. Suggestions come from many, but the responsibility for the final text, with whatever inadvertent omissions or errors, is entirely mine. I wish to thank the Research Council of the University of Nebraska-Lincoln for their support in granting me a stipend for a revision of this text. I am also indebted to my former department chair, Tice Miller, for his encouragement throughout this project. The final revision was completed at Indiana University. For the use of unpublished materials I must thank the Special Collections division and Law Library of the Library of Congress, Mary Ellen Brooks and the Hargrett Rare Book and Manuscript Library of the University of Georgia Libraries, and Mary Ann Jensen and the William Seymour Theatre Collection, Department of Rare Books and Special Collections of the Princeton University Libraries.

My thanks to the interlibrary loan staff of the Love Library of the University of Nebraska for tracking down a number of the unusual items my research always seems to require. I also wish to thank Gary Jay Williams, editor of *Theatre Survey*, and Robert Schanke, editor of *Theatre History Studies*, for permission to reprint material from my articles on the tax controversy and *The Demi-Virgin*, which appeared in those periodicals in the issues of May 1990 (volume 31) and 1990 (volume 10), respectively. I also wish to thank Judith Milhous and Ron Engle, the former editors of those journals, who published the original articles. Thanks also to co-editors Ron Engle and Tice Miller and to Sarah Stanton and Cambridge University Press for permission to use material from my article on commercialism that appears in *The American Stage: Social and Economic Issues from the Colonial Period to the Present* (1993).

I offer special thanks to my graduate students at the University of Nebraska who made suggestions and asked pointed questions, thus leading me to ideas or to new questions that had a significant impact on portions of this book. In particular, Michael Solomonson and Layne Ehlers uncovered materials that made their way into text or notes and enhanced the manuscript. To my California colleague Al Weissberg—one of the few people I have encountered who shared an interest in the sex farces without my prodding—I give thanks for helpful suggestions about theatrical producer Al Woods. I also extend my thanks to Kim Marra of the University of Iowa for bringing an unpublished manuscript to my attention and to Rosemarie K. Bank of Kent State University for inviting me to present a paper on Eugene O'Neill that led me to new assessments of several of his plays. Tom Postlewait of Ohio State University provided helpful suggestions after his reading of the text in an earlier form, and I am indebted to him for introducing me to the essays of Warren Susman and emphasizing the importance of cultural history to my work. The keen editorial eye and helpful suggestions of Otto Bohlmann and Susan Laity of Yale University Press are much appreciated.

To my wife, Kathy Fletcher, I cannot properly acknowledge my gratitude for her direct contributions, such as offering incisive suggestions after reading portions of the text, or her indirect contributions: affording me precious periods of uninterrupted writing time without bombardment from our two wonderful but loquacious children, Jeremy and Kendra. As I have expressed before, the unrepayable debt endures. I must also thank Jeremy Fletcher Wainscott, my inquisitive son, who at the ages of four and five spent many an hour with me at this computer keyboard entering functions (his favorite seemed to be creating footnotes), usually with accuracy. Without his talkative presence (replete as it is with a barrage of questions) I suspect the text would have been quite different.

1

Introduction

Acknowledging and living with ambivalence is, in a way, what America was invented to do.

—Roger Rosenblatt

"After years of war," an anonymous review observed in 1919, "the audience is coming back to the theatre ready for anything." Theater artists in the 1920s redefined the direction of American theater for decades to come, especially in terms of playwriting, stage direction, and scenic design. These ten years of turmoil featured conflicting cultural, social, economic, and political events (both foreign and domestic), clashing artistic tastes, dramatic upheavals, and dynamic theatrical experiments that shaped and promoted a distinctly American theater practice and dramatic form. The theatrical problems and developments explored here began earlier, most in 1915 or 1917, but each came to a head after—often well after—the Armistice. Although the increasing popularity of film (especially following the advent of motion pictures with sound), the fascination with radio, the skyrocketing popularity of commercialism as part of the "culture of abundance," and the economic crash each played a role in the inevitable decline of live theater as a popular form after 1929, even victories, like the successful struggle to defeat the new theater tax that mobilized a nationwide audience in 1919, can also be linked ironically to the fading of the theater.[1]

Most of the memorable American theatrical work between 1915 and 1929 is characterized by the violent, the pathetic, the satiric, the outrageous, or the incomprehensible. By *incomprehensible* I mean a dramatic literature or theatrical event that reflects the inability of characters, and sometimes playwrights, to comprehend the pervasively violent or overwhelming nature of the world being dramatized. Such drama raises many troubling but poignant questions yet rarely supplies answers. Conversely, much dramatic literature of the 1930s glibly, if angrily, takes the opposite position, providing facile answers thought to be readily apparent in, for example, left-wing socialist ideology. Although some playwrights offered occasional solutions to American social and economic problems in the 1920s, providing plays with all the answers in the 1930s created simplistic drama. Not surprisingly, many left-wing playwrights and critics of the 1930s considered the ambivalent 1920s a limited theatrical era because the playwrights were "unenlightened." This point of view has persisted long beyond the 1930s, resulting in the dismissal of the social efforts of the 1920s as trivial by most critics who prefer 1930s drama. By such reasoning Ibsen, Strindberg, and Chekhov (who likewise provided difficult social and domestic questions without offering solutions) would be considered inferior to the French thesis writers Alexandre Dumas fils and Emile Augier.

From 1919 to the stock-market crash, Broadway theater could boast of being the most prolific and profitable of the professional performing arts in American life. But the theater never completely recovered from the losses it suffered in the Great Depression. Both the tax rebellion of 1919 and the closing of legitimate theaters after 1929 were inextricably connected with economics and shifting social and cultural forces, as well as with the rapidly changing status of film and radio.

These chapters comprise a critical and historical examination of significant plays and productions, along with nontheatrical events, of the era, concentrating on the contradictory nature of theatrical incidents in an age that represents Broadway at its most commercial and extensive, but also Broadway as an intrepid theatrical experimenter. The postwar, pre-Depression era represents the only period in which one could find experimental plays opening in Broadway houses as a matter of course. It was the heyday of American expressionism, although this term was less the description of a movement or specific style than an artistic umbrella for a host of nonrealistic experiments.

Examination of the theater in this period reveals trends, aberrations at first assumed to be trends, and conflicting lines of dramatic development that we can understand by acknowledging the unusual cultural, social, economic, or political issues of the period. Contradictory and ambivalent elements (both inside and outside the theater) contributed to—and sometimes dictated—dramatic form and content, theatrical styles, and the success or failure of artistic products. Much of this activity can be characterized as the clash of modernism versus tradition, or what was assumed to be traditional. What American postwar society produced, in cultural historian Michael Kammen's words, was a "revival of traditionalism" rather than a continuation of tradition, that arose simultaneously with the more familiar "intrusive thrust of modernism" to create an eccentric symbiosis. Modernism and traditionalism "flourished, in part, as a critical response to the other. Most of the time, however, there was little if any recognition that an oxymoronic condition persisted: nostalgic modernism."[2]

The after-effects of World War I, for example, and the American experience in Europe clearly advanced a growing seriousness in the subject matter deemed appropriate for the New York stage. New attempts at tragic, violent, and psychologically scathing material filled American theaters, yet from 1919 until 1924 most treatments of the war experience itself were comic, farcical, or heroically melodramatic. In 1924, when *What Price Glory,* by Maxwell Anderson and Laurence Stallings, appeared, the play was perceived by most critics as a violation of a barrier that was all but imaginary. This play was nonetheless momentous as an expression of the war experience, and along with the plays of Eugene O'Neill it broadened the acceptable limits of stage language and contributed unwittingly to the theater's struggles with censorship. These attempts reached a crisis in 1921 before censorship spiraled out of control in late 1924 with the formation of a citizens play jury system, which was replaced in 1927 by the ominous Wales Padlock Law.

World War I and its consequences are central to an understanding of the development of American theater in the 1920s. Before the war, in the words of Paul Fussell, the world was comparatively static, "the values appeared stable and . . . the meanings of abstractions seemed permanent and reliable."[3] Afterward no one could be quite confident of the rules. In spite of the proverbial devil-may-care spirit associated with the twenties, the effects of the war and the memory of that debacle were perpetuated pervasively in American drama until the next cataclysmic event, the Great Depression. One supreme irony informs most of the examination of the history that follows: the Allies engaged in World War I purportedly to defend and preserve the society, values, culture, and way of life, as well as the democratic principles of the European and

American countries. Yet that very war, owing in large part to its massive number of participants and its four-year duration, destroyed or enabled the destruction of these social forms and cultural expressions.

Throughout the decade following the Great War the word *civilization* and what it seemed to represent was repeatedly attacked or redefined by myriad intellectuals, artists, and journalists. Many wondered whether the character of modern civilization had permanently changed or whether it had indeed vanished—a victim not only of the war but of the onslaught of the industrial complex, the destruction of manners, and the creation of a crass, consumer world. Cultural historian Warren Susman relates this as an obsession of many writers of the period: "The great fear . . . is whether any great industrial and democratic mass society can maintain a significant level of civilization, and whether mass education and mass communication will allow any civilization to survive."[4]

Many American theater artists regarded their transforming world as a way of life destroyed, a culture dispossessed. For some, adjustment to such loss proved not only difficult but impossible. Consequently, a majority of the plays examined here express the confusion, anger, nihilism, celebration, and reactionism inevitable under such circumstances.

The defense of the American theater by the commonweal against the ravages of Congress just after the Armistice could lead one to believe that the tenets of the prewar theater were being defended, yet Americans were unwittingly standing up for an anachronism. The American theater was already irrevocably remodeling itself in darker and more experimental tones and images. Simultaneously, the position of the theater as the popular center of the performing arts had become endangered by the burgeoning popularity of film, which would soon demonstrate its superiority in fabricating realism and naturalism. Yet few envisioned that the theater, which continued to increase in popularity throughout the 1920s, was on a joyride, much like the stock market of the same decade. The reduction of the theater to a minority art form was inevitable with the rise of film, radio, and later television—even without the horrendous blows given it by the Great Depression.

The postwar, pre-Depression theater was not only the most prolific in American history (the high-water mark quantitatively was reached in the season of 1927–28, when Broadway theaters opened 264 different productions) but, in terms of experiment, perhaps the most exciting.[5] This period may also be the most difficult to assess politically and socially. Remarkable, conflicting, reactionary and liberating forces assailed dramatic criticism, playwriting, spatial and decorative interpretation, directorial authority and conceptualization, and anachronistic acting. Perhaps most important, commercial management was often caught between a business-as-usual exploitation and the newly enshrined values of the art theater. Nonetheless, this is a period that is usually simplified and generalized in popular histories so that it is difficult for most of us to imagine the 1920s without invoking the icons of Lucky Lindy, Charlie Chaplin's Little Tramp, soaring hemlines, bobbed hair, open roadsters, and wild Prohibition revels in bathtub gin—images that so swamp the popular notion of the period that these cosmetic reflections, these shadows of excess, *become* the history of the period.

For many students of drama, the history of the American theater in the 1920s is Eugene O'Neill. As dynamic as he was in this period, such a perception is unfortunate, for his work is rarely emblematic of the period. He forged his own fascinating trail, which wound through the 1920s without necessarily characterizing it. As critic Alan Downer writes: "No play that survives its generation is altogether typical of that generation."[6] Because his work is so familiar and expressive, however, O'Neill is useful as a gauge for evaluating or comparing the work of others, and I employ him as such throughout. The other theater artists examined here include both experimenters and popular Broadwayites, whose contributions resulted in modern tragedy and sex farces, Red-baiting and paeans to socialist ideology, worship of big business and gloomy depictions of the depersonalization of workers. I also analyze the litigation that jeopardized the integrity of artistic expression as well as the gaudy but riveting real-life melodrama of the courtroom that sometimes turned to disputatious farce.

Many of these theater artists reflect European influences that invaded the American artistic landscape during and especially after the war. Once the Atlantic had been traversed by so many American neophytes (soldiers, nurses, and entertainers), the European artistic and cultural changes that had been developing since the 1880s infiltrated the isolationist and artistically conservative United States. The New Stagecraft, symbolism, expressionism, and grittier realism premiered together, as if they were simultaneous, even related, developments. On the professional American stage, for example, expressionism and surrealism were blurred into a single theatrical style—as they continue to be in television advertising and music videos.

Much of what characterizes the American theater between the wars, however, bears little reference to Europe. The notorious sex farces of the era simultaneously entertained, bored, outraged, or titillated American audiences. Concomitant with the escalating openness and sexuality of these popular entertainments were the calls for censorship, which continued to affect serious plays of social or political import long after the success of the sex farces. Censorship struggles reflected an insistence on transforming the performing arts into an arena where any idea could be discussed or dramatized. As is usual with American reactionaries, the focus remained on sexuality, profanity, and public morality.

In the prewar twentieth century many immigrants from outside the traditional Anglo-Saxon Protestant sphere arrived on American shores. Alarmed conservative responses to this influx led to severe restrictions on immigration, beginning with the time of the American entrance into World War I. At the same time, the women's movement was gaining strength. In 1920, while America was struggling with a postwar economic recession, the Nineteenth Amendment (women's suffrage) achieved ratification, and the following year the American Birth Control League, spearheaded by Margaret Sanger, appeared. Immigration as well as women's rights and suffrage contributed to cultural conflict along racial, religious, political, and gender lines that found artistic expression in the theater.

Equally prominent after the war, and certainly related to the immigration "problem," was the American Red Scare following the Russian Revolution. Although the collective paranoia appeared to recede in a few years, it returned after World War II. The wartime Espionage and Sedition Acts and Trading with the Enemy Acts had been passed in 1917 and 1918, but fears about the Russian Revolution kept some of these laws in force beyond the Armistice. Especially alarming was the Spartican Revolt in Berlin, which suggested to many a global spread of Communism, a fear that was reinforced by the Wall Street bombing in 1920 believed to be the work of foreign anarchists. For a few years the journalistic and theatrical responses to revolutionary events were extraordinary in scope, and they continued throughout the 1920s, even as they underwent a metamorphosis. What was first expressed as near panic and scare tactics by anti-Communists became Bolshevik jokes and caricaturish Russian revolutionaries, which eventually became sympathetically drawn rebels and socialists—even anarchists.

The development of the stage revolutionist in the 1920s bears an inverse relation to the evolution of the big-business magnate, who was so characteristic of the 1920s. While the image of the revolutionist evolved from a negative to positive, that of the commercial zealot altered from social role model to obsessive monster. These shifts appeared just as the United States was transforming to a mass-consumption society and economy—the first successful such society in the world. These changes in artistically perceived political and commercial figures preceded the stock-market crash, and they were not confined to radical voices in Greenwich Village. The commercial drama and theater of Broadway transformed itself. What follows is an account of that theatrical renovation.

2

Drama in the Trenches from *War Brides* to *What Price Glory*

[Before World War I] there were few problems incapable of solution in this oversize Eden.
—Alan S. Downer

There ain't going to be any after-this-war.
—Maxwell Anderson and Laurence Stallings, *What Price Glory*

At the close of *The Proud Tower,* Barbara Tuchman writes that after the Great War, "illusions and enthusiasms possible up to 1914 slowly sank beneath a sea of massive disillusionment. For the price it had paid, humanity's major gain was a painful view of its own limitations."[1] It is difficult to ignore some 8.5 to 10 million dead combatants and 20 million dead civilians scattered across Europe, as well as two hundred thousand wounded soldiers who returned to the United States. The aftershocks of World War I reverberated in the American theater, not only in plays about warfare, the American experience in France, and homecomings both melancholy and farcical but in the growth of seriousness in subject matter now deemed appropriate for the stage, in the grittier language, and in the newfound freedom of American playwrights and theatrical practitioners to experiment. Although there were some fresh attempts at tragic, violent, and psychologically scathing material, most treatments of the war experience were comic or sentimentally melodramatic until *What Price Glory* shocked its first audience. *What Price Glory* remains seminal in terms of its honest and scorching portrayal of the war experience, but this play was by no means the first to treat the war seriously.[2]

Traditional analysis of postwar American drama assumes that the war was all but ignored until *What Price Glory*. The following 1991 assessment is typical: "The extensive social upheavals of wartime prompted a swift departure from the past; but, like all catalysts, the war contributed to the process without becoming an integral part of it. The conflict itself faded into the background. [*What Price Glory* is noted as the exception.]. . . On the whole, the war was largely ignored by American dramatists in developing their ideas and themes."[3] On the contrary, the parade of World War I plays professionally produced in New York alone numbered at least twenty-eight from the outbreak of war to the American declaration of war on April 6, 1917. From this date to the Armistice, another thirty-four war plays were added. And yet another thirty-four were produced before *What Price Glory*. By the fall of the stock market the Broadway stage had mounted at least 112 plays and revues about World War I, and many of these were periodically revived.

The subject of war in American drama outstripped all other subjects of the postwar decade with the exception of business, yet it took a long time for playwrights to abandon patriotic fervor and speak honestly about the anguish of warfare. Few ventured into such dolorous territory before 1924. If one trusts the accounts of many of these plays, America suffered an epidemic of husbands who had been reported killed turning up years later; an alarming number of soldiers returning with amnesia, wandering aimlessly but fortuitously into the arms of those who loved them; and a plethora of German or Allied spies. During the war the melodramatic spy plot was the most prolific on the New York stage. After the hostilities ended, its popularity waned as the homecoming play rose to prominence. Somewhat prophetically, an unsigned review of *Under Fire* in 1915 observed that "the great conflict is too huge, too near, too overwhelming for the perspective of serious drama. Probably we shall not have the great war play until the Captains and the Kings depart." More to the point, however, many believed that it was incumbent upon the theater to divert its audiences. A 1917 article, for example, proclaimed: "In war time . . . it is of the utmost importance that the theatre should realize its opportunity. The theatre's greatest mission is to take men out of themselves. . . . In war time the horror of real life presses upon us. . . . Against this we need the spiritual elixir of the theatre, we need the revivifying touch of the world of fancy."[4]

It is nevertheless true that the doughboy as farceur, melodramatic hero, or even villain was an important expression of the American experience, even if his presence was primarily therapeutic. The warring and postwar nation, having passed through what seemed Armageddon, was hemorrhaging, losing much of a young generation, yet such emblematic titles as *Doing Our Bit, Out There, Over the Top, An American Ace, The Luck of the Navy,* and *Mother's Liberty Bond,* all produced during the war, ironically suggest the spirit of much of the work of the theater. *Mother's Liberty Bond* (1918), in fact, was used as a fund-raiser to supply cigarettes to American soldiers in France, and *Out There* (1917), by J. Hartley Manners, was a vehicle for actress Laurette Taylor, who played a nurse to the British wounded in this "simple chronicle of a soul that finds itself through service, . . . a study in patriotism."[5]

To explore the impact of the war only through the weighty drama and to dismiss the comic and traditional fare is to miss the import of the catastrophic events of 1914–1918 on the American public and its dramatic arena. Edmund Wilson wrote that the war effort, which focused Americans on the "relentless machinery of destruction," also made Americans "appreciate human things, the commonest human fellowship." More to the point perhaps, A. H. Woods, a producer who specialized in sex farces, defended his tastes, claiming: "I should be considered a public benefactor when I attempt, by means of a zippy show or two, to drag people up out of the depths of despond." Much of the spirit of such escapism, however, was expressed in poetic doggerel by Parmlee Brackett in 1918:

> Player folk! Take us where pain is forgotten!
> Sinless thy fairy-land! War unbegotten!
> . . . .
> You are the anchor to hold us from drifting.
> Keep ye the Dream bright 'neath Death-ashes sifting![6]

I examine here both escapist and serious plays, exploring the war experiences and their social and cultural context and drawing on some of the most intriguing American war plays. These were first produced in 1914, but I focus my attention here primarily on the plays produced between U.S. mobilization and 1924. The offerings include musical revues, farces, melodramas, serious plays, and attacks, and they are by both men and women, focusing on both soldiers and civilians.

The serious plays produced between demobilization and *What Price Glory* dramatized what happened to war participants after their return to the United

States, not during hostilities. Recalling the recurring messenger of Greek tragedy (like the herald in the *Agamemnon* of Aeschylus) who recounts horrors that took place offstage or previously fought battles, many plays before 1924 describe the war or demonstrate the effects of war on the domestic front. All fall short, however, of rolling out the ekkyklema. Nonetheless, returning combatants often demonstrate cynicism as they describe bloody encounters in the trenches and other events of the war. There seems to be not a need to forget the war but rather a desire to refocus the bellicose acts in terms of where the survivors find themselves in the aftermath. Characters, and perhaps the playwrights (many of whom served in the war), were more profoundly changed by the events or inextricably locked in the past than they seemed to recognize. Innocence could not be restored. Reclamation of Progressive-era sensibilities in the spirit of Teddy Roosevelt, and a return to a neutral, isolated America were impossible, despite the successful efforts of the Senate to reject the League of Nations. Three thousand miles was no longer a safe distance from the battle front. The telephone, transatlantic cable, air flight, and wireless transmissions rendered the globe a much smaller place.[7]

Melodramatic or comic structure undoubtedly had an impact on the ultimate reception and message of the plays, perhaps undercutting much that was cynical or graphically described. Furthermore, trying to domesticate a hellish, outdoor, almost geographically limitless, experience by fitting it into an indoor, boxlike space with a polite audience was challenging. It was impossible for the proscenium theater to capture the stench and the grotesque images of dead men and horses that sometimes lay for months, even years, in the No Man's Land between the claustrophobic "temporary" trenches full of rats and lice; or the continuous noise of bombardment, snipers, and machine guns; or the ridiculous charges over the top that usually ended in carnage, with no discernible victory or advancement. Yet much about the war was theatrical, and it was often seen by its participants as so irrational or melodramatic as to be tolerable only if the soldiers approached their task as if they were playing roles in a grotesque play. Paul Fussell's brilliant study of the British literary interpretation of the war includes a chapter entitled "Theater of War," which tells us that "seeing warfare as theater provides a psychic escape for the participant: with a sufficient sense of theater, he can perform his duties without implicating his 'real' self and without impairing his innermost conviction that the world is still a rational place."[8]

Nonetheless, a collective picture emerges from these plays that shows a remarkable sweep of martial violence and imminent social change. The shifts in dramatic writing were evident to some critics as early as 1918, by which time it was clear that the war promised to inspire an impressive outburst of dramatic writing. Some efforts had shown, in theater critic John Corbin's words, "how rich and deep are the veins which the war has already opened up to our theatre." At the same time he wondered whether "we have playwrights able to explore the new leads to the depths and a public capable of appreciating the result."[9]

In spite of the efforts of Eugene O'Neill, whose work since 1916 had imbued the stage with the tragic experience, it is not surprising that after scores of productions that simply reported the horrors of war, *What Price Glory,* which dramatized them, was so startling. After all, O'Neill had pointedly avoided the war experience in his professionally produced work, except for the brief one-act *In the Zone* in 1917 and *Diff'rent* in 1920, while Maxwell Anderson and Laurence Stallings thrust the spectators into a comparative maelstrom of military profanity and senseless violence.[10]

Nonetheless, a number of antiwar plays and cautionary dramas like *Across the Border* (1914) and *Moloch* (1915), by Beulah Marie Dix; *The Spoils of War* (1915), by Hilliard Booth; and Marion Craig Wentworth's *War Brides* (1915) appeared on the American stage soon after hostilities broke out in Europe.[11] *War Brides,* the text of which survives in a periodical, is a one-act set in German territory about Hedwig, a young woman who kills herself rather than bear children whom her militaristic government can use as cannon fodder in future wars. The leading character, played by Alla Nazimova, who toured the play for a season, attacks the military machine as an insult to womankind; in addition, she denounces a system and a war that enslaves women, reducing them to working drudges and "breeding machines." The young women, in fact, are ordered by the priests and military officers in the name of the emperor to marry men they hardly know and bear children "for the fatherland [because] it is your patriotic duty." When Hedwig talks some of the young women out of becoming war brides, living symbols of their servitude with iron wedding rings, she is accused of treason. Although she is pregnant, she shoots herself before she is arrested. Her last words are intended for the emperor: "I refuse to bear my child until you promise there shall be no more war."[12]

Moloch survives only as fragments, but it may have been the most influential of these antiwar plays, with its aria-da-capo ending in which the war horrors are brought to a conclusion—until the unnamed country (clearly England) declares war on yet a new enemy, its former ally. One reviewer noted that "a year ago we would have considered it . . . rather exaggerated. Today it becomes poignantly real." Dix dramatized "a war without glory, chivalry, heroism or manly virtue," a picture that disgusted one jingoistic reviewer, who proclaimed *Moloch* "the handiwork of hysterical womanhood[,] a purely feminine creation which . . . has failed to interpret the moral of silent devotion to duty . . . and the glory of heroic immolation upon the altar of patriotism." Others, however, were moved, especially by a scene in which a British servant, whose sister has been killed by the Germans, cuts the throat of a German lieutenant who is billeted on the family she serves. A German major orders his troops: "Take her down into the street. Shoot her! Let the neighbors see. . . . Clear the house at once. Then burn it." He forces the whole family, including a sick child, who soon dies of exposure, to vacate their house, allowing them to take nothing. One of the family exclaims, "There is no God," and the execution is heard offstage. Many of the characters are benumbed by the horrors and can no longer grieve: "There's an ocean of tears been shed already—an ocean of blood. Doesn't make any difference. We're fighting still. No end to it. God's a joke."[13]

Such well-known war plays as Shaw's *Arms and the Man*, which inspired the Americanized *Arms and the Girl* in 1916, were revived at this time, and *Major Barbara*, although ten years old, received its first American professional production in 1915 and was interpreted as a voice against military preparedness—which was, until 1917, an ongoing controversy. Once the United States entered the fray, however, antiwar and cautionary productions ceased, and alternative voices did not reappear until 1919. John Corbin, writing in 1918, recalled that with the arrival of the war, "the first instinct of managers and playwrights was journalistic: they rushed into the midst of things. But they soon found that they were hopelessly outclassed by the correspondent at the front. . . . The pacifist horrors of *Moloch,* and the belligerent thrills of *Under Fire* alike fell short of the sensation that awaited us daily with breakfast."[14]

A combination of factors, including American enthusiasm for the war once the U.S. declaration was made (despite strong efforts by peace movements and conscientious objectors)[15] and a wave of patriotism from many theatrical producers and actors who spearheaded the war-bond effort, contributed to this prohibition of antiwar plays. In characteristic fashion, Alexander Woollcott, reviewing the flag-waving *Out There* shortly after American mobilization, claimed that early antiwar efforts "depressed and bored the audience by exposition of war's waste, war's horror, and war's futility." In this same review Woollcott noted that perhaps war plays with the heart-warming tone of *Out There* would not "long survive after the soldiers are mustered out."[16]

The most significant force working against antiwar plays, however, was the U.S. Congress, which passed the Espionage Act and the Trading with the Enemy Act in 1917 and the Sedition Act in 1918. These forbade any expression of contempt for the government, Constitution, flag, or military uniform. The government exercised its power "over speech and printed opinion, regardless of consequences." One could not defend the German cause at all. It became impossible to publish or produce an antiwar play without risking arrest for "disloyal utterance." At least one production, *The Little Belgian* (1918), was closed in tryouts in Philadelphia by federal authorities. The play, by Arthur Reichman, was reported to be a slur on British troops. Even before mobilization, however, some were calling for more circumspection in subject matter on the stage. One call for restraint in sex farces was linked to taking care during wartime. "Between the war and the competition of the movies, the stage needs to exercise common sense in what it offers," an anonymous reviewer proclaimed.[17]

As the war progressed, ethnic distrust and repression were enhanced by creating doubt of anyone associated racially or culturally with the enemy. The censorship laws inspired occasional tongue-in-cheek responses from the theatrical community, however. *Theatre Arts* in 1917, for example, published a photograph of the interior of a German theater, which was intended to shame American theater managers into improving their houses. "Now that everybody is busy showing up the barbarism of the Germans," the note began, "we wish to expose their cruelty as seen in the playhouse. For many years the Germans have been building theatres so much finer . . . that a comparison is extremely humiliating to all the Allied peoples. . . . We must say—even at risk of being jailed for giving aid and comfort to an enemy nation—that the Germans have the best theatres in the world. However we may dislike their politics, we must grant that they are decades ahead of us in stage production, in theatre administration, and, most of all, in theatre architecture." This comment led the Detroit Arts and Crafts Theatre to remove its subsidy of *Theatre Arts*, thereby forcing the magazine's move to New York.[18]

Before American mobilization, the war was a distant, intriguing spectacle of someone else's problems. Europe seemed to have gone mad, and President Woodrow Wilson assured Americans that the United States would maintain its traditional neutrality because the war had nothing to do with America. After all, neutrality in foreign wars had been the traditional U.S. position since the presidency of George Washington. Foreign-relief efforts, however, were popular. All-star revues were mounted to raise money for war charities, especially for relief of Belgian women and children in the wake of the German invasion. On December 8, 1914, for example, a host of international stars appeared in scenes or monologues recalling their most famous characters. William Gillette, Ellen Terry, Viola Allen, Ethel Barrymore, Annie Russell, William Faversham, Alla Nazimova, Mrs. Patrick Campbell, and twenty-two others shared the stage of the Strand Theatre. After American mobilization these fund-raisers were replaced by Liberty Loan rallies in theaters that featured such tableaux as a crucified madonna figure representing "the spirit of heroic Belgium" or "Columbia guarding her fighting men." These tableaux were also popular in revues like Ziegfeld's Midnight Frolics.[19]

Sympathizers with both Germany and France supported and produced an unusual number of German and French plays in New York during the war years, many of which were geared specifically to improve American relations with the belligerent nations. Plays of Gerhart Hauptmann and Eugène Brieux, for example, were rarely absent from the stage between 1914 and 1917. The European struggle for the allegiance of Americans and the onslaught of propaganda by all sides led many to label World War I "the first press agents' war."[20] Most of the plays of this preentry period that did not attack war were melodramas like *Inside the Lines* and *The White Feather* (both 1915), which tended to feature infiltrating spies, double agents, beautiful, brave heroines, and martial music. Although O'Neill's *In the Zone* belongs to this period, it explores the fear of submarine attack held by paranoid civilian seamen who jump to erroneous conclusions about a loner in their midst whom they presume to be a spy. No combatants or scenes of war appear in this melodrama. The only commentary is on the stupidity and the crude, thoughtless behavior of frightened men who will turn on those they do not understand. The behavior of the sailors is similar to the xenophobic antics of anti-Communist characters that I shall explore in chapter 8.

As early as 1915, however, some war plays were siding with England or raising suspicions about the loyalty of German-American citizens. *The Hyphen* (the title refers to hyphenated nationalities of immigrants or second-generation families with foreign roots), by Justus Miles Forman, gives a characteristic portrayal of the growing fear throughout the country that reached its peak when a series of apparent German espionage plots against the United States was exposed by the Secret Service in the summer of 1915. Plays about German-Americans continued to appear throughout the war, culminating in the most popular, *Friendly Enemies* by Samuel Shipman and Aaron Hoffman, which was produced in 1918 by Al Woods (who also produced most of the successful sex farces of the period).

Although not really speaking for the German cause, *Friendly Enemies* was interpreted by some reactionaries as propagandistic. It is clear in the flurry of letters to the editor attacking this play that the letter writers were anti-German and anti–German-American, not just opposed to the German government and its military machine. Moderate critics viewed the play as an attempt to humanize German-Americans without aiding the enemy, while reactionary critics saw in it yet another opportunity to attack the evil Germans. The following commentary is representative: the play "is a typical answer to all the miserable lies and damnable scheming of the traitorous pro-German propagandists, of which there are still too many at large in this country." The play was defended by most drama critics, however, and allowed to run.[21]

The text of *Friendly Enemies* makes the play's patriotic position clear. Billy, the son of Karl Pfeiffer, a wealthy, militant German-American who glorifies Hindenburg, joins the U.S. Army and goes to war, much to the horror of his father. Billy infuriates Karl by attacking Germany's atrocities: "They are guilty of every outrage they are charged with. . . . Their record of savagery is written with human blood in the ashes of Belgium and France." Pfeiffer is subsequently fooled by a German spy into financing sabotage that results in the sinking of Billy's troop ship. Thinking that the Germans have killed his son, Pfeiffer finally turns against the German cause: "We gave him to the curse that wipes out that damnable Hindenburg and brings back the beautiful Germany we used to know—the Germany of Goethe, Lessing and Schiller!"[22]

Beautified depictions of war also appeared in many musical revues and musical comedies both before and after American entry, and they often included rousing patriotic songs like George M. Cohan's "Over There" and bouncy trench ditties like "Pack Up Your Troubles in Your Old Kit Bag."[23] One revue by Irving Berlin, entitled *Yip, Yip, Yaphank* (1918), played at the Century Theatre, although it was not a professional production. The cast included active duty soldiers from Camp Upton at Yaphank, where Private Berlin was stationed. Drawing on minstrel shows, transvestism, and military drill, this patriotic and comic extravaganza gently poked fun at military rigors (the already famous "Oh, How I Hate to Get Up in the Morning" was sung by Berlin himself), but it really functioned as "fun-coated propaganda," a stellar recruiting tool. The end of the war was only three months away when this revue appeared in August, but this was not evident to Americans, who were preparing for another major draft.[24]

In other revues, flamboyant, even outrageous scenic numbers featured scantily clad chorus girls, often impersonating Allied troops on the march "in dress and undress uniforms;" the shows alternated between armaments and violins, between guns and roses. Before American mobilization, the *Ziegfeld Follies* presented a beautiful chorus girl as white-winged, diaphanously gowned Peace flying in like an angel to dispel the world of mass violence. Most of these successful musical extravaganzas involved a book or lyrics by Harold Atteridge and music by Sigmund Romberg, who went on to write the music for such popular musicals and operettas as *Maytime* and *The Desert Song*. In *Doing Our Bit* at the Winter Garden in 1917, the action centers on the exploits of chorines who run "a Girl's Hotel" and wear nearly backless dresses because of "the wartime shortage of material." A Fred and Adele Astaire rooftop revue with music by Romberg entitled *Over the Top* (1917) depicted a club that serves no food or cigarettes because "patriotically [everything goes] over the top to the trenches." In the most martial scene of this Shubert production, a formation of American airplanes bombed the German trenches.[25]

Inspired perhaps by *Ben Hur* as well as the war, *The Passing Show of 1916* ended its first act "with a stirring cavalry charge that show[ed] a troop riding at full speed directly toward the audience." Treadmills were used for this scene, but many of the horses in the first few ranks were dummies, with live performers resembling Rough Riders wielding sabers and the Stars and Stripes. Most of the multitudes filling out the charge were actually two-dimensional cutouts.[26]

Much more contemporary in its technology, however, was a playlet entitled *The Show of Wonders* in the Winter Garden revue of 1917, which depicted an American submarine (in cross-section) sinking an enemy ship (aided by film projection)—only to be imperiled by counterattack, followed by the apparently doomed sailors losing oxygen (yet singing "My Country 'Tis of Thee"), and a dramatic, last-minute rescue.[27] Some of the most spectacular revue scenes, however, in which "the Hun was assaulted with all the resources of the English language," featured aerial dogfights onstage as American planes on wires looped-the-loop after dispatching their Teutonic adversaries to fiery graves. Although musical and spectacular tributes to the Allied efforts continued throughout the war, most were produced in the first year of American mobilization, almost as if they were a theatrical sendoff of the doughboys.[28]

Many of these extravaganzas, as well as patriotic melodramas, were used not only to entertain but to raise money for war charities and sell war bonds. *The Passing Show of 1918* actually sent chorus girls singing and dancing down the runway and into the aisles to sell war stamps to the audience. *Getting Together* (1918) was used to recruit new military volunteers. This successful war melodrama by J. Hartley Manners and Ian Hay starred Blanche Bates and toured the country after only a few performances in New York, specifically as a recruitment tool. It alternated such up-to-the-minute entr'acte music as "You've Got to Go in or Go Under" with stirring scenes of trench warfare representing Allied victories (one included a tank: a terrifying but intriguing war novelty introduced by the British in late 1916). Although not really a war play, *Johnny Get Your Gun* (1917), written by and starring Louis Bennison, capitalizes on the war spirit and with its all-American, shoot-'em-up hero, sets the tone for most of the nonmusical war plays that appeared after mobilization.[29]

Shortly before the Armistice war plays were assured of reasonable success. A review of a comic-melodrama entitled *Watch Your Neighbor* (1918), for example, observed that "any subject connected with the war is so timely, so perfectly in tune with what is uppermost in everyone's mind, that the theatregoer swallows every war play greedily and cries for more." After the Armistice was declared, however, many war plays were still on the boards, and several in rehearsal were duly mounted in late November and early December. "And still they come," a reviewer quipped with some surprise.[30]

Yet by December it was clear that the flag-waving type of war play was no longer surefire, and perhaps passé. Some Broadway producers were even reported as depressed or angry because many of their wartime properties would have to be withdrawn from production. A different expression of the war experience was now in order; a shift in focus was demanded, resulting in some nine months of dramatic activity without a single new war play. Then a plethora of them descended on New York. Most dealt with the return of the soldiers, transformed by conscripted service, indescribable combat, and exposure to European culture. As a popular song of the period inquired: "How 'ya gonna keep 'em down on the farm, after they've seen Paree?" The soldiers, in turn, were no less surprised to see the transformations at home.[31]

In the popular farcical spirit of *Johnny Get Your Gun,* but taking full advantage of the war effort and homecomings, *Clarence,* by Booth Tarkington, opened on September 20, 1919, in New York.[32] This play is usually noted solely for launching Alfred Lunt's luminous career on the stage and bolstering that of the young Helen Hayes, but its wild popularity was not due to acting accomplishments alone. Many critics were just as enthusiastic about the play as were audiences. Alexander Woollcott, for example, when reviewing the reopening of Sem Benelli's *The Jest,* mentioned that *Clarence* "should be seen at least once a week." When Tarkington was writing the play, he anticipated accurately that the following season would have floods of plays "with soldiers in 'em." The popularity of his effort rose above most of the competition.[33]

The title character is a recently discharged, eccentric soldier in search of employment. The vicissitudes of the army have damaged him, but Tarkington uses military ordeals more to heighten the mystery of the character and to create misunderstanding among the other characters than to explore the war's aftermath. By appearing in uniform, for example, Clarence can always obtain a job interview—as a secretary says, "We want to show consideration to any *soldier*"—but he has no luck finding a position except through extraordinary serendipity. Clarence's plight, though comically presented, was a common and disturbing one for most Americans in 1919. The secretary goes on to state what was reportedly common practice in American business after the war: "We've taken on more returned soldiers . . . than we have places for." When the United States entered the war, the civilian unemployment figure was 4.6 percent; as the war ended it had fallen to 1.4 percent, only to rise quickly to 5.2

percent; and in 1921, the height of the postwar recession, the unemployment rate soared to 11.7 percent, the highest until the second year of the Great Depression.[34]

When Clarence first appears, he shambles in, hat in hand, a "friendly sort of friendless creature." Tarkington describes him as bespectacled, sallow, stooping, limping vaguely, wearing an ill-fitting, "faded old shabby khaki uniform of a private of the Quartermaster's department." It turns out he was a successful entomologist, who was drafted and then wounded in artillery target practice; he never came closer to France than Texas. Nonetheless, the teenage children are fascinated by Clarence and pester him for advice, while the adults are mystified and often put off by his language and behavior, yet find him curiously useful. No one understands him.[35]

Throughout most of the farce Clarence is treated as an incomprehensible outsider, one of the many cited by Joseph Wood Krutch as having "lost all dignity as individuals and all right to any ultimate control over their lives or destinies."[36] In the spirit of comedy and the perhaps naive optimism of the playwright, however, Clarence regains dignity and control. By the play's end he is not only fully integrated into the now healthier social unit—much stabler because of his contributions—but he is reunited with the larger society by being rewarded with his prewar entomology job and, not insignificantly, the love of the heroine. This play celebrates a return to "normalcy," as President Warren G. Harding would soon have it, and a wouldbe end to the global upheaval. Harding's regular refrain of normalcy perhaps best describes the hopes of vast numbers of Americans after the war, who wished to return to things as they were. Such a "hopeless hope," as Eugene O'Neill might call it, was soon shown to be a pipe dream.

On December 22, 1919, just three months after the opening of *Clarence,* James Forbes unveiled his dramatization of the homecoming of another person in uniform, but this time from the Allied Expeditionary Forces (AEF) of the French front. Forbes's authority may have come from his own experience; he was recently demobilized himself, having served as a director of AEF entertainment in France. The demobilized figure in *The Famous Mrs. Fair* is a woman, however, and the tone of this melodrama distinguishes it as the first serious effort to grapple with the effects of the war on private citizens. Critic Louis Reid reports that this play was the first to link dramatically military demobilization and "the neglected family." Arthur Hornblow called it a timely and overdue "drama of war reaction . . . the banner bearer of a distinct after-the-war class of entertainment." As in *Clarence,* the action takes place in luxurious surroundings, the home of Major Nancy Fair, who is returning to her husband and grown children after serving four years, as her eighteen-year-old daughter, Sylvia, puts it, "to save the world for Democracy." This paraphrase from Woodrow Wilson's message to Congress asking for a declaration of war (his actual words were "the world must be made safe for democracy"), is one that recurs in nearly every war play. The line is sometimes used seriously, but it is often presented with an ironic tone.[37]

The war effort reportedly put on hold many domestic issues that returned to prominence after the peace. The play, which nearly ends with a divorce, tells us that "not a soul" has been divorced during Nancy's sojourn in France. "This war has done that for the country. Fighting in France has given a lot of husbands a rest from battles at home," according to Nancy's son, Alan. Since 1900 the divorce rate had been rising steadily before escalating alarmingly in 1919. (By the late 1920s the divorce rate was approaching 20 percent.) After the war, a stigma still attached to divorced people, but Americans were growing more tolerant of the condition.[38]

Upon her return Nancy, who was decorated for bravery, is offered the opportunity to undertake a lecture tour to share her experiences with the American people. Although her husband and children claim to detest snobbery ("it isn't being done since the war"), they consider lecture tours vulgar, a feeling that reveals their own snobbery and a hypocrisy that, given Forbes's point of view, may be unconscious on his part as well. Forbes makes Gillette, the lecture-tour manager who devised the whole affair, an embezzling cheat who tries to "ruin" Sylvia and cash in on the family fortune in traditional melodramatic style. Forbes also describes Gillette as a young man "of good appearance and address, but not a gentleman. His manner is over-suave, his clothes too correct." The implication is that if he is not born a gentleman Gillette cannot pass as cultured. It makes no impression on the family Fair (note the name) that Nancy will donate her entire $30,000 fee (a considerable sum in 1919) to charity. The family ungenerously want Nancy, now a public figure, to themselves, yet they accuse her of selfishness.[39]

Unlike the unprepossessing entrance of Clarence, Nancy Forbes's first appearance is "in her Overseas uniform of horizon blue, Sam Browne belt, beret and ribbon of the Croix de Guerre," awarded for her valorous duty driving an ambulance through heavy enemy fire. Forbes describes Nancy as "a vividly arresting figure, the personification of those American women brought into prominence during the war because of their executive ability, gay courage and unselfish devotion." Alan, who served in France as a captain and is reportedly "full of the brotherhood of man," which he got from the trenches, predicts accurately that his mother will soon tire of her return to domesticity, just as he did. The experiences of war are something the survivors cannot ordinarily discuss openly, especially to those who never served and are not likely to understand. Although Alan comprehends, he cannot approve her predicted behavior, apparently because she is his mother and a woman.[40]

When the women of the ambulance unit are reunited, they can talk of little but the war and how boring they find things at home. "If somebody would only drop a bomb I'd feel perfectly at home," says one as they reminisce. All complain of sitting around with "time to burn and no matches." When Gillette urges Nancy to commence the tour after only a month at home, one of her unit jibes, "Isn't that punishment enough?"[41] The freedom and exhilaration many women found as nurses and ambulance drivers at the front were frequently expressed in letters and literature after the war. "'Frontline fever,'" we are told, "infected almost everyone. . . . American women competed to get as far forward in the war zone as they could." Some 25,000 American women served in Europe during the war, many of them working as nurses, ambulance drivers, and other volunteers long before American military mobilization.[42] Literary critic Sandra M. Gilbert describes their delight in their dangerous work: "These once-decorous daughters had at last been allowed to prove their valor, and they swooped over the wastelands of the war with the energetic love of Wagnerian Valkyries, their mobility alone transporting countless immobilized heroes to safe havens."[43]

Just as he is recounting these female heroics, Forbes shifts the focus and turns the play into a domestic struggle about a woman's duty to her family. In his introduction he writes that "the realization is brought home to [Nancy] tragically that a wife and mother can have a career but not at the expense of her obligations to her home and family."[44] This may now strike us as curious, for the family obligation that turns Nancy around is the necessity of coping with the waywardness of her eighteen-year-old daughter—who is a little old to need child care.[45] Yet the melodrama's resolution is keyed to this event. When Nancy returns from some four months of American touring, she discovers that her once-proper and innocent daughter is "completely transformed. In dress, coiffure and manner, she is the modern 'cutie.'" Sylvia now saunters and speaks slang, but the effect is cosmetic, a child playing dress-up rather than a deep-seated change. Complete transformation is what the playwright suggests in his stage directions, but Sylvia's behavior belies this. Nonetheless, Nancy's reaction on first seeing her is speechless shock.[46]

Nancy's capitulation is similar to the reversal of the artist mother Ann Herford in Rachel Crothers' prewar play *He and She* (1912). Ann gives up her chance for a commission, handing the job over to her husband, to take up her obligations to her neglected sixteen-year-old daughter. *He and She* was revived less than two months after the premiere of *Mrs. Fair*, and it served as something of a companion piece to the Forbes drama. Hornblow's review of the revival, which featured Crothers herself as Ann, reflected the reaction of many men to both plays: "It is the common belief, overwhelmingly justified, that the genius of most women lies at home."[47]

Forbes appears to be attempting to feed widespread reactionary fears inspired by the rise of the flapper while professing traditional values and sensibilities that were fading in the wake of the war. Forbes further undercuts Nancy by aligning her professionally with the unscrupulous Gillette, thus demonstrating her poor judgment of character when she is the center of sycophantic activity. Ultimately, Forbes is using the war as a platform to propagandize his interpretation of a woman's domestic duty. In spite of his personal feelings, however, Forbes gives Nancy a convincing speech in the climax of act 2 that dynamically connects the domestic struggle and women's position with the impact of the war: "I give up everybody and everything belonging to me and endure privations, horrors, because I think it's my greatest duty, and then I am neglecting my family! . . . Must I secure the approval of my husband and my son for what I think best to do? . . . This war has settled one thing definitely. A woman's work counts for just as much as a man's and she is entitled to all the rewards it brings her."[48]

Curiously, most of the plays dealing with homecomings demonstrate changing mores regarding the expectations of young women vis-à-vis men and male treatment of women. The high incidence of these plays may surprise readers now, but postwar audiences probably found it less so, for women's rights was a topical issue. The Nineteenth Amendment, granting women's suffrage, was passed by Congress in 1919 and ratified in August 1920, just in time for the election of Warren G. Harding that launched twelve years of Republican leadership and the concomitant enshrinement of commercialism—not the results envisioned in the rhetoric of those either strongly favoring or strongly opposing women's suffrage. The anticipated large-scale mobilization of women into politics never came.

The theme of the domestic place of women occurs in three major homecoming plays: *The Famous Mrs. Fair, The Hero,* and *Hell-Bent fer Heaven,* but the women in question are of vastly different socioeconomic classes, and the plays offer quite different interpretations of their problems. The differences can also be linked to the plays' temporal distance from the homecoming; they were produced in 1919, 1921, and 1924, respectively.

By act 3 of *The Famous Mrs. Fair* the men in the family are struggling with a transfigured world for women. They are not accepting it, but they are trying to understand. Alan is apparently functioning adequately but cautiously in a two-career marriage. "If a wife wants to work these days," he informs his father, Jeffrey, "you have to let her." Jeffrey, often alone when his wife is on the lecture circuit, responds, "Yes, but sometimes I wonder in the modern scheme of things where in hell the husband belongs." In Nancy's absence Jeffrey takes to cheating on his wife, and when she discovers his betrayal, he expects her to "be big enough to understand." He considers her "craving for a career" to be as serious, if not more damaging, a sin against their marriage than his affair. Nancy is prepared to divorce him until her daughter's attempt to run away with a cad leads the family to call the police and drag Sylvia back. As a result of this crisis Nancy decides to abandon all plans of a divorce and dedicate herself to her family.[49]

In spite of the popularity and favorable reception of this play as well as *Clarence,* it was clear to many that a profound expression of the war experience was unlikely to come soon. One wag in fact predicted that "an immortal play on the Great War" was an impossible dream, no more likely to be realized than "anybody making money on Broadway with a Strindberg play."[50] The impossible dream was five years away, but several plays demonstrated significant advances in honest portrayals of war.

Less than two years after the appearance of *The Famous Mrs. Fair,* the first play by Gilbert Emery (pen name of Emery Pottle), an actor and writer who had served as an Army first lieutenant in France during the war, opened in trial matinees. When the play proved popular in March 1921, it was withdrawn, reworked, and partially recast with stronger actors in several roles for a September opening. *The Hero* (1921) is another serious melodrama about a returning soldier and his impact on his family, but the social class of the principals is lower than that of the Fairs, their quarters are more modest, and the events of the play are more catastrophic. The action never leaves the home of the Lane family nor extends to characters beyond the family circle. Emery wrote that he was more interested in demonstrating the effects of the war on those who stayed than on those who served overseas, and one review considered this play a plausible exploration of a prominent "phase of the war reaction in America . . . where many a black sheep won all the glory."[51]

The previous year, Eugene O'Neill had also created a crass returned soldier, Benny Rogers in *Diff'rent,* who is likewise corrupt and makes occasional references to France, but Benny says nothing of combat or the war experience. Unlike Oswald, Benny is not fully developed, and he is not the cause of the conflict. He does not appear until the last act, where he is used as a foil to belittle and further expose the central figure, Emma Crosby. His Uncle Caleb says of him: "I thought when the war come, and he was drafted into it, that the army and strict discipline'd maybe make a man o' him. But it ain't! . . . It's killed whatever mite of decency was left in him. . . . If you put a coward in one of them there uniforms, he thinks it gives him the privilege to be a bully! Put a sneak in one and it gives him the courage to be a thief! That's why when the war was over Benny enlisted again."[52]

The action of *The Hero* takes place in the cheaply decorated rental house of Andrew and Hester Lane in the suburbs near New York. Andrew, "a faithful and honest insurance clerk" who will never get farther on, struggles to support his family. The war spirit is made manifest immediately, as Andrew's mother, Sarah, laments that her younger son Oswald has not yet returned from the war, and Marthe, a Belgian war orphan taken in by Hester in 1915, now grown up, quietly observes, "The world is full of ghosts since the war." Hester describes her humanitarian act as "our little bit," a common war phrase borrowed from the British. Her bit, however, aligns her with the many Americans who gave generous support to Belgian refugees before the United States entered the war. [53]

The unscrupulous character of the returning soldier Oswald is established before his first entrance. The prodigal son ran away from home twelve years earlier after forging a large check, which his family struggled to repay in his absence, and "ruining" a girl who eventually fell into prostitution. Eventually, Oswald fought for the French Foreign Legion, was wounded, and was decorated for bravery. Hester is fittingly overwhelmed by the horror of war described by Oswald, but it is Hester, not Oswald, who relates the battle imagery to the audience, removing us another step from the awful events: "All the cold, and mud—and suffering—and disease—and wounded—and the dying. . . . Oswald—you really advanced right over the piled-up bodies of your comrades, as they lay there—dead and dying, in the trenches? . . . There isn't anything in the whole world too good for you—not *anything*." She claims that she can never forget the war, nor can any feeling American. Andrew in his turn forgives Oswald for past crimes, saying, "I guess you've about wiped out all that tomfoolishness—or worse—by what you've done over there—in the war." Combat is perceived here as penance or even an act of purification, a notion that persists in our culture's contemporary popular media.[54]

In stark contrast to both Clarence and Nancy Fair, Emery describes Oswald as attractive but slightly lame and "somewhat marred by dissipation, rough living, and vagabond wanderings." He is at once charming, impudent, reckless, and morally weak. Some reviewers were relieved to finally see in a play a war hero "whose shining glory is a bit tarnished." In the second act he appears in his worn blue, French poilu uniform, indicating a frontline soldier, complete with decorations that include the Croix de guerre (like Nancy Fair) and Medaille militaire. He usually feigns flippancy about his war experiences, quoting the oft-heard remark of returning soldiers, "'Twas a hell of a war, but 'twas the only war we had!" Nonetheless, he takes every opportunity to remind others of his contributions or arouse guilt in those who did not serve.[55]

The Lanes open their home to Oswald, who does no work. Rather, he seduces and impregnates Marthe, claiming that she should reward him for getting wounded while fighting for her country. When Andrew suggests that Oswald seek employment, even secures a job for him, the latter angrily invokes his war efforts again and calls Andrew a slacker (the term then current for draft dodger).[56] "You're like all the rest of 'em," he yells at Andrew, "fight for 'em, get wounded for 'em, croak for 'em, by God! Save their old country for 'em . . . and then have 'em tell you to go to hell." In Oswald's cynical mouth, "keep the world safe for democracy" means sacrificing so the slackers can maintain their cozy way of life safely distant from the war. Ironically, in his review Alexander Woollcott turned the name-calling on Oswald, describing him as "a spectacular soldier, but . . . such a miserable slacker in every other obligation a man incurs while transient on this planet."[57]

Although Oswald is at the structural center of the play, serving as both antihero and catalyst for all dramatic action, much of the play uses Hester to focus on the changing roles of women and the impact the war has had on these roles. Hester's longing for real achievement is harnessed to her sexual desire for Oswald; the two yearnings are probably inextricably linked. Sandra M. Gilbert suggests that "the revolutionary socioeconomic transformations wrought by the war's . . . role reversals did bring about a release of female libidinal energies, as well as a liberation of female anger, which men usually found anxiety-inducing and women often found exhilarating." Emery wrote elsewhere that "the real problem of the play is Hester," whom he describes on her first entrance as having an expression that indicates "some inner dissatisfaction." Hester is envious of the women who served in France with the Red Cross, but her mother-in-law simply quips: "Women better stay to home where they belong. If the men want to fight, let 'em." Yet Hester longs for something that gives "women a chance to look outside their own little dooryards . . . to be something. Something that counts more in the world." Like the men in The Famous Mrs. Fair, Sarah attacks Hester for failing to acknowledge that domestic duty can bring fulfillment. "I dunno what women's comin' to nowadays," Sarah exclaims. "I s'pose you'll want to be votin' too—an' dancin'! . . . and a smokin' of them nasty cigarettes! . . . Next thing you'll want to get a divorce, I s'pose—like all the rest of 'em." This moralizing fundamentalist, however, is shown by the last act to be as selfish and duplicitous as her son Oswald.[58]

Hester's frustrations with confinement to the distaff sphere result in her coveting Oswald's war experiences and feeling shame that neither she nor her husband volunteered for service. Oswald exploits the sexual tension between Hester and himself as well as her thwarted ambitions in order to seduce his sister-in-law. But, although Hester finally offers her body to Oswald, he cynically refuses her in an act of humiliation.

When Oswald is called on to help Andrew's church raise money for "the suffering infants of devastated France," he basks in the celebrity and attention garnered by speaking in uniform from a pulpit. His speech is such a success that Andrew compares his effort to a trench charge: "You went right over the top this time!" Five hundred dollars is collected, but Oswald steals the money before the night is over. Hester catches him and attempts to stop him, but Oswald once again uses the war to excuse his criminal behavior: "[Andrew] didn't go to war, did he? Let him pay, then. I'm a soldier. I'm his brother. Let him pay!"[59]

Unfortunately, Emery yields to sentiment by having the corrupt Oswald, after absconding with church money, rush into a burning kindergarten to save his nephew, only to perish when the building collapses. His producers wanted Emery to pervert the conclusion even more absurdly by saving Oswald and wedding him to Marthe. Emery refused.[60] Apparently, Oswald is living up to his definition of a hero: "a guy that does somethin' he wouldn't a-done, if he'd stopped to think." Andrew laments the passing of the "impulsive hero" and must remain to mop up after Oswald "has gone over the top and out in a blaze of glory." More unfortunate, perhaps, Hester privately repents and realizes how well off she has been with lackluster but honest Andrew. Like Forbes with Nancy Fair, Emery paints Hester Lane as selfish before bringing her to an eleventh-hour conversion to traditional domestic subservience.[61]

Many of the homecoming plays open on a note of celebration, but it only ushers in renewed violence or pain, almost as if the reunited families must now undergo yet another severe rupture to recover their prewar status. The war turned domestic and political life topsy-turvy, and recovery was possible only after considerable change and damage to the participants. In 1955 literary critic Frederick Hoffman wrote that "three reactions are prominent in the war literature of the 1920s." One of these categories, "the war as a violent re-education of the soldier," if enlarged to include the changes and reeducation of the civilians as well, would be appropriate to many of the homecoming plays. Another of Hoffman's three categories, "the war as a means of testing the true nature of men," however prominent in novels, is all but invisible in postwar plays. But Hoffman's leading category, "the war as a monstrous hoax," emerged as the most memorable theme on the American stage.[62]

Although most war plays of the era concentrated on returnees and their friends or families, a few plays dwelt on those who never returned. *Aria da*

Capo (1919), by Edna St. Vincent Millay, was probably the first antiwar play to be produced after U.S. involvement in the war.[63] This harlequinade, forceful though it is in its poetic and stylish attack on territorial warfare, does not specifically refer to World War I. Yet the play presents prewar and postwar activity as well as the conflict itself.

The playwright opens the action with the merrymaking of Columbine and Pierrot, who proclaims, "Let us drink some wine and lose our heads / And love each other." Yet the frivolity is soon interrupted by Cothurnus, the Masque of Tragedy, who expels the harlequinade and forces two pastoral youths to kill each other, against their will and before their time (recalling the hyacinthine generation of young men—especially European—lost to systematic slaughter). Their territorial dispute begins as a game; their wall of division is arbitrarily drawn; their deaths are effected with farcical props; but the conclusion is irreversible. Ironically, the tragedy is not sustained. Throughout the building tension the farcical characters periodically invade the action, offstage and on. With the killing completed the farceurs are called back, but the bodies remain onstage. Pierrot protests: "Come drag these bodies out of here! We can't / Sit down and eat with two dead bodies lying / Under the table! . . . The audience wouldn't stand for it!" Cothurnus, of course, tells the clowns to "play the farce. The audience will forget." Although the absurd society figures attempt to return to their stylish but meaningless lives as if nothing has happened, the carnage cannot be hidden. As Pierrot and Columbine repeat their opening, empty lines about macaroons (hence the title), they do so astride the unburied dead.[64]

The allegory was clear to early audiences of this popular play, but allegorical it remained. Woollcott reminded his readers, however, that although some unthinking playgoers might miss the point, "no mother from a gold-starred home [families who lost sons to the war put a gold star in their window], who saw the war come and go like a grotesque comet and who now hears the rattlepated merriment of her neighbors" could fail to understand.[65] The play, unlike the others discussed here, is not specific to the Great War; but it is an impressive response to it and a warning that global warfare can and will happen again.

After Millay's emblematic assault, which she directed herself for the Provincetown Players, there was no further attack on the war until 1921, when another woman with the Provincetowners, Susan Glaspell, presented her play *The Inheritors*.[66] Although this four-act drama stretches from 1879 to the early 1920s, and the agenda is primarily an appeal for tolerance of other points of view at a time when America found itself in the midst of a Red Scare, Glaspell attacks warfare in general and American involvement in World War I in particular. "Seems nothing draws men together like killing other men," an aging grandmother complains in act 1. And in time of trouble, with hypocrisy and patriotism out of control, a student muses about the Great War: "The war must have been a godsend to people who were in danger of getting on to themselves."[67]

The play supports the right of conscientious objection during World War I by creating opposition from an inflexible right-wing state senator and a gang of ruthless young college toughs who wish to deport or imprison anyone who does not share their point of view. Holden, a moderately radical professor, supports the objector: "It's a disgrace to America that two years after the war closes [a conscientious objector] should be kept [in prison]—much of the time in solitary confinement—because he couldn't believe in war. It's small—vengeful—it's the Russia of the Czars." It is Madeline Morton, however, a twenty-year-old student and champion of the First Amendment, who best sums up Glaspell's evaluation of the young, dead heroes of World War I. When challenged by her uncle, who tells her she is not free to say what she pleases even though she lives in America (the Espionage and Sedition Acts were still in force), she speaks of her brother Fred who died in trench warfare in France: "Fred had—all kinds of reasons for going to France. He wanted a trip. . . . Wanted to see Paris—poor kid, he never did see Paris. Wanted to be with a lot of fellows—knock the Kaiser's block off—end war, get a French girl. It was all mixed up—the way things are. . . . One thing I do know! Fred never went over the top and out to back up the arguments you're making now!"[68]

By 1921 it was already clear to Glaspell and many others that the supposed noble cause of World War I was a sham, and democratic principles had been sacrificed to finances and expediency. "The world had broken; it could not be mended." The only advice Madeline's isolationist father can give her is, "Mind your own business, that's all that's so in this country." All the characters, including Holden, try to frighten Madeline away from any idealism that does not conform with mainstream beliefs.[69]

The father's phrase reflects a traditional attitude associated with Americans, especially before the war, but also afterward. With the official stance of neutrality in the early years of the war, "Mind your own business" became governmental policy. In spite of the spread of internationalism throughout American culture, arts, letters, and theater, in particular, after the war, the American government embraced isolationism once again, until Pearl Harbor forced a change.

The following season Glaspell attacked again, but this time with a stronger play that dealt less with the war than *The Inheritors* but that struck blows both at what the war represented and at its aftereffects, which were still catastrophic for many. For most, however, the war stood as an imposing cataclysm that disrupted and destroyed but that taught humanity nothing. Like the clowns of Millay's *Aria da Capo,* most of the characters in Glaspell's *The Verge* (1921), also produced by the Provincetown Players, have learned nothing from the war and have attempted to carry on with business as usual, almost as if the violence of the war were a spoiled dish that could be discarded, allowing us to return to the same meal at the same table, just as Millay's clowns resume their repast over the bodies.[70]

Only the heroine of *The Verge,* Claire, who is on the brink of insanity, can see the conditions fabricated by the Western world clearly enough (hence her name) to acknowledge the hypocrisy, and emptiness of her reactionary family and friends—and by extension the world—who assume that sanity has been restored and that it is possible to roll back the clock, to return to "normalcy." In this respect, Claire personifies the struggle of modernism with tradition in the postwar world. "The war didn't help," Claire startlingly informs the men. "Oh, it was a stunning chance! But fast as we could—scuttled right back to the trim little thing we'd been shocked out of. . . . Showing our incapacity—for madness." The cacophony, the utter chaos of a world war was for Claire a period of madness that offered a chance, an opportunity to destroy the shackles of the past and begin anew. To create new forms, to "break through," as she often says, in order to free not just the imprisoned women but the men as well who remain incarcerated by their own patriarchal dogma. "Why need I to be imprisoned in what I came from?" she asks. Ironically, Claire, who is the only character to lose emotional control of her life, is the most liberated and creative, yet she is clinically depressed because only she can recognize how limiting the postwar world remains. Clearly, tremendous changes had transpired since 1914. For Glaspell, however, most of the alteration was cosmetic. "It's hard to—get past what we've done," Claire observes almost pathetically. "Our own dead things—block the way."[71]

After *The Inheritors* the war plays continued to arrive in a steady stream, but little appeared that was new in content, structure, or point of view until the advent of two Southern playwrights in 1923 and 1924, Lula Vollmer and Hatcher Hughes, both of whom specialized in what was then characterized as folk drama. Vollmer's *Sun-Up* (1923) is set in her native North Carolina in the western mountains among ignorant people who confuse the Great War with a new outbreak of the Civil War and treat it for some time as rumor. They think of the Germans as Yankees and think France is "'bout forty miles 't'other side o' Asheville." On hearing this, Mrs. Cagle, the protagonist replies, "Goin' a mighty long way to fight, seems ter me."[72] This play departs from most of the others in this examination in one important respect. Rather than concentrating on the homecoming or reflecting on the war as past, *Sun-Up* is set in 1917 and 1918 and focuses on the men marching off to war and the dreaded news of death on the battlefield, with neither heroics nor understanding of the import of the war achieved by the characters. The unusual time frame is probably owing to the play's composition during the war—it may have been written in 1918.[73] It took Vollmer five years to find a producer, at first because the war was still on and the play would have been viewed as defamation of the government, but afterward because there was no taste for modern American folk drama; the vogue did not arise until 1923.[74]

Although laced with occasional crude humor, the tone of *Sun-Up* is serious, and the action encompasses considerable pain in the last act until final moments of forgiveness and redemption. The central conflict is domestic: Rufe Cagle, a young farmer, is drafted and leaves his widowed mother and new wife to struggle with the land; he dies "somewhere in France" (the official location for all American soldiers overseas). News of his death brings on catastrophe when his mother discovers that an Army deserter (another conscript) she is harboring is the child of the man who killed her husband years before. She lashes out at war before preparing to murder the deserter in revenge. "This [war] ain't no feud whar ye have a chance. Hit air murder, and the law air back of hit." The play takes a mystical turn in the climax, however, as Mrs. Cagle believes that she hears the voice of her dead son instructing her to let the deserter go. With the rising sun, the final tension of the play yields to selflessness and reconciliation. Like the homecoming plays, *Sun-Up* calls for healing and coming to terms with the pain of great loss.[75]

Hatcher Hughes, a playwright and professor at Columbia University, is primarily remembered for one folk play, *Hell-Bent fer Heaven* (1924), which concerns an Appalachian youth returning from the war. Hughes won a Pulitzer Prize amid some controversy when the selection committee's choice of George Kelly's *The Show-off* was overruled, but this backwoods melodrama of phony religious zealotry and North Carolina mountain feuding moved numerous audiences and was one of the most popular in the wave of folk dramas appearing on or off Broadway in that decade.

In the play, Sid Hunt, who has a reputation in his rural community for fighting, returns from the French front. His family wonders whether the war has altered him. In his restlessness, egotism, and celebrity, Sid bears many similarities to Oswald in *The Hero*, but unlike his forebear, Sid is basically good at heart. Also like Oswald and Nancy Fair, Sid has been reported a hero in the papers for bravery on the battlefield. Hughes seems to be borrowing a leaf from *Sun-Up* when he has Sid's grandfather David muse, "From what I've hyeard o' these here Germans, they're jist a bastard breed o' Yankees." David goes on to claim that Sid probably did not even know what cause he was fighting for. Sid's retort that he fought "to lick t'other side," is an answer that David apparently takes as complete. The suggestion in much of this conversation is that many Americans did not understand the causes of the war or the goals sought by the combatants. The unclear goals of the war were further complicated by President Wilson's recurrent assertion that the results of the war "must be a peace without victory," a phrase that would haunt postwar negotiations.[76]

The introduction of souvenirs from Europe not only reveals the ignorance of the Hunts (including Sid, whose war experiences have made him only slightly more sophisticated than the rest) but links the war and its aftermath with the changing roles of women—even in this rural society. Sid offers a French lace brassiere to his mother, Meg, but she has no idea of its purpose. Ironically, David chooses that moment to announce for Sid's edification that the girls and women at home have gotten bolder since before the war. His complaint is exemplified when Sid's old girlfriend Jude Lowry says, "I've noticed that all the things that men want to do are a man's job; an' them they don't, like washin' dishes an' milkin', are a woman's." David laments that if women continue as they are now, "I dunno how men are a-goin' to live 'ith the next generation of 'em." Even in traditional Appalachia the women's movement is contesting patriarchal dominion.[77]

Among Sid's war mementos is a German automatic pistol he liberated from a soldier he killed. This infuriates Meg, who forbids him to use it and demands that he throw it in the river. Sid's robbery of a dead soldier makes the killing too personal for her, although she and the others applaud Sid's military accomplishments.

Rufe Pryor, a thirty-year-old who stayed out of the war by claiming that he was physically unfit to serve, has become an evangelical zealot. David, however, suggests that Rufe waited "till the war broke out an' skeered him afore he got his [religion]." It is Rufe who is both a hypocrite and "Hell-bent fer heaven." With the aid of all the war talk, Rufe starts to stir up old family feuds between the Hunts and the Lowrys. Rufe goes so far as to induce a drunken Andy Lowry to attempt to murder Sid, and failing in that, he attempts to kill Sid himself by dynamiting a dam and flooding the area. The disheveled Sid returns and convinces Rufe that he is a ghost, terrifying the villain into confessing his treachery. Sid tells Rufe that God's "almighty tired o' bein' the scapegoat fer folks that do all the meanness they can think of an' call it religion." Ironically, the flood Rufe unleashes is the agent of his own death, which is imminent as the play ends. This is the conclusion of the play as written and published. For the production a rescue of Rufe was added that undermined the ironic ending that would have linked this to the final curtain in the plays of O'Neill or the early Maxwell Anderson. A condensation of the produced version was published while it was running in New York.[78]

In the play, the "God-fearing" people are dedicated to vengeance. God, they believe, must work through a human instrument. "Even God cain't smite evildoers 'thout a fist!" David intones. Their violent way of life seems to offer little change for Sid, who is beset by treachery and killing as soon as he returns from the institutional, mass violence sanctioned by the Allied forces of Europe and America.[79]

Like nearly all the war plays since demobilization, this one focuses on the homecoming. The social status and behavior of the soldier and his family are considerably poorer and less sophisticated than those in the other plays. Yet the catastrophe at the play's end is more devastating and the consequences much deadlier despite the melodramatic construction. As in *The Hero* the opening tone is one of celebration of the end to fighting, but the rejoicing seems to usher in a renewed wave of violence. None of the homecomings in these plays, even in the comedies, are allowed to be celebratory events. The war has turned domestic, political, and social life topsy-turvy, and recovery is possible only after considerable change and damage to the participants.

In spite of the reversion to traditional values at the ending of most of these plays (*Aria da Capo* and *The Inheritors* are notable exceptions), the plays preceding *What Price Glory* clearly demonstrate that the war was immediately recognized as a line of demarcation. The world was changing rapidly, and many, perhaps most people felt powerless in the storm of events. Many plays tried to grapple with evolving social issues or to gloss over the damage to nineteenth-century or progressive-era values while capitalizing on the topicality of women's rights, the suffering of wounded (or homeless or unemployed) soldiers, and the role of women in the workplace.

Perhaps most surprising is the picture of the returning combat veteran that emerges from these plays, which usually endorse traditional values without succumbing to flag-waving. The plays do not yield to oversimplification in detailing the plight and confusion of returning combatants. Rather, they depict serious adjustment problems and renewed domestic strife, even though the goal of most of the plays seems primarily to be escapist entertainment.

When Corporal Kiper uttered the words "There ain't going to be any after-this-war" on the evening of September 5, 1924, shortly after the curtain rose on *What Price Glory*, those in the audience of the Plymouth Theatre who had served in the Allied Expeditionary Forces must have felt a chilling reminder of the hopelessness, the ceaseless violence, the hell they had survived six years earlier. The life expectancy for enlisted soldiers in the trenches was about six weeks, and many soldiers who survived beyond the average began to think of the war as endless, a "permanent condition" of the future world.[80]

If the auditors read their programs before the house lights dimmed, they had already been warned of what to expect by the director Arthur Hopkins: "*What Price Glory* is a play of war as it is, not as it has been presented theatrically for thousands of years. The soldiers talk and act much as soldiers the world over. . . . In [the] theatre . . . war has been lied about, romantically, effectively—and in [this] city . . . the war play has usually meant sugary dissimulation."[81]

This statement is often quoted, and it has contributed to the critical and historical dismissal of previous war plays. Similarly, Burns Mantle said of the play in his theatrical yearbook of 1924–25, somewhat hyperbolically: "It has served the theatre as a bolt of lightning that has struck and blasted for all time the war play that is no more than romantic hokum, prettily heroic and sentimentally untrue." More accurately, nearly six years earlier John Corbin had written prophetically, "If the life of our army at the front is ever adequately portrayed on the stage it will be by some of the lads who are now turning their faces westward." Steps in this direction were taken by Forbes, who supported the troops in France, and by Emery who was a soldier, but it was the veteran Laurence Stallings, a Marine Corps captain who lost a leg in combat in 1918, collaborating with Maxwell Anderson (who had no combat experience), who took the audience back to the front and over the top. Captain Flagg of the play is not based on Stallings but is a composite of at least two captains he served under in France.[82]

Although numerous war plays had appeared since the conflict ended, the war, as Joseph Wood Krutch observed, had yet to be assimilated emotionally. In this respect *What Price Glory* served the public in much the same way that the film *Platoon* served post–Vietnam era audiences. *Platoon* differed from earlier successful films like *The Deer Hunter* and *Coming Home,* which focused, not unlike *The Hero* and *The Famous Mrs. Fair,* more on the readjustments after the war than on the war itself.[83]

Heywood Broun was certainly precise in calling *What Price Glory* "the best use which the theatre has yet made of the war," but he too succumbed to overstatement in asserting, as if he were the play's press agent, "It is entirely possible that it is the best American play about anything."[84] The play had its detractors as well, but even they admitted that it was exciting, atmospheric, and effectively produced. The chief criticism, beyond that of profanity, was that the play presented no heroics, the very thing Anderson and Stallings meant to undermine. Arthur Hornblow, for example, wrote, "We are shown only the sordidness, the stark horror, the filth and bestiality of war. . . . The other side of the picture—the spiritual exaltation of the young warrior as he responds to his country's call, buckling on his armor to defend home and loved ones, the individual deeds of heroism, the self-sacrifice of the badly wounded soldier emptying his water flask to slake the thirst of a dying comrade, the noble work of mercy done by the women nurses—all that is conveniently ignored."[85] Not only is the play antiheroic, it is cynical and sometimes comic in nature, keeping the action and tone more in line with trench life than with depictions of glum despondency.

Although the minimal plotline in the episodic *What Price Glory* concerns the struggle of two soldiers over a woman, there is nothing romantic about it, and most of the play is dedicated to describing or dramatizing war conditions and how military life and expectations had changed in this war. Charmaine, the woman in question, is described as "a drab"; she is the only female character in a play that contains twenty-six men, all but two of whom are soldiers. Although the soldiers fight over her, they never cease to recognize Charmaine as a cheap trollop. "It's love in a manner of speaking," Quirt quips. "It's a small world . . . but the number of soldiers' sluts is numerous." Virtually every soldier in the play has a cynical worldview, and it is for Charmaine alone to be romantic about the soldiers: "They are beautiful," she says. "They go into hell to die—and they are not old enough to die." But Sergeant Ferguson undercuts her: "I shouldn't think it would matter much to you, dear. Some get killed, but plenty more come in to relieve them. Never any shortage of soldiers." Such a statement was especially true of the Great War, which was a war of attrition, with few decisive battles and a more or less static Western Front throughout most of the war.[86]

The soldiers, in turn, although carefully drawn, are less individualized than in previous war plays. That is, the play focuses less on specific character development and more on group dynamics. We see a sweeping cross-section of military personnel: enlisted men and officers, veterans and conscripts, career soldiers and volunteers, staff officers and field officers. The onstage soldiers' ranks include a brigadier general, a colonel, two captains, seven lieutenants, three sergeants, three corporals, and five privates, plus a Navy medic and a chaplain. Captain Flagg, the most fully developed character, along with Sergeant Quirt, calls his company "a rough crowd of old men and little baa-lamb recruits. . . . They're mostly Bible Class boys, and God knows most of 'em haven't got long to live."[87]

The tension between staff and field officers is perfectly dramatized and reveals the basic distrust and contempt of each rank for everyone above and below them along the chain of command. When Flagg, for example, learns that Headquarters staff officers are visiting his command he launches into a tirade:

"Damn headquarters! It's some more of that world-safe-for-democracy slush! Every time they come around here I've got to ask myself is this an army or is it a stinking theosophical society for ethical culture and the Bible-backing uplift! . . . I'd like to rub their noses in a few of the latrines I've slept in, keeping up army morale and losing men because some screaming fool back in the New Jersey sector thinks he's playing with paper dolls."[88]

The staff gives orders that are essentially suicide missions, and some orders are apparently arbitrary, yet the leadership insists on minimizing casualties. The commanding general's refrain is "hold down the losses . . . and give 'em the steel." Some critics, notably those without military experience, found the staff scene absurd in its depiction of ranking officers as inept and self-protective, but those with military service, especially at subordinate levels during this or any other war, can recognize the truthful picture the play's ridiculous series of exchanges captures. Furthermore, as Fussell puts it, "No soldier who has fought ever entirely overcomes his disrespect for the Staff." After weathering the staff visit, Flagg, like Oswald in *The Hero*, falls back on the popular quotation used to remain philosophical about impossible situations: "It's a hell of a war, but it's the only one we've got."[89]

Act 2 contains the most strident action and introduces the effects of combat. Strictly speaking, it is set not in the trenches (almost impossible to render realistically onstage) but in a cellar in the combat zone of a disputed town that is used as sleeping quarters and where the wounded and dying lie before evacuation.[90] The soldiers are filthy, and most are wounded or exhausted. One, for example, who is dragged onstage by Flagg, has been shot in the belly and is "holding half his guts in his bare hands and hollering for somebody to turn him loose so he could shoot himself." Flagg also drags in a lieutenant who has lost an arm: the man is soaked through with blood, "an indescribable mess of dried blood and dirt." Lieutenant Moore starts to crack under the pressure of incessant attack and little sleep: "God DAMN them for keeping us up in this hellish town. Why can't they send in some of the million men they've got back there and give us a chance? Men in my platoon are so hysterical every time I get a message from Flagg, they want to know if they're being relieved. . . . They look at me like whipped dogs. . . . . What price glory now? Why in God's name can't we all go home? Who gives a damn for this lousy, stinking little town but the poor French bastards who live here? . . . God damn every son of a bitch in the world who isn't here![91]

In miniature the scene demonstrates what many felt at the time, that the world had gone mad. "The whole damned universe is crazy now," Kiper observes. In spite, or perhaps because of the graphic, truthful depiction, many prudish voices arose in outrage over the profanity in the play and demanded it

be censored. The production survived intact, but otherwise responsible critical voices continued to object from time to time. Arthur Hobson Quinn, for
example, wrote three years later that the profanity "was perhaps unnecessarily
violent for the purpose of art."[92]

Flagg, in turn, almost careens out of control when even as he is losing good,
experienced men he has to deal with two new green lieutenants. His cynicism,
however, keeps him on top of his emotions. "I am a lousy, good-for-nothing
company commander. I corrupt youth and lead little boys astray into the black
shadows between the lines of hell, killing more men than any other company
commander in the regiment, and drawing all the dirty jobs in the world. . . .
We are all dirt, and we propose to die in order that corps headquarters may be
decorated." In the midst of the cacophony, suffering, and death, some of the
soldiers try to be philosophical, but their attempt is gloomy. Kiper, for example, complains, in an oft-heard question, devoid of any patriotism, "Well, if
there is a God . . . Why the hell doesn't he win the war for one side or the other
and get this mess over?"[93]

Quirt and Flagg are both no-nonsense soldiers, yet they fight over a woman
they don't love and drink themselves into oblivion. They reach for anything to
turn off the madness, anything to anesthetize the pain. After getting back
from the front line, Flagg complains, "Jeez, but I'm off war for life. . . . There's
so many little boys along with me ain't got any business here at all. . . . Gimme a
bottle to drink in bed. I don't want to think tonight." When Quirt and Flagg
finally have it out over Charmaine, Quirt remarks, probably with some truth,
"First time in six months I've had a good reason for fighting. The Germans
don't want my woman. I been fighting them for eight dollars a day."[94]

When the company is called back up, although they have had no rest, Flagg
is outraged but knows he will not buck orders. "There's something rotten
about this profession of arms, some kind of damned religion connected with it
that you can't shake. When they tell you to die, you have to do it, even if you're
a better man than they are. . . . We're shoving off. Follow us, because we don't
know where we're going. Nobody knows."[95] This cynical, almost nihilistic
view of the futility of warfare is seconded by Quirt, who utters the play's famous benediction: "What a lot of God damn fools it takes to make a war!"[96]

Perhaps the singularity of *What Price Glory* has been oversold to later generations, but not its import. Certainly it was shocking, and it was the first honest attempt to recapture the confusion, arbitrariness, and senselessness of the
Great War, known almost exclusively by the combatants. In these things the
play stands rightfully apart, but we can now recognize that a significant number of plays before *What Price Glory* ventured into the therapeutic region of
the war at home and sought to heal or explore (perhaps with less candor than

we would prefer) some of the new wounds of the war's aftermath. Finally in 1924, via the theater, the ex-soldiers themselves, along with those who remained at home, could begin to venture back into the trenches and with distance evaluate what the war experiences signified and what the costs, consequences, and lessons were for American character, American drama, even the American way of life.

Through the remainder of the decade plays from both the United States and abroad like *The Enemy* (1925), *Spread Eagle* (1927), and *Wings over Europe* (1928) continued to attack warfare and battle heroics in general and the Great War in particular with cynicism and realistic portrayals of combat experiences and the commercial underpinning that makes war possible. The character Joe Cobb in *Spread Eagle,* by George Brooks and Walter Lister, for example, observes: "Nine years ago. . . . All us damned fools marchin' away. . . . Thinkin' we were patriots. Marchin' away to make money for somebody." As John Anderson put it in 1930, *What Price Glory* and other plays that followed "mocked savagely the whole system of government butcher boys." By decade's end, however, the wave of contempt and sneering was diminishing and yielding once again to nostalgia, heroics, and romance for the war years, as we see in parts of *Journey's End* (1929) and the whole of *Waterloo Bridge* (1930). Few at the time of the Armistice would have disagreed with the assertion: "Won or lost, the war is the most dramatic crisis in the history of civilization." Yet it was soon too clear that the war that was fought to make the world safe for democracy had not done so and that the war to end all wars did not.[97]

3

The American Theater Versus the Congress
of the United States

When the theatres get started as a political organization [Congress] is going to hear
something. What [Congress has] done is a dastardly treacherous outrage.
—Marc Klaw

Two months after the Armistice, hostilities broke out again. For eight days in
January 1919 the theater industry waged war with the U.S. Congress, a nationwide event that, surprisingly, has been overlooked in theater histories. Theater managements and workers joined with the public to carry out a
well-orchestrated campaign in the newspapers and mail, in the theaters and
on the streets to stop what was perceived as a gross injustice to the American
theater and its paying audience.[1]

The Congress had framed a 6 billion dollar tax revenue bill to recover exor-
bitant war costs from the Great War; in this bill, Congress attempted to slip in
a new tax that would raise theater admissions by 10 percent in order to raise
between 75 and 81 million dollars. What Congress was unprepared for was
the highly organized backlash engineered by theater management, as well as
the groundswell of support for the theater's predicament from all regions of
the country. The Ways and Means Committee of the House of Repre-

sentatives unwittingly unleashed a public rebellion and an eight-day demonstration that verifies the profound importance of professional theater to the American people in the early postwar days of 1919. The event also demonstrates the power held by theater managements of the era and the surprisingly efficient, rapid, and far-reaching networking and public relations possible among them, a networking that owed a great deal to the organization of the road begun by the Theatrical Syndicate in 1896 and perpetuated by the Shuberts and leading managers of the United Managers Protective Association until the Great Depression.[2]

As the House bill, H.R. 12863, went into conference committee with the Senate in mid-January, the public issues of the day were immense, so much so that it seems surprising that the theater dispute managed to garner press coverage and public demonstration so quickly and forcefully. Not only was the recent war effort continuing to take its toll, but the Eighteenth Amendment (Prohibition), which was everywhere either supported or decried with vigor, was formally ratified on January 16. The United States and Europe were hotly debating the incipient League of Nations, and President Wilson was spending more time in Europe than in Washington. Wilson left for France to conduct negotiations himself beginning in December 1918; he was the first American president to visit Europe while in office.

In addition, the Russian Revolution and the Spartican revolt in Germany had appalled and frightened many across the United States. Rosa Luxemburg and Karl Liebknecht, chief figures in the Spartican revolt, were murdered in Berlin on the same day that the Dry Amendment was passed. Beginning in January and recurring periodically throughout the year, xenophobia and anti-Bolshevism erupted, taking the form in early 1920 of a full-blown Red Scare, in which thousands of citizens and foreign nationals were persecuted. Widespread fear of a long-predicted postwar recession soon became a reality. In April all American citizens had to pay income taxes for the first time. Furthermore, it was clear that a great deal of new revenue had to be raised to pay for the war, which had driven the federal government almost irretrievably into debt. Growing unemployment was a chronic problem, especially because soldiers had been returning home in large numbers since the Armistice. In January 1919 there were still many more waiting to come home.

The Spanish influenza pandemic had attacked the nation with devastating results in the fall of 1918, and it was only just subsiding in January. In many countries, including the United States, the disease caused more deaths than the war. This deadly strain of flu, which attacked nearly everyone between the ages of twenty and fifty, had severely hurt the theaters as well, felling both actors and potential audiences and leaving many houses dark, especially outside of New York. In New York as well, many theaters did poor business, which caused good plays to fail. Arthur Hopkins's production of *Redemption* succeeded only because Hopkins, in an unusual move, kept the play running for more than a month, despite poor houses, in hopes of finally drawing well. Most producers and theater owners were not so intrepid. Furthermore, throughout the last year of the war many theaters had lost money because of the dark nights enforced on them to conserve fuel. New York was lightless four nights a week during much of 1918, and the Great White Way ceased to be until after the Armistice. Numerous theaters had experienced six-figure losses in the fall and were hoping for a theatrical boom now that the war was over and the flu fading. Then Congress struck.[3]

During the Great War, Congress passed revenue bills each year in order to gather emergency funding. Four major bond drives in 1917 and 1918 had been successful in relieving some of the war deficit, and a fifth drive was planned for April. One particular bill, the Revenue Act of 1917, had levied a 10 percent admission tax on the theaters; managers were concerned but did not seriously protest the measure because many things had been taxed to support the war effort. Some theater managers protested that the government was vague about how the tax was to be collected, and some objected that the theaters themselves should not be tax-collecting agents, that the government should find a way to collect the tax itself. But no group except the motion picture industry seriously objected to the tax. Their lobbying failed, although they did achieve the exemption of nickelodeons (the five-cent theaters). After the tax went into effect, however, it was seen that the theater box office suffered severely throughout the country. In the first week there was a 50 percent drop in attendance at some theaters. It was widely believed that once the war was over the tax would be rescinded.[4]

In the fall of 1918, however, the House of Representatives passed a new war revenue bill to recoup losses after the war's conclusion. This bill, introduced by the conservative Democratic chair of the Ways and Means Committee, Claude Kitchin of Scotland Neck, North Carolina, proposed not only keeping the theater tax but doubling it. Nearly a year before mobilization, in July 1916, Kitchin had proposed a revenue bill designed to tax the gross receipts of the theater, a bill that the House passed but the Senate killed. That bill was designed to tax theaters in cities much more heavily than those in small towns. The theater managers worked together to defeat the bill but did not take their appeal to the people. The Senate action on this bill also predisposed the managers to believe that the Senate would kill the new tax bill in 1919.[5]

Although alarmed by the new House bill, theater managers calmly appealed to the Senate, which drew up its own version in December. After extensive lobbying and testimony by theater managers at hearings, the Senate, led by Finance Committee chairman F. M. Simmons, decided to retain the theater tax but not increase it. Theater managers decided that they could continue satisfactorily under these conditions, especially since men in uniform (a substantial portion of the audiences, particularly during the war) were exempt from paying the tax. When the two bills went to the conference committee of the Senate Finance and House Ways and Means in January, however, the House contingent convinced the senators to agree to the 20 percent tax. It was reported that the House conferees "threatened a deadlock" if the increased theater tax was not reinstated.[6]

According to the *Congressional Record* the original bill, as well as the law passed in February, carried "the greatest monetary burden ever imposed upon any people at any time." This was a gargantuan, labyrinthine bill that taxed almost everything imaginable, much of it for the first time. One representative quipped that "to wander through its [406] pages is suggestive of a journey through the chamber of financial horrors." Between September 3, 1918, and February 6, 1919, most parts of the bill went through many versions and amendments, but the section affecting the theater remained comparatively untouched until the conference committee came under attack in mid-January. The original bill levied a 20 percent tax on all tickets of admission above thirty cents (thus, most movie houses were exempt). Box-seat holders at theaters and the opera were to be taxed 25 percent. These figures were announced by conference committee on January 15, 1919.[7]

As the Revenue Bill was being argued in Congress a typical Broadway theater ticket in the orchestra was $2.00, the top admission in most legitimate houses. A few managers sometimes charged as high as $2.25 or $2.50 for large musicals and spectacles. In January 1919 top prices of $2.00 were being paid to see John and Lionel Barrymore in *Redemption,* Frank Bacon in the popular, sentimental *Lightnin',* and suggestive farces and dramas like *The Woman in Room 13* and *Up in Mabel's Room.*[8]

When theater managers heard that the Senate committee had yielded to the House, they created an uproar that reached the front pages of many newspapers. Some of the producers who had believed the optimistic report given them by the Senate in December gathered on January 15 and called an emergency meeting of the membership of the United Managers for Thursday, January 16. Meanwhile, several managers held news conferences to attack the congressional activity. John Golden, for example, asserted: "It is nothing less than an outrage. . . . After all the theatre has done to aid the war it is now proposed to mortally cripple it. No agency has worked harder, more unselfishly or with less prospect of individual gain than have the theatres in helping the winning of the war. . . . The treatment it is now receiving . . . would make one think that the theatre was a useless luxury that Congress wishes to wipe out of existence."[9]

The theater during the war years had indeed raised 200 million dollars "toward the sinews of war and the solace of the afflicted." Of this figure an estimated 10 million was donated by the theaters themselves. The funds, which do not take into account the participation of 2,280 actors in more than 2,000 free entertainments for wounded soldiers, were raised for the Red Cross and Liberty Loan drives, the Jewish War Relief, the Catholic War Work Fund, the Salvation Army, the United War Work Campaign, and many smaller war charities. One of the most forceful arguments concerning the revenue the theater had already generated for the war effort was presented by producer William A. Brady. "During the twelve months of 10 percent tax the theatre and moving-picture industry poured into the treasury of the United States $50,000,000. It is the third contributor in the list of industries." The Treasury Department issued a statement verifying "that the box offices of the country returned the third largest amount credited to any single industry during the war—railroads and steel alone exceeding the theater's sum total."[10]

"Thousands of actors and all sorts of persons allied with the theatre are going to be thrown out of work just when the nation is striving with all its resources to avoid unemployment," Golden lamented, allying the theater's problem with an important national concern as thousands of soldiers returned to civilian life. Producer A. H. Woods worried that Congress was attempting "to wean people away from the theatre. . . . I notice that what are termed luxuries are to be taxed five percent. . . . But the theatre . . . has not been looked on during the war as a luxury, but a tremendously valuable and helpful necessity. . . . The public faces the possibility of losing perhaps its greatest source of amusement and agency for morale. Hundreds of managers of small touring companies will be obliged to see their business ruined at once."[11]

Nearly all the managers painted a black picture, but director David Belasco, always the actor in life, was the most adept at emotional speech: "It will be the death blow not only to theatrical managers, but to the entire theatrical profession. It is such a ruinous and drastic thought that I myself am quite overwhelmed by the unspeakable sorrow of the picture which I see and which I am sure would become a reality." Florenz Ziegfeld solemnly projected the statistic that "two-thirds of the houses" would be closed. "Even now," he said, "expenses have gone up so that only the enormous successes are making any money." Ziegfeld even quoted specific inflationary problems brought on during the war: canvas for flats and drops, for example, had risen from 34 cents to

$1.04 a yard, while chorus girls' shoes had increased from $3.50 to $10.00 a pair. At present, he reported, the Ziegfeld Follies was paying the government $350.00 a night.[12]

Lee Shubert also noted that "it is a habit of most managers to keep plays running in New York often at enormous losses in order to be able to send them upon successful road tours later. This practice will have to be abandoned. . . . Only the sensational success will be able to survive a New York season, and one unhappy result of that will be . . . throwing out of work many thousands of people." Shubert predicted theater closings and "a severe hardship on the public," a common refrain linking the theater with the general populace that was heard throughout the controversy. Producers Bruce Edwards and Sam Harris presented what became a related, and ultimately more forceful, argument in the campaign by claiming that the tax "is going to lay such a burden on the public . . . that theatre-going will be discouraged and this will reduce audiences." The reduction in audiences would diminish potential revenue well below the current levels, and "the aim of the bill will be defeated."[13]

As early as January 16, newspaper editorials in support of the theaters began to appear. No New York newspaper supported the congressional proposal. The *New York Herald,* for example, called the measure "a slap in the face." The editors were certain that "every one will admit that the theatres and the actors have been good to the government since the United States has been at war. Propaganda, bond drives, war fund drives have been carried on tirelessly in the playhouses with the hearty co-operation of the managers." Also stressing the monetary and personal sacrifices of actors and managers both at home and abroad, the *Sun* wrote: "Actors have repeatedly appeared for war benefits of every kind; many theatres are always open to the soldiers and sailors [a reference to free theater admission for military personnel in uniform], in addition to the special performances given for their exclusive enjoyment."[14]

The *Herald* editorial expanded on the idea presented by producers Edwards and Harris, wondering not only whether much of the public would be *unable* to pay, but whether it would be *unwilling* to pay. The increase seemed prohibitive to the editors. The *New York Globe* likewise castigated Congress for its "shortsighted policy," which would create a staggering load for the theater, especially since the "war hit the theatres heavily," and production costs were "the highest ever." The *Brooklyn Daily Eagle* published an editorial insisting that the theater not be treated as a luxury. "Recreation is a necessity to public well-being. This is especially true in cities where congested population compels a more or less artificial life." Producer Marc Klaw summarized the predicament of the theater. "Now that the war is over and the best friend the theatre had in the United States [Woodrow Wilson] is in France, the other departments, simply finding no further use for the theatre, have invited it to go to hell." During the war, President Wilson, realizing the theater's importance to public and military morale, had classed it as "a necessary occupation." After the war, he declared that "the theatre was one of the most potent contributing factors to American victory."[15]

Satisfied with the original outpouring of laments and charges, the managers settled down to more constructive and imaginative action. One of the first orders of business was to cable Wilson and his chief economic adviser and head of the War Industries Board, Bernard Baruch, in Paris, begging the president's intervention. Although the Democratic president was friendly to the theater, he was now battling a hostile, Republican-controlled Congress, which he had already offended by virtually excluding the Republicans from the peace treaty negotiations in Paris. The cables from the managers warned that the tax legislation would "seriously cripple a profession in which hundreds of millions of dollars and the employment of many thousands of people are at stake." The managers also sent a telegram to the Conference Committee urging the need for hearings at which the managers could be represented. Manager William Brady produced the master stroke. He proposed holding mass meetings throughout the country to mobilize the public and "protest against taxing the theatre out of existence." Every theater, after all, already had an audience to exploit.[16]

Forty managers attended the open emergency meeting, came to a unanimous decision (a minor miracle for this group), and persuaded the actors and supporting personnel to back their efforts. "For the first time on record," the *Sun* reported, "the theatrical employees combined with their employers in a fight." Seven months later the two groups would be divided again during the first bitter Actors' Equity strike. Although the managers were the heroes of the tax conflict, by August they would be cast as villains again. Writing of the successful Equity strike just after management capitulated, theater critic Kenneth Macgowan noted that public support had shifted since January. "The sympathetic public which the actors immediately won built its faith in the actors' cause largely at first on the unsavory reputation of the 'commercial manager.'"[17]

The anti-tax strategy called for "audiences in every theatre in the United States ... to sign petitions to Congress to stop the measure." The standardized petitions, which began, "We theatre patrons hereby desire to respectfully make a protest against the proposed legislation," needed to be distributed effectively and aggressively. The method employed for securing supporting signatures was one developed for Liberty Loan fund-raisers in the theaters during the war. At Brady's suggestion, preceding each performance, "'four-minute speakers' appear[ed] before the curtain in theatres all over the country." During the war the White House had operated a propaganda program that organized volunteer "four-minute men," some 75,000 nationwide, who spoke at public gatherings, often in theaters, to encourage registration and enlistment, sell Liberty Bonds, dispel rumors, or disseminate official information from the office of the president. Actors and managers were often used in this capacity and were practiced in the technique.[18]

Most of the anti-tax speakers from the stages of New York were the managers themselves or such prominent actors and actresses as Minnie Maddern Fiske, Ethel Barrymore, William Faversham, Margaret Anglin, DeWolf Hopper, and Robert Mantell. A prepared speech was sent to all theaters by telegram. The speech began: "Now it is proposed to put the theatre out of business," and it linked the audience's welfare and needs to the continued survival of the theaters. "The theatre is the nation's playground. The theatregoing public in this country is the greatest in the world. And now it is proposed to tax that public—to tax you—to a point that will make theatregoing prohibitive." Petitions on cards were circulated by ushers, actors, and chorus girls among audiences and forwarded daily to the Conference Committee in Washington. On the first night of petitioning at the Hippodrome alone, some three thousand signatures were secured. "In many houses . . . the audiences were asked for an audible expression of opinion, and in several instances audiences rose to their feet en masse to thunder their disapproval" of the tax hike. More than five hundred theaters participated in the first twenty-four hours. By the second night of the campaign every theater in America was involved.[19]

Furthermore, "a telegram was . . . sent to every prominent actor and actress in the country, asking for a personal appeal to the White House." Entreaties were also made to the public at large to send telegrams and letters to the Conference Committee. Fledgling Actors' Equity sent a telegram to Congress reiterating the feared loss of jobs and the predicted loss of theater to smaller communities if the tax was raised. Equity also noted the violence already done to the theatrical profession by the flu epidemic and reminded Congress of the theatrical profession's patriotism during the war.[20]

The United Managers formed a special national committee of protest chaired by manager Morris Gest. The protest committee, which included not only six prominent young managers but a representative from Actors' Equity, the Stage Hands Union, the Musicians Union, and opera, vaudeville, and burlesque management, met for at least four hours every afternoon throughout the crisis to compose protest statements, plan new strategies, and mobilize supporters.[21]

An editorial in the World sympathized with the theater but feared that the implacable Claude Kitchin would only delight in thinking that his legislation might destroy the wicked theater and hurt those living north of the Mason-Dixon line. It should be noted that Kitchin's North Carolina town had no theater. *Variety* glibly asserted that Scotland Neck had the highest illiteracy rate in North Carolina.[22]

On the third day of protest, Friday, January 17, Ziegfeld sent a lengthy cable to Wilson in France. As part of the strategy of the protest committee, most of the letters and cables sent by the managers became open letters that were distributed to the press. The cable stressed the coming financial ruin, as well as unemployment and chaos in the entertainment industry, that would be caused by the new legislation. The cable also noted that under the 10 percent tax, road companies were reduced in number by one-third, and it was such "a heavy exaction that only the most prosperous and successful theatrical organizations could withstand" it. The managers also sent a telegram to Carter Glass, secretary of the treasury, urging his aid to the theaters "so they may be able to help in the Fifth Liberty Loan Campaign." The veiled threat, of course, was that the theaters would no longer help raise money for federal campaigns if the tax were passed. The Musicians Union began petitioning the American Federation of Labor to join the protest, but the AFL was already concerned, recognizing that some forty thousand stage hands as well as eight hundred musicians' locals might be adversely affected. On Saturday Frank Morrison, secretary of the AFL, began lobbying on the theater's behalf in Washington.[23]

Perhaps more significant, other business concerns in the public eye and outside the theater became involved. The Merchants Association of New York, the Broadway Association, and the Hotel Proprietors Association organized meetings to endorse the protest. The New York Real Estate Board sent a protest to Washington stating that "considerable depreciation in real estate values would follow any crippling of the theatrical business."[24]

By Friday morning it was estimated that the theaters had amassed 560,000 signatures, with 375,000 coming from New York. In addition it was reported that thousands of individual letters and telegrams were filling the boxes of the Conference Committee in Washington. Furthermore, theater managers had organized at least five hundred committees across the country to circulate petitions. As early as Saturday, letters from playgoers protesting the tax were appearing in newspapers. By Friday, however, it had become clear that the senators on the Conference Committee already strongly favored returning to a 10 percent tax, but the House contingent held so inflexibly that the *Times* reported: "There seems little likelihood of bringing about a change of heart." The Committee conferees were at an impasse.[25]

After Saturday night the number of signatures on petitions had risen to more than 1.5 million, and the protest committee was predicting at least 20 million total. By the weekend the organization and activity were so widespread and efficient that managers estimated that they could accumulate a million signatures a day. Even the state legislature of Indiana quickly passed a resolution condemning the Congress for attempting to increase the theater tax. Within a few days twenty-one more state houses passed similar resolutions. Mass rallies were planned throughout the country in every city that possessed a theater. The protests were scheduled for Sunday afternoon, when most theaters were dark. So many letters of protest were pouring into New York that the postal authorities appealed to the United Managers to help them redirect the mail to Washington. The producers were happy to comply, supplying twenty volunteer clerks.[26]

On Sunday, January 19, the *Washington Post* joined the protest. "The great, profit-paying mass of theatergoers in the United States do not expend money for amusement from an unrestricted purse," the editorial warned. "There is, therefore, a limit to what the 'traffic will bear.'" The newspaper went on to proclaim that the theater should not have to make up government deficits brought about by the loss of revenues from alcohol. Prohibition, which the paper dubbed this "highly moral decision of thirty-six States in the Union," had "borne a direct relation to the country's credit balance." This fiscal argument against Prohibition, in surely its first media use since its inception, reappeared throughout the 1920s whenever politicians complained of limited revenues.[27]

Although atypical of the polemics raised by others, an important artistic argument was introduced by theater critic and columnist Heywood Broun in the *Tribune:*

> The drama is a necessary form of expression. It is the most popular of all the arts, and if it is impaired the country will be so much poorer that the result cannot possibly be estimated in dollars and cents. . . . [A] tax as onerous as the one suggested encourages the production of "sure fire" plays. . . . The only production which has a chance to live under the 20 percent schedule is the play which is certain of a huge popular appeal. Such a play is not very likely to be one of the highest order. It will be impossible for managers to attempt anything new. They must play as safe as they can while the tax lasts. . . . The legislation would be singularly unfortunate just now, when there is a possibility of a definite awakening in American drama. The nation has been so profoundly stirred and shaken by the crisis through which it has passed that it seems fair to predict that some fine expression of all this emotionalism must come to the drama if only Congress will refrain from sawing the head off the theatre.[28]

Notably, Eugene O'Neill's first full-length production, *Beyond the Horizon,* lay only twelve months in the future.

The *Tribune* also published a political cartoon on the front page of the Sunday paper entitled "Exacting a Pound of Flesh That Lies Very Near the Heart." Depicting the climactic court scene of *The Merchant of Venice*, it labeled Antonio "Theatre Business," Portia "Public Opinion," and Shylock (of course) "Congress." His huge knife was marked "20% Tax on Theatres." Portia inquires of him, "Hast a surgeon, Shylock—to stop his wounds lest he bleed to death?" It is telling that the activists in this cartoon are public opinion and Congress, while the theater is a kneeling victim.[29]

It comes as no surprise that many in the theater industry were given to hyperbole that reached the level of absurdity. Several managers, for example, tried to frighten the public with the threat of possible Communist rebellion at home, presaging the Red Scare that reached alarming proportions just a few months later. Morris Gest noted that the tax "is the greatest boost the Bolshevik could have in America! It will put the poor man out of the theatre." John Golden added to this the inflammatory remark: "The spring will . . . see a considerable Bolsheviki unrest throughout the country. I am sure that for every dollar the government takes in on the new tax, it will have to pay out ten dollars on repressive measures."[30]

By Monday morning the protest petitions boasted well over 3 million names, including the signature of Mayor Hylan of New York. On Sunday more than 4,500 soldiers and sailors had joined thousands of civilians in signing petitions, cheering the theater, and jeering Claude Kitchin at public meetings in three Manhattan theaters. Also over the weekend a quarter of a million soldiers and sailors, based or hospitalized in the New York area, signed petitions circulated by the Red Cross. Pointedly, the theater managers and employees themselves did not sign the petitions, insisting that all their support come from outside their own industry.

After a meeting on Sunday, the protest committee issued a new statement, perhaps inflated but effective, in which they estimated that a million theater people nationwide would join the unemployment rolls, while losses in salaries from those jobs would reach about a billion dollars after the tax went into effect. "It's the little towns which will suffer most," Gest asserted, hoping that more of small-town America would join the protest. The road, "the backbone and the sustenance of the theatrical industry," he was sure, would be destroyed.[31]

The crux of the managers' new appeal, however, lay in their hopes of engaging more support from businesses indirectly associated with the theater. "Transportation lines of the country, including railroads and street car lines, hotels, cigar stores, florists, [and] candy shops" were sought out by the managers, who attempted to persuade the service industries that they would "find

"Exacting a Pound of Flesh That Lies Very Near the Heart," New York Tribune, Sunday, January 19, 1919, p. 1.

their receipts depleted to a very large degree." On Sunday afternoon sixteen chorus girls worked the streets of Manhattan, canvassing pedestrians and boarding taxis to garner increased support. Because the result of these tactics was "overwhelming success," all chorus girls not currently in rehearsal (more than a thousand) hit the streets on Monday to appeal personally to offices and businesses. Even the theater scrub women, "who number[ed] about 4,000 in New York City alone, [gathered] to circulate petitions among their grocers [and] butchers."[32]

The citizens of Omaha, Nebraska, decided to demonstrate against the tax, but they confused their priorities, much to the alarm of theater managers, by staying away from the theaters. New York managers hoped that this kind of protest would not catch on. Nonetheless, personal telegrams of protest reached Washington from Omaha as well as many other midwestern, western, and southern cities.[33]

By Tuesday morning, the petition signatures had swelled to 5 million, but the managers introduced yet another tactic. On Monday night the producers had ordered the immediate cessation of all preparations for seventy-one productions planned or in progress for the 1919–20 season, and a few that were already in rehearsal or under scenic and costume construction. This jeopardized the jobs of sixty thousand people and a million dollars of production money, which had already been invested, with another 4.5 million dollars yet to come. An additional two hundred road shows and a dozen new theaters scheduled for erection outside New York were also placed on hold. The managers insisted that these productions could not be mounted if the 20 percent tax were passed.[34]

Meanwhile, Washington's postal service was reported to be nearly swamped by the barrage of mail protesting the theater tax. The *Times* described a scene that could later have played in a Frank Capra movie starring Jimmy Stewart or Henry Fonda celebrating the victory of the common people over the powerful. "There was not sufficient storage space in the ante-room of the conference quarters and batches of the petitions and letters were shoved inside the room. Clerks piled heaps of them upon the table where they [would] be the first objects to greet the eyes of the conferees in the morning."[35]

The police and fire departments of New York now offered their services to help circulate petitions. The 250-sailor crew of the *USS Sierra* drew up its own petition and forwarded it to Washington. The Merchants Association and Hotel Men's Association of New York sent resolutions to Washington condemning the tax. The hotel proprietors wrote that "vast financial loss . . . would fall . . . upon the hotel men, the restaurant men, real estate owners and hundreds of others."[36]

Professor Thomas Proctor of Cornell University sent his personal appeal strongly urging the repeal of the tax because "the theatres were instrumental in keeping many of our students from saloons before the town went dry." The letter continued with what could be read as a veiled allusion to prostitution. "It would not only cause hardships on the students who are working their way through college, but also the working class, particularly the working girls, who otherwise . . . would stand around for lack of amusement."[37]

As the Stage Women's War Relief allied with star performers to open "protest booths" in New York's hotels, cabarets, and restaurants, Claude Kitchin fell suddenly and conveniently ill, and the Conference Committee had to recess. Other committee members took this opportunity to register their incredulity at the public outcry, and "each member approached [on Monday] declared that while he had not made up his mind regarding his own vote, he was informed that other members had decided that the 20 percent levy was unjust and would vote against it."[38]

In spite of this encouragement the United Managers did not soften their attack. Producer Marc Klaw, for example, made his message to Washington overtly political and even threatening. "The Democratic Party is riding for the biggest fall it has had since 1861," he warned.[39]

The newspapers of Wednesday morning reported 6 million petition signatures; the campaign was a week old. The postmaster general wired the United Managers asking them to mollify the assault, "inasmuch as a whole room in the post office building is at present filled with these letters and lists of protests." The producers, however, would be moved by nothing less than a reversal by congressional committee. "This fight," Gest claimed, "is going to be kept up until it is won." Even churches began to join the protest. The Reverend Christian Reisner and 120 members of the choir of Grace Episcopal Church in New York sent a petition to Washington. Other New York Catholic and Protestant clergy followed suit.[40]

The United Managers were surprised when on Tuesday afternoon Kitchin telegraphed asking the managers for "a brief statement of their contentions." They immediately complied and sent their report by special messenger to Washington on Wednesday morning. Meanwhile, the mothers of 25,000 chorus girls and actresses in road shows began to organize into delegations to march on Washington. New York taxi companies as well as chambers of commerce, rotary clubs, and literary clubs throughout the country wrote protesting letters to Washington, and all the editors attending the annual conference of the New York Associated Daily Newspapers went on record as opposed to the 20 percent tax. On Thursday the protesters were due to begin arriving in Washington.[41]

With a host of senators and representatives begging in vain for clerks to relieve their offices of mountains of protest mail, the Conference Committee finally surrendered. In a closed meeting on Wednesday, Senator Simmons reportedly proposed killing the 20 percent increase, and all but stubborn Claude Kitchin and Representative Joseph Fordney of Michigan voted to revert to 10 percent. "The conferees have been greatly surprised at the unanimity of the public's opposition to the burdensome tax," the *Morning Telegraph* reported. "They never expected such a protest as the public has made under the stimulus of the theatre managers. Only after the telegrams and letters began pouring in on Congress did they wake up to the serious injustice they had done." The United Managers immediately sent a message to all professional theaters: "The people have won the fight and the protest committee . . . requests that you discontinue all public announcements, except to have speeches made from stages of all theatres tonight announcing the victory of theatregoers and general public and to thank the public and the local press for their splendid assistance in winning the fight." The *Washington Post* warned that there was "still a chance that the House [would] insist upon the 20 percent tax" when the bill returned to the floor, but Kitchin failed to reintroduce the matter. When the bill was finally discussed in the House on February 8, he simply said, "If I had my way, this bill would not have been quite as it is now." The bill was finally passed on February 15 and signed by President Wilson February 24, the day following his return from France.[42]

Although the United Managers employed many tactics, two primary factors appear to be responsible for the reversal in Congress: the degree and scope of the protest (which suggested loss of voter endorsement) and the threat of actual decline rather than gain of revenue. The "storm of protest from all parts of the country" was not only surprising but overwhelming. The "sentiment of the public" seemed "almost universal" in support of the theaters and against the tax. The states of Maryland and Connecticut, for example, produced signatures equal to one-third of their populations. The fear, first raised by managers Bruce Edwards and Sam Harris, that doubling the admission tax would actually decrease the recoverable revenue because of severely reduced theater attendance was persuasively argued and perpetuated in the press.[43]

Variety was most impressed by the theater's accomplishment. "Organized in six hours, and in full swing overnight, America's theatrical . . . managers set in motion the giant protest to Congress, . . . so far flung in expression and so voluminous in size that it will go down in record as the most spontaneous crystallization of public opinion ever sent into Washington." In the wake of victory many editorials appeared congratulating the managers and restating the importance of the theater to the American people. "Public protest, managerial tact and newspapers," wrote the *Herald*, "have saved the theatre. . . . This immediate and nation wide campaign . . . reveals the American theatre as a real force in public life. Though hardly suspected by managers until now, it is a far reaching audience and can be made more powerful as the producer progresses by realizing the importance of dealing fairly with his patrons."[44]

Theater managers of the era routinely assumed a comprehensive grassroots support for the theater that transcended regional, social, and economic boundaries. The magnitude of the popular response emphatically designated the theater an exemplar of American culture. At the United Managers meeting on January 17, for example, "it was the contention of all present that the proposed [tax] is a bigger question than prohibition, because while there are many persons who never drink anything, everybody goes to the theatres." For years before and after this event it was not unusual to see the theater matter-of-factly enshrined in widely disparate criticism and journalism as "the most vital and persuasive of all the arts."[45]

If this were not so it is unlikely that the theater would have undergone such severe censorship trials as it did in the 1920s. The theater was perceived as—and, in fact, was—a powerful instrument for communicating ideas and mobilizing people. Sound motion pictures and network radio programming would diminish its role by the end of the decade, only to be usurped in their turn by television and music videos. Radio had begun to steal some of the theater audience, especially on the road, by about 1923. Experimental stations opened in 1920, and at the end of 1922 there were 576 radio stations nationwide, prompting commentators to inquire whether radio would undermine the theater. After the 1920s the theater gradually dwindled (with occasional atavistic activity) to an important but minority art form, patronized primarily by the upper-middle classes.[46]

But in the week following the rescinding of the proposed theater tax the United Managers made a final tally of the petitions signed before management sent the signal to stop. From a current perspective, the 8,762,420 signatures, representing 2,465 cities, that were accumulated in eight days of formal protest seem miraculous in the absence of radio, television, computer networks, and opinion polls. The theater was staggered by its own power and popularity. Yet what a difference inflationary recession makes. Just three years later, as the postwar recession was ending, Broadway patrons, without an apparent whimper, paid $3.40 to see John Barrymore in *Hamlet*, an increase of more than 35 percent.

4

She Would Be Erotic:
The Virtuous Role of the Postwar Sex Farceuse

Mother—Father—Son and Daughter
Don't you think you really oughter
See them
Getting
Gertie's
Garter?
—Advertisement for *Getting Gertie's Garter,* 1921

Long before the Great Depression threatened to destroy the financial stability, if not the cultural expression, of a flamboyant, exuberant, and sometimes artistically anxious Broadway theater, a great deal of popular entertainment was characterized by risqué frivolity and the absurd, suggestive antics of the idle rich, which tested the common definitions and acceptable limits of prurience and pornography. Journeying from the bedroom to the hayloft (both made remarkably public by glib playwrights), the sex farce, popular during and just after World War I, offered escapism from troubled times; indeed, the sex farce was what the tax rebellion of 1919 was in part defending.

We can now see, however, that the sex farce reflects a distinctive set of social assumptions, values, and artistic principles by playwrights, producers, and theatergoers. For some seven years America's fascination with this genre was unequalled by any other Broadway entertainment, with the exception of musical comedy (such as it was, in those pre-*Showboat* days).[1]

Under such titles as *The Girl in the Limousine* and *Up in Mabel's Room*, producers (chiefly A. H. Woods and Selwyn and Company) and playwrights (like Avery Hopwood and Wilson Collison) exploited sexuality (both real and imaginary) and pushed the sex farce near the limits of public taste and morality. Inevitably, censorship followed, beginning in 1921 with Hopwood's *The Demi-Virgin*, an event I examine in the next chapter. By 1923 John Corbin could write, "The time is past when anything goes in farce."[2] Of course Mae West had not yet unveiled her provocative 1926 comic hit, bluntly entitled *Sex*. This play, written by West under the pseudonym Jane Mast, also starred the controversial performer and ran for 375 performances before her arrest and imprisonment in 1927 for writing an indecent entertainment.

I explore here the formulas incorporated in twenty of these sex farces (a complete list of which is given in the Appendix), as well as the social assumptions and theatrical principles of the people who created these forays into physically frenetic, but never graphic, erotica. Although French sex farces, which undoubtedly inspired the American species, were occasionally presented on the American stage (most notably, Feydeau's *Breakfast in Bed*, produced by A. H. Woods in 1920), I concentrate only on the plays written by American playwrights and produced on the Broadway stage. My choice includes the most popular and conspicuous sex farces, as well as five box-office failures, presented between 1915 (when the vogue began) and 1921 (when the popularity faded after the trial of *The Demi-Virgin*). I examine all the plays in this genre by Avery Hopwood, who was the most prolific and successful. Beginning in 1915 at least one money-making sex farce appeared in each Broadway season. Six of the eight hits, however, came in the three years after the end of World War I. And six of these eight hits were produced by A. H. Woods.[3]

In making my assessments I focus primarily on the dramatic presentation and the critical and popular reception of the heroines of those farces that were set against a social and political maelstrom of world war, a burgeoning women's rights movement and the reactionary responses to it, economic recession, and the new commercialism. I note that despite the right-wing attacks on the sex farces for their suggestive content and corruption of the values of women, the farces were themselves in part reactionary in their attempt to restore women (perceived as growing forceful and rebellious) to their "rightful" place in the traditional home and marriage. In consequence, the sex farces were self-contradictory in both intent and production, while eliciting the ambivalent, contradictory public reception that typified other theatrical experiences of postwar America as well.

Of all the successful writers of the sex farce Avery Hopwood reigned supreme in style, language, suggestiveness, and popularity, and the "exclusive pedestal" of this "potentate of playwrights" was never seriously challenged. A sophisticated traveler and bon vivant, he was credited by Alice B. Toklas with helping to create "modern New York." The city in this era, like Hopwood, "became . . . gay, irresponsible and brilliant," she wrote.[4]

The American rage for sex farces began in 1915 with Hopwood's enormously successful *Fair and Warmer*, which set the standards for structure, tone, and subject matter. Farces modeled on the French like *Twin Beds* (1914), by Margaret Mayo and Salisbury Field, were popular before 1915, but they flirted only momentarily with sexual misunderstanding. American farces that centered structurally on sexual shenanigans really began with *Fair and Warmer*, which featured actors John Cumberland and Madge Kennedy, who also starred in *Twin Beds*. Critical response to Hopwood's "little masterwork of farce writing" was nearly universally laudatory, praising the playwright's skills and finding the racy subject and character machinations great fun. Merely mischievous rather than wicked (a charge laid to later sex farces), *Fair and Warmer* was found to be "perceptibly improper [but] flagrantly entertaining."[5]

As the genre persisted, however, and Hopwood as well as his fellow practitioners reached for ever-more suggestive material, critics began to reconsider the appropriateness of the genre. Reviewers were fond of describing Hopwood's efforts as skating on thin ice—that is, when he "manipulate[d] the suggestive in such a way, indirectly and skillfully, that actual immorality is avoided." The *Dramatic Mirror,* for example, in reviewing Hopwood's *Sadie Love* (1915), reported that he "dallies with situations which avoid only by a hair's breadth what in most hands would probably shock the dignity of the purists. . . . [He has] the happy faculty of setting the nerves atingling in nervous expectancy of something shocking that is always just beyond reach." Likewise, his language in *Our Little Wife* (1916) raised eyebrows: "Line after line convicts him of trying to see just how far he can go without having the police raid his theatre."[6]

Usually writing alone but sometimes in collaboration, Hopwood created eight sex farces (most of them popular successes) that were produced on Broadway between 1915 and 1921. His two-time collaborator, Wilson Collison, a former Kansas City druggist who never achieved success in the genre

by himself, wrote five between 1919 and 1921, and their colleagues Otto Harbach, Charlton Andrews, Martha Stanley, Adelaide Matthews, C. W. Bell,
Mark Swan, Lawrence Rising, Margaret Mayo, Martin Brown, Jack Larrie,
Gustav Blum, Fred Jackson, and George Hobart contributed one or two such
farces apiece after the outbreak of the Great War.[7]

Of the twenty plays written by these playwrights, two were enormous hits
(more than 300 performances), six were very successful (more than 100),
seven had modest runs (40–80), and five failed (fewer than 30).[8] Many of
these farces earned additional money with successful road tours. But only
Hopwood, among the five playwrights who attempted sex farces without col-
laborators, created hits, and the first of them, *Fair and Warmer*, was the most
commercially successful of all. This play ran for 377 performances, and according to Hopwood's biographer it earned the playwright almost a quarter of
a million dollars.[9] Hopwood also collaborated with Charlton Andrews on the
second longest-running sex farce, *Ladies' Night* (1920), which ran for 360 performances. For Hopwood's two other collaborations he was hired by the producer to doctor the ailing scripts of Collison. It appears that producers
assumed that Hopwood's contribution would assure success. Curiously, none
of the playwrights failed in collaboration. Except for Hopwood, most playwrights began in successful collaboration but thereafter created solo flops.
Both Collison and Harbach failed when writing alone, yet when they collaborated on *Up in Mabel's Room*, the result was a hit. Apparently, all were emulat-
ing Hopwood's proven formula and smart style, but the style seemed
approachable only when they worked as a team.

The titles of these farces are meant to suggest loose character or behavior,
and most of them include a reference to the heroine, or to the character whom
the playwright and producer wished the ticket buyer to believe was the central
female character. Consider *Sadie Love, The Girl in the Limousine* (in prepro-
duction entitled *Betty's Bed*), *The Girl with the Carmine Lips, Our Little
Wife, The Naughty Wife, Up in Mabel's Room, The Demi-Virgin*, and *Getting
Gertie's Garter*. *Ladies' Night, No More Blondes*, and *Scrambled Wives* also
refer to women, but in a more general way. *Scrambled Wives* was written in
1920 by Adelaide Matthews and Martha Stanley, a women's playwriting team
which added to the list of sex farces just before the genre waned in popularity.
Even subtitles usually exploit the feminine. *Up in Mabel's Room*, for example,
is subtitled *A Frivolous Farce of Feminine Foibles*.[10] *The Naughty Wife*
opened in 1917 as *Losing Eloise*, but after three weeks of middling business,
the management attempted to improve the box office by altering the title to a
more suggestive one.

Only six titles are gender neutral, and but three refer to men. All titles except one, however, feature sexual suggestion: *Fair and Warmer, His Bridal Night, Nightie Night, A Sleepless Night, Double Exposure, Parlor, Bedroom and Bath, A Bachelor's Night,* and *What's Your Husband Doing?* The subtitle for *Fair and Warmer* underscores the intent: *A play of Temperature and Temperament.*[11] Martin Brown's *An Innocent Idea* (1920), which did not provide a provocative clue in its title, closed after seven performances.

On occasion a play's title is misleading—as with *Nightie Night,* which, despite numerous scenes featuring a woman who has lost her dress, and another concerning a confrontation with a former lover, is comparatively tame and has no bedroom scene at all. It could be argued that this 1919 play by Stanley and Matthews is merely masquerading as a sex farce. The *Times* claimed that the "indecorous" title was intended to mislead the public. It is also telling that the play's pre-production title was the safer "Oh, How Could You!" Similarly, in *The Girl in the Limousine* (1919), advertised as "fun in a four-poster," an automobile figures in the action of the play, but its passenger is the play's hero (or, rather, victim of the playwrights' complications), not heroine. Neither the heroine nor any other woman was involved with actions taking place in the limousine. The heart of the conflict in *The Girl in the Limousine,* however, is definitely sexual. Strictly speaking, the titles of *The Girl in the Limousine* and *Nightie Night* have nothing to do with the plays; they seem to have been created to arouse interest. The sex-farce vogue also inspired producers and playwrights to use sex-farce titles for plays that did not belong in the genre; sex-farce popularity was used to draw attention to harmless comedies like *Exchange of Wives* and *Six Cylinder Love.*[12]

The sex farces are written in three acts, usually with one or more acts, often the second, transpiring in a bedroom. Customarily, this is the heroine's room, like the "pretty pink boudoir" for actress Doris Kenyon in *The Girl in the Limousine,* and invariably the settings are realistically designed and furnished in the latest trends, such as a wealthy, "gay young woman would fancy." Typically, the bed and surroundings are adorned with frills and coverlets that both aid the concealment of interlopers and accentuate the femininity of the heroine. Through myriad misunderstandings and coincidences the playwrights manage to troop all the characters through the bedroom, trapping various people of opposite sexes in or under the bed in compromising positions.[13]

In *Getting Gertie's Garter* (1921), by Hopwood and Collison, the bedroom is avoided, but it is replaced by a barn hayloft that functions in the same suggestive way. This shift in locale was specified in the tryout title of the play: *Come up to the Haymow.*[14] A similar switch in location is effected in *Ladies' Night* by supplanting the bedroom with a Turkish bath populated by women wearing nothing but towels most of the time. After bedrooms, the most frequently used setting is the luxurious drawing room of a Long Island estate house or chic New York apartment. The exposition of act 1 usually transpires there, although in *His Bridal Night* (1916), by Rising and Mayo, the action opens in the bedroom of the heroine, Vi Damorel.

The action of the sex farce is fast-paced, relying on misunderstandings, half-heard conversations, and narrow misses by the characters. A critic for the *Evening Journal* stressed the athletic nature of the proceedings by observing that Bertram Harrison, the director of *Getting Gertie's Garter*, must have "had a strenuous time . . . for what the actors did during the play was enough to tire out any ordinary person." Almost continuously, one or more characters is in a panic, desperate to procure or return an item or to avoid being caught in a sexually compromising situation, although the predicament usually has an innocent origin. *Parlor, Bedroom and Bath* (1917), by Bell and Swan, for example, is "based upon such apparently secure foundations as lies and lingerie." A review of *The Girl in the Limousine* provides a ready explanation of the misunderstanding as a plotting device: "The action is based upon the theory that a person surprised in a strange predicament does not believe anyone will believe the obvious truth."[15]

Not surprisingly, the misunderstanding creating the most devastating results always occurs near the end of the second act. In *Fair and Warmer*, Laura Bartlett returns from a flirtatious night at the opera only to find her husband, Billy, and best friend Blanny passed out after an apparent evening of drunken licentiousness and sexual debauchery, with their "appearance calculated to furnish first class evidence in a suit for divorce." Actress Madge Kennedy, who played Blanny, epitomized what one critic called "devilish innocence". Even the age-old mistaken-identity device is central to several sex farces, most notably *His Bridal Night*, where the heroine, Vi, marries a young man who finds himself on his honeymoon with Tiny, her indistinguishable twin.[16]

Like *Fair and Warmer*, most of the sex farces make liberal use of alcohol, even after passage of the Eighteenth Amendment, when the plays begin to include many references to "Prohibition cocktails." In *The Demi-Virgin* the heroine remarks that she did not know the hero was "so fond of things to drink." "I wasn't," he replies, "till they took it away from me."[17]

In keeping with standard stage farce every set included numerous doors, wardrobes, and novel hiding places, such as laundry tubs and rolled-up rugs, to abet the would-be liaisons and mad escapes. In the case of *Getting Gertie's Garter* the entire stage offered limitless possibilities for concealment in act 2 because the barn loft was covered with mounds of hay. The other two acts, however, provided a "red-letter night for nooks and crannies," featuring interior action replete with slamming doors, pratfalls, and rain-drenched characters fleeing through two hours of nearly ceaseless errors. The review by S. Jay Kaufman asserted that he had never seen "a play in which there was so much action. I shudder to think what would have happened if one of the doors had suddenly refused to allow itself to be opened."[18]

At the center of this structured mayhem we find the heroine/farceuse, who is treated differently from the other characters, both male and female.[19] In what image are the playwrights creating this most fascinating and enigmatic of all the dramatis personae? The heroine is always pretty, designed to lure well-heeled men who either seek a liaison with her or are mistakenly believed to be carrying on sexually with her. In the former case the leading or secondary male character desperately attempts to effect an illicit assignation; this is always ultimately denied by the playwright, although the attempted act comes close to completion. In the latter case the result is a frenzied display of musical beds, closets, hampers, and trunks. When there is no deliberate attempt by a couple to engage in sexual intercourse, the manic and surreptitious activities of hero and heroine are invariably misinterpreted by others as an illicit affair. The heroine may sometimes delight in being frantically pursued by a host of men (married or not), and she frequently allows her reputation to suffer, but she is always fundamentally wholesome. She is thus morally acceptable at the end, even if she has been considered "naughty" throughout most of the play. The audience is often privy to her virtuousness even if all the other characters are mistaken. *The Demi-Virgin* is an important exception.

The Hopwood heroine in particular is not only beautiful and young (a typical age range is mid-twenties), but high-spirited and witty. She is generally more serious in manner and deed than other characters of both sexes and more mature than at least one naive or frivolous woman. On the other hand, she is usually contrasted with an aging, conservative matron as well. *The Demi-Virgin*, for example, has Aunt Zeffie Wilson, a Mrs. Malaprop type who blocks the love interest of the secondary couple in the play. Zelda Sears, a popular character actress and playwright, assayed many of these virtuous spinsters, like Aunt Cicely in *The Girl in the Limousine*, who in the midst of the would-be sexual shenanigans exclaims that she doesn't know whether "she is in Greenwich Village or Sodom and Gomorrah." One reviewer quipped that the school of American sex farce "insists upon the pernicious presence . . . of a chaperon."[20]

Providing further contrast with the heroine, sensuous vamps and empty-headed, giggly women of easy virtue are also included in many of these plays. In Hopwood's plays, in fact, they seem to be a necessity. But these characters are never the protagonists, and they are usually dismissed by the play's heroine. Female roles that suggest a looser morality than that of the heroine are usually introduced in the first act and given their most extensive and sexiest action in the second act only to vanish or, at most, dress the stage in the finale. In act 1 of *The Demi-Virgin,* for example, two bathing beauties, hired principally to decorate the movies, discuss their jobs: "Gee, I wish they'd give me a part where I could wear some clothes," one complains. Her companion later philosophizes, "Take enough off when you're young, and you'll have enough to put on when you're older!" In the play's second act these girls play strip poker, and a certain Bee La Rose is introduced as "an extremely pretty girl, in a costume so décolleté, that one can only gaze at her—and gasp." All of these characters are conveniently absent (offstage in another part of the house) at the play's end, when the vicissitudes and mistakes of the night are happily and morally resolved.[21]

Many other plays of the period that include such characters similarly insist that they be absent at the final curtain. The farce *We've Got to Have Money* (1923), by Edward Laska, and the comedy *The Advertising of Kate* (1922), by Annie Nathan Meyer (discussed in chapter 7), are good examples of this disappearing act. In more serious dramatic work, no matter how prominent the loose woman, she is usually absent during the resolution. Even O'Neill in *The Great God Brown,* for example, who brings on the sympathetically presented prostitute Cybel for the climactic death of Billy Brown, returns to his virtuous Margaret for the restoration of order in the epilogue.

Typically the sex farceuse is recently wed or in her second marriage following death or, more frequently, divorce. Therefore, she is sexually experienced in a socially sanctioned way. In several plays, such as *Scrambled Wives,* the heroine comes unexpectedly face to face with her embarrassed new husband's ex-wife, or finds herself trying to explain to her startled husband the inexplicable reason for her ex-husband's sudden appearance in her bedroom. It is not coincidental that she is an experienced woman of the world; she may have been modeled on the leading women of Restoration comedy, especially those of Congreve, rather than the women of late nineteenth- and early twentieth-century French farces that were frequently used for comparison to the Broadway plays by American critics of the teens and twenties. Although Restoration comedy did not appear on the Broadway stage in this period, Hopwood's level of sophistication makes him likely to be familiar with it. He and his colleagues would certainly have known, however, the late eighteenth-century heroines of Sheridan and Goldsmith, whose major work was regularly revived on Broadway between 1909 and 1915. Clearly, French farce was an important model for the plays' situations, as we can see in the farces of Labiche, Sardou, and Feydeau, at least three of which appeared on Broadway in this period. Perhaps the most important character model for the sex-farce heroine, however, was the "simultaneous siren and angel" of so much Victorian literature and art, a woman like George du Maurier's Trilby, from the book that had left an indelible mark on the dramatic vision of the generation following the war.[22] This model of woman is clearly evident in both comic and serious work of the best and least on Broadway after the Great War, from the tragedies of Eugene O'Neill to the revues of Florenz Ziegfeld.

The heroine's economic status is always high; she moves among her fellow socialites and dresses impeccably in expensive and often alluring gowns and negligees while she holds or attends large private parties, usually on Long Island. (Only *The Demi-Virgin* ventures into the decadent world of Hollywood house parties.) In the plays of Hopwood, Collison, and Harbach the heroine has a quicker wit than any other character (including the men); the most quotable lines usually belong to her. Again, one may look to Congreve's Millamant in *The Way of the World* or Etherege's Harriet in *The Man of Mode* as a model. In the world of postwar Broadway, as in that of Restoration England, the playwrights were creating characters who talked, moved, and behaved in the sophisticated and glamorous manner that they and their audiences would like to think they themselves did. Hopwood, in talking of his own plays, stressed that he sought to create characters whom people would like to know. Like the heroines of nineteenth-century melodrama, however, the heroines of the sex farces, despite their apparent independence, abilities, and wit, were cast in a position that reinforced conventional, patriarchal views when order was restored at the conclusion of the play. As we shall see, the casting of specific actresses and actors in these productions further reinforced this view of women, a view that conflicted with the growing independence women were really experiencing.[23]

Brief pictures of the predicaments of several heroines should demonstrate their typical action, wit, and style in nearly all the farces. Mabel Essington, the title character in *Up in Mabel's Room* (1919), by Harbach and Collison, is a widow whose previous suitor, Garry, now married to Geraldine, a jealous young woman, tries to recover an autographed pink chemise he once gave her. Mabel describes the chemise as "the record of the only naughty thought I believe Garry ever had." Mabel, of course, is usually wearing the incriminating garment, and her conversations with Garry are misinterpreted by various eavesdroppers, who believe she is bestowing sexual favors on the married man. Throughout all the silly doings of the misdirection, only Mabel maintains her equanimity. Even when Mabel is caught in what appears to be "the act" with Garry and is attacked by a hysterical Geraldine, Mabel remains cool. "Oh if I'd known there were such creatures in the world as you, I'd never have wanted to be born," Geraldine screams. Mabel replies, "What a pity you weren't informed in time."[24]

Mabel's level-headedness is nearly matched by that of Trixie Lorraine in *Nightie Night*. When confronted by the virtuous but jealous wife Mollie Moffat, who angrily claims that Trixie has "always wanted my husband—now I hope you're satisfied," the heroine replies, "I don't want your husband. I wouldn't take him for a gift. . . . If you had any sense you wouldn't worry about your husband's old love-affairs. The time for you to get excited is when he starts a new one."[25]

Laura Bartlett of *Fair and Warmer* is a bright but bored banker's wife. Our first glimpse of her is smoking and playing the piano, a picture that informs the audience that she is not an innocent. She is stylish and talented, attends the opera regularly, indulges in the latest dances, and likes to flirt. Superficially recalling Hedda Gabler, Laura is exasperated with her husband, Billy, who seems to be a "perfect person," a homebody with no rough edges. Her home life lacks intrigue and danger. What Laura seems to hate most, however, is the fact that other women are not interested in Billy. Even after Laura discovers Billy and Blanny in their compromising drunken pose, she remains the most serious and forceful character, through the bedroom chase scene of act 3 and up until the inevitable nuptial reconciliation before the final curtain.

On the night of her marriage to Teddy, Gertie Darling of *Getting Gertie's Garter* is confronted by Ken, an old flame, who is now married to Pattie and anxiously trying to get back a bejeweled garter with his photograph on the buckle. As with Mabel's chemise, the object of Ken's quest is usually on Gertie's person until she loses it, thus causing Ken no end of difficulties as the item passes from one confused character to another. He believes that if Pattie finds out she will know that Ken and Gertie have been, in his words, "more than romantic." Gertie is a woman with a past, but her activities in the play are all virtuous.[26]

Although many of the actresses who attempted these heroines came under attack from critics for either their lack of acting ability or their inappropriateness for the role, it never seemed to lessen the popularity of the productions. Periodically, a film actress with little affinity for the stage was cast to exploit her notoriety. American theatrical producers were beginning to recognize that they could capitalize on the growing popularity of film. Until this time film had been raiding the legitimate stage, while New Yorkers sneered. The tables were turning, however, and by the end of the decade and the advent of talking pictures, the ascendancy of film would be complete and irreversible. The changing tide was subtly in evidence in show-business periodicals like *Dramatic Mirror*, which from 1915 to 1921 devoted ever more space to film.

By 1920 almost all the cover illustrations were of movie, rather than theater, stars.

The casting of film performers was also important professionally for the actresses, for it was supposed to endorse their ability to act with their voices as well as bodies in the legitimate theater. Doris Kenyon, a popular, much-photographed movie queen, who took the lead of Betty Neville in *The Girl in the Limousine,* primarily decorated the production displayed "in a new negligee every minute," as the *Times* put it. If a cinema personality were not cast in the leading role, she would almost certainly be cast in an exotic or highly visible supporting position. One such film star "familiar to fans the country over," Claire Whitney, made her stage debut in *An Innocent Idea* as a flirtatious wife. This also occurred in *Up in Mabel's Room* with the casting of Enid Markey as the frenetic Geraldine. Heywood Broun complained that Markey "quite overdid the part. . . . Even ingenues should be restricted to a certain number of grimaces and squirmings."[27]

A typical dramatic use of the secondary female character is that of Pattie Walrick in *Getting Gertie's Garter.* This young, impressionable new wife misinterprets her husband's pursuit of the garter as an attraction to Gertie. Consequently, she seeks revenge by proposing a scandalous affair with another house guest, "to be written up in the papers as a married woman driven to an unvirtuous affair because [of] . . . a deceitful husband." The attempted comic seduction in the hayloft of the barn is, of course, never consummated, but Pattie does manage to lose all her clothes and spend most of the second and third acts wrapped in a horse blanket, screaming and fleeing.[28]

The Dolly Sisters, Rozsika and Yansci, were not actresses but popular dancers in music halls, extravaganzas, and midnight roof revels and Ziegfeld Frolics. Nonetheless, Al Woods cast them as Vi and Tiny in *His Bridal Night,* capitalizing simultaneously on their notoriety, beauty, and virtually identical faces. The *Times* noted that the dancers "have left the merry-merry and gone into the naughty, naughty." Their attempts at characterization, however, were apparently unsuccessful, as they failed to "grasp the shadings and subtleties of acting." Although the Dollys' acting deficiencies were loudly decried (at best the two were described as "well drilled" but "tiresome"), the sisters performed in this farce for months.[29]

Most often an actress like Hazel Dawn, who was considered wholesome rather than sensual, was cast by A. H. Woods, apparently to make the heroine less offensive to those who might be appalled by too much salaciousness. Dawn, who "achieved the dubious distinction of being the leading bedroom farceuse," had a manner of presentation that nullified much that would be considered lewd in another actress' performance. Percy Hammond, for example, wrote that "Miss Dawn's cleanly personality enables her to overcome the compromising situations in which the nympholetic farceurs involve her, and she is, despite her sexly assignment, pretty and wholesome. . . . [She] always puts a saucy halo upon her most forward impersonations." Nonetheless, in negligee and pajamas she made, according to one critic, "a sufficiently alluring figure, even for a Woods audience."[30]

Dawn was apparently a poor actress, however; she was repeatedly attacked for her strident voice and lack of talent for anything save modeling clothes or removing them. But she could play the violin and sing well enough to perform in musicals. Leo Marsh described her as "highly ornamental and at times not inadequate."[31] Others were harsher. In spite of the criticism, Dawn played the heroines in *The Demi-Virgin, Getting Gertie's Garter*, and *Up in Mabel's Room;* we must therefore ask whether the poor or limited acting of so many actresses in the farceuse roles undermined or defused the sophistication and social control of the heroines. Were producers like Woods simply trying to make the roles safer because of the controversial nature of the plays, or were they subverting well-wrought roles that celebrated the intellect of women? Or were both intentions contradictorily in play?

Dawn herself, while performing in *Up in Mabel's Room*, wrote an article that articulately described her passive approach to "naughty parts," an approach that can be seen either as explaining the safeness of her stage appearance in such roles or undercutting the negative criticism she often received for her acting. Her technique, she explained, consisted of

> being innocent on stage . . . [whereby] the naughty part can be lifted into an appearance of conventional propriety. The point of a naughty line must not go beyond the lips. It should not be in the eyes, or in the mind. It must be articulate, that is all. . . . Add to this, the baby stare, and if appropriate, the baby voice, and you have a naughty part played at its best. The audience is always delighted to observe that the actress is saying something that she appears to believe is perfectly innocent. . . . If the actress spoke the lines . . . with an obvious wink, the audience would resent it. . . . Ignore the suggestive idea and you put the responsibility of moral delinquency upon the audience.[32]

The shift of moral burden from the performers to the audience, from the sellers to the customers, is an effective discursive device that has sometimes been used in later years by pornographers under attack for corrupting the morals of the community.

Dawn went on to explain that it was vital for her in such roles to project a personality "that is entirely different from the play's idea of a suggestive character." This, she claimed, had "been a great advantage." Woods seemed to understand this as well; he also appeared to be undercutting the suggestiveness of Dawn's character by calling attention to her reputation as an actress even while she was performing. At one point in *The Demi-Virgin*, for example, Dawn pulled out a violin and played a short piece from her most popular previous musical comedy, *The Pink Lady*. This business, of course, was not in the written play. Dawn had in fact played this same song many times before, and most of the regular theatergoers recognized the reference, a tactic that called attention to the stage personality and took the audience out of the world of the play.[33]

Likewise, the Selwyns habitually cast serious actresses who had little experience with comedy and were better known for playing heroines in melodrama. Margaret Illington, the flirtatious Dodo Warren in *Our Little Wife*, was described as "one of our most tear-stained actresses . . . now seeking to disport herself in a role that calls for airy irresponsibility."[34] Apparently the producers were attempting to defuse possible backlashes against the productions by either dressing up the farce with the appearance of sophisticated respectability (the Selwyns) or (Woods) with the spirit of good, clean fun. In spite of complaints by the critics, the producers continued this practice throughout the reign of the sex farce. Only in *Sadie Love* was an accomplished actress (Marjorie Rambeau) cast who projected a wholesome image as well as being adept at the farcical style.[35] The *Times* compared her favorably with Ethel Barrymore; others praised her tenderness, vivacity, beauty, grace, authority, and refinement. Many reviewers, however, found the casting a mistake and ill-suited to the farcical humor of the play.[36]

In contrast to the actresses usually cast as heroines, the leading male actors were talented, veteran farceurs like John Cumberland, who worked repeatedly in this genre. He performed so frequently in these plays that he soon had difficulty obtaining any other kind of role. "Though it was most profitable," he wrote in 1926, "the 'bedroom period' of my career is one that I am striving earnestly to forget." Cumberland's character Tony Hamilton in *The Girl in the Limousine* was labeled "an immoral little Jack-in-the-box," which perhaps best describes his physical activity in these farces. The moral nature of his usual farcical character, however, was revealed in his depictions of "worried innocence," for which the *Times* said he had "a positive genius." Hornblow described his "super-clowning" in *Up in Mabel's Room:* he "slouches or prances through his moments of defeat or triumph, looking for all the world like a melancholy or an elated frog." This diminutive farceur became so adept at these roles that critics began to refer to them as "John Cumberland parts." He and such other performers as Roland Young, Ernest Truex, and Charles Ruggles performed the anxious, embarrassed, but likable male leads with complete abandon and little concern for their physical well-being. Most other characters in the play assume that the heroes are sexually active and committed adherents to the double standard. As the maid Norah in *Nightie Night* philosophizes, "When you find him out, the man don't live that ain't leading a double life."[37]

Whether deliberate or not, the practice of casting accomplished actors in the male roles further undermined the integrity of the women presented in the sex farces and underscored the patriarchal model, not only in the world of the play but also in the production practice itself. We must remember that the patriarchal model and the stereotypical life roles for women were under attack at this time on many fronts. Not only was women's suffrage a pervasive issue, resulting in passage of the Nineteenth Amendment in 1919 and its implementation in August 1920, but advocates for birth control, led by Margaret Sanger, were enmeshed in battles with the courts, police, newspapers, churches, and the public at large from just before the Great War and throughout the 1920s. The extensive grassroots movement supported "free sexual expression and reproductive self-determination," yet the legislature of New York declared it a violation of "the public interest to have contraceptive information disseminated," and the state supreme court approved a municipal government's right to forbid screenings of a silent film advocating birth control. Illegal birth-control clinics began to open in 1916, resulting in prison sentences for the women who operated them. Opponents, including many feminists who were divided over this issue, claimed that publication of contraceptive methods would undermine the institution of marriage.[38]

What was deemed suitable in women's fashions and public behavior was not only changing rapidly but also debated in both public arenas and private quarters. Women shucked off yards and pounds of garments (both outer and under). Many cut their long hair, thus eradicating another symbol of vulnerability and a traditional emblem of beauty. Smoking in public was becoming more common, with women often lighting up deliberately to cause a stir and reopen the controversy. So-called indecent dances like the shimmy were performed not only privately but publicly, often in the sex farces. In *Nightie Night*, for example, when the heroine is caught trying to bolt from the married hero's apartment clad in borrowed pajamas, she breaks into the shimmy to mask her attempted escape.[39] Like birth control, the suggestive dances were contested by clergy and the new wave of community and undergraduate purity leagues that sprang up in opposition to these challenges to the old models. Much of the younger generation especially embraced an iconoclastic fashion and revolutionary sexuality; they were bored by many of the issues and values that had preoccupied their Victorian and Edwardian forebears.

The prewar way of life was under siege, and the sex farces took a curious position that straddled the old and the new by exploiting the new fashions, language, and openness while enshrining many traditional values. Superficially the farces seemed to assault the old lines of decorum and inhibition, but actually they adhered to many of the tenets of nineteenth-century morality concerning the appropriate position of woman in society. The appearance and language of the flapper were celebrated, but the plays did not allow her to be truly liberated—to, for example, enjoy sex "as much as men had enjoyed it for centuries," as Sanger put it. The plays ultimately denied the genuine individuality of the evolving postwar age while perpetuating the proverbial but entrenched double standard. In spite of their potential for power through the use of intellect and wit, Hopwood's glib-tongued heroines remained imprisoned by convention and powerless in the face of moral expectations dictated by playwright, critics, and much of the audience. The female characters with less wit or physical charm fit the stereotypes engendered by the Victorian world, such as "tendency to brain fever, ubiquitous maternal instinct, raging hormonal imbalance . . . meant to shackle female experience to male convenience."[40]

The New York Call, a socialist workers' newspaper that regularly published articles on feminism, sex education, and birth control, observed that the sex-farce playwrights were "dealing with past standards, with the sniggering modesty of Mid-Victorians."[41] Perhaps most of the humor appeared sophomoric and the material passé to the Call's well-read and progressive readers, but not to the voyeuristic audiences who made the physical displays of fashion and bodily charms so successful.

Further subversion of the female character's potential power is evident in the formula plotting devices, which encouraged displays of the female body in vulnerable, compromising, and revealing positions and costumes. Critics clearly enjoyed and happily reported the exhibitions. Making typical reference to the feminine charms onstage, Bernard Sobel said of Andrews and Hopwood's Ladies' Night: "The settings are simple, but the women players are simply beautiful." His remark reduces the women to stage dressing, as did many reviewers who coupled scenic investiture with the attractiveness of actresses. Eileen Wilson, who played the heroine in Harbach's No More Blondes (1920), was reviewed more for her "magnificently dramatic lingerie" than for her performance. Exposing some of the physical splendor of beautiful young women was typical in nearly all of these farces, but it was especially exploited by Woods, who for six years "paid his annual tribute to Aphrodite." Rennold Wolf said of him, "There is none who gauges the spiciness of this sort of entertainment, its limitations and its possibilities, quite so accurately," observing later that the Woods production of *Up in Mabel's Room* was "embellished [note the scenic word choice] by several comely women in a state of considerable underdress." In this case, and in many others, the heroine as well as the looser women appeared in suggestive attire, ranging from pajamas to negligee to chemise.[42]

When attacked by would-be censors for his strip-poker scene in *The Demi-Virgin,* Woods claimed that a display of scantily clothed women onstage should offend no one since there were no male characters present. "Had a man come on the set," he said, "it would have precipitated a suggestive situation."[43] Woods describes the onstage action as if it were a real event, ignoring the voyeuristic presence of a male and female audience. It appears that the onstage female presence and the pretense by the characters that the situation is private is used to justify the voyeurism. Furthermore, to these practitioners the possibility that a woman might be attracted to her own sex was apparently unthinkable.

Many reviews, written by men, even when they condemned the play, commented on how attractive the women in the cast were. "There are enough pretty women in the company [of *The Demi-Virgin*]," we are told, "to fill the front row of any first class musical comedy." By contrast, when the plays were reviewed by women, the sexual or suggestive nature of the actions of the female characters might be described or references made to their minimal attire, but there were no references to their attractiveness. Also, it was frequently reported that women in the audience reveled in the parade of bedroom fashions as well as in the revealing gowns. A reviewer observed that *Up in Mabel's Room* had "fascinating feminine clothes" and Mabel's lingerie especially "brought out expressions of admiration from every woman in the house." It was also common for reviewers to report on the stage fashions in detail. Alan Dale described Hazel Dawn in *The Demi-Virgin* as "gowned in pure silver, plus a magenta plume emerging from her pricelessly peroxide locks."[44]

For commercial purposes the producers often exaggerated the prurient interest and erotic nature of the staged material, but when under attack by the public, press, or legal system, they usually confessed to the truth about how safe the product really was. By safe, producers referred only to the plays' sexual message; but the plays were subversive to women in the implied hegemonic discourse. Occasionally producers advertised material as risqué but denied the danger of the piece once the theatergoer had a ticket. With *A Bachelor's Night* (1921), for example, the public was told to expect a sexy farce of lingerie, slamming doors, and screaming women. Yet the program noted that "this is a farce containing nothing but the good old stuff." No matter how closely the dramatic material might approach suspect moral behavior, the farces always endorsed traditional social values in the final scene. The playwrights also acknowledged the safeness of their plays, especially in interviews. Hopwood declared that it was impossible for him to corrupt anyone and that he was mystified that "the prurient come to be shocked. . . . [*Ladies' Night*] is not meant to appeal to those people who cover up the legs of their pianos and veil their eyes at the sight of a well-turned ankle." He claimed, perhaps sarcastically, that he was listening to the voice of the audience, for he was but "a servant of the public." Those who would censor him, however, "the Uplifters . . . persist in looking down upon the public and decrying the wisdom of the many."[45]

Whether critics called for censorship, condemned the plays as inartistic, or praised them, the results were the same. Criticism had little or no impact on the popularity of the sex farces except to promote them; the producers managed to use all notices as publicity. The lack of critical control here was typical of the cultural partitioning under way during and just after the war. Historian Ellis Hawley notes that as modernists (like Heywood Broun and Kenneth Macgowan, who championed O'Neill and theatrical experiment) and traditionalists (reactionaries Arthur Hornblow and Alan Dale, who strove to recover the halcyon days of the Progressive era) "fought over the custody of high culture, both were losing contact with the emerging popular culture."[46] Nonetheless, the contemporary criticism provides insight into the import of the sex farces on, or their reflection of, cultural forces of the period.

Although many critics of the period attacked these plays for licentiousness, finding them "vulgar in the extreme," just as many stressed what the play manuscripts bear out: not only are the heroines without serious fault, but none of the characters commits a sexual act (although a few make the attempt). Most of the suggestiveness, humor, and conflict revolve around misunderstanding, double entendre, and flirtation. Heywood Broun observed that in *Up in Mabel's Room*, "although the fact is firmly planted in advance that every one in the play is wholly without guilt—no opportunity is lost for coarse innuendo." Even conservative Alan Dale wrote that "'The Demi-Virgin' was peopled with boys and girls presumed to be of the risqué-est. There they were trying, oh, so hard, to shock us—the dear things . . . but we were 'on' to their little game." At the beginning of the era, in 1915, a critic observed that in *Fair and Warmer*, Hopwood "uses beds, nightrobes, and quarts of alcohol as theatrical properties, but he sees to it that the hearts of his puppets are all pure as the driven snow."[47]

The most scathing reviews of the era call for censorship, claiming that the action and language are offensive and "shocking . . . [and] a blue pencil would cleanse" them. Reviewer H. Z. Torres goes on to say, however, that *Getting*

Gertie's Garter is very funny. This same reviewer, who published the most outspoken attack on *The Demi-Virgin*, observed that "one who loves the theatre must wax wrathful to see it so prostituted." But extreme responses were to be expected; as Warren Susman wrote of the 1920s: "Virtually every popular cultural form inspired instantly an opposition that urged its banning or at least its censorship."[48]

It is curious that many critics complained of the sex farces yet provided the producers with titillating publicity gratis by dwelling on their off-color or scandalous elements. A pan of Collison's *A Bachelor's Night,* for example, stresses that a young wife spends most of the play in her underwear, that the play strikes "a daring note of suggestiveness both in action and speech," and that "the show is actually vulgar." Hornblow complained that *Ladies' Night* went beyond the acceptable limits of decorum, yet he noted that "the women go around wearing little more than a smile," and he described the bare beauty of the actresses: "the willowy lines of the stately vamp, the more than generously displayed charms of Jimmie's wife and friends." He also wondered naively—or sardonically—how so many actresses could be found who were "willing to make such a show of themselves." Another critic claimed that *His Bridal Night,* an "overindulgence in nuptial humor, . . . is not only no play for the graduating class at Miss Minchin's Academy; it is no play for the fastidious." Unable to envision the liberation of stage language and event that lay ahead, the *Sun's* reviewer of *Getting Gertie's Garter* claimed that "when a . . . blanket was pulled off one woman . . . she was left with nothing but hay for lingerie. . . . The limit in farce had been reached."[49]

Of course, some reviewers provided positive assessments that reveled in the plays' naughtiness. The following passages are typical: "When the curtain . . . arose [on Collison's *The Girl with the Carmine Lips* (1920)] and revealed the mysterious Girl . . . nonchalantly smoking a cigarette and revealing a shapely ankle, we sat up and took notice. Instinctively we felt that there would be some saucy doings—and there were." *Up in Mabel's Room* is "an excellent farce of the 'naughty-naughty' type . . . [that] lives up to all that the title and the subject matter threaten." *Ladies' Night,* we are told, began "where other lingerie plays stop. . . . It disappoints no one who wishes to be shocked, for it presents all the old thrills and a few more—bare legs, the shimmy, jokes with double meanings, vampires, bath-room scenes, underwear and infidelity."[50]

Both positive and negative reviews that enumerated the sins of the plays clearly overwhelmed attempts by a few reviewers to undermine the productions' appeal by calling them "moderately amusing," or to condemn them with the claim that the proceedings were "deadly dull," or to take a stance of neutrality amid assurances that the so-called erotic material was in fact innocuous. Woollcott, for example, noted that *The Girl in the Limousine* was "not much more indecorous than 'The Merry Wives of Windsor' and almost as void of any furtive or steamy licentiousness." *The Demi-Virgin,* according to the *Herald,* in both title and action attempted to suggest "a wickedness which is never achieved." The *Times,* however, undercut its own attempt to soft-pedal *Sadie Love* by claiming first that "the improprieties . . . are nothing to get excited about," but then that the play "keeps its audience always on the verge of a blush."[51]

Frequently a critic claimed that a play's actions or language were unfit to repeat or impossible to include in a daily paper. Kenneth Macgowan, for example, declared that *Getting Gertie's Garter* was driven by "the injection of some lingerie and some jokes that no American newspaper dare print." Others noted the need to protect women from the suggestive goings-on. Such calls were picked up by local government officials, which led to the legal struggles over *The Demi-Virgin.* Writing shortly after the play's obscenity trial Chief Magistrate William McAdoo lamented, "There are certain farces on the stage in this city . . . to which it would be an outrage to take a decent young girl, or allow her to go there." Clearly there was a split in the way the public perceived women vis-à-vis the sex farce. Their presence in the audience and their ostensible attraction to the fashions sanctioned the voyeuristic act for men, yet the suitability of the material for them remained an open question. Percy Hammond, in reviewing *The Demi-Virgin,* suspected "that no one who attends . . . will be harmed by what he sees and hears." He may, however, have been referring only to men, because his review refers to protecting female newspaper readers from the details of the strip-poker scene. On the other hand, he may have been silently assuming that the type of woman who attended such a play was beyond being harmed by the proceedings.[52]

What persisted, among both critics and producers, was an assumption that women attended such plays for reasons very different from men's. Woods himself later asserted that it was men, not women, who wanted to see naughtiness on the stage. He underscored this by referring to *The Demi-Virgin,* which increased ticket sales considerably after the production was attacked by the courts. "The matinee business thereafter didn't jump," he explained; "it was at night, when the men go to the theatre, that we sold out." If Woods's report here is accurate, however, this fact did not deter him from adding an extra matinee when the overall patronage for *The Demi-Virgin* surged in late 1921.[53]

The need to protect women is also assumed by the playwrights, who present marriage as an institution that shelters women from the cruelties of the world. Even the female writers of these farces adhere to stereotypical gender behavior and approve activities like breach of promise suits and archaic, unequal marriage laws. The playwrights assume that the unexposed maiden must not be left to fend for herself. Even when experienced women of the world are presented in the plays, they often opt for or wish for marriage in order to gain security and protection.

Clearly, the predominant impulse behind the near scandal, the revealing of women's bodies, the racy language, and the suggestive action was commercial exploitation and box-office success via exaggerated publicity. Critical overreaction was probably expected and definitely exploited by producers, as we shall see in the next chapter. The plays promised the audience more than they delivered, yet audiences frequently were made to believe that they had witnessed something shocking or rebellious, even though it did not actually challenge their moral stance or beliefs. The audience was invited to escape into the fantasy of would-be erotica without genuine embarrassment or discomfort. Yet audiences arrived anticipating these very reactions. Perhaps the experience was similar to that of attending freak shows at a carnival, most of which deliver something other than the fascinating promise of the showbill.

Jane Cowl, a popular serious actress of the time, who usually performed in classical tragedy or contemporary melodrama, wrote an essay in which she attempted to demonstrate that the audiences saw through the sexual shenanigans, even while flocking to the sex farces. "In the end," she claimed, the plays make the audience "realize what nonsense stage sex really is. They come out of the theatre with a keener enjoyment of the fresh air, the steady calm of the stars overhead, and a gradual relief from such stifling fiction."[54] This was probably wishful thinking, however. Cowl overlooked the obvious audience identification— the imitation of contemporary mores, fashion, and design— and the shock or humorous delight they often registered in response to the apparent naughtiness and near-calamitous events of the farces.

In this marketing of a flamboyant, commercial, sexist vision, everything was attempted with style and panache, elevating the tone so the characters would never be associated with the have-nots in society. Such an identification would have altered the mood and the fun and undermined the commercial, up-scale ethic promoted by the world of these plays. Audience identification with the wealthy, well-dressed, sophisticated character of the heroine bears a skewed resemblance to Restoration comedy as a reflection of how people wished to be perceived or think of themselves, even if the dramatic product, although set in realistic, up-to-date interiors, and the characters, dressed in contemporary high fashion, bore scant resemblance to daily reality. Perhaps more

significant historically, the sex farce, with its hybrid heroine and mixed message of permissiveness and moral conservatism, stands as an emblem of
postwar change and the forces that abhorred the new—the passage and
transformation of cultural symbols and values as the nation was about to
embark on the jazz age.

The withering of the sex farce after 1921 did not nearly end the role assumed by these plays, legitimate or not. In fact, suggestive material continued
in three major theatrical ventures: girlie shows, topical popular melodrama,
and serious drama. Controversy continued to rage over musical revues like
the *Ziegfeld Follies* and the Shuberts' *Artists and Models, Earl Carroll's Vani-
ties,* and *George White's Scandals,* in which suggestive dancing and prome-
nading, near nudity, and in many cases above-the-waist nudity in tableaux and
action scenes were exhibited purely for physical tantalization: no longer
framed by characterization, plotlines, or play structure. Now, theatergoers
were explicit voyeurs, and the censors directed much of their attention to the
flesh revues. Even Al Woods seemed disturbed by the new frolics. "After looking over some of the undressed revues on Broadway today," he observed in
1927, "I'm more than ever convinced that I have never produced an off-color
show."[55]

Commanding a somewhat more respectable position among the Broadway
offerings were popular melodramas with topical sexual subjects designed to
draw the curious and perhaps offend the shockable. Most of these plays appeared after mid-decade, and for the sake of sensation and box-office they incorporated petting parties, trial marriages, open marriages (*free love* was a
popular term), abortion, and even lesbianism. Some were closed by the police, but most managed to run if they could draw an audience. Titles like *Marriage on Approval* (1928) and *Her Unborn Child* (1928), which recall the
suggestiveness of the earlier sex farces, give the flavor and tone of the plays.

Simultaneously, serious American drama came into its own through the efforts of Eugene O'Neill, Elmer Rice, Susan Glaspell, John Howard Lawson,
Maxwell Anderson, Sidney Howard, Sophie Treadwell, and others, who insisted on dramatizing all levels of society, the woes of the destitute and the
fallen, and the vicissitudes of daily existence in authentic language. Venturing
into violence, prostitution, profligacy, miscegenation, incest, abortion, and a
host of other once-marginal or prohibited themes with integrity, the new playwrights brought a validity and urgency to these subjects. The grim vista revealed in the early 1920s by these latter-day *sturm und drangers* rendered the
once-scandalous efforts of Hopwood and his associates rather harmless and
redefined what was acceptable on the American stage, just as Tennessee Williams would do to the sexual content of the plays of O'Neill's generation. Even

in Hopwood's day, critic Heywood Broun, reviewing *Getting Gertie's Garter*, found himself wishing to stand and shout "louder and dirtier" at the actors who were pretending their material was scandalous.[56] Nonetheless, it was the sex farces that inspired the new wave of censorship that continued throughout the decade to plague both important and frivolous attempts to dramatize the American experience.

5

Popular Culture at the Crossroads:
Wooing Censorship with *The Demi-Virgin*

Oh Hollywood, my Hollywood, that you should have come to this at the hands of Avery Hopwood!
—*Variety*

Moral and cultural ambivalence in the United States perhaps reaches its zenith in the periodic censorship struggles that pepper the historical American landscape from the seventeenth century to the present. The result might be called America's ongoing cultural split personality—freedom of expression versus moral legislation. Warren Susman characterized the typical American as "a reformer" and his history as "a series of reforms." He goes on to describe the rhetoric of most reform movements of the 1920s as reflecting "a desire to maintain the older family patterns of an agrarian and preindustrial order."[1] This characterization aptly describes those reformers who wish to censor theater and drama, but many theater artists were also reformers, who wished, like Maxwell Anderson and Eugene O'Neill, to transform the stage and redefine what was acceptable dramatic fare. Standing between the censorship reformers and the artistic reformers, however, was a host of theater practitioners who sought to exploit the climate of reform for publicity and economic rewards.

Although censorship and artistic suppression had threatened the theater before, over George Bernard Shaw's *Mrs Warren's Profession* in 1905, two "white-slavery" dramas in 1913, and stage profanity in general throughout the teens, it was in the early 1920s that censorship skirmishes escalated to open warfare. Shaw's play about a successful prostitute was produced by Arnold Daly and closed by the police after one performance. Most critics railed against it for offending public morality. Daly, along with Mary Shaw, a feminist who played Mrs Warren, was arrested and later acquitted, but the production did not reopen. Mary Shaw, however, began a crusade for the play and appeared in it again in 1907 without trouble from the authorities. The white-slavery dramas, also called red-light plays, were *The Fight*, by Bayard Veiller, and *The Lure*, by George Scarborough. Both were closed in 1913 by the police for indecency and corruption of public morals. The producers and playwrights were forced to rewrite the plays before they could reopen. Throughout the teens conservative critics like Alan Dale accused the theater of suffering from "mania blasphematoria," whereby the stage was littered with cursing, which caused corrupting laughter in the audience. He and numerous others begged for an end to such "shameful practice."[2]

The decade of the 1920s, however, featured a liberation of subject matter and language in the dramatic efforts of both art theater and commercial playwrights—experimental as well as traditional—that made previous "shameful practices" appear rather tame. Tentative struggles over important plays like O'Neill's *The Hairy Ape* (1922) and Maxwell Anderson's *What Price Glory* (1924) yielded to full-blown public battles over O'Neill's *All God's Chillun Got Wings* and *Desire Under the Elms* and Sidney Howard's *They Knew What They Wanted* (all 1924). Apparently sparked by reviews that called these plays "morbid, cheap, naked nastiness," the district attorney of New York City responded to censorship calls from such organizations as the Actors Association for Clean Plays and the Society for the Suppression of Vice. *They Knew What They Wanted* and *Desire Under the Elms* were justly acquitted by a citizens play jury following public complaints against their indecency.[3]

Ultimately the New York State Legislature passed the Wales Padlock Law in 1927, under which the police could arrest producers, playwrights, and actors if the authorities disapproved of the play. If the courts subsequently found the play obscene, indecent, or immoral, the theater could be padlocked for a year. The law was first invoked in February 1928 against the play *Maya*, by Simon Gantillon, which explored the world of prostitution. This was followed by many unfounded complaints that year against plays regardless of artistic merit, including O'Neill's *Strange Interlude*. Most of the complaints were dismissed, and thereafter the district attorney acted with more restraint. Trouble emerged again, however, over Lillian Hellman's *The Children's Hour* in 1934. The Wales Padlock Law was not repealed until 1967. But this furor had begun in earnest with the obscenity trial of A. H. Woods's production of Avery Hopwood's *The Demi-Virgin* in 1921.

"Shades of Fatty Arbuckle!"[4] So commenced Alan Dale's review in the *New York American* of *The Demi-Virgin*, the last dynamic example of the American sex farce discussed in chapter 4. At least eight of these farces (not counting several adaptations from the French) were produced by Woods. Dale, like several other reviewers, was reacting to the scandalous court proceedings taking place in California as well as to the new wave of censorship that hit the New York stage in the fall of 1921. It can be argued, however, that Woods did not so much fall victim to increasing censorship interests as succeed in attracting censorship to *The Demi-Virgin* and enticing reactionaries to attack him, solely to bolster his box office.

As the 1921–22 theatrical season in New York was getting under way, Warren G. Harding was quietly mismanaging his first year as president and the United States was attempting to pull out of the postwar economic recession. Nonetheless, a typical theatergoer, as he or she had been throughout the war, was assured of encountering suggestive and smart-looking sex farces from the dramatic factory of A. H. Woods (known to most around Broadway as Al, although he called everyone "sweetheart"). Woods always had many plays running at once in and out of New York (at one time twenty-three simultaneous productions), and since 1916 one could almost always find at least one bedroom farce running under his aegis in New York as well as on the road.[5]

The popular producer, aged fifty-one when *The Demi-Virgin* opened, had broken into the theater with low-priced productions of sensational, blood-and-thunder melodramas, or "spine thrillers" in Woods's terminology, beginning with *The Bowery After Dark*. Collaborating with Owen Davis, his chief playwright after 1905, Woods made a fortune introducing formulaic melodramas under such titles as *Nellie, the Beautiful Cloak Model; Bertha, the Sewing Machine Girl;* and *Edna, the Poor Typewriter*. After the popularity of this type of play began to wane, the cigar-chewing producer, noticing the success of Hopwood and the Selwyns, switched to sex farces, the popularity of which reached a peak in the season that preceded *The Demi-Virgin*. After his labors to squeeze one more profitable season out of sex farces with *Getting Gertie's Garter* and *The Demi-Virgin*, Woods abandoned the bedroom farce as passé and centered his producing activity on safer domestic comedy and murder mystery. He would go on to produce *The Trial of Mary Dugan, The Night of*

January 16th, and, most notable, *The Green Hat,* starring Katharine Cornell—he had produced more than two hundred shows by 1943. It is telling that a Broadwayite in 1920 would call "an A. H. Woods production with an unhappy ending" an impossible dream.[6]

Recognizing Avery Hopwood's talent for the sex farce, Woods added the already successful playwright to his stable, where Hopwood remained supreme in volume and style as long as the vogue persisted. At thirty-nine, the "playboy playwright" had been writing regularly for Broadway since 1906 under the guidance of many different producers. He collaborated not only with sex-farce contributors but with writers of comedies and mysteries like Mary Roberts Rinehart, with whom he wrote his longest-running production, *The Bat.* Hopwood also wrote the popular comedy of chorus-girl life *The Gold Diggers,* produced by David Belasco in 1919. Not unlike the sex farces, this comedy also features a central character, Jerry Lamar (played by Ina Claire in the role that made her a star), who is apparently a loose-moraled gold-digger but who turns out to be virtuous. The text is filled with quips meant to be racy, but many of them reveal the virtue of the chorus girls: "A man will pay a lot more for a thrill," Trixie informs us, "than he will for the real thing!"[7]

Hopwood was also frequently called upon to doctor ailing plays of various genres. He had contributed thirty-three plays to the New York stage (and in 1920 had four Broadway shows running simultaneously) before his untimely death in 1928. He called himself an entertainer whose forte was writing comic dialogue specifically "to please Broadway." In the same interview he went on to say, "I've the perhaps queer idea that playwrights who have counted have been primarily showmen." It is reported that Woods once announced that Hopwood had adapted Shakespeare's *Othello* to his Broadway style and had entitled the contrivance "Up in Desdemona's Room."[8]

The style of the Woods-Hopwood farces was one of slick presentation in attractive surroundings, usually staged by Woods's house director Bertram Harrison. The dialogue was racy, laced with light profanity and double entendre; attempts at sexual exploits never quite came off. Woods himself claimed: "Most people want to see something naughty on the stage. . . . Not that they get it—except on rare occasions. But the public does want to see things which it has been led to believe are a bit off-color." Similarly, his lawyer argued that the shocking action forecast in *The Demi-Virgin* "turned out to be all anticipation and no realization." Woods sought to entertain and make money; he never called himself an artist. Perhaps an interview with Woods published just two months before the opening of *The Demi-Virgin* best captures his approach to dramatic art. Woods had just opened the opulent Apollo Theatre in Chicago, with elaborate dressing rooms and baths for the performers. "Are you putting on the kind of plays that go with such grandeur?" the interviewer asked. "I'm putting on the kind of plays that pay for such grandeur," Woods replied. "Ibsen wouldn't buy a shampoo spray. Isn't it better to keep your actors clean than to be mentioned four times in a book by Brander Matthews?"[9]

An advance New York notice of the play published while *The Demi-Virgin* was in an Atlantic City tryout explained that "Mr. Hopwood is trying to tell a naughty story in a nice way."[10] Actually, the reverse was true. Hopwood harnessed a reasonably moral tale to the trappings of naughtiness.

Although the play was never published, two manuscripts of 1921 have survived at the Library of Congress and New York Public Library, the important details of which are verifiable from reviews of the production. It is clear that some changes were made for production, but they had little effect on the plot. In brief, the action takes place in Hollywood, opening on a silent film stage reminiscent of Mack Sennett's, in which the director is busily grinding shots; it moves on to a noisy weekend house party at the luxurious quarters of film star Gloria Graham, who is divorced from Wally Deane, another screen idol. Gloria had left her husband only three hours into the first night of marriage when he received a phone call from an old flame, thus setting a "short-distance matrimonial record." Naturally, the gossip columnists have been exploiting the scandal ever since, wondering whether the marriage was ever consummated. Hence, Gloria is now labeled a demi-virgin.[11]

The ensuing, convoluted action brings the two errant lovers together again, even as each pretends to love another. As in all such Woods-Hopwood pieces, the production sported a number of female beauties running about the stage displaying their physical charms in gowns and lingerie that were "the last word in fashion and daring," and cracking risqué jokes "with the elegance of fishwives" about Hollywood lifestyles, Prohibition, and film making.[12] During the house party at Gloria's, for example, one of the starlets refers to a fire at a recent Hollywood house party with the remark, "You should have seen the right people coming out of the wrong rooms."[13] In the opening scene two starlets lament that they never have the slightest idea what their movies are about. They simply know that they can always find work as long as their costumes cover only tiny portions of their bodies. The supporting cast also includes a Charlie Chaplin clone, a "Perils of Pauline" serial heroine, and, of course, an innocent-looking Mary Pickford pixie who is the secondary love interest. Of special interest is the detailed presentation of silent film making, which is not only unusual for the stage at this time but often quite humorous. Several reviews pointed to the originality of this touch. The critics seem to have forgotten *Johnny Get Your Gun* (1917), the prologue of which is dominated by a farcical film-making sequence in a movie studio. Critics of the earlier production likewise commented on the originality of the device.[14]

Two scenes in *The Demi-Virgin*, however, were of central importance to most of the production's would-be censors. In the second act Hopwood called for a strip-poker game called "stripping Cupid," played by five young women. In the manuscript one of the gamblers loses all but her last and most vital item of undergarments, a move Woods was not yet prepared to risk. Onstage the character, Dot, was reduced to two, rather than one, pieces of clothing. Woods was later to claim that this scene should not have been objectionable because he and Hopwood "were careful not to introduce a male character" during the proceedings.[15]

This giggly shimmy-dancing and stripping scene is immediately followed by an encounter between Wally and Gloria in which it seems that the divorced husband is going to force himself on his former wife. He roars at her: "You owe me a debt . . . a marriage debt . . . and now you're going to pay!"[16] As it turns out, Wally's behavior is a devious performance, but the audience is led to believe for some time that the rape will take place. In the final act the audience learns that the divorce had never been legal, a fact known only to Wally, who reveals the truth at the appropriate moment—when Gloria returns to him. Even after knowing that Wally was still married to Gloria, it is hoped that audiences today would see the scene as a threatened rape, but most theatergoers at the time (Margaret Sanger and a few "radical" birth-control advocates excepted) were likely to interpret the threat as only a demand for the husband's conjugal rights.

One of the most striking aspects of the play for out-of-town audiences was the presence of the character Fatty Belden, an undisguised Fatty Arbuckle character, who chases any woman, young or old, guzzles three drinks at a time, tells off-color jokes, and tries to dance the night away with several women at once. He attempts to entice women (any woman in fact) to sample his prowess by claiming, "I taste just like a martini!"[17] Like the indecorous supporting female characters discussed in chapter 4, Fatty does not appear in the final act of the play. Also in keeping with the other sex farces of the era, Fatty's most suggestive dialogue and actions occur in the second act.

Although Fatty Arbuckle's reputation was well known and the character was part of the written play by June 24, the terrible events of Arbuckle's life filled the headlines on September 11, just fifteen days before the first Pittsburgh tryout. Arbuckle, who sat atop the comic film world, making a thousand dollars a day, suddenly found himself on trial for manslaughter after the death of the young film actress and model Virginia Rappe. She died of abdominal complications from a ruptured bladder following a drinking party in Arbuckle's room in the St. Francis Hotel in San Francisco on September 5. The popular press and the public chose to believe that Arbuckle was responsible. Although he was acquitted, Arbuckle's popularity and film career were over. Paramount canceled his contract and scrapped his completed films, and movie theaters throughout the country banished his films from the screen. The first of three Arbuckle trials began on November 21, only a few weeks after Woods and Hopwood found themselves in court defending *The Demi-Virgin* against charges of indecency. In his opening-night review of the production Louis De Foe wrote that if the account in the play was "faithful, then recent happenings now engaging the attention of the California courts are not, after all, so surprising."[18]

Hopwood and Woods were always in search of a suggestive title, and in *The Demi-Virgin* they succeeded almost too well. Many theatergoers expected a risqué play and perhaps saw more in this one than it actually delivered. There is little here that was not previously explored by Woods and Hopwood in *The Girl in the Limousine* and *Getting Gertie's Garter*. Certainly no more flesh was exposed, but the strip-poker scene seemed to promise forbidden erotica; the language of Wally's demands on Gloria was no more profane but perhaps more forceful than that in previous work. *The Demi-Virgin* did offer an exception to one important pattern of previous sex farces, in which the audience had been privy to the heroine's virtuousness even when all the other characters misjudged her. In *The Demi-Virgin,* Gloria's virtue is not revealed until the final scene.

At any rate, Pittsburgh was not ready for *The Demi-Virgin*. After opening on September 26 at the Pitt Theatre, where it was billed as a "farcical romance," the play was met by mixed reviews: one found it familiar and essentially harmless, if distasteful in its Arbuckle jokes; the *Pittsburgh Post,* however, attacked it viciously, claiming that "Hopwood . . . has gone where there are no lengths left to go," that the play was "reeking with indecencies," and that "the theme's too risqué and [the] innuendo too rampant for clean enjoyment." Apparently taking his cue from this response, Robert Alderdice, director of public safety, warned the managers that certain cuts had to be made in the text. When Hopwood refused to comply, Alderdice closed the show just before the final performance of the one-week run. Although Alderdice claimed that "there was no question about the smutty features of the piece," Hopwood was incensed and thanked the official for giving his play "a million dollars worth of advertising." He went on to claim to the Pittsburgh press that New York audiences would "crowd to see the play that Pittsburgh police objected to" and would henceforward "brand Pittsburgh as a yokel district."[19]

Hopwood did indeed get his publicity, for the story was picked up by New

York newspapers, and reviewers and columnists continued to refer to the police raid for months to come. Only the *Pittsburgh Dispatch* tried to bury the story, placing it in an article on Prohibition raids carried out by the police at the same time. The play is not mentioned by name, and the article merely says that "the show at a local theater was closed because of risqué lines and scenes."[20]

It is likely that Woods was hoping for out-of-town scandal by selecting Pittsburgh as his first tryout city. In the spring of 1921 Alderdice had announced to the press his new program to ban all morally objectionable plays. Since the theatrical trade papers carried this news beyond Pittsburgh, Woods or his staff must have been aware of the threat, carried out for the first time against his production.[21]

The Demi-Virgin went on to two more tryouts in Stamford and Atlantic City, where the play was labeled a "salacious farce" but allowed to run.[22] After moving into New York for a few days of revision, *The Demi-Virgin* opened at the Times Square Theatre on October 18 and transferred a few weeks later (November 7) to the Eltinge Theatre, where it remained through the fuss that followed. The most notable revision Hopwood had made on the road was to combine the Arbuckle character with the Chaplin character so as to make the Arbuckle jokes less offensive, for these gags fell flat out of town. Thus Fatty Belden melded with Chicky Chatterton to emerge as Chicky Belden. Although New York reviewers continued to draw parallels to the Arbuckle case, no one seemed bothered by the presentation of this amalgamated character. The offense lay in other quarters.

Rarely is one likely to read such a mixed collection of reviews as those that met *The Demi-Virgin*. The descriptions range from clever fun and games to an evening full of belly laughs to an innocuous comedy, to a boring piece of drivel, to "unadulterated smut, bordering on the pathological." A few critics chose to ignore it, and one found the play beneath his dignity to describe although he saw the production. J. Ranken Towse's entire review follows: "There is not the slightest reason or excuse for wasting space upon any description of this concoction which was decanted upon the stage of the Times Square Theatre last evening. It is quite sufficient to say that it was mixed by Avery Hopwood and introduced by A. H. Woods. This statement will prove to all theatre-goers of any experience the nauseating antiquity of the flavors."[23]

Several critics, hoping to hurt the production, noted accurately that Woods was anticipating advantageous publicity even from reviewers who panned the production. The *Sun*, for example, reported that the play was "not as shocking as Manager Woods would like theatre goers to believe," while De Foe noted that "to describe the various details of the farce or to classify them candidly would probably be gratifying to Mr. Woods. But it might be misleading to future playgoers." On the other hand, both of these critics as well as many others dwelt upon the implied vulgarities and double meanings as the play "manage[d] to balance on two wheels around the dangerous curves of dialogue"; they also noted the coarse situations that resulted in what one critic called the play's dissolute environment: "passion's playground." This review continued: "The program quite boldly admitted that the first act passed in a moving picture studio in Hollywood. The public was then prepared for anything."[24]

In spite of such charges, however, many reviewers insisted, quite truthfully, that the play presented little of real harm to the public. Dale, for example, stressed that the production was toiling hard "to give us the exquisite sensation of being shocked," but with slight success. The *Times* noted that the people of *The Demi-Virgin*, "while a bit gaudy and prankful, seem to be a moral lot." For these critics, the play's title was the "most provocative detail."[25]

Described by reviewer Percy Hammond as the first strip-poker game on Broadway, the card game featuring "a quintet of lens lizettes" was mentioned by most reviewers in disgust, fascination, or horror, but Woods was no doubt delighted that the newspapers were mentioning this highlight of the production. According to Maida Castellun, "the dear little serpents" disrobed "within the law and little more." Often described as the climax of a Hollywood orgy, the "fleshly frolics" of the party game were said to bring into question "whether or not the majority of the young women fall enough below the prevailing physical standard to justify police interference." Hammond simply stated that he could not describe the game because "the details are a bit ruddy for a home paper involving as they do our women folk."[26]

Overwhelming in many papers, however, was the level of disgust felt by reviewers, who bombarded the production with a plethora of abusive epithets. "A brazen and obvious piece of pornology," wrote Kenneth Macgowan, who claimed that the "smutty farce" could appeal only to "the paranoiac portion of the public." Ironically, Macgowan would soon find himself under attack for presenting "obscene" material as the producer of O'Neill's *Desire Under the Elms.* Torres of the *Commercial,* however, in the spirit of reform, launched the most virulent broadside, which openly called for censorship. "The movement for dramatic censorship received a powerful impetus last evening," he wrote. The production, Torres continued, "beckons to smut hunters. . . . The so-called play serves only to amuse the vulgar element and hasten censorship for indecent classes of shows." Warming to his mood, the critic asserted that such productions "not only invite censorship, but fling insolent defiance in the face of decency. . . . It is a blot on the escutcheon of the city and the theatre that a play so flagrantly and odorously vulgar, dirty and stupid should be permitted on its busiest thoroughfare."[27]

Woods was undoubtedly thrilled that *The Demi-Virgin* became a controversial topic throughout the city while generating in the opening week box-office receipts of about $12,000 (a high but not stunning figure for a nonmusical show at the time). According to several reviews, "the success of the play is bound to depend on the daring scenes." This sense of daring was exploited by both reviews and Woods's publicity, and the box office responded well until New York's Chief Magistrate's Office became involved. Then ticket sales soared.[28]

In the first few weeks of the play's run occasional editorials and letters had appeared in the newspapers complaining of the theater's declining standards, of the liberties taken by sex farces on the New York stage, and of *The Demi-Virgin* in particular. The *Herald* argued that "the metropolitan stage has this year offered more dramas objectionable in their moral character than any previous season." The editorial went on to describe the sex farces as "a menace to manners." There had been some talk of censorship even before the play opened, and many critics and managers began to discuss self-censorship. They also raised the question of whether the state legislature should try to enforce government censorship of the theater similar to that controlling the film industry. The opening review in *Variety* best laid out the scenario to come: "Dear old Hollywood . . . certainly will manage to increase the bankroll of A. H. Woods, that is, providing that the authorities will let him get away with the performance. . . . It will also mean that there is going to be a run on the box office."[29]

On November 3, two weeks after opening, Woods and Hopwood were summoned before Chief Magistrate William McAdoo to answer to complaints that *The Demi-Virgin* "constitutes an immoral exhibit." (McAdoo was the police commissioner responsible for closing the first New York production of *Mrs Warren's Profession* in 1905 as well as the white slavery plays in 1913.) It was rumored that the *Demi-Virgin* complaints arose from a newspaper critic (Torres was the obvious choice), and the production had been visited by members of the police morality squad. Before the hearing began, Woods intimated to the press that he might refuse to make any changes to the play. Because Woods's lawyer, Max D. Steuer, had not yet read the play, the hearing was postponed until November 7. By the end of the first week of the hearing, *Variety* reported *The Demi-Virgin* as the leading farce moneymaker in New York.[30]

Members of the press seemed to enjoy the hearing proceedings, which often had a circuslike atmosphere; reporters reveled in describing the poor grammar of police witnesses, the discomfort of Avery Hopwood, and the attention sought by Al Woods. The source of the complaint finally appeared in one John S. Sumner, notorious evangelical secretary of the New York Society for the Suppression of Vice, who liked to call plays like *The Demi-Virgin* "professional commercialized indecency." He was known by reputation to nearly everyone in the hearing, but few knew him by sight until he was sworn in. The most entertaining witness, however, was police lieutenant Albert Duffy, who had attended a performance and was charged to report on his findings. He recalled the stripping Cupid scene, but noted that once one of girls was down to her "she-meese" he "didn't pay so much attention" after that. When the policeman described Wally's forceful scene with Gloria in act 2, "Hopwood, who dotes on writing elegant boudoir dialogue, shuddered visibly." Duffy quoted Wally as charging Gloria to "take off them clothes!" Even the prosecution seems to have been somewhat unsophisticated, for when the assistant district attorney, reading from the manuscript, pronounced a phrase "Maw Cherry," Hopwood reportedly turned to the press and said, "He means mon cherie." Throughout most of the hearings, however, Hopwood "was sunk in a mournful contemplation of the ceiling" while Al Woods smiled.[31]

When Woods was allowed to speak, he declared that "if the police feel called upon to interfere in any way with my production they should cite me not for producing an indecent play, but for blocking traffic outside my theatre, where the people are fighting each other to get in and buy tickets." Four days later *Variety* reported that *The Demi-Virgin* was still doing very well and that the censorship publicity was a factor. In the midst of the first hearings Woods's publicity began openly to exploit the situation. A typical advertisement read, "If you have not yet seen *The Demi-Virgin*, or heard it discussed or read about it, you haven't been anywhere. Now is the time to see this most talked-of, original, amusing play in town."[32]

McAdoo read the play and listened to testimonies of people disturbed by the production, but he stubbornly refused to admit testimony from people in the field of theater. He claimed that it was his "duty under the law . . . to judge this play as it would appeal to the intelligence of ordinary men and women and not experts or those connected in any wise with theatrical productions." Although Woods and Hopwood made some unspecified changes to the script at the magistrate's insistence, on November 14, McAdoo rendered a decision finding Woods in violation of the penal code for presenting an obscene play that "would tend to the corruption of the morals of youth or others" and thus guilty of a misdemeanor punishable by up to a year in prison and a thousand-dollar fine. The specific statute was section 1140a of the Penal Law of New York State, which read in part: "Any person who as owner, manager, director or agent or in any other capacity prepares, advertises, gives, presents or participates in, any obscene, indecent, immoral or impure drama, play, exhibition, show or entertainment, which would tend to the corruption of the morals of youth or others, and every person aiding or abetting such act, and every owner or lessee or manager . . . who leases or lets the same or permits the same to be used for the purposes of any such drama . . . shall be guilty of a misdemeanor."[33]

The magistrate condemned the play and handed Woods over for trial by three judges in Special Sessions. Bail was set at a thousand dollars and McAdoo published an attack on the play, but because he was presiding over a hearing rather than a trial, he had no power to take the production off the boards. McAdoo's judgment stated that the play was "deliberately, painstakingly, and for the purpose of gain, coarsely indecent, flagrantly and suggestively immoral, impure in motive, word and action, and in every respect offensively illegal under the statute governing such matters." Woods reported that the worst part of the play for McAdoo was the strip-poker scene, which the producer nonetheless refused to eliminate. This assertion is supported by McAdoo's own account, published in January 1922. McAdoo went on, speaking as if he were an official play doctor, that other producers of questionable plays had sometimes allowed him to "collaborate" in the "sterilization of certain plays." Note that McAdoo uses the word *sterilization* as a positive term.[34]

On the same day, in a move that recalled the early response to Ibsen's *Ghosts,* Dr. Royal S. Copeland, New York Commissioner of Health, issued his own attack, announcing that plays like *The Demi-Virgin* needed to be closed for the health of patrons of the theater. Such corruption, he said, "is as surely undermining the public health of impressionable theatregoers as an exposed sewer would if placed in the middle of the auditorium."[35]

Four days later *Variety* reported the public response: "The reaction of the McAdoo opinion had almost immediate demonstration at the Eltinge, the fully worded reports bringing a golden stream to the *Demi-Virgin* box office. Wednesday afternoon the matinee line was out on the pavement and continuous until there was a turnaway." From this time until final judgment was reached in late December, the show ran at capacity, even after an extra matinee was added. McAdoo ordered Woods to remove the offensive play at once, but the district attorney's office did not force the issue, preferring to continue preparation of its case for Special Sessions court. By November 20, Woods could declare in his ads, perhaps accurately, that *The Demi-Virgin* was "the most famous play in America."[36]

A trial date was set for November 28, but Woods did not wish to take his chances with more judges; he sought a jury trial in General Sessions. Meanwhile, the city's license commissioner complicated the proceedings. Apparently in sympathy with McAdoo, Commissioner John Gilchrist warned Woods that he had to remove *The Demi-Virgin* by November 25, or the Eltinge Theatre would have its license revoked. Although Woods at first said that the show would not stop unless the police "backed up the wagon" to the theater, it appeared that he would have to comply. At the last moment, however, his lawyer convinced him to fight the mandate. Notably, Woods showed no open defiance to the commissioner until the New York Supreme Court began considering an injunction filed by his lawyer. "With only a few hours to spare before the expiration of the time limit," Woods received a temporary injunction against the license commissioner. The play could continue to run until a verdict was reached in court.[37]

In the meantime, Woods was preparing his case by polling his audiences with paper ballots. He reported that only two people in every thousand polled found the play immoral. Unfortunately, these findings never had to be verified in court. At the same time Woods began to give the press financial figures, asserting that he stood to lose $40,000 or more if he were forced to close the show. He continued to warn of financial losses for several weeks until the trial.[38]

The trial in Special Sessions was postponed, then Woods's lawyer Steuer succeeded in having the case transferred to General Sessions, where it would go before the grand jury. Woods wished to guarantee the maximum press coverage; he also wanted to be judged by citizens rather than magistrates. His pre-trial affidavit had called *The Demi-Virgin* "a proper play," and it had included his financial statement for the production, which listed an initial investment of $26,000 and weekly expenses of $13,700. Because Woods's typical weekly gross at this time was $14,500–$15,000, he may have been inflating his expenses to claim poor-mouth. When the extra matinee was added, the production could gross about $17,000. "If I am found guilty," he announced, "it will take from me the possibility of a return on my investment." Apparently, Woods's emphasis on financial affairs paid off in the decision to transfer the play to General Sessions. "Where property rights were involved," a judge ruled, "such a course should be taken." The next step was the grand jury.[39]

During the slack time, however, Woods found other ways to keep his name and *The Demi-Virgin* in the press. On November 29, for example, he audaciously announced five new productions at once, including a new play by Hopwood. Early in December he suddenly proclaimed that he had resigned from the Producing Managers Association (PMA), a descendant of the United Managers Protective Association (UMPA) discussed in chapter 3. The resignation of Woods was the first since George M. Cohan departed in an unsuccessful protest over the new Actors' Equity in 1919. Woods let it be known publicly that he was disturbed that the PMA was not supporting him actively in his struggles against censorship. By December 14, however, it was formally announced that he was reconciled with his friends and fellow managers after they "passed a resolution of sympathy with Mr. Woods in his hour of trial." *Variety,* with accurate aplomb, referred to the entire affair as a "press stunt."[40]

The grand jury finally initiated proceedings on December 23. They heard the testimony of McAdoo, Sumner, and several policemen, listened to the play read by an assistant district attorney, and abruptly gave Woods an unexpected Christmas present by dismissing the case. Woods, however, may have been disappointed, for he did not get the fight he was clearly anticipating. The producer was never called, despite his application to testify. Characteristically, Woods's newspaper advertisements for *The Demi-Virgin* that weekend were decorated with vine leaves.[41]

Although *The Demi-Virgin* was now free to run, Woods's struggles were not quite over. On December 13, the day it had been announced that the production would go to General Sessions, the editors of the *New York Times* decided to stage a protest of their own. Apparently finding *The Demi-Virgin* not among "all the news that's fit to print," the editors refused to include the title of the play in advertisements or articles. This continued long after the play was exonerated by the grand jury. Consequently, Woods found ways to continue advertising without the title, such as: "Have you seen the most successful comedy in town now playing at the Eltinge Theatre?" Later in the spring Woods began to use numbers: "Are you one of the 140,281 people who have already seen A. H. Woods's production of the most wonderful play in America now at the Eltinge?" The totals changed with each day's advertisement. Despite the *Times's* silent lifting of the ban on March 12, Woods continued to advertise as if he were still forbidden to use the title. In other papers Woods changed the advertisements each week, always looking for new enticements: "Complete your education by seeing *The Demi-Virgin.*"[42]

Woods's production ran until the end of the season, closing quietly of its own volition on June 3, 1922. *The Demi-Virgin* enjoyed good houses to the end, having drawn a total audience of more than 200,000 to nearly three hundred performances and having outlasted all but three productions of the season. As the play was closing Woods announced that he would send four road companies on tour beginning in the fall of 1922. As of September 1923 the hinterlands (save Pittsburgh) were still witnessing *The Demi-Virgin.* The final remnants of *The Demi-Virgin* appeared in a 1927 MGM film entitled *The*

Demi-Bride, a slickly-made farcical romance starring Norma Shearer and directed by Robert Z. Leonard.[43]

After the Broadway closing Woods announced that the bedroom farce had had its day, that he would produce no more such shows for at least seven years. Woods had made this announcement before, in late 1919, but only as a publicity stunt: he had a sex farce, *No More Blondes,* in rehearsal when he disseminated the press release. This time, however, he kept his word and was quick to note that he was not responding to the previous trials but to a waning interest on the part of the public. From the production side, *The Demi-Virgin* seems to have been a last-ditch effort to squeeze one more hit out of the sex-farce formula before putting it to rest. Woods appears to have recognized the end of this phase of his career and decided to conclude it with a splash.[44]

In the wake of *The Demi-Virgin* controversy the press fought over the question of censorship. Conservative periodicals like *Theatre Magazine* and *Literary Digest* called upon lawmakers to present tough legislation; they demanded support from members of Actors' Equity who should, according to these reactionaries, be ashamed to perform in indecent productions. Making reference to the Actors' Equity strike of 1919 and once again invoking the need to protect women, one article asked, "Having protected the actor against thieves, can [Equity] not now protect him, and especially her, against the immoral harpies among the producers?" Another even called for a "boycott of those managers and those theatres that continue to offend against good taste and good morals." Conversely, other magazines and journals, such as the *Nation* and the *New Republic,* loathed productions like *The Demi-Virgin* but warned that audiences must tolerate them in order to avoid worse disasters inherent in state censorship. "The reason these terrorists resort to censorship," ran one editorial, intending to link the censorship with familiar Red Scare xenophobia, "is precisely because they mistrust liberty. They live a life of fear—fear of sex, fear of the Reds, fear of human nature, above all human expression. And they are gradually getting this country by the throat." Perhaps as a sane response to all the furor, Mary Shaw revived *Mrs Warren's Profession* in February 1922 along with Ibsen's *Ghosts,* another important play that had been maligned by emotional reactionaries.[45]

The day after the reprieve for *The Demi-Virgin* the Authors' League of America joined with the American Dramatists and Actors' Equity to campaign against legislated censorship, but as a compromise offered to allow a citizens play jury to judge suspect plays. The jury was duly created and called upon from time to time, most notably for *They Knew What They Wanted* and *Desire Under the Elms.* Sumner attacked these plays as he had *The Demi-Virgin,* referring to Sidney Howard and Eugene O'Neill disparagingly as "certain literary lights" who needed to be prosecuted. Owen Davis, president of the American Dramatists, which at that time numbered 276 members, announced that "the majority of us now accept [the play juries] only because some form of censorship seems necessary and inevitable, and the jury plan is considered far preferable to censorship by three paid politicians." This concession satisfied government for a few years, but the play juries acquitted productions far more frequently than they censured, a practice that inspired the vice societies and district attorneys of Manhattan and Brooklyn to lobby the state legislature to create the harsh Wales Padlock Law in 1927.[46]

After the Wales Padlock Law was finally enforced, Sumner, repeatedly under attack from voices for moderation or liberality, proceeded doggedly in his "constant warfare against commercialized indecency," serving the district attorney as an always "complaining witness," envisioning himself as "a proxy for the ordinary citizen." Sumner and his New York Society for the Suppression of Vice are striking examples of what Sumner's contemporary Frederick C. Howe in his *Confessions of a Reformer* (1925) called "evangelistic psychology" and "evangelical mindedness" that sought "a moralistic explanation of social problems."[47]

Although Woods's involvement in the censorship struggles of the 1920s was more a function of economics than artistic integrity (the issue in several subsequent trials of the era), Woods nevertheless was instrumental in providing an impetus for moral crusaders attempting to vent their wrath on and promote their values in the American theater. With his eye on his own box office Woods unwittingly and naively opened Pandora's box. Yet Woods was a measure of historical change, especially as a monitor of shifting tastes and topicality in what he produced and what he exploited. In an article published two months before the premiere of *The Demi-Virgin*, Woods provided not only a suggestion of his own theatrical tastes but also a hint of things to come. "Should [the critics] praise a show of mine," he wrote, "I shall, of course, begin a big advertising campaign to combat the ill effects such praise might have on the public." As Hugh Leamy described him in 1927, "Al Woods, for all his years, is still a boy."[48]

6

The Vogue of Expressionism in Postwar America

*Are we to emerge from the war into a new theatre? . . . One thing is certain: if we go
anywhere, we shall go far.*
—Kenneth Macgowan

For the work of the future let us have a bare platform.
—Jacques Copeau

The appearance of theatrical expressionism on the American stage in 1921 resulted in confusion among critics and theater artists over what distinguished it
from its predecessor, German expressionism, as well as from other stylized
forms simultaneously invading U.S. theaters. Consequently, American expressionism in the 1920s was often identified as any method that objectified the
subjective. More specifically, both American and German expressionism were
methods of presenting theatrical event, character, language, and location that
objectified and externalized theatrically either what is subjective and internal
for the characters in the play or the point of view of the theatrical artists presenting the work. Objectification of the subjective and externalization of the

internal were accomplished through scenery, performance, use of space, and interpretation of events. The result on stage was an "extreme subjectivism" that distorted, abstracted, and fragmented representational event, location, and character, often leading to depictions of destruction, madness, and irrational emotional expression.[1]

Just as frequently in America, however, *expressionism* was used by artists and critics to identify any kind of theatrical experiment except symbolism— the only stylized form that was well-established in the New York before 1921. Although expressionism as drama has been widely explored, we lack a careful examination of the visual and spatial dimensions of American expressionism that would allow us to discern its relation to European practice. More important, perhaps, we shall see that although expressionism celebrated modernism, its vogue in the United States bears a direct relationship to anxiety over the Great War and reflects growing cynicism with commercialism in American society. (German expressionism, of course, predated the Great War, but Americans delayed adopting it until 1921, when the recession was waning.) Both the war experience and the parade of modern European theatrical experiments arriving in New York from 1911 to 1917 inspired the hybrid American expressionism.

Defining expressionistic space is complicated because artists take eclectic approaches to visual expressions of form. To find enduring principles we must examine contemporary staging and designs as well as suggestions for them in surviving dramatic texts of experimental productions and in American interpretations of European plays. The American species often maintained the cacophony and sometimes the angularity of German expressionism, but centered more vividly on locating and enhancing identifiable character and family conflict. Furthermore, directors and designers employed more surrealistic scenic designs and staging techniques to reflect the protagonist's point of view in American productions, especially after 1922. These devices give the world of the play a sense of the dream world coexisting with or superseding the real one.

As an exemplar of modernism, American expressionism in its visual realization was defined more precisely by the development of the New Stagecraft in design than by the German expressionist designs, which were usually dedicated to extreme angularity and obvious symbolism. These effects often overshadowed the image of the performer and reinforced anonymity of character. American New Stagecraft celebrated simplicity and emphasized the presence of the actor/character. Impressive American productions of European plays that had never been performed in America (some even decades old) began to appear regularly from 1918, leading Alexander Woollcott to observe: "It is an interesting thing to see the avid curiosity of New York and the new life astir in its theatre quicken" after the former neglect of these plays.[2]

If we are to search for seminal European influences on American expressionism, we must look to European visitors and the publications that appeared periodically between 1911 and 1917. Between these years American audiences were exposed for the first time to three major directors, Max Reinhardt, Harley Granville-Barker, and Jacques Copeau, from Germany, England, and France, respectively, whose aggregate work comprises the principal production model (enhanced and inspired by the theories of Gordon Craig) for creative American staging and design after World War I.

PREWAR INFLUENCES

The productions and designs of the European directors were predated by an extensive engagement of the Irish Players of the Abbey Theatre, beginning November 20, 1911, at Maxine Elliott's Theatre. The stagecraft and acting in the nineteen Irish productions emotionally overwhelmed some of New York's most creative young playwrights, designers, and directors, who not only consciously referred to this experience throughout their lives but reflected significant aspects of it in their own dramatic work. Robert Edmond Jones and Eugene O'Neill, especially, saw these performances as landmarks in their lives.

John Millington Synge's *Riders to the Sea* stands as the jewel of the 1911 repertory, the most influential Irish production in its simplicity of staging, design, and dramatic action. It inspired Ridgely Torrence in his *Three Plays for a Negro Theatre* in 1917 as well as many American folk-playwrights of the mid-1920s like Hatcher Hughes, Paul Green, and Lula Vollmer. The setting for *Riders to the Sea* demanded that American audiences radically change their customary expectations of stage design; it would now be "confined to the fewest of absolutely necessary accessories." More poetically and more fitting to the spirit of the play, designer Robert Edmond Jones later described the impact of the setting on himself: "Neutral-tinted walls, a fireplace, a door, a window, a table, a few chairs, . . . a fisher's net perhaps. Nothing more. But through the little window at the back one saw a sky of enchantment. All the poetry of Ireland shone in that little square of light, moody, haunting, full of dreams." This image informs not only some of Jones's own designs but many of the New Stagecraft settings that dominated the next decade, including those of Lee

Simonson, Woodman Thompson, Cleon Throckmorton, and Mordecai Gorelik. These artists contributed the most momentous American expressionistic designs of the 1920s.[3]

Late in 1911 Gordon Craig's *On the Art of the Theatre,* which had first appeared in Europe in 1905, was finally published in America; it provided an interesting counterpoint to the Irish Players' aesthetics as well as inspiration to designers and directors. Impressed by the ideas and designs in this book, American theatrical experimenters embarked on a metamorphic journey in both the little theaters and the Broadway stage. Craig's call for an all-powerful regisseur, who would be responsible for unifying all elements of the production, was stimulating: "It is impossible," Craig wrote, "for a work of art ever to be produced where more than one brain is permitted to direct." Most consequential to American practitioners were Craig's designs themselves, which startled viewers with simultaneous visions of simplicity and grandeur—elements that earlier had seemed antithetical to American producers, directors, and designers wedded to ornate and detailed verisimilitude. American designs and staging before this time (since the passing of the Italianate wing and drop) were literal in their reality, enslaved to specific locale. Physical realism continued to dominate and win praise, as this *Theatre Magazine* article attests: "Naturalness is the keynote of modern stage setting. The rooms of the stage are as habitable as are those of the best houses, for it is such homes that form the basis of up-to-date stage decoration."[4] Of course, many audiences have continued to expect, and many directors and designers have continued to produce, verisimilar detail, especially when designing domestic environments, throughout the twentieth century.

Perhaps most dynamic among Craig's visual offerings were his productions of *Hamlet,* with its open stage, tall curtains, and partially revealed moon, and a *Macbeth* that not only presented two contrasting architectural styles but invited simultaneous staging of different events in different locations. Craig *interpreted* rather than dressed the play; he offered screens, platforms, curtains, and imagination. All would become standard elements of American expressionistic staging.[5]

Part of Craig's remarkable challenge was first fulfilled in America by Max Reinhardt, Europe's strongest representative of the super director demanded by Craig. Throughout 1911 pseudo-Asian and Middle-Eastern plays, such as *Kismet* and *The Garden of Allah,* garnered popularity on the New York stage through their opulent and exotic productions. When Reinhardt's *Sumurun* (first performed in Berlin in 1910) was transplanted by American producer Winthrop Ames on January 16, 1912, at the Casino Theatre, however, the extravaganzas of the past instantly paled. "Of all these Oriental entertainments," one review observed, "*Sumurun* affords the most complete relief from the contemporary realistic drama. . . . In treatment, it is the most exclusively esthetic."[6]

Based upon *Tales of the Arabian Nights*, the erotic symbolist play by Friedrich Freksa was performed entirely without words, except for a brief prologue. The production's designer, Ernst Stern, referred to it as a "pantomime musical." Reinhardt's spokesman and staging assistant Richard Ordynski announced that this was the director's attempt to present sweeping emotions that were too powerful to find expression in words. Sans reference to particular time and place, the production employed dance, mime, and stylized movement in a series of tableaux vivants and processions. The production reflected the vibrant qualities of silent film, but here they were made three-dimensional; Reinhardt even expanded the action beyond the usual confines of the proscenium.[7]

Inspired by Japanese Kabuki theater, Reinhardt built a version of a hanamichi, a narrow runway extending from the front of the stage through the audience to the back of the house for processions and entrances and exits, thus breaking the fourth wall and increasing intimacy between audience and actors despite the large space and spectacular nature of the scenery and pageantry. The most immediate impact of this device, however, may have been to inspire J. J. Shubert to add a runway for his show girls in the *Passing Show* series.[8]

Reinhardt also employed a revolve, one of his favorite devices, also borrowed from Kabuki. Rather than dazzle the audience with minute scenic detail, Reinhardt and Stern eschewed perspective and produced monochromatic backgrounds with large splashes of vivid color (deep blues and indigo skies, for example); vistas of white, off-white, and pink walls; or silhouettes of mosques and minarets, usually in single colors or deep black. "In consequence," Clayton Hamilton wrote, the settings "stop the eye, and fling into vivid relief the [detailed] costumes of the actors."[9] This isolation of the performer working on platforms set against two-dimensional expanses of color became a defining motif of American New Stagecraft designers and, by extension, of expressionism.

Writing some twelve years after witnessing the production, Marsden Hartley recorded the importance of the event for American audiences: "Until then we were ignorant of that kind of simplicity, that kind of directness, that kind of theatrical relativity." *Sumurun*, described by the *New York Times* as "the most frank and unreserved exhibition of passionate abandon that has ever been seen in this country," was unquestionably the theatrical event of the season, and it was powerful enough to sustain Reinhardt's reputation until he returned to the United States in 1924 with *The Miracle*.[10]

WARTIME EXPERIMENT

Inspired by both Gordon Craig and the success of the famous Armory Show of 1913, which boosted modern art in America, the New York Stage Society presented the first American exhibition of New Stagecraft designs by mostly native artists in an empty shop on Fifth Avenue. Opening on November 9, 1914, the exhibit created a stir in the theatrical community. The standout design projects seemed to be those of Robert Edmond Jones and Sam Hume, who had recently returned from Italy, where he studied with Gordon Craig. Failing to draw professional offers in New York, he departed for Detroit, where he founded the Arts and Crafts Theatre in 1916, which featured his pioneering adaptable settings—arrangements of component platforms, curtains, pillars, screens, and stairs. Hume's emblematic approach to design was quickly disseminated throughout the American theatrical world because of articles and photographs in various theater publications, and it found resonances in the work of Lee Simonson and Norman Bel Geddes in the 1920s and beyond.[11]

One of the highlights of the exhibit was a Hume model of a plaster sky dome, or *kuppelhorizont,* a creative alternative to the cyclorama that had been developed in Germany. The exhibit included a special hour-long display of lighting effects on the model dome. Because its reflective properties were prodigious, it was greeted with considerable enthusiasm, but only the Neighborhood Playhouse tried it out, installing a partial dome in 1915. In 1920, when George Cram Cook added a complete dome to the Playwrights' Theatre of the Provincetown Players, the results were so surprising for such a small theater, that his project was treated by most critics as an innovation when it was unveiled for *The Emperor Jones.* It was also used dynamically for at least four prominent expressionist productions in the 1920s.[12]

The most famous item in the 1914 exhibit, however, was a project by Robert Edmond Jones—who had spent a year in Europe in 1913–14 studying informally with Reinhardt, Stern, and others—that was immediately adopted by British director Harley Granville-Barker. By insuring him against financial loss, the New York Stage Society induced Granville-Barker to leave Europe and direct a series of productions in New York. Seeing Jones's rendering for *The Man Who Married a Dumb Wife,* a slight one-act by Anatole France, convinced the director of the young designer's artistry and theatricality; he immediately hired Jones to execute the same design for production (Jones's first professional job). The piece served as a curtain-raiser for the initial production of the series, Shaw's *Androcles and the Lion.* In keeping with the spirit of the times and the leadership provided by Europe until the mid-1920s, this talented American artist was given his first opportunity to design for an American audience by a European producer-director with a European play.[13]

In its American debut, January 27, 1915, *The Man Who Married a Dumb Wife* attracted more attention than the Shaw play it was intended to herald. The *Times* recognized it as "the new art of the theatre." The play itself is a light comedy of small import, but the Jones design was striking in its beauty and simplicity. The dominant feature was a huge window, fronted by stage-length steps and a walkway for street processions on the apron, which lay just above the heads of the front row of the audience. Through color and line Jones gave the New York stage its first home-grown stagecraft in the Continental manner. Designer Mordecai Gorelik has left us a vivid picture of the effect: Jones "symbolized [the play's] comic spirit in primary colors, light frame construction and an almost Japanese architectural style. . . . The costumes, scissored out of richly colored felt cloth, had the stiffness of medieval woodcuts." Vivid reds, oranges, and yellows predominated in the costumes, colors that contrasted sharply with the black and grayish-white setting, embellished with gold.[14]

The key to the labors of Jones and those who followed in his wake was simplicity. The *Dumb Wife* design was likened to poster art. From Toulouse-Lautrec until well into the 1920s poster art tended to employ simple detail and large expanses of color. This is true of European art and theatrical posters as well as of American illustrated magazine covers and recruiting and propaganda posters for the war.[15] Identifying the design with "sophisticated modernism," and setting the production apart from what was defined as traditionally theatrical, critic Francis Hackett observed that it was "hard to praise too much a visual pleasure in which there is richness without congestion and artifice without perversion."[16]

Although most reviewers and theater professionals were excited by the design and its execution, an anonymous mossback of *Theatre Magazine* (about to be upstaged by *Theatre Arts*) summarily dismissed the show as a trifle, "staged after the manner of *Sumurun*."[17] Fortunately, his was not the prevailing opinion, and it was soon apparent that changing trends in staging were not fads but momentous alterations destined to dominate American theatrical production. By the mid-twenties the New Stagecraft and the physical elements of expressionism were so common to productions that they often went unnoticed in reviews.

Granville-Barker, along with his designers Albert Rutherston and Norman Wilkinson, modified the stage and house of Wallack's Theatre by extending an apron over the orchestra pit and the first two rows of seats; the old stage boxes became entrances for actors. A revolving stage, reportedly inspired by Reinhardt, was installed, while footlights (standard at the time) were eliminated, and large spotlights were mounted on the horseshoe balcony's edge in plain view of the audience. Most of these innovations, especially the visible lighting instruments, which garnered much attention at the time, are now standard practice. Although it is also now typical of Broadway productions, renovating a theater specifically for a production was far from usual in 1915; it was possible because Wallack's was old and had been condemned. Through enhanced theatricality and self-consciously manipulated aesthetic distance, the anti-illusionist director insured that his audience never forgot that the dramatic event was being staged. In retrospect, much of Granville-Barker's approach may strike us as Brechtian. When committing his theories to paper later, Granville-Barker wrote that actors should interpret, not impersonate. "Any identification of the player with the part implies a lowering, not a heightening, of artistic achievement."[18]

On February 16, 1915, just four days after the Neighborhood Playhouse opened its doors, Granville-Barker added Shakespeare to his New York repertory, giving Americans their first view of one of the three productions with which he had startled the British public—his stripped-down vision of Elizabethan drama on an unlocalized platform stage. His direction of *A Midsummer Night's Dream,* designed by Wilkinson, was the first in America to avoid a verisimilar but romantic sylvan glade for the fairies and a sumptuous palace for the Athenian court. The nonrepresentational forest was suggested by green strips of diaphanous cloth swaying from above, and the Athenian palace of Theseus was emblematized by a flight of wide steps and towering, exaggerated, silver pillars—there was no other scenery except for a starry backdrop in the final scene.

Even the reviewers who did not wholeheartedly endorse this treatment of Shakespeare—one called it "a bizarre creation"—agreed that it was cleverly and skillfully accomplished. One critic, who was not prepared for the inevitable shifts in artistic taste, hated the scenery and compared it with a revolutionary contemporary painting for which he also felt contempt: "The wildly decorative starry welkin of another occasion is as permanent and genuine a contribution to art as [Marcel Duchamp's] 'Nude Descending a Staircase.' Plain curtains would be more attractive." Posterity's celebration of Duchamp's rebellious art places Granville-Barker and Wilkinson's iconoclasm in good company and underscores the change that was about to take place in American directing, design, and criticism. In recent scholarship Cary Mazer called Granville-Barker's *Dream* "the production in which he succeeded most completely and consistently in creating a new language of theatrical presentation."[19]

Granville-Barker's opening productions in 1915 represented the most comprehensive employment yet of the New Stagecraft. Together with Reinhardt and Copeau, Granville-Barker forged the path that many forceful American directors of the 1920s would take, and it was in the work of Arthur Hopkins that Granville-Barker's preponderance would first become consistently evident in the commercial American theater.

The year 1915 also marked the birth of three of the most important art theaters in the history of American theater: the Neighborhood Playhouse, the Washington Square Players, and the Provincetown Players. It was not until after the war, however, that these amateur groups began to influence the professional theater and to convert to professional organizations themselves. This same year witnessed two more events that signaled momentous change for experiment in the American theater: the premiere of the movie *Birth of a Nation* and the sinking of the *Lusitania*.

When D. W. Griffith's *Birth of a Nation* first appeared in New York in March, the twelve-reel monument triggered an unexpected sensation. Reviewed by many periodicals that had previously dismissed the cinema as trivial entertainment for the lowest common denominator, Griffith's film made it clear that detailed realism on the stage could not compete with realism on the screen. Although film would be without a voice for another twelve years, the pictorial verisimilitude—especially of mass spectacle, the vast scale and violence of troop mobilization, parades, and Civil War battles (including trench warfare, Sherman's march, and the destruction of Atlanta)—its close-ups alternating with long shots, and its myriad location shots rendered the stage a more appropriate arena for stylization and open theatricality. It would take most practitioners and producers of the theater some time to acknowledge this, however. Theatrical producer William A. Brady realized that year that film had the power to usurp the theater's primacy. "The public likes the pictures on their merits. If it ever was purely a matter of cheap admission charges [five to twenty-five cents was typical], that has been dissipated by the genius of D. W. Griffith, who devised and executed a picture which commands top prices [two dollars—equal to top tickets in Broadway theaters] and plays to more money than any regular attraction I know of."[20]

The film features a series of historical facsimiles based on paintings or photographs of such famous events as Lee's surrender to Grant at Appomattox. The most prominent scene for our purposes here, however, is the assassination of Abraham Lincoln at Ford's Theatre. In this scene, which focuses eerily upon the violent act, Griffith regularly intercuts moments from the stage action of *Our American Cousin*, sometimes showing us simultaneously both the action around Lincoln's box and the performance on the stage. The sense of the reality of the theatrical event is quite convincing, but I am struck by the ironic juxtaposition of the stage event that lends counterpoint to the "real life" of the assassination and audience reaction.

The stage has a realistically decorated box set with unraked side walls that run perpendicular to the curtain line. A generous apron extends below the proscenium arch, with all scenery and properties save the edge of the carpet placed above the curtain line. Griffith makes sure that we see the gaily painted grand drape go up and the play proceed, only to stop utterly when starring actress Laura Keene comes onstage. In fact, she must interrupt the play's action several times to acknowledge the audience and accept flowers. Lincoln's late arrival also interrupts the play as the audience shifts its focus to the presidential box. Also, almost all the stage action we see is placed on the apron, below the scenery. Consequently, most of it is performed in front of the box set, not within it. Furthermore, the leading actors are covered by follow spots (ostensibly limelight) as they move about the stage.

Thus the "realistic" staging is highly theatricalized and very unbelievable compared to the events within the auditorium. The only exception to this is the artificial behavior of John Wilkes Booth, but he was a stage actor, a fact that does not escape Griffith, who enhances the character's actions with theatrical flair, unlike the conduct of Lincoln and his entourage. Nonetheless, Griffith seems not to be making fun of the theatrical event but attempting historical accuracy. The result is not only haunting emotionally but a graphic display of conflicting styles. This scene demonstrates, perhaps without intention, the almost diametrically opposed optimum possibilities of filmic versus theatrical art.[21]

Based on The Clansman (1906), an unsuccessful, bigoted play and novel by reactionary Baptist minister Thomas Dixon (who also wrote The Red Dawn, which I discuss in chapter 8), Birth of a Nation shares in the racism of its literary source. Although part 2 of the film is melodrama, complete with villains and heroes, just like nineteenth-century Western and frontier plays, many accepted the work as docudrama. An enthusiastic reviewer, who was apparently not a historian, reports that the scenes "are one and all faithful to historic fact . . . so that, looking upon them, you may feel that you are beholding that which actually happened." The finite stage could hardly compete with such perceptions; a different theatrical direction was necessary.[22]

While Birth of a Nation was enjoying long lines at the box office, the conflict of the Great War delivered its first major blow to the United States when the ocean liner Lusitania was torpedoed and sunk by a German U-boat off the coast of Ireland on May 7, 1915. Among the 114 dead were many Americans, including two playwrights, Charles Klein and Justus Miles Forman, as well as Charles Frohman, the principal member of the Theatrical Syndicate and the most consistently successful commercial producer in New York.[23]

Led by producers Frohman, Marc Klaw, Abraham Erlanger, and four others (all businessmen), the Theatrical Syndicate had been created in 1896 as a trust to control the theater of New York as well as that of the touring road. The syndicate opened a central booking office to control engagements nationwide. In doing so, they restored order to a haphazard business. For the most part, such proficient systematization was advantageous to both management and performers, as we saw with management's triumph over Congress in 1919, but the inflexibility of the monopoly undermined the artistic level of theatrical achievement. Light, popular entertainment constituted most programs, and the advancement of serious art in the theater was significantly curtailed by the pedestrian tastes and assumptions of the producers. Frohman, for example, who was not an artist, yet was dubbed "the Napoleon of the drama," believed that it was only stage tricks and unusual "situations which count with the public."[24]

Because the syndicate's power had already been challenged by the Shubert brothers and independent producers, Frohman's death was its breaking point. The monopoly formally disbanded and liquidated on August 31, 1916, but its essential expiration coincided with the fate of the *Lusitania*. The passing of the syndicate signaled an era of organization within labor ranks (Actors' Equity crippled Broadway and effectively closed it in 1919), changing popular tastes, expanding audiences for the movie industry, and increased artistic freedom for directors and independent producers. Without the dissolution of the syndicate, the expansion of theatrical experiment—including expressionism—to Broadway theaters would have been unlikely.

Some two years before the sinking of the *Lusitania,* a minor vaudeville writer and producer named Arthur Hopkins had directed his first successful play, *The Poor Little Rich Girl* (1913), by Eleanor Gates. This pre-expressionistic novelty, dominated by the "phantasmagoria of [a] child's delirium," marked his incipient stirrings toward experiment. A little girl under medication falls into a strange dream in which figurative situations become literal: her nurse suddenly has two faces, her governess becomes a snake, and her father is leashed to a moneymaking machine. Almost from the beginning Hopkins rebelled against stage realism.[25]

At the close of the 1912–13 season Hopkins departed for a summer-long European expedition. He was especially anxious to see unusual German staging devices, and he was drawn to the symbolist plays of Gerhart Hauptmann and Frank Wedekind (the chief German precursor of expressionism). Visiting

Reinhardt's Deutsches Theater, he saw many designs inspired by Gordon Craig as well as Tolstoy's *Living Corpse,* which Hopkins staged himself three years later under the title *Redemption.* "Everywhere I went in Europe," he reported, "the audiences were moved to a passionate intensity of interest and stirred to an eager and often violent discussion of the play they were attending. . . . I want people to leave my theatre actually quarreling about what they have seen."[26]

When Hopkins returned to New York, he wrote a series of articles for *Harper's Weekly* recounting the notable productions of his tour. Subsequently, he emerged as the foremost American professional director of new dramatic and design forms and remained so throughout the 1920s. He directed Elmer Rice's first success, *On Trial,* the first play to experiment in the use of flashbacks, and the following year distinguished himself as the first American to hire Robert Edmond Jones, thus creating a directing-design team that stood for many years as the preeminent one in America—all with commercial productions.[27]

The first Hopkins-Jones production, *The Devil's Garden,* by Edith Ellis, opened December 28, 1915, at the Harris Theatre. It was a tense domestic drama in which a man murders his benefactor who is also the seducer of his wife. The design for this play set the tone for much staging and scenography to follow. Expressiveness was achieved by the application of the simplest imaginable means at the time (deliberate fragmentation and selective realism had not yet been introduced); the opening scene featured stark, bare walls, broken only by a map and two doors. The judges in this litigious action clustered about a table, sometimes with their backs to their subject, while the accused man sat far apart, in a small, isolated chair. More than twelve feet of unadorned gray wall divided the defendant from the agents of his tribunal. The bold simplicity of the design underscored and exacerbated the anxiety and brooding of the play as well as the division of the opposing characters. For some time the setting served as "a classic example of the . . . heightening of dramatic reality by abstract means." Such was the key to much of the dynamic but simplified scenic design mounted and exploited by Jones and Hopkins. Lee Simonson rightly pointed out that the play failed to live up to the scenery: the austere setting "loomed stately and mysterious. . . . And the room stood waiting, while the play literally expired in it, as a sick puppy might die whimpering in the aisle of a church." Such blank rooms were waiting for American expressionist plays.[28]

In addition to occasional appearances of austere stagecraft that celebrated simplicity, during the Great War the American stage was periodically bombarded by symbolist explosions in both design and dramaturgy. The much-heralded Ballets Russes of Serge Diaghilev, which opened for four weeks of performances in New York on January 16, 1916, was recognized by many, especially in the little-theater movement, as manifesting "a profound influence on [what was still perceived as] the young American theatre." The work of this company reflected a predilection for the exotic. One of Diaghilev's principal designers, Leon Bakst, created intricate, decorative, symbolic, Asian, and often sensuous lush costumes and ornamental, painterly settings for such productions as *Scheherazade* and *L'Après-Midi d'un faune*. His imaginative and densely crowded designs combined a sense of danger, even the sinister, with scenes of erotica and debauchery and were said to represent "the exuberant fantasy of ornamentation and colour which overruns the stage." He liberally splashed the stage with vibrant color, which suggested an impromptu, unstudied vision completed by the subjective and often erotic choreography of Michel Fokine and Vaslav Nijinsky. Those who witnessed the kinetic display could not easily remain unmoved by the intensity of the experience.[29]

The most immediate effects were noted not in direct emulation of the Ballets Russes, but in an innocent boldness and often primitive (one could argue, self-consciously so) expression that permeated the work of the experimentalists and youthful little theaters. Unafraid to fail, delighted to shock, and eager to create new forms (often for the sake of newness), the art-theater innovators distinguished 1916 with their exploration of virgin theatrical territory. The Neighborhood Playhouse and Washington Square Players were already under way in 1915 and added *A Night at an Inn* and *The Magical City* in the months following the Ballets Russes. Percy MacKaye's *Caliban by the Yellow Sands*, with vibrant designs by Joseph Urban and Robert Edmond Jones, appeared in May. The Provincetown Players moved to New York in October and added Susan Glaspell's and Eugene O'Neill's experiments to the Greenwich Village cauldron. The following month Stuart Walker's Portmanteau Theatre first appeared with its traveling repertory of symbolist plays.

In November 1916 the magazine *Theatre Arts*, founded by art-theater proponent Sheldon Cheney, made its appearance. Established in Detroit, the periodical was dedicated to art theaters, little theaters, theatrical experiment, and the New Stagecraft. An article in the first issue is entitled "Acting and the New Stagecraft," and the foreword to this issue explained that *Theatre Arts* was determined to offer an alternative because theater as big business had made "existing dramatic publications its trade journals." Cheney was acutely aware of the sea change the theater was undergoing, and he sought to make his journal "a permanent record of American dramatic art in its formative period."[30]

In spite of its championship of the community and professional theater outside New York, *Theatre Arts* moved to New York in 1918 after censorship became an issue. Throughout the period we are exploring *Theatre Arts* remained the chief journalistic exponent of experiment in theater and drama, and the periodical provided one of the earliest efforts to define American expressionism. Its illustrations alone provide a stunning overview of several decades of theatrical creativity. This was a conscious effort on the part of Cheney and the editors who followed him; the first issue states: "It is part of the plan of *Theatre Arts Magazine* to reprint pictures of the best stage settings hitherto designed by American artists."[31] The elevated tone of this publication suited the current American theater, which not only took itself more seriously than earlier theaters but was having a greater artistic influence abroad. Nonetheless, the title *Theatre Arts* was viewed by some as pretentious or even oxymoronic. Inspired by the publication, theatrical mavericks and dissenting professionals joined amateurs of the little-theater movement in transforming stagecraft, directing, and dramaturgy.

Movement toward the American style of expressionism can be discerned in the Washington Square Players' presentation of the allegorical, episodic *Life of Man*, which opened January 14, 1917, under the direction of Philip Moeller. One of the most dynamic symbolist plays of the Russian Leonid Andreyev, it borrowed heavily from the morality play (as did the German expressionists). An impassive, anonymous, half-veiled Being in Grey delivers a prologue in which the futility of existence is pronounced; this is then dramatized. Throughout the episodes of Man's life, the Being stands watch as a candle burns down, paralleling Man's demise and accentuating the morbidity of the play. All the characters are types; they have no names (another characteristic of expressionism), and each of the five acts combines images of death with laughter, gossip, and displays of greed. The action culminates in the final scene, in which the front lighting is extinguished. The body of the dying man is brightly illuminated on an elevated bier upstage, while the faceless, avaricious relatives and acquaintances (backlit only) perch on chairs or move about the space, starkly silhouetted against the white wall and the equally white corpse. The actors' faces are never visible during their final chatter and chant around the body.[32]

The play's pessimism makes *The Life of Man* an appropriate example of much Continental drama that "mirrored what many European intellectuals believed to be the failure of their culture," but Americans were not as convinced of the collapse of their own.[33] Nor were they the immediate and indissoluble heirs of European culture—only partially so. Consequently, the American artistic and theatrical legacy was a contradictory morass that included fascination with stylization from symbolism on, continuing adjustment to Ibsen and modern realism, and a deeply entrenched penchant for optimistic melodrama (also begun in Europe and perpetuated in the United States long after its vogue was past on the Continent). Americans, then as now, were hard-pressed to abandon romantic notions, grounded in the belief in democratic principles as the world's salvation and the pursuit of the American Dream.

Other symbolist work, like Maurice Maeterlinck's *The Blue Bird,* performed in 1910 at the New Theatre; Edmond Rostand's *Chantecler,* produced by Charles Frohman the following year; or even James Barrie's *Peter Pan* (1905) had preceded *The Life of Man,* but all had shared an optimistic vision. Furthermore, all were presented in spectacular displays that safely literalized the fantasy of the plays—they illusionistically and representationally staged and costumed the romantic fairy-tale forests and fantastic events and characters. Such interpretation was consistent with the staging of classics like Shakespeare's *Midsummer Night's Dream* as it had been traditionally presented on the nineteenth-century stage. American producers typically reduced the symbolist plays to commercial vehicles for popular stars like Maude Adams, who performed in both *Peter Pan* and *Chantecler.* All prewar, American-produced symbolism was enslaved to pictorial representation.[34]

In the fourth year of the Great War Jacques Copeau, dedicated to the bare platform, which could emphasize the actor and by extension the primacy of the text, exemplified for New York the European directorial model fashioned from the experiments of Germany, England, and France. Copeau, with his Théâtre du Vieux Colombier in Paris closed by the war, brought his company to New York under the auspices of the French Ministry of Fine Arts and rebuilt the stage of the Garrick Theatre, which after a few productions was renamed the Vieux Colombier and often referred to as the French Theatre throughout Copeau's tenure.

Assisted by Louis Jouvet as both actor and designer, Copeau built an apron and proscenium doors with stairs and windowlike openings above, elevated upstage platforms, and added numerous steps reminiscent of the design projects of Adolph Appia and Gordon Craig, with whom he had met to exchange ideas in 1915–16. The Garrick project was an intermediate step between his bare stage of the first Vieux Colombier of 1913 and the final theater built in 1919–20 in Paris. Like Granville-Barker he left the stage essentially bare, yet went even further than the English director in elimination of scenic detail. Unlike those of his European predecessors, however, Copeau's architectural setting was permanent; it was used for all productions, usually incorporating only minor changes, such as hanging cloths. For Molière's *Fourberies de Scapin,* for example, the space was "open to its white-washed back wall, with the big Elizabethan-looking balcony and no wings." Some critics, in fact, even when they appreciated the experiments, failed to recognize his facade as scenic and revealed their inseparability from the illusionistic tradition of specific locality that still governed most theatrical production. "Copeau," we are told, "uses combinations of flat surfaces, columns, and curtains instead of what is commonly called scenery."[35]

Copeau's staging allowed the play uninterrupted flow from scene to scene without altering the setting. Already the tone of popular criticism was beginning to change to a more welcoming one, as it became increasingly evident that open staging was not an aberration but a trend among important theatrical innovators. *Les Fourberies de Scapin,* the opening production of November 27, 1917, was performed in French, as were all the Copeau productions during his two-year stay. For *Les Fourberies* Copeau added a *tréteau nu,* a bare trestled stage on top of and in the center of the existing platform stage. The result was a stage within a stage, an elevated central arena having many of the same stylized qualities as the later boxing ring of Bertolt Brecht and the central resonating square in Peter Shaffer's *Equus.*[36]

In spite of the language barrier, Copeau, by attention to detail, achieved impressive, mobile stage pictures that appealed in their austerity and formality to growing numbers of designers, directors, and critics. The first fully staged, commercial American response to Copeau's methods appears to be *Richard III* (1920), directed by Arthur Hopkins and designed by Robert Edmond Jones, who included versions of the tréteau nu, though Copeau's influence on little theaters in the United States was greater than this.[37]

As the American theater entered the postwar period some distinctions between European and American theatrical experiment began to blur. What was distinctly American is not always easy to discern. Such blurring is evident at least as early as 1918 and 1919 with Arthur Hopkins' productions of *Redemption* and *Night Lodging.* Occasionally, theater artists conducted experiments only for the sake of venturing into forbidden or unknown territory. During and following the war many New York artists, both within and beyond the theater, were driven by "a new cultural 'modernism' that attacked the very notion that art should promote established moral principles." As Ellis Hawley describes it, newness was often glorified, "especially if it embodied the virtues of spontaneity, intuition, and sensuality."[38] The Bohemian spirit infused commercial artists as well with a desire to innovate. In spite of record numbers of misfires, the intrepid efforts of the earliest modern American directors, playwrights, and designers shaped the direction of much theatrical experiment for decades.

In 1918 Hopkins added a remarkable actor to his production team, John

Barrymore, whom he acquired for a production of *Redemption*, which opened on October 3. Ideas for this production, which Channing Pollock labeled "the most artistic, sympathetic and atmospheric ever given a play in America," had lingered with Hopkins since his European tour of 1913. Even Hopkins could see that his production had opened a new era: "Everyone knew that something vital and disturbing was happening."[39]

The play's dark themes of dissipation, alcoholism, divorce, bigamy, and suicide were realized in naturalistic performances, especially Barrymore's as an alcoholic. But all the action transpired in simplified, highly suggestive settings that reflected economy of line while maintaining the gloomy presence. A Jones sketch for the second scene is characterized by chiaroscuro and stark contrasts in light values on opposite sides of the set. Photographs also reveal large expanses of unadorned walls broken only by simple doors. John Corbin wrote of the settings, "No attempt is made to realize any locality in its literal detail. Walls are rendered as flat surfaces. . . . Essentials are emphasized by eliminating nonessentials." The squalid scenes especially, usually featuring shadow and glaring pools of light or apparent candlelight in half-seen rooms, became, for many, unforgettable images.[40]

What the production team had managed to do was beautifully meld accomplished acting performances with new approaches to design and staging. "The atmosphere of lights and movement that [the settings] create about the extraordinarily vivid and tortured performance of John Barrymore," Kenneth Macgowan wrote, "marks high water in American production." Hopkins, Jones, and the Barrymores would accomplish similar but more striking results with Benelli's *The Jest* in 1919, *Richard III* in 1920, and a fully expressionistic (at least scenically) *Macbeth* in 1921, the year that expressionism conquered the American stage. It was clear that the American theater was entering a new era: "It is given to few industries and fewer arts to blossom into such fullness or such meaning within six months of the cannons' roar and six weeks of the diplomats' whisperings," Macgowan wrote. Most significant for the American theater, the postwar spirit seemed to stimulate native tragedies for the first time. The genre began in earnest with O'Neill's *Beyond the Horizon* in 1920 and quickly grew.[41]

POSTWAR EXPERIMENT

The first of Eugene O'Neill's major experimental plays to reach a commercial audience, *The Emperor Jones*, opened November 2, 1920, at the Playwrights' Theatre of the Provincetown Players in Greenwich Village, but the next month it transferred to the Selwyn, a Broadway theater. In this semi-expressionistic drama, as well as in his later fully expressionistic plays, it is clear that the playwright demanded deliberately esoteric stagecraft, which at times worked to mystify rather than clarify the action, a practice that intrigued audiences and heightened his notoriety during the 1920s. His approach was echoed in similar practices of other American playwrights who contributed expressionistic plays to Broadway. *The Emperor Jones* shares some characteristics of expressionism, such as the journey motif and structure, the death of the protagonist, stylized scenery in the nightmare scenes (at least as produced, though not as written), and a pervasive dark mood. As others have observed, however, *The Emperor Jones* bears remarkable similarities to Georg Kaiser's *From Morn to Midnight*, which was written in 1912, produced in Germany in 1917, and available in both German and English before the composition of O'Neill's play.[42]

O'Neill's correspondence verifies that he assumed that audiences and critics could easily misunderstand his intent with each new play. In spite of this perception, or perhaps to exploit this perceived condition, O'Neill frequently called for specific staging that was designed to confuse or mystify audiences, whom he believed were unlikely fully to understand his plays. When the plays were well-written and emotionally charged, the mysterious content and staging served to intrigue and engage the audience even while confusing them, thus contributing to the mystique that grew up around this reclusive playwright, who exemplified the serious American drama of his decade.

O'Neill insisted on assaulting the audience's senses and mixing styles while stringently protecting his dramaturgy and meaning. He seemed to cultivate obscurity. Like Samuel Beckett, who also fostered his mystique, O'Neill did not like to explain his work and often refused to clarify. On the few occasions when he chose to offer public clarification, as he did in the *New York Times* after public confusion over *The Great God Brown*, he further muddied the already murky waters by offering unsatisfactory explanations.[43] Nevertheless, O'Neill seemed to succeed at his unwillingness to adhere to whatever dramatic style or convention he established early in a given play. He would sometimes create expectations by introducing a style like expressionism only to violate it or contradict its use later in the action. This stylistic inconsistency and contradictory dramatic patterning was not only emblematic of O'Neill's plays; it helped define the hybrid vision of all American expressionism.

With *The Emperor Jones,* directed by George Cram Cook and designed by Cleon Throckmorton, O'Neill created such fascinating images of darkness and mystery as the vaguely defined but tangible, little formless fears that haunt Brutus Jones on his journey to the heart of racial and personal darkness. In his first scene alone in the dark, threatening jungle (scene 2 of the play), these childsize grubwormlike creatures creep and squirm toward the oblivious Jones. "They are black, shapeless, only their glittering little eyes can be seen. . . . They move noiselessly, but with deliberate, painful effort, striving to raise themselves on end, failing and sinking prone again." Their only sound is "low mocking laughter like a rustling of leaves," a sound O'Neill repeats in *Desire Under the Elms*.[44]

Stimulated by constant but slowly accelerating drumming, Jones, through dream, hallucination, racial memory, or overblown imagination, reverts to the primitive and conjures up a ritual, cultural past. Or is it created for him by the voodoo drums? The truth is unclear. O'Neill calls for pantomimic dumbshows of Jones's past and of events emblematic of African-American history to drive Jones to panic (and fascinate his audience), but these scenes do not clarify the action: they only deepen the mystery.

Except for the first and final scenes, the play functions as a nightmare, whose surrealistic images fill so many of O'Neill's plays of the 1920s, although usually with more subtlety than in the work of European surrealists and expressionists. Here I use the word *surrealism* to signify a full invasion of the dream or subconscious world of the character into the drama; an intrusion that allows neither the central character nor the audience to discern the difference between what is real and what is dream. This device, typical of European surrealism, recurs in American expressionist and semi-expressionistic plays. In American plays preceding *The Emperor Jones*, like *Poor Little Rich Girl,* the use of dream was always clarified for the audience: dream images were always separated from reality-based images.

In spite of his flights of fancy with stagecraft, O'Neill remained committed to realistic character at the center of *The Emperor Jones* and most of his plays. The image of a nightmare, however, also pervades much of O'Neill's experimental work and may help to explain the esoteric, sometimes contradictory images, devices, or techniques he fabricated. The model presented in *The Emperor Jones* and in most of the early American expressionist plays follows the same line: well-defined, realistically drawn central characters are trapped in a nightmarish or highly stylized and threatening world.

Also capitalizing on nightmarish imagery, Hopkins and Jones offered their second foray into Shakespeare with *Macbeth,* on February 17, 1921, this time starring Lionel Barrymore. "In our interpretation," Hopkins reported before opening, "we are seeking to release the radium of Shakespeare from its vessel of tradition. . . . We have left behind all compromise with realism."[45] Break with tradition they did, and rarely has a popular failure garnered such contemporary critical examination—due in part to a remarkable degree of public anticipation.

The Jones settings were marvels of stagecraft, but audiences frowned at the gigantic symbols and were disturbed by the absence of literalism. Jones and Hopkins attempted to avoid both specific time and place with scenery and staging, yet inexplicably, the actors were costumed in "conventionally barbaric" garb, which resembled the costumes of a nineteenth-century Wagnerian production. The entire stage was enveloped in black, and three large silver masks (corresponding to the masked, red-clad, human witches) hovered in the air, as if watching over the proceedings on the stage. It was a "witch-infested space." In some scenes shafts of light streamed through the openings in the masks, like "vast daggers . . . [which] poured down, crossed, pierced, flooded the action below." On these occasions the stage seemed to Woollcott "a glowing platform [suspended] in space." Hopkins and Jones envisioned the witches as a dominant force in the play. They showed this by creating an extended, extraphysiological presence for them through oversize representations that were theatrical and anthropomorphic by being both scenic elements and abstractions of functional masks—unknowable, mysterious personae that remove us even farther from the enigmatic witches than Shakespeare did in his sketchy characterization.[46]

The principal design form was the Gothic arch, often distorted, appearing in various sizes and locations—large and looming, gold on black, often tilted, leaning or collapsing to accentuate Macbeth's rise and fall. Some reviewers, who had little respect for the experiment, described Macbeth's castle as "a giant molar tooth pitched rakishly in space." The most vituperative attacks seemed to be attempts to stave off the onslaught of modernism. Hornblow considered the sets "a fadistic combination of futurist effects and imaginative conceptions so eccentrically bizarre as to be quite without the ken of human comprehension." The designs nevertheless were exciting, beautiful, and stimulating, especially in retrospect, even if difficult for many to understand. Apparently, Jones was attempting to "suggest an emotional idea, instead of a physical reality," but few who witnessed the production were able to get past the scenery.[47]

Hopkins devised interesting staging for many scenes, using the forestage extensively, in the manner of Granville-Barker, and including simultaneous actions and unexpected dissolving movements, such as filling the stage with action before suddenly isolating the witches or Lady Macbeth. Because the stage was so dark, actors could make sudden appearances as in a nightmare, seemingly materializing in the stark pools of light and just as quickly vanishing. The entire production, even more than that of *The Emperor Jones*, conveyed the feeling of a distorted dream, a primal journey "into the fogs of abstraction."[48]

Most disturbing was the stylistic dissonance of Barrymore's performance, which did not meld at all with the open, figurative design and staging. It appears that he internalized the character to such a degree that he seemed to be performing in a different production. Hopkins later described the actor's approach to the role: "Lionel . . . becomes the character he assumes. . . . Macbeth's tenancy of Lionel produced an almost unbearable effect of horror." Furthermore, a central concept of the production, enhanced by the gigantic witches' masks but apparently unconveyed by the actors, was the interpretive decision to show the Macbeths as possessed by the witches, who represented "the evil forces of life" over which we have no control.[49]

Walter Prichard Eaton blamed the audiences and their traditional expectations of Shakespeare, seeing this kind of staging as the theater of the future. "The public," he wrote, "is not yet ready to accept the scenery of pure mood rather than that of place."[50] It is curious, however, that just a year after the failure of *Macbeth,* Lionel's brother performed to great acclaim a beautiful Hamlet in another symbolic, "unlocated" setting by Jones under the direction of Hopkins.

After considerable preparation, the American theater was primed for the aesthetic and emotional attack of expressionism. It was not a play or theatrical production that introduced expressionism to the American public, however, but a German film, *The Cabinet of Dr. Caligari,* which arrived in the United States in the year following its 1919 German release but did not have wide U.S. screening until after its New York premiere on April 3, 1921. Directed by Robert Wiene, the film incorporated techniques common to the Habima Theatre, which New York did not see until 1926. *Caligari* is usually regarded as the best early example of expressionism in film and was certainly the first exposure to the style in the United States. As late as 1925 one critic of theater still claimed that "the entire production achiev[ed] a unity which has been our best guide to the real aim of the Expressionistic in the theatre."[51]

The silent picture revealed the distorted, nightmarish fantasy of a villainous asylum doctor-sideshowman, often from his point of view. This is the standard interpretation of the film's stance. If we note that the film came postwar, following the hellish period viewed by most expressionists as an era of mass insanity, however, we may agree with Lenny Rubenstein's interpretation of the film's distortion. Perhaps the world we see is not the fevered view of a particular madman, but "an abstracted view of a society on the brink of lunacy."[52]

In the action of the film, Dr. Caligari releases his creation, his somnambulist Cesare, to stalk through the town committing nighttime murders. (The name Cesare was frequently used during the war by Allied propagandists to

characterize Germany and the German character as both militaristic and barbaric.) Mordecai Gorelik describes the action as moving "in spasms, while the
unnatural scenery writhes in tortured lines or is broken into creased, angular
planes." The settings are obvious constructions, dominated by deformed geo-
metric shapes and outsized, recognizable theatrical properties for both interiors and exteriors: they are theatrical spaces, which set up a tension between a
coherent story, its mad characters, and the almost incoherent settings. Pene-
trating images include fantastically elevated working stools and tables; an
oblique, spinning carousel; and a feverish escape across impossibly angled
rooftops. In fact, it is sometimes difficult to distinguish interior from exterior
scenes, as if the images were the result of unstable minds; Perhaps, as Michael
Minden suggests, such scenes are perceived as both exterior and interior by
the madman narrating and framing the action. Chiaroscuro is often created
not only with light but in patently painterly ways, emphasizing the obvious
theatricality of the presentation. The results, even when confusing, or perhaps
because they were perplexing, fascinated American playwrights, designers,
and directors, who gravitated to expressionism throughout the 1920s and
filled the American stage with dissonant images, convoluted scenery, and distraught, sometimes mad, central characters.[53]

German expressionist plays and paintings preceded *Caligari*, of course,
and the texts of some of these plays were available in the United States, but
none had been staged. *Caligari* was the first visualized, theatricalized mani-
festation of the movement. In addition, many stills from the film were published in American periodicals, including *Theatre Arts*.

Although most contemporary critical reactions to *Caligari* concentrated
on the visual impact of the film and its uses of stylization, at least one critic,
Robert Sherwood in his pre-playwriting days, connected the film's shocking
qualities to habitually complacent American intellectualism. "The picture itself questions, makes sanity relative as insanity is relative—and constitutes a
valuable offset to the American tendency to oversureness of intellectual values."[54] The popular and critical impact of the film underscored the postwar
embroilment of American intellectual and artistic thought and expression.

By the time of *Caligari* it was clear that visual interpretation of dramatic
events in nonrealistic plays was almost as important as the linguistic content of
the plays themselves. Although this alteration of focus had been developing
with the ascent of the New Stagecraft since about 1912, it was also part of a development in American culture in general. During the Great War, the use of
visual imagery in various communication media had steadily escalated—especially in advertising and film. A survey of American newspapers through this
period demonstrates a remarkable increase in illustrations. The shift to visual

focus in American culture, which is usually blamed on television, began much earlier, and expressionism was a salient exploiter of and contributor to this shift.

On April 20, 1921, just seventeen days after the New York premiere of *Caligari*, Frank Reicher directed a twelve-year-old Eastern European play for the Theatre Guild, *Liliom*, by Hungarian Ferenc Molnar, which opened at the Garrick (Copeau's old space) to near-universal applause. What makes this production particularly dynamic is its successful study in contrasting styles, which characterized much American dramaturgy and production to follow.[55]

Although Reicher insured that the "folk-character is preserved . . . so its people retain their fine, concrete humanity," the play mixes sentiment and satire, realistic and expressionistic styles. Most critics were fascinated, but a few were confused by the hybrid play. One bewildered critic wrote, "After five scenes of ironic realism the play suddenly shifts to fantastic farce." The success of this mingling of styles was due not only to the sensitivity of the playwright but to the imagination and harmonious labors of the two heterogeneous creators, Reicher and Lee Simonson. The designer, especially in this era, had no superior in evoking exterior scenes in simple strokes that suggested free, unburdened space and open air. His *Liliom* designs, intended to "invest the squalor of [the thief's] world with beauty," produced impressive depth of field without painted perspective, a technique especially emblematic of the New Stagecraft. Although hyperbolic, Woollcott's paeans to Simonson's efforts with the railroad embankment set of scene 4 suggest how far American theatrical design had developed in a short period. "Mr. Simonson has worked in beauty a magic picture which five years ago would have been beyond the wildest dreams in the American theatre."[56]

Simonson nevertheless created realistic designs (albeit simplified in line and texture) for most of the play before shifting the scene to a heavenly courtroom for suicides, which became in effect "a petty police court, because the dramatist is allowing his audience to see it through the mind's eye of his principal character." Yet the upper reaches of the walls of the room—too austerely unadorned and untextured to be realistic (recalling Jones's *Devil's Garden*)— were eliminated, to reveal the skies of heaven, thus connecting the final scene to the open skies from the preceding scenes, which were exteriors. The walls of the courtroom extended only about five feet above the floor level at room entrance, hence the tops of the doors and large window rise into the open air.[57]

Although not as characteristic of German expressionism as the settings of *Caligari* had been, the principle of scenic distortion owing to the anxiety and point of view of the protagonist in *Liliom* is certainly at the heart of expressionism as well as of this production. The fantasy sequences in which the dead Liliom is "arrested" and escorted by two men in black ("God's police"), the entire heavenly court scene, and Liliom's return to earth for a day carrying "a glittering star from Heaven" in his red handkerchief were played with verisimilitude rather than broad stylization—yet the events were irrational. The play and production served to ease American audiences into the field of expressionism; it probably influenced the afterlife scenes in Elmer Rice's *The Adding Machine* (1923) and inspired the romanticized Rodgers and Hammerstein musical adaptation of it, *Carousel* (1945).[58]

AMERICAN EXPRESSIONISM

On November 14, 1921, the Provincetown Players produced a fascinating play by one of the company's founders, Susan Glaspell. Just a year earlier O'Neill had written that Glaspell was "the only true writer of real comedy in this country," yet she quickly revealed with *The Verge* and *The Inheritors* that she could also produce serious drama. *The Verge* stands in part as an early American experiment in expressionistic technique, predating all American dramaturgical attempts (unless we label *The Emperor Jones* expressionistic). *The Verge* probably influenced *The Hairy Ape*. Strictly speaking, the play is not expressionistic in the way German plays of the style are, but the scenic needs, especially of the second act, and the protagonist's spiral into madness, which is complicated at times with her breaking into spontaneous lyrical verse, sets it apart from realistic presentations, including the productions of all Glaspell's other plays.[59]

The play explores the psyche of emblematically named Claire Archer, a woman on the edge of insanity (David Sievers diagnoses her as manic depressive), who seeks refuge in her escape from reality or, more accurately, seeks to cross over to "otherness." She is terrified of dying "on the edge." Her condition is symbolized by her botanical experiments—the Edge Plant (a failure, which she destroys) and Breath of Life (which Ellen Gainor calls "a metaphor for female creativity"), plants that she has cultivated in a quest for new forms. She is searching for a way to break out of the stifling, deadly sameness of feminine tradition, social repetition, and patriarchal expectations. Her husband will not take her work seriously, deeming creativity "unsettling for a woman"; and her nearly grown daughter is a washout in whom Claire can see nothing but a parade of old men—her imprisoning ancestors. At one point, Claire, horrified by what she sees, bluntly says of and to her daughter: "To think that object ever moved my belly and sucked my breast!"[60]

Critic Barbara Ozieblo notes that "Claire is selfish—a male prerogative in the 1920s," and it is probably this that not only makes the male characters in the play confused and threatened by her but disturbed many male critics, who expressed bewilderment or hostility. Woollcott, for example, wrote that the play "can be intelligently reviewed only by a neurologist or by some woman who has journeyed near to the verge." He went on to remark tellingly that the play "provokes combativeness in the onlooker."[61]

In the first act, Glaspell represents Claire's psychic disturbance with an intriguing visual image. Claire's husband, Harry, is locked inside her greenhouse, while Tom, the man she loves but cannot touch, is locked outside. The two men can see each other through the glass but cannot communicate. Neither can open her door. The result is both frustration and comic absurdity, reflecting the same states that dominate Claire's condition throughout much of the play.

Glaspell's husband, George Cram Cook, directed; for the confusion and anxiety of Claire's mind, he used an expressionist environment designed by Cleon Throckmorton. Sievers calls it "the first expressionistic distortion of scenery in our theatre for a subjective effect—that of unconscious 'regression to the womb.'"[62] (This honor should probably go to the production of *Macbeth* or *Liliom*, however, both of which opened earlier. *The Verge*, however, was the first American play to be so mounted. *The Emperor Jones*, also designed by Throckmorton, does not fit Sievers' description because the distortion only accompanies hallucination or dream, a device that had been on the American stage at least since *Poor Little Rich Girl* in 1913).

The physical refuge of act 2, Claire's "thwarted tower," was an incomplete, circular room in a tower lit as though by a single lamp, which cast strange, waterlike patterns on the curved walls. The only entrance was a spiral stair, the top of which rose out of the floor (the published play calls for a trap door, which would make the space even more prohibitive as a retreat). The audience looked into this room through the suggestion of a wide, leaning, curving window. One might compare the effect to that of looking through the mouth of an illuminated jack-o'-lantern. After this private sanctuary is invaded by people Claire despises she finally breaks down, crossing the line of control that results in her murder of the man she comes closest to loving. Unlike in *Macbeth*, the milieu and acting were compatible in conveying what was described as "normality verging on insanity in its attempt to escape from the conventional patterns of life into a new design," or as the playwright put it, verging into otherness.[63]

A theatrical experiment that opened on February 27, 1922, introduced a scenic device that proved invaluable to future expressionistic productions. The Theatre Guild and the Neighborhood Playhouse staged the world premiere of George Bernard Shaw's impossible *Back to Methuselah* at the Garrick Theatre. The monumental collection of plays opened in three parts on three different evenings, each guided by different directors. The "philosophical fantasy" was considered almost unplayable, not only for its massive length but because of its dense verbosity devoid of dramatic action.[64]

Lee Simonson simplified the multitudinous scenic needs by employing colorful, projected scenery—a European invention at which the designer had marveled on his trips abroad. Economizing with time and money, Simonson virtually painted with light, projecting his images onto a translucent gauze backdrop that was foregrounded by a series of levels and simple set properties, which varied throughout the action. To suggest the Garden of Eden, for example, a four-stepped circular platform on top of which dwelt the large Serpent, horizontally filled the stage opening narrowed by partially opened curtains that accentuated the vertical. Above the platform, a huge image of the Tree of Knowledge, which faded into the flies, towered over the action and dwarfed Adam and Eve. It was the scenery that was lauded by the critics and that had the most influence on future American productions; particularly in designs like Jones's for *The Ancient Mariner* and *Beyond* and Simonson's for *Adding Machine* and *From Morn to Midnight*.[65]

In the midst of the three premieres of *Methuselah* Eugene O'Neill and the Provincetown Players offered a more thoroughly defined American expressionism than had thus far been attempted. Their production opened on March 9, 1922, and soon moved to Broadway's Plymouth Theatre under the guidance of Arthur Hopkins, although James Light was the director. With *The Hairy Ape*, O'Neill continued his esoteric assault on the audience and escalated the level of violence. It was as if this production answered a reported fear of Woodrow Wilson's in the aftermath of the Great War: "To fight you must be brutal and ruthless, and the spirit of ruthless brutality will enter into the very fibre of our national life."[66]

In the play, both as written and as first produced, expressionism through scenery, movement, and sound slowly crept into the action and steadily escalated, until it was interrupted by a realistic Industrial Workers of the World (IWW) Union encounter in scene 7, which employed a fully staged interior-exterior setting that was prop-heavy, "decidedly cheap, banal, commonplace and unmysterious as a room could well be." Thus the audience might be confused about the play's style; more important, questions are raised about whose perception of the dramatic world they are watching at any given time. Is it the protagonist Yank's? He is at the center of the play, and it is he with whom the audience must emotionally connect if the play is to work dramatically. Like many Americans after the war, Yank feels aimless and lacking in purpose. His

Emperor Jones, *by Eugene O'Neill (1920). Charles Gilpin as Brutus Jones confronting the Witch Doctor* ⋯ision. *Produced by the Provincetown Players. Directed by George Cram Cook. Designed by Cleon* ⋯ckmorton. *(Photo courtesy Billy Rose Theatre Collection, the New York Public Library for the Perform-* ⋯rts, Astor, Lenox and Tilden Foundations)

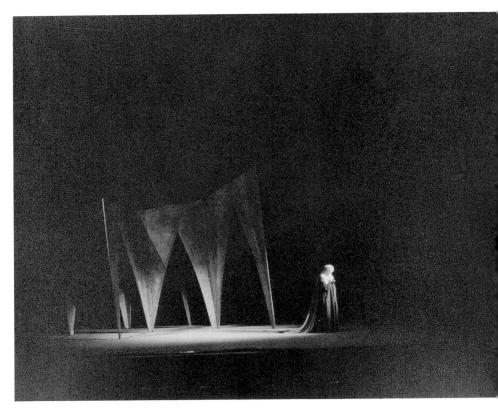

Macbeth, *by William Shakespeare (1921). Julia Arthur as Lady Macbeth in the handwashing scene in fro*
of the "bicuspid" arches. Produced and directed by Arthur Hopkins. Designed by Robert Edmond Jones.
(Photo courtesy Billy Rose Theatre Collection, the New York Public Library for the Performing Arts, Aste
Lenox and Tilden Foundations)

Back to Methuselah, *by George Bernard Shaw (1922). Adam and Eve beguiled by the Serpent in front of projected scenery. Produced by the Neighborhood Playhouse and the Theatre Guild. Directed by Agnes Morgan, Alice Lewisohn, Philip Moeller and Frank Reicher. Designed by Lee Simonson. (Photo courtesy Billy Rose Theatre Collection, the New York Public Library for the Performing Arts, Astor, Lenox and Tilden Foundations)*

The Hairy Ape, *by Eugene O'Neill (1922). Louis Wolheim as Yank in an expressionistic jail cell. Produced by the Provincetown Players and Arthur Hopkins. Directed by James Light. Designed by Cleon Throck morton and Robert Edmond Jones. (Photo courtesy Billy Rose Theatre Collection, the New York Public Library for the Performing Arts, Astor, Lenox and Tilden Foundations)*

R., *by Karl Capek (1922). The robots defeat their masters and take over the world. Produced by the*
...tre Guild. Directed by Philip Moeller. Designed by Lee Simonson. (Photo courtesy Billy Rose Theatre
...ction, the New York Public Library for the Performing Arts, Astor, Lenox and Tilden Foundations)

Roger Bloomer, *by John Howard Lawson (1923). Satirical expressionistic scene: identical business office* containing automated clerks lead to the boss's office. Produced by the Equity Players. Directed by Shelley Hull. Designed by Woodman Thompson. (Photo courtesy Billy Rose Theatre Collection, the New York Public Library for the Performing Arts, Astor, Lenox and Tilden Foundations)

The Adding Machine, *by Elmer Rice (1923). Dudley Digges as Mr. Zero, who is on trial for murder before a masked judge in an expressionistic courtroom. Produced by the Theatre Guild. Directed by Philip Moeller. Designed by Lee Simonson. (Photo courtesy Billy Rose Theatre Collection, the New York Public Library for the Performing Arts, Astor, Lenox and Tilden Foundations)*

The Spook Sonata, *by August Strindberg (1924). The expressionistic ghost supper scene in the round room. Produced by Experimental Theatre, Inc. Directed by Robert Edmond Jones and James Light. Designed by Robert Edmond Jones and Cleon Throckmorton. Masks by James Light. (Photo courtesy Billy Rose Theatre Collection, the New York Public Library for the Performing Arts, Astor, Lenox and Tilden Foundations)*

cessional, *by John Howard Lawson (1925). George Abbott as Dynamite Jim in his two-dimensional jail*
. Produced by the Theatre Guild. Directed by Philip Moeller. Designed by Mordecai Gorelik. (Photo
rtesy Billy Rose Theatre Collection, the New York Public Library for the Performing Arts, Astor, Lenox
Tilden Foundations)

Beyond, *by Walter Hasenclever (1925). Walter Abel and Helen Gahagan as ill-fated lovers stand in fron of fragmented and projected scenery. Produced by Experimental Theatre, Inc. Directed by James Light. Designed by Robert Edmond Jones. (Photo courtesy Billy Rose Theatre Collection, the New York Public Library for the Performing Arts, Astor, Lenox and Tilden Foundations)*

The Great God Brown, *by Eugene O'Neill (1926). William Harrigan as Billy Brown and Anne Shoemaker as Cybel self-consciously discussing their masks. Produced by Experimental Theatre, Inc. Directed and designed by Robert Edmond Jones. Masks by James Light. (Photo courtesy Billy Rose Theatre Collection, the New York Public Library for the Performing Arts, Astor, Lenox and Tilden Foundations)*

Spread Eagle, *by George Brooks and Walter Lister (1927). Osgood Perkins in uniform as Joe Cobb, the assistant of Fritz Williams as Martin Henderson, the captain of industry, aboard Henderson's private railway car at the beginning of the war Henderson has created. Produced by Jed Harris. Directed by George Abbott. Designed by Norman Bel Geddes. (Photo courtesy Billy Rose Theatre Collection, the New York Public Library for the Performing Arts, Astor, Lenox and Tilden Foundations)*

The Front Page, *by Ben Hecht and Charles MacArthur (1928). Lee Tracy as newspaperman Hildy* *Johnson is manhandled by the cops. Produced by Jed Harris. Directed by George S. Kaufman. De-* *signed by Raymond Sovey. (Photo courtesy Billy Rose Theatre Collection, the New York Public Li-* *brary for the Performing Arts, Astor, Lenox and Tilden Foundations)*

Machinal, by Sophie Treadwell (1928). The Trial of the lonely Young Woman, played by Zita Johann, in a stylized courtroom. Produced and directed by Arthur Hopkins. Designed by Robert Edmond Jones. (Photo courtesy Billy Rose Theatre Collection, the New York Public Library for the Performing Arts, Astor, Lenox and Tilden Foundations)

s of the Lightning, *by Maxwell Anderson and Harold Hickerson (1928). The realistic courtroom setting _ides a marked contrast to the courtroom of* Machinal. *Produced by Hamilton MacFadden and Kellogg _y. Directed by Hamilton MacFadden. (Photo courtesy Billy Rose Theatre Collection, the New York Pub-_ibrary for the Performing Arts, Astor, Lenox and Tilden Foundations)*

Meteor, *by S. N. Behrman (1929). Lynn Fontanne and Alfred Lunt as Ann and Raphael Lord. Produce[*
the Theatre Guild. Directed by Philip Moeller. Designed by Raymond Sovey. (Photo courtesy Billy Ros[
Theatre Collection, the New York Public Library for the Performing Arts, Astor, Lenox and Tilden Foun[
dations)

burning question is "Where do I belong?" As in German expressionism and *From Morn to Midnight*, in particular (which is often compared to this play), is it the protagonist's rising anxiety that distorts the scenic investiture? If so, how to explain the interruption of the mounting confusion and despair of Yank by the apparent realism of the IWW scene?[67]

O'Neill himself said that the play was a stylistic admixture that combined the guttural naturalism of Yank with the gritty stokehold language, which is at one moment naturalistic with its hodgepodge of dialects and expletives, at the next chanted in choral measures. The playwright calls for automaton movement, masks, and scenery that is sometimes expressionistic, sometimes representational, despite the fact that in the play's opening directions he wrote: "The treatment of this scene, or of any other scene in the play, should by no means be naturalistic."[68] Yet some scenes are realistically drawn. Although scene 5 presents a chorus of featureless socialites, socialites appear in scene 2 fully individualized. O'Neill apparently enjoyed combining dissonant stylistic choices with little regard for the resultant disconcertion or perplexity. Nevertheless, audiences and critics alike were fascinated by the experiment and flocked to witness the remarkable production, with its stunning, naturalistic performance by Louis Wolheim, and the play was everywhere praised by the critics.

As if to demonstrate the triumph of the methodologies and artistic philosophy promulgated by Gordon Craig, as well as cement the European trends making their way to American stages, Kenneth Macgowan and Robert Edmond Jones published *Continental Stagecraft* in 1922. The critic and designer had taken a ten-week tour of European theaters beginning in April of that year and witnessed almost sixty productions, most of which were recorded in renderings by Jones and descriptions with commentary by Macgowan. The book stresses the work of directors and designers, giving special prominence to German productions, although France, Austria, Sweden, Czechoslovakia, and the Moscow Art Theatre (on tour in Stockholm) are represented.

An antirealistic aesthetic permeates the writing and illustrations and foreshadows the spirit of much of the best theatrical work accomplished in the American theater in the 1920s. "There is something in the nature of the theater that makes Realism a natural and a thoroughly unsatisfactory method of expression," Macgowan wrote. "Especially when the heart of the whole business is an elaborate pretense that there really isn't any actor, and there really isn't any theater." The book proved invaluable to American directors and designers, who were attracted by theatrical innovation, demonstrating the work of Copeau in his newly redesigned Vieux Colombier; more work by Reinhardt, including "found spaces" like the Redoutensaal in Vienna; and Georges

Pitoëff's stylish theatricality in Paris. Perhaps most significant, this publication brought the work of expressionistic director Leopold Jessner with his *Jessnertreppen*, as well as of Jürgen Fehling, a director of similar aesthetics, to the attention of American practitioners. Jessnertreppen were flights of steps used as the primary playing space. Much of Jessner's *Richard III*, especially, was played on red steps, which were peopled by crowds in red or white costumes, depending on whether Richard was in power or not. The pyramidal staircase appeared downstage of "a wall all across the stage, with a platform along the top at the base of another wall." All of Jessner's productions at the Schauspielhaus in Berlin, conceived with his designer Emil Pirchan, were presentations with stairs, platforms, myriad levels, and often huge expanses of wall towering above the actors. He used light, not just to define action and set mood, but "as a parallel expression to the play." In *Richard III*, for example, the designer suddenly cast huge shadows of Gloucester on the walls when the character figuratively referred to buying "a glass / That I may see my shadow as I pass."[69]

In short, Jessner was directing nonexpressionistic plays expressionistically, while Fehling at the Volksbühne, with designer Hans Strohbach, probably inspired by some of Jessner's methods, was applying them to contemporary expressionistic plays like Ernst Toller's *Man and the Masses*, many of which would find their way to the American stage. The legacy of Jessner's and Fehling's work would become most obvious in Arthur Hopkins' direction of *Hamlet* later in 1922, designed by Jones and starring John Barrymore, and in *Man and the Masses* directed and designed by Lee Simonson in 1924.

Before the influence of Jessner was seen directly on the American stage, however, the Theatre Guild and independent producers introduced straightforward German expressionism in the wake of O'Neill's *The Hairy Ape*. Although *From Morn to Midnight*, by Georg Kaiser, was written ten years before *The Hairy Ape*, it did not reach the American stage until two months after it, opening at the Garrick Theatre on May 14, under the direction of Frank Reicher. The works of Kaiser, Toller, and other German expressionists had reached American playwrights like O'Neill and Rice in written form and inspired American expressionism, but hitherto the German and American strains always demonstrated great disparity. Compared to O'Neill's and Rice's experiments, Kaiser's play appeared to be a completely subjective treatment of a victimized, nameless worker—the Bank Teller (called the Cashier in the Ashley Duke translation used by the Guild).

Typical of expressionism in its pilgrimage, fruitless search, and the destruction of a lowly protagonist, *From Morn to Midnight* stressed the progress of a man who attempts to escape his dehumanized, exploited existence. After embezzling sixty thousand marks, the Cashier says he has come "from the grave. . . . The living keep on sinking deeper and deeper." A later speech, which appears to have inspired John Howard Lawson as well as O'Neill and Rice, underscores the plight of the masses caught up in the machinery of society and business: "The procession is endless. An eternal pilgrimage. Like sheep rushing into the slaughter house. A seething mass. No escape—none—unless you jump over their backs." Like the anti-heroes and hero-victims of the American expressionists, the Cashier breaks out of lockstep only to spiral down into the abyss.[70]

As he had with *Back to Methuselah,* Lee Simonson designed the production with projections that quickly changed in keeping with the cinematic sequence of events. Projections were especially useful for the tree that turned into a skeleton and back into a tree in scene 3. The action moved about the playing space, much of which was left in darkness, "letting the surrounding gloom . . . suggest the dark womb of the scenes to come."[71] This well served the play's seven scenes, which included isolations (only part of the stage is illuminated) like the steward's box of the bicycle races and the penitents' platform of the Salvation Army hall.

Reicher appeared to work more enthusiastically with this expressionistic form than with any other of his assignments for the Guild, driving the action at a breakneck pace, thus underscoring the relentless, unequivocal course of catastrophic events. He accentuated the subjectiveness by not allowing the audience to forget that the grotesque action and bizarre, modulating surroundings were projections of the Cashier's state of mind. Some critics understood the images precisely: "These racing visions must remain visions yet be real. . . . The world is this actual world but it is in the fevered brain of one creature. . . . There is no periphery."[72]

Reicher reinforced his intention and could control the distressed Cashier's anxiety by playing the maddened central character himself, yet many critics were confused or troubled by the structure of the play. Perhaps the schematic nature of the central character was not personalized enough for many Americans; and the swiftly changing episodic form of the play left the traditionalists with no fully developed character to unify the action for them. American playwrights, although inspired by the Germans, rarely created anonymous central characters like the Cashier; they were also more successful at garnering critical American support than the Germans. Nevertheless, many audiences were intrigued by this experiment, more, in fact, than the Guild had expected, with the result that the planned short series of special performances at the Garrick expanded to a regular run at the Frazee Theatre.[73]

Not surprisingly, the vogue of expressionism also inspired tangentially related dramatic themes that permeated melodramas and films examining the machine age. Fritz Lang's *Metropolis* (1927) is probably the best-known film of this genre, but one of the most popular stage incarnations originated in Eastern Europe and reached America as *R. U.R.*, opening October 9, 1922, at the Garrick Theatre. Czech playwright Karel Capek's melodrama, which introduced the word *robot* to our language, intrigued and fascinated audiences with its story of the triumph of Rossum's Universal Robots, a victory that spells the demise of humankind at the hands of androids. The ominous, pallid makeup and padded, forbidding uniforms of the robots in Simonson's designs brought comparisons with Frankenstein's monster and the Golem to many reviews. Philip Moeller's direction of the movement of the robots in revolt in act 3 was particularly well-executed. All the action was presented in bare, cold, industrial rooms, which heightened the sense of threat that loomed until the "happy" conclusion brought about by sensitive, self-sacrificing, counterrevolutionary robots, who opt for a return to "human" love.[74]

"The true enemy of civilization is not the machine," John Corbin wrote in response to this production, "but the mechanized human being." Set in the near future (what appears to be the 1950s and 1960s), all the action takes place in and near the factory that manufactures the robots, creating a sterile atmosphere that is underscored by the crass commercialism and technological preoccupations of all but one of the human characters. The anti-capitalist themes are so prominent, in fact, that had the play been American I would have included it in chapter 7, on plays that attack big business. Harry Domin and his fellow human managers and engineers are all business and technology. Their worldwide supply of robots keep production and labor costs to a minimum. Consequently, it is not in their interests to give the robots the capacity for human emotions. Robots become indispensable for all labor—even fighting wars. "So many robots are being manufactured," a scientist finally observes, "that people are becoming superfluous." In the end, some of the humans realize that the business ethic and blind allegiance to technology have led to the annihilation of civilization: "For our own selfish ends, for profit, for progress, we have destroyed mankind."[75]

Although Eastern European, the play addressed what was becoming emblematic of the American way of life and finding concomitant expression in American plays like *The Hairy Ape, The Adding Machine*, and *Processional*. In *R. U.R.*, Capek, whose "armies of robots . . . struck a chord in postwar America," had combined cynicism with sentiment—for example, having a robot pronounce in the epilogue: "Slaughter and domination are necessary if you would be human beings. Read history," apparently as a preamble to a sentimental scene of newfound love. Macgowan found the play's "atmosphere curiously repulsive. Yet it remains fascinating." This response is typical of many theatergoers, who turned the dark experiment with its surprisingly sentimental conclusion into a hit for the Theatre Guild. Such a formula was almost certain of success in New York in the 1920s if the play was well-written, as witness *Anna Christie, Processional, They Knew What They Wanted,* and a host of others that explore unpleasant themes only to offer hopeful, even comic conclusions. The American taste for dark melodrama, even tragic action, laced with sentiment underpins the contradictory nature of the artistic predilections that characterized the 1920s and persist in the 1990s. As Hodge wrote, "While the process is to uncover American problems at the roots, there are often optimistic conclusions; . . . though the uncovering is gloomy, the possibility of survival and correction is still possible."[76]

It is not surprising that this ruling aesthetic did not dominate, in fact barely existed in, American drama before World War I. Although its most immediate precursor is the sensational melodrama of the nineteenth century, with its restoration of order and rewards for the good, we should not equate the two. Many American artists and audiences were attracted to *part* of the darker European experience. Most American expressionistic plays are infused with violence, often climaxing or reaching a crisis with a violent death, yet a hopeful upturn in a final scene or epilogue is common. It is telling that a more pessimistic Capek play, an allegorical satire on the inhumanity of humanity and the futility of war called *The Insect Comedy* (produced in New York as *The World We Live In*), opened a few weeks later in a well-mounted production by William A. Brady to good reviews but fared much more poorly with audiences than did *R. U.R.*

VISUAL EXPERIMENTS

The Jessner-inspired and critically anticipated Hopkins and Jones production of *Hamlet,* which opened November 16, 1922, at the Harris Theatre, proved to be John Barrymore's premiere moment in the theatrical sun. This presentation stood as the emblematic *Hamlet* of an era just becoming fascinated with psychoanalysis.

Visually, the action was concise, unified by Jones into a multilevel unit setting that, as with *Macbeth,* was emblematic and suggestive of no specific location but that had an austere, gray-stoned structure onstage similar to the Tower of London used in his successful *Richard III.* Commanding the space was an impressive, wide flight of steps running directly upstage, leading upward to a towering Romanesque archway, that opened out against the night sky. The skydrop was frequently lit in deep or silver-blue hues that provided dynamic contrast with the almost colorless walls. Upward climbing steps continued on the left and right beyond sightlines that were stopped by the walls of the arch. This archway was also fitted with drapes to close off the facade, which was flanked by two high, narrow windows on the left and right walls that traveled downstage to the proscenium. An apron extended over the orchestra pit bringing some of the action very close to the audience, and for some compartment scenes several formalized curtains dropped in front of the platform, leaving only the apron for a playing space. That was all. The effect, akin to that of the spatial projects of Adolph Appia, was unity of place rhythmically modulated by light, shadow, and the kinetic composition of the actors and space. Although the archway gave the impression of deep space and openness when it was open to the skydrop, when it was draped, the room that was created was confining. For the most part, changes of scene were indicated by lighting shifts, familiar to late twentieth-century audiences but quite uncommon in 1922. The result was dynamic open staging reminiscent of Copeau and Granville-Barker. Macgowan called it "half symbolic, half actual . . . always frankly artificial and theatrical. It was never reality, but always a place where players acted a play."[77]

Hopkins' staging made repeated use of the stairs, often placing entire scenes on the staircase, in a manner similar to Jessner's, or using the staircases for compositionally intriguing scenic groupings of actors in the court scenes. The ghost of Hamlet's father was unseen except for a shaft of green light or a projection high on the skydrop beyond the archway; an actor spoke his lines offstage. Stark Young described an interesting piece of staging in the suggestive closet scene: as Hamlet crawled toward the light of the ghost, he was "caught in his mother's arms, weaving together the bodies of those two, who, whatever their sins might be, must belong to each other at such terrible cost." Macgowan proclaimed the heightened acting "stylized. Like expressionism, it is almost the poster."[78]

This stunning production was the zenith of Continental stagecraft given native expression—an interpretation that finally freed American designers to apply the lessons from abroad without being mere imitators. It was the maturity of the New Stagecraft, thus rendering the term passé. The New Stagecraft was no longer new—it had been fully ten years since *Sumurun* and seven years since *The Man Who Married a Dumb Wife*—and it was now a fully integrated style, free to evolve in its own way apart from the shadow of Europe.

Near the end of 1922 New Yorkers saw the most outwardly expressionistic production of the decade. *Johannes Kreisler,* by Carl Meinhard and Rudolph Bernauer, opened on December 23 at the Apollo Theatre under the direction of Frank Reicher, this time working independent of the Guild with Swedish designer Svend Gade, who had designed the original production in Berlin.

Called a "fantastic melodrama" in forty-two scenes, the play unfolded its disjointed episodes quickly, and in many cases as flashbacks. The play buried a
romantic plot and *Tales of Hoffman* hero, Kapellmeister Johannes Kreisler,
beneath a facade of bizarre action and nightmarish hallucinations and fanta-
sies. In one scene, for example, Kreisler envisions that the woman of his inspiration, Undine, is being flogged beneath a huge cross by a priest, only to
awaken and find her taking communion; in another scene Kreisler's enemies
are decapitated by his conductor's baton. The action was superbly and imagi-
natively orchestrated by Reicher and stands as the first of its kind in the
American theater—an experiment in staging, the substance of which subsequently became standard practice in ensemble productions well beyond
the 1920s.[79]

For the play's "gargantuan orgy of scenery," the stage was subdivided into
six movable stages on two levels, some raised more than ten feet above the
stage floor. All six units were mounted independently on tracked wagons that
moved both up- and downstage and left to right. In addition to the six stages,
the full stage was used for certain scenes (the wagons were pulled off). Between the audience and the staged action was a painted scrim (bowed toward
the house), which also served as a curtain when lit from the front. Yet the
scrim never rose. Much like what Tennessee Williams called for in *The Glass
Menagerie* (1945) or Martha Clarke used beautifully in *Vienna Lusthaus*
(1986), all action was viewed through the haze of the scrim. Intense, bright
lights (many with mirrors) flooded the desired stage areas, which were lit in
complete isolation, aided by black velvet drapery and the scrim (which allowed the wagons to be changed on the darkened stage while the action, lit
elsewhere, proceeded). It was never necessary to stop the action between
scenes. All effects were stark, and shifts were usually made abruptly with
blackouts. The action moved quickly about the stage, left and right, high and
low, or in a moment would fill the entire playing space. The actors, unaccus-
tomed to blackouts and trying to take their places on multiple levels in darkness or within the harsh glare of lighting instruments, often were assisted by
stagehands dressed in black, who also shifted the wagons and scenic units.
The production style was emulated only a few months later by the Equity
Players, with their much smaller production of John Howard Lawson's *Roger
Bloomer*.[80]

Because *Johannes Kreisler* confused many theatergoers, but most of all
because the play was slight in content, its run was brief, although several
critics were fascinated rather than troubled by the dislocating experience. The
production, Ludwig Lewisohn wrote, "is not calculated to project a taut or
reasoned dramatic action. . . . The scenes are like a series of paintings," with

each fulfilling its "specific purpose." Likewise the *Times* critic lamented that "just a little of the genius that went into the scenery should have been devoted to the play." Regardless of the play's merit as dramatic literature, the production, in its risks and excesses, helped prepare for, or at least augured, modified expressionistic staging for nonexpressionistic plays, a practice that became increasingly popular and expedient beyond the 1920s. Much stagecraft of the future lay in the aesthetic that inspired the interpretation of *Johannes Kreisler*.[81]

NIGHTMARE AESTHETICS

In the year 1923, an increasing number of expressionistic plays attacked American commercialism and greed, a trend that continued until the stock-market crash. Lawson's *Roger Bloomer*, which opened March 5, 1923, is a quasi-expressionistic exploration of adolescent anxiety and America's preoccupation with making money. The play is intriguing, but the production was disappointing. Lacking the funding and resources available to *Johannes Kreisler*, and without the services of an experienced director (Shelley Hull is credited), the Woodman Thompson design of *Roger Bloomer* was a much smaller, low-budget version of shifting scenes set simultaneously across the stage of the Forty-Eighth Street Theatre.

Visual expressionism appeared in two scenes. A stylized Wall Street setting in which the protagonist Roger is seeking employment appeared as a series of identical offices in which all the workers "move in unison like wax-works throughout the scene, turn over papers, pick up telephones, rise and walk around their desks . . . with [the] appearance of organized haste, giving [the] impression of choral movement."[82] The image has also survived in production photographs and was revived for the satirical *Beggar on Horseback* the following year.

The final act, in a jail cell, is dominated by Roger's expressionistic nightmare brought on by the false accusation of murder against him. The dream is dominated by exaggerated versions of many of the characters with whom Roger had difficulty earlier in the play, and like so many American expressionistic plays, it ends with a hopeful upturn as Roger gains the opportunity to start over. Few people saw this production; just two weeks after *Roger Bloomer* opened, however, New York experienced a play that now stands as the classic of American expressionism.

The Adding Machine, by Elmer Rice, might have disappeared from theatrical memory had it not garnered a critical attention that lasted long beyond its moderate first run. Opening on March 19, 1923, under the auspices of the

Theatre Guild at the Garrick Theatre, Rice's play attracted attention without reaping the financial rewards of his enormously popular *On Trial*, directed by Hopkins in 1914.

Philip Moeller's direction helped *The Adding Machine* stick to its American roots and idiom, as Rice had intended that it should. This made the production a significant departure from German expressionism, but in ways different from O'Neill's work. Rice and the production were criticizing specifically American commercialism, industry, and civilization, rather than European, or even industrialized, civilization in general, as European expressionism tended to do. *The Adding Machine* also differed from its German models because its departures from reality through dialogue, design, and characterization were geared to social inequities and middle-class small-mindedness, or even to cosmic jokes, as opposed to the searing political upheaval and psychological anguish common in the drama of wartime and postwar Central Europe. Also, Rice's protagonist Zero was revealed to be not just a victim of the commercial machine and the industrial complex but a despicable, racist, pedestrian nonentity whose lot would never change, in part because he was incapable of or unwilling to change. His fate is a bit like that of Turgenev's superfluous man, but Zero is drawn without the Russian's compassion. Like the protagonists in *Roger Bloomer* and *The Hairy Ape*, Zero finds himself lost in a mass of indistinguishable, purposeless humanity. As a self-improvement manual of the 1920s observed: "We live now constantly in a crowd; how can we distinguish ourselves from others in that crowd?"[83] Even Zero's act of murder, which leads to his execution, gives him no particular distinction.

Human depersonalization was presented in the social gathering of the *number* people, but Moeller had already achieved success with a similar device in *R.U.R.* earlier in the season. Here, however, the robotlike behavior of the Zeros' social acquaintances was substituting for the artificial, conditioned behavior of real, ignorant people, who, through group dynamics, perpetuate prejudices and meaningless social intercourse masquerading as both articulate interaction and healthy entertainment.

Lee Simonson designed novel, exaggerated settings and stage properties, such as the gigantic adding machine of Mr. Zero's torture in the afterlife, the stage-left-leaning walls and right-leaning defendant's rail of the austere courtroom, and Zero's lifeless workplace, devoid of any memorable features other than high wooden stools and workbenches for the harried scribes. Most likely the image for this scene was inspired by the police-station and town-clerk scenes from *The Cabinet of Dr. Caligari*. For Zero's brainstorm (just before he murders his employer), Simonson used projections, as he had done in *Back to*

Methuselah, to fill the blank walls with numbers. When Zero strikes out blindly in retaliation at the Boss, the setting is spinning, "the noise is deafening, maddening, unendurable," and through the use of projections, "all the figures he has ever added whirl madly in the Zero brain." The violent climax of the scene, of course, is the murder, which is also presented stylistically: "Suddenly in a great tumult everything is blotted out with two bloody splashes." After this catastrophe, the sound of the adding machine dominates Zero's sensibilities, even replacing such ordinary daily sounds as a doorbell, as the audience sees and hears the distortions experienced by Zero's fevered consciousness. Simonson, however, shared credit for the brainstorm with his director, noting that it grew out of Moeller's need for the scene: "If the whole scene could go mad, blood you know," Moeller told him, "something to show what's happening inside the man."[84]

Although this play received considerable critical attention for years as an important exponent of American expressionism, at the time of production it rated mixed reviews and a number of pans. Perhaps viewers were thrown by the cynically ironic conclusion, which was neither hopeful nor tragic. One review, even though tongue-in-cheek, captured what may have been the heart of the problem: it was an *American* experimental play by a *commercial* playwright who had no background in the little- or art-theater movements. "*The Adding Machine* is a play which, coming from Prague, would excite the townsfolk to prayer and feasting. A hullabaloo would be sent up about it which would result in the issue of a special edition of *The Nation* and a riot call by the Drama League. But being the work of an American, incidentally, not of the esoteric order, we can expect a merely mild critical reception and a patronizing attitude."[85] Be that as it may, the play captured symbolically and stylistically the heart of social and economic problems, dilemmas central to American life, and exploited them artistically. Rice offered no solutions, but he graphically demonstrated the destructiveness and cyclic, enervating condition that threatened to perpetuate itself, especially in a country that was growing increasingly more commercial. In 1923 Rice wrote another fascinating experiment in expressionism, *The Subway,* but in part because of the mixed reception of *The Adding Machine,* it was not produced until 1929.

After 1923, the Theatre Guild itself moved steadily toward commercialization, despite occasional brave play choices and periodic stagings in a creative or innovative manner, sometimes in spite of the Guild's organization. The Guild, along with other producers, was clearly attracted to expressionism, which was in part a reaction to increasing industrialization and, especially in America, to the glorification of mass-production and the practice of advertising and salesmanship. It is curious that the form and style of expressionism captivated many in the commercial theater despite the contradictory nature of the polemic established by the artistic object itself (the anti-commercial play, like *The Adding Machine*, in a commercial production) and the popular advertising and selling of that same object by the producer or producing organization.

Nightmarish visions continued to bombard New York audiences. Although Experimental Theatre, Inc. (ETI), founded by Kenneth Macgowan, Eugene O'Neill, and Robert Edmond Jones in 1923, was dedicated in part to producing O'Neill's new plays, the ETI dreamed of developing a repertory theater, as had its forerunner the Provincetown Players. The first ETI season opened with a European play that had served as an inspiration to many American playwrights, directors, and designers, O'Neill chief among them: August Strindberg's phantasmagoric *The Ghost Sonata* (translated by Edwin Bjorkman for this first American production as *The Spook Sonata*).

This production, described as "Strindberg's strange vision of the springs of sin in the human soul," opened January 3, 1924, in the renamed Provincetown Playhouse, and its choice and expressionistic style paid homage to the principal European progenitor of Eugene O'Neill. Three of America's most dedicated experimenters created the production: Robert Edmond Jones co-designed with Cleon Throckmorton and co-directed with James Light, who also built masks, the first ever used for a Strindberg play. Although the Provincetowners had used masks in one scene of *The Hairy Ape*, *Spook Sonata* made a much fuller use of masks than previous American expressionistic productions. *Spook Sonata* seemed to invite literal masks with its symbolic unmasking in scene 2 and this line spoken by the vampire Hummel: "Now and then a favourable chance will reveal the most cherished secret, stripping the imposter of his mask, and exposing the villain."[86]

While adhering to the pervasive death imagery in a play that is dominated by vampirism and the idea that truth can kill, the production avoided some of the obvious choices and opted instead for lighter, ethereal fancies. The stage, bathed in "a symphony of ghostly blues," was a modified open platform suggestive of the work of Copeau and Granville-Barker. The play's scenic pilgrimage through the spectral house was abandoned for this production, but the choice of open staging on a raised, curving platform exploited the tiny theater's skydome, exposing most of the dome and breaking its sweep only with side wings and occasional isolated set pieces like the Mummy's statue and closet (combined in the design). The actors' masks, also used selectively, were all white, as were the death screens that lent the production a sepulchral, funereal dimension similar to the conclusion of Washington Square's 1917 production of *The Life of Man*.[87]

Strindberg's eerie, protracted silences at the ghost supper were not only effective in production but influential on O'Neill, whose work—*Welded*, for example—immediately showed experimentation with increased silence and cross-talk, such as Strindberg creates in this play. "What is the use of talking, when you can't fool each other anyhow?" the Young Lady quotes her father as saying of his awful circle of family and acquaintances.[88]

Although considered depressing and confusing by many, the play of "crime and guilt and secrets," in which stage metaphors assume life and become the dramatic reality, still lends itself to manifold conflicting interpretations.[89] Critics usually think of it as an original experiment that provoked difficult questions and helped to heighten American awareness of the author, whose plays had rarely been performed here before this production. (Strindberg's *A Dream Play* followed in 1926.)

COMIC EXPRESSIONISM

Glaspell, O'Neill, Lawson, and Rice had hardly established American expressionism before the form assumed a new character in self-parody: a carefree, satirical attack on materialism, politics, the judicial system, and the tasteless manipulation of the fine arts. *Beggar on Horseback*, which opened February 12, 1924, at the Broadhurst Theatre, was written by George S. Kaufman and Marc Connelly, who were no doubt satirizing the expressionistic form as they freely adapted from an outline of a minor German play by Paul Apel. The expansive comedy (another rarity among expressionists) was directed by Winthrop Ames, who was artistic director of the ill-fated New Theatre in 1910, sponsored Reinhardt's *Sumurun* in America, and created a minor vogue for intimate professional theatrical houses after 1912 with his Little Theatre. Like romanticism, most expressionism dwelt on melancholy, violence, and serious subject matter. *Beggar on Horseback* was to expressionism what Ludwig Tieck's outrageous comedies like *Puss in Boots* were to romanticism.[90]

The cacophonous *Beggar on Horseback* is often characterized as the first expressionistic Broadway hit. Called a "super-revue . . . with the music left out," it was performed with the externals of expressionism but without the seriousness that usually accompanied the disjointed fury so typical of the plays—and that was present here as well, though with something of a devil-may-care, sarcastic manner. Nonetheless, the play and production effectively attacked commercialism while ironically reaping profits as a successful commercial venture.[91]

Kaufman and Connelly quickly dispense with a realistic expositional scene, creating an expressionistic dream sequence that dominates most of the action of the play. Actually the dream itself is a satirical, absurd response to serious expressionism. In the dream "one sees the crudity and garish ineptitude of the successful expressionistically intensified." Composer Neil McRae, the protagonist, is literally pulled into the dream sequence by a dream character, whereupon the dialogue "turns into a rhythmic chant, to an orchestral accompaniment." Kaufman critic Jeffry Mason calls Neil a romantic hero, an odd character type for an expressionistic play, but one that both identifies the protagonist as displaced, gives the audience a traditional hero to root for in a nontraditional play (despite the fact that he is an artist), and ultimately makes his rejection of the commercial world, as envisioned in the dream, the only appropriate and life-fulfilling choice when his integrity and artistry have been restored.[92]

At his dream murder trial, where the travesty of justice is literal and the court proceedings are treated as if they were the premiere of a new play, the Cady family, whom Neil kills in impulsive frustration to preserve his art, become judge, prosecuting attorney, and witnesses. Neil's punishment is his being forced to work in an art factory, a fractured combination of a prison, the industrial assembly line, and the Hollywood screenwriters' work ghettos, where mimicry, mass production, and pop tastes are the order of the day. No originality and imagination are allowed to enter his music. Neil explains the routine: "The ideas are brought from the inspiration department every hour on the hour. After I turn them into music they are taken to the purifying department, and then to the testing and finishing rooms." Unable to endure his fate, Neil begs to be executed and at this point mercifully awakens from his nightmare.[93]

The clever settings, designed by Woodman Thompson, one of the "second wave" of New Stagecraft designers, ranged from the protagonist's realistic apartment to a series of dream locations, some fragmented (like the courtroom), others fully realized (such as the confining art factory). A railway station suddenly became the setting for the wedding; the Cady home, where Neil is condemned to live, was defined only by columns and drapes ("a perfect forest of marble columns" matched at times by a forest of identical servants), through which Ames conducted a series of mad chases and sudden appearances.[94]

Ames violated the fourth wall by sometimes bringing up the house lights and making full use of the aisles; there was a bridal procession, as well as an invasion of newsboys, who appeared just before the intermission informing the audience of Neil's conviction before the trial was over. The courtroom for Neil's trial functioned like a theater; the trial even had an overture and ushers. The artist factory, of course, appeared jaillike and recalled the lockstep activity and mirror-image office settings for Lawson's *Roger Bloomer,* also designed by Thompson.

Ames, Kaufman, and Connelly clearly intended their audience to enjoy the novelty afforded by such a production scheme, and because the play pretended to bear no abstruse meaning and was perfectly executed, it went far beyond *Johannes Kreisler* or *The Adding Machine* in acclimatizing American audiences to expressionistic techniques. *Beggar on Horseback* actually attracted, rather than distanced, viewers by its alienating devices. Consequently, unlike burlesques of the past, this play contributed to the perpetuation of the form and style it mocked.[95]

RADICAL EXPRESSIONS

Just two months later, another American production of German expressionism appeared, which provided maximum contrast with *Beggar on Horseback,* verifying the homage to European forms but underscoring what by 1924 was an obvious need to domesticate alien methods and styles. The value of Jessnertreppen made itself most apparent in Lee Simonson's earnest production for the Theatre Guild of Ernst Toller's *Man and the Masses* (*Masse-Mensch*), which opened April 14 at the Garrick Theatre. Toller, first represented in the United States by this production, embodied the "chief exponent of the political side of expressionism [seeking] social and political reorganization."[96] The play, while sympathizing with the plight of the proletariat being exploited by the moneyed classes, is a critique of revolution and a call for restraint and peace; it presents a well-meaning leader of the oppressed workers, called the Woman, who tries mobilizing workers to strike, only to see her control usurped by the Nameless One, who drives the workers to kill and destroy. Of course, it is the Woman who is executed by the establishment. Structurally, the play's seven scenes are alternating pictures of reality and dream or vision: each vision underscores the preceding scene and introduces the next.

Simonson, who both directed and designed, had been ruminating over this play since first seeing Fehling's *Masse-Mensch* produced in Berlin in 1921–22. He also saw Jessner's *Richard III,* and in both productions he was struck by the "almost orchestral sense of controlling the dynamics of actors and all their movement." He stressed Fehling and Jessner's "sensitiveness to the symbolic power of . . . human movement." Simonson was an exponent of the directing techniques of Reinhardt and used similar methods for the obviously choreographed crowd scenes in his production. He presented much of the action on a flight of black steps (wide at the top, narrow at the stage floor), running low to high from stage right to left, flanked and backed by black curtains. The action swept up the stairs as the crowd was incited to riot by the Nameless One while the Woman at the foot of the stairs heedlessly appealed to the mob's humanity. The director described the physical interpretation of the shift in authority: "The mob looking up toward a leader who plainly dominates it, finally voic[es] itself in one cry and a single gesture of aspiration." Simonson's chorus of thirty-two characterized the masses that suppress or destroy any sense of individuality and create a collective organism that functions as one, many-tentacled character that can be manipulated by a powerful individual.[97]

In scene 2 Simonson cleverly and fittingly combined visual and aural staccato patterns for the masked bankers and brokers of the stock exchange, who orchestrate political, military, even social events for the sake of making more money—"to keep our machinery going"—and assure that "the system is safe." In this highly stylized dream sequence, Simonson built on the action until the bankers broke into a fox-trot, dancing around the staircase, using the mechanical sounds of the stock ticker as musical accompaniment, and "ending in a riot of ticker tape."[98]

Simonson was drawing on a theatricality rarely seen on the American stage before this time, except in visiting European productions or in a few American expressionistic works like *The Hairy Ape* or *The Adding Machine*. Above all, however, he provided, if not the first, then the most obvious production drawn from the methods of Leopold Jessner that were promulgated in print by Macgowan and Jones.

By 1924 it was clear that the ruling theatrical influence on American production came from Germany and that the movement most effectively transforming American staging was expressionism. Yet Americans did not like to admit such things about a former enemy. Sheldon Cheney's observation on the superiority of German theater architecture during the war, which got his publication into trouble (see chapter 2), underscores the ongoing contradiction of American tastes and artistic pursuits and their ideology and political beliefs, as well as what they claim to think important as opposed to what they really prefer.

When R. P. Blackmur wrote in 1925: "It is almost as if to make trouble had become the creative habit of the general mind," he could have been thinking about John Howard Lawson, whose *Processional* opened January 12, 1925, under Philip Moeller's direction with the Theatre Guild at the Garrick, and inspired a level of controversy usually associated with plays or films deemed sexually indecent. The mongrel nature of the play's structure, dubbed a "symphonic miscellany," and the frequent use of "the jazz tempo" seemed appropriate to critic Richard Dana Skinner, who observed that the tinny, funky music "symbolizes so aptly the confusion of our lives since the close of the war . . . as if everywhere a circus parade were to meet a funeral and each convey something of its own spirit to the other." Robert Littell likewise grouped it with recent American expressionistic plays "which testify to the curiosity and uneasiness of Americans about themselves." These views are in keeping with the confusion, the grappling for comprehensible patterns, that the playwright in his postwar emotional dilemma seemed to be seeking while struggling to reject a nihilistic philosophy. The effect is a bit like watching a clever, sincere man have a nervous breakdown while keeping his sense of humor.[99]

Even the significance or appropriateness of the expressionistic play's settings were argued about in the press. The stage designs of Mordecai Gorelik, one of the most dynamic American designers of the second generation, inspired by the cheap, two-dimensional backdrops of burlesque and music hall, lent sinewy support to Lawson's imaginative hodgepodge. Gorelik used bright colors and painterly settings in order to exploit a Fourth of July spirit, which ironically underpins the play. The irony was further enhanced by his decoration of the entire proscenium frame with stars-and-stripes bunting, advertising placards, and symbols of Americana. Most of the settings had an open stage below the shallowly placed drops. Even when Dynamite Jim, the protagonist (or the closest the play has to one), is in jail, he looks out through a window that has obviously been cut into a drop.[100]

Resembling a theatrical collage, the production revolted against accepted dramatic form, as the playwright bombarded his audience with contradictions and incongruities concerning what Lawson saw as both what was wrong and what was right in his country's public struggles. Sadie Cohen, a childish seventeen-year-old who becomes the love interest for the jazz wedding in the play's conclusion, reflects the vibrant spirit and jumbled structure of the play: "They're gonna kill lots a' people, oo . . . lots a' people! . . . It's martial law an' everybuddy can be kilt . . . an' the soldiers has taken the mines an' the strikers has got music an' they're marchin' an' they're marchin."[101]

Lawson's thesis was the need for social reform because of the conflict caused by insurgent groups like the Ku Klux Klan and by the insensitivity of management toward labor that had been exacerbated by the Red Scare. This theme at times was in danger of being overwhelmed by the lively, extravagant form and shifting moods. Brooks Atkinson's labelling the play a revolutionary prank is probably unfair; nonetheless, the cacophony clearly was the result of cramming somewhat naively, if energetically, too many ideas into a single play. Although guilty of oversimplification of the problems it attacked, and occasionally marginally coherent in its deliberate dissonance, *Processional* was unlike anything New York audiences had witnessed. More important for

Lawson, this fascinating and successful production allowed the playwright to continue his assault on capitalism, cronyism, and commercial exploitation while enshrining socialism and labor.[102]

For months critics and theatergoers argued the play's value in terms of content as well as dramatic form and style. Three weeks after the premiere a columnist wrote that the play could "be regarded as a step toward that self-analysis from which as a nation we have been apt to shrink."[103] Even a public debate about expressionism, theatrical art, the status of America's social problems, and the merits of *Processional* was held in the theater, on February 1, 1925.

TOWARD SURREALISM

While the controversy raged over *Processional,* New York's final example of radical German expressionism was produced by ETI on January 26, 1925, at the Provincetown Playhouse. *Beyond,* by Walter Hasenclever, presented only two characters in twenty-two scenes. James Light directed the performers through quickly transmuting, indefinite locales that bore no relation to time or specific place. It was as if the characters were suspended outside normal existence in order to associate disjointed episodes from an imagined or introspective life. Much of what transpired was an expression of the thoughts of the characters; therefore the director accentuated the characters' vocal dynamics and overpowering emotionality.

The settings by Robert Edmond Jones, however, were executed in a style more akin to Copeau or Granville-Barker, with minimal scenic elements, "using the plaster dome of the Provincetown Playhouse as a background and . . . placing in front of it only the most significant abstract details." By omitting walls and creating as much open space as possible, settings were often emblematized selectively by a few set properties like a bed or table with a screen, or simply by "a window or a door adroitly placed which evokes the entire interior." It was as if "material objects of the decor existed only in relation to the thoughts of the characters." The results were, in Stark Young's words, "as beautiful an arrangement of scenery and lighting in the expressionistic style as you will be likely to see anywhere."[104]

Typical critical responses, however, reflected confusion and the difficulty of having just two characters carry the emotive dialogue, written in a spare, linguistic style. *Beyond* lasted only sixteen performances, but it was materially one of the most perfectly, if simply, executed productions of the 1920s, reflecting unity and harmony of production elements; it may have been, along with *Desire Under the Elms* and *The Great God Brown,* the finest work of ETI and

one of the most complete Greenwich Village productions of the decade. Perhaps more to the point here, *Beyond* demonstrates an advanced synthesis of
European and American experimental theatricality.[105]

By mid-decade the productions of both *Beyond* and O'Neill's *The Great
God Brown* represented a high-water mark of mysterious stage action in expressionism. These plays also took a strong turn toward surrealism where illusion and reality competed for primacy. Perhaps inspired by the plays of Luigi
Pirandello, which began appearing on the New York stage in 1922, O'Neill's
new play explored autobiographical anxieties, split character, personality confusion, and public versus private masks. Audiences who began attending performances on January 23, 1926, of the austere production directed and
designed by Robert Edmond Jones were perplexed and fascinated. As Joseph
Wood Krutch wrote: "At no time during the course of his career has Mr.
O'Neill given us a play more powerful or more confused than this."[106]

A dual tragedy of self-loathing and psychological introjection (which is the
disturbing result of adopting the personality of another), *The Great God
Brown* makes use of both the actor's face and masks that let him or her confront or hide from others. The split is apparent not only in the division of Dion
Anthony and Billy Brown (two characters who may be halves of the same person) but also in separate characters who are themselves split: Dion Anthony is
at war with himself over religious, artistic, and erotic issues as well as in a life
and death struggle with his Dionysian mask. Brown, on the other hand, does
not feel conflicted until he takes over the mask of Dion, thus adopting Dion's
personality—that is, that part of the personality of Dion of which Brown is
aware. The ultimate tragedy seems to be one of possession—wanting to possess or be what another has or is, and once having or becoming that, being destroyed by it. The stagecraft of the play often supports this reading, but it
frequently confuses the issues through mystification and contradiction.[107]

The settings O'Neill called for suggest lonely, ascetic, interior islands of
professional and domestic activity. In production they were backed by two-dimensional, obviously painted and stylized drops, which suggested without de-
lineating specific locations. The action takes place in a mid-sized to large
American city. Little other than the slang of the youthful principals and the incidental music locates the play in the 1920s. Nearly all is in service to an anywhere, anytime, generic arena for the action of the mystery.

The masks point up the characters' vulnerability and people's inability or
unwillingness to honestly confront the people (they think that) they love.
Margaret, for example, is shown to be in love with Dion Anthony's mask, not
the man beneath. When he unmasks, she automatically dons hers for protection, screaming, "I don't know you! You frighten me!" What is most confusing

about the mask device, however, is the inconsistent way it is used throughout the action. Although masks are employed first of all to suggest private versus public personae, it becomes quickly clear that the mask itself is seen by other characters when a character is wearing one but not when it is in a character's hand. This is especially true of Margaret, who loves first Dion and then Brown, believing the latter is Dion simply because he wears Dion's mask. Early in the play masks are recognized only when on the face. In later scenes, however, the mask is seen by some characters, such as Cybel, the almost clairvoyant prostitute, when off the face. The dialogue often revolves around Cybel and Dion's arguments about masking and unmasking. At one point she physically removes his mask: "Haven't I told you to take off your mask in the house?" Although creating a comic moment, she seems to have violated the mask conventions set up in the early scenes.[108]

Later still the characters Dion and Brown can even address, read to, and kiss their own masks—threatening, goading, beguiling them, as if the masks have a separate personality or power. The most confusing and contradictory mask usage comes when the disembodied mask of Brown is taken by a crowd for the entire body of Brown, a moment that always confused the audience, especially when four actors carried the mask "two on each side, as if they were carrying a body by the legs and shoulders." In the final moments of act 4 Margaret also treats the mask of Dion as if it were the whole body of her husband, although the character has been buried for two months. In the epilogue, however, some four years have passed, and Margaret produces the mask of Dion as if it were a photograph or eternal shrine to his memory. The stage direction reads: "She slowly takes from under her cloak, from her bosom, as if from her heart, the mask of Dion . . . and holds it before her face."[109]

A turning point for both the dramatic action and the mask work is the death of Dion, which leads Brown to remove Dion's mask and don it himself, a rather impossible act if taken literally except as objectification of personality introjection. The action points up how unknowable we really are, but onstage the moment was at once confusing and electrifying. This psychic hijacking is further mystified by having Brown create a mask of himself, which he wears when he is not wearing the mask of Dion. Therefore, Brown appears to be playing the role of Dion as well as the role of himself. This psychic manipulation is achieved through physical action, masks, and staging—not through dialogue. The intended "meaning" therefore remains verbally unexplained, hence deliberately ambiguous, like a dream.

Recalling the moods of *The Emperor Jones* and Hopkins' *Macbeth*, *The Great God Brown* is ghostly, haunting, spectral. It begins and ends at night, in the moonlight on a pier. All that comes between prologue and epilogue is interior, but they are stark, stylized interiors that suggest modernity and under-score isolation and impersonality. Like Brutus Jones, Billy Brown ends in des-peration, physically stripped and murdered by a bullet. Unlike Brutus, however, Dionysus, if you will, first as Dion then as Brown, must be tortured and die two times. The play represents, in effect, twin tragedies, as we play through similar action twice, ending with an uneasy but quiet synthesis of the two characters—spiritually and physically—presided over by Cybel, the seer prostitute who names the final hero-victim Dion Brown. The contradictions of the stagecraft and dramaturgy seem to imitate, if not celebrate, an irrational world. Like Dionysus, O'Neill seems to be attempting to cast a spell over his audience, to force them to accept the irrational and the contradictory because they are intrigued and mystified by the ritualistic proceedings.

EXPRESSIONISM AS POLITICS

Until the stock-market crash every season continued to present expressionis-tic productions, but after *The Great God Brown,* only a few offered anything new in style or content. Some of the productions of the New Playwrights' Theatre provided a forecast for the 1930s, melding aspects of Russian con-structivism (and possibly the stylization of space in the productions of Vsevolod Meyerhold) with American expressionism to present a socialist agenda.[110] Unfortunately, all but one of the expressionistic productions were theatrically disappointing.

On October 19, 1927, the New Playwrights' Theatre premiered Paul Sifton's *The Belt,* a satire on the automobile industry with socialist themes. The interesting device here was the realistically presented living room of a la-bor family that acted as the foreground for a stylized factory assembly line (the belt). At first we only hear the machine sounds, but ultimately we see the belt take over as primary performance space. Unfortunately, the setting by John Dos Passos and the direction of Edward Massey were too confined by the small stage and the production faded quickly.[111]

John Howard Lawson's *The International,* mounted at the New Play-wrights' Theatre on January 12, 1928, graphically depicted a Communist revolution centered in New York City that combated the forces of big busi-ness. Using a sixteen-woman chorus, which alternately represents stenogra-phers and Communists, Lawson invokes both modern jazz music and contemporary rhythms as well as the stateliness and tragic spirit of Greek drama. By mounting the play with an unchanging unit-constructivist setting in shades of gray (designed by Dos Passos), Lawson, as both playwright and di-rector, placed the capitalists in the same space as the Communists, which may have (unintentionally) underscored the similarities rather than the differences of opposing ideological camps.[112]

Also at the New Playwrights' Theatre in 1928 Michael Gold presented an intriguing look at racial hatred in *Hoboken Blues*. Gold calls for a unit setting in a modified constructivist manner (he had seen some of Meyerhold's work on a recent visit to Russia), but the execution of the play was crude. More significant, it calls for an all-black cast, with whites played by black actors in white masks. In production, this scheme was abandoned for an all-white cast, who parodied African-Americans in blackface. Not only was the choice insensitive, but much of the point of the play was perverted. Like *Beggar on Horseback,* the play presents a satirical dream sequence in the second act, but Gold's play climaxes with a pervasive image: a stereotype of black culture imitates white commercialism.[113]

In a special production at the Provincetown Playhouse, the New Playwrights' company finally staged an expressionistic play well, under the direction of Em Jo Basshe. Upton Sinclair's radical *Singing Jailbirds,* which opened December 4, 1928, attempted to glorify the plight of the working class and attack the evils of the capitalistic system. The play mixes styles and includes expressionistic sequences; some of the scenery, designed by Manuel Essman (especially the jail cell), recalled *The Hairy Ape.* Unlike that play, in which Yank sits solitary in his cell, however, the strikers are packed in the cells "so tightly that not all can sit down." The staging here was impressive to the critics as a "spectacle of man's notorious inhumanity to man." Much of the play, however, is realistic in terms of character, event, and location. As the action enters its crisis, emotional moments include dream sequences that bleed into other scenes. The protagonist, in fact, although confined to a prison cell, moves in and out of the hallucinations and visions, projecting himself into remembered or imagined events.[114]

A strange parody of justice occurs when Red, the protagonist, imagines himself on trial in the Hall of Hate. The almost comic rendering, in which the judge is a tiger and Red's defense lawyer a treacherous jack-in-the-box, recalls the dream trials in *Roger Bloomer* and *Beggar on Horseback,* but here the imagined event is the product of a fevered brain on the verge of death. Unlike those two plays, *Singing Jailbirds* has no hopeful ending.

A WOMAN'S EXPRESSIONISTIC CODA

The pessimistic conclusion of *Singing Jailbirds,* unusual in American expressionism, also underscored one of the most powerful expressionistic plays of the decade, *Machinal,* by Sophie Treadwell, a journalist-playwright who had served as a war correspondent in France between 1916 and 1918. Recent feminist criticism and a New York revival in 1990 have returned focus to this play, which was largely ignored or minimalized in the decades following its production, especially by critics writing about expressionism. At the time of production—September 7, 1928, at the Plymouth Theatre, under the direction of Arthur Hopkins with designs by Robert Edmond Jones—the play's well- interpreted theatricality and topical themes made it popular. *Machinal* included an argument about abortion and a scene with an older gay man attempting to seduce a young, inexperienced man (or "boy" in Treadwell's parlance). The play's unusual title, which in French means "mechanical," refers to habitual human behavior characterized by automatic personal responses; it perfectly describes the repetitive, dissonant, fragmented style of performance called for in the drama. The title also underscores the social and commercial machines that destroy possibilities of joy and freedom for women.

In production Hopkins walked a fine line between stylization and realism—the character portrayal was realistic. In the office scene at the play's opening, for example, the playwright's stylized repetition of duties and vocalization by the office workers was maintained, but the actors never seemed to become automatons as in so many earlier expressionistic productions. Nonetheless, their business and line delivery, designed to overwhelm the protagonist (played both stridently and sympathetically by newcomer Zita Johann), were carefully choreographed and orchestrated.

The play's locations were set in front of a permanent background of framed curtains, surroundings that altered primarily through changes in lights or shifts of set properties and by the elimination of all but the most essential details, techniques not unlike Jones's in *Beyond*. Some scenes, however, featured fragmented bits of realism that in photographs appear to be realistic settings; full-stage views reveal the anonymous surround. The designer was clearly responding to the playwright's call for generic scenery, offering two entrances for the first four scenes but only one way out for the last five, as the protagonist's world closes in on her. The intimate postcoitus scene of episode 6 actually begins (and proceeds for some time) in the dark, while the final scene, the execution, is likewise played in darkness until the Young Woman's final screams for "Somebody!" are cut off by death. In Hopkins' production "only a pulsating flood of terrifying crimson light, like a still flame, makes reply." The rapidly shifting, cinematic scenes effectively paralleled "the emotional course of the story." By the late twenties, general audiences could readily appreciate cinematic scene shifting and emblematic, suggestive setting without being distracted by what was once considered peculiar.[115]

Treadwell's dark drama was loosely based on a sensational murder case, and it stressed the emotional upheaval, social paralysis, and crisis-borne act of violence forced on the Young Woman by commercial and domestic exploitation and patriarchal dominance. In a love affair she finally finds some freedom and pleasure only to discover that she has been exploited once again.[116]

Structurally, the play is deliberately episodic—in fact, Treadwell labeled the nine scenes episodes—and each scene has a generic title like "To Business," "Prohibited," and "A Machine" that underscores the emblematic and momentous events or conditions that resulted in the destruction of the protagonist, known only as Young Woman or Miss A. until late in the play, when we find out that her name is Helen Jones (I refer to her throughout as the Young Woman because this is in keeping with the Everywoman, anonymous tone of the play). Unlike other female playwrights of the 1920s, Treadwell, anticipating many women writing for the theater in the 1970s and 1980s, experimented openly with form. Hers is one of the few major expressionistic plays of the era to avoid a dream or hallucination sequence. The action centers on the confusion of the Young Woman, who is virtually immobilized much of the time until near the end, when she commits an act of violence and is condemned by an insensitive society to which (like Yank in *The Hairy Ape*) she feels she does not belong. The play ends with her execution in the electric chair; no restoration of order follows.

Although she is in many ways the opposite of the intelligent and articulate Claire in Glaspell's *The Verge,* Treadwell's Young Woman is similarly disturbed, depressed, and driven to murder by social impulses and her treatment by men. One could argue that Claire goes mad when she kills but that the Young Woman kills in order to avoid madness. Like the expressionistic plays of O'Neill and Lawson, much of the action is heavily dependent on responses to sound and music that provide ironic or pathetic counterpoint to the onstage action and frequently serve to overwhelm the protagonist. At the time, however, most critics compared *Machinal* to Rice's *The Adding Machine,* both because the five-year-old play was already viewed as a model for American expressionism and, most of all, because of the similarity of title, acts of unseen murder by the protagonists (along with their subsequent trials and executions), and the oppressive depiction of the worker caught up in the machinery of commercialism and industry.

Unlike any of these plays except *The Verge,* however, former suffragist Treadwell had a radically different agenda, which resulted in a play that was at its core subversive to patriarchy. Nearly everyone, but especially the Young Woman's husband, mother, doctor, and lawyer, dominates her conversationally, and each constantly interrupts, forcing his or her own views. No one recognizes her pain or understands her confusion. The Young Woman is desperate and cannot adjust, making her subject to claustrophobic attacks: "I had to get out!" she complains of the subway. "In the air! . . . All those bodies pressing." Often the stage directions indicate that the Young Woman is looking for a way out of the room (no setting is an exterior), and in production it was said that "wherever life touches her, it swamps her in mediocrity." Her marriage functions like a jail, which she exchanges for a real prison cell after killing her husband. Yet Treadwell fittingly, if surprisingly, calls her "an ordinary young woman, any woman," thus stressing the plight of women in 1920s society and the anxiety and danger of destruction or self-destruction under the patina of domestic normality.[117]

Although *Machinal* was not the last American expressionistic play of the 1920s, it was the last prominent one, both as drama and production. In essence, then, though dominated throughout the decade by male dramatists, the American expressionistic movement began and ended in the 1920s with the work of two women, Susan Glaspell and Sophie Treadwell, who harnessed a strident and painful form and style, usually reserved for male protagonists, to explicate a very different kind of inhumanity and isolation for their women protagonists suffering in a confusing and inhospitable postwar world.

7

The Calvin Coolidge Grand Tour

This is the most commercial time in the history of the world. Money technique is the essence of the age. And I shall be master of it.
—S. N. Behrman, *Meteor*

Sing for him, sing for a rich man,
'Cause he's richer than God.
—John Howard Lawson, *The International*

The commercial spirit and acquisitiveness of Al Woods was emblematic not only of much that drove the producers of Broadway but also of what was coming to be the American way of life in the postwar United States—a recurring part of the American dream. Like much 1980s popular theater (*Glengarry Glen Ross, Other People's Money, Hurlyburly*), popular cinema (*Working Girl, Wall Street, The Secret of My Success*), and pop music ("Sweet Dreams," "Simply Irresistible," "Material Girl"), the popular theater of the 1920s featured plays that celebrated or attacked the flood of commercialism and advertising that inundated the United States after recovery from the postwar recession.[1]

After the recession ended, by late 1921 and early 1922, the mass-consumption society and economy defined themselves with a rocketing stock market and the modern advertising industry. As Warren Susman observed: "Advertising became not only a new economic force, . . . but also a vision of the way the culture worked: the products of the culture became advertisements of the culture itself." At the same time some 40 percent of the wealth of the world came under U.S. control, while the government went to work reducing corporate taxes. Even when greed-driven corruption in government was exposed, it failed to diminish the new god of commercialism. The Teapot Dome scandal, for example, occurred in the early and mid-1920s, during the term of Warren G. Harding. After Harding's death, his vice-president, Calvin Coolidge, completed his term and was elected to another term riding on the slogan: "The business of America is business." This compares crassly with Woodrow Wilson's more humane but less catchy phrase of 1914: "The idea of America is to serve humanity."[2]

Throughout the decade of the 1920s playwrights never seemed to tire of dramatizing commercialism and big business, although the point of view, style, and genre shifted radically. Unlike the other categories of plays examined in this book, however, the business plays, whether pro or con in their view of commercialism, rarely make direct references to the Great War. Even during the war, business plays like *It Pays to Advertise* (1914) and *Good Gracious, Annabelle* (1916) usually eschewed direct references to the global cataclysm. Most of the business plays from the turn of the century to the Armistice were comedies and farces. Serious dramas about business did not appear until 1923, but by the end of the decade Broadway theaters had produced more than one hundred business plays since 1918. Some of the plays I discuss here and in the final chapter have already been analyzed in earlier chapters; I view them now from a different perspective.

The models for pro-business plays of the early 1920s can be found in the previous decade. Farcical business plays had appeared periodically in the manner of *Get-Rich-Quick Wallingford* (1910), by George M. Cohan. The objective of all the characters in these dramas was to make as much money as possible as quickly as possible, with no regard for moral scruples. The protagonists of most of these plays would agree with the character Jim Hutton in Philip Barry's *Paris Bound* (1927): "Just keep cool with Coolidge." Likewise, *Johnny Get Your Gun* (1917), by Louis Bennison, presages postwar commercialism by comically setting the tone for unscrupulous—in this case life-threatening—acts, which are celebrated as all-American (but similar to the methods of the business world). At the play's climax the hero, Johnny, holds a gun on manipulative businessman Milton and threatens to kill him unless he signs over the money he managed to pilfer from the heroine by deliberately devaluing her railroad stock. After begrudgingly signing the documents Milton tells Johnny, "Young man, you are wasting your talents—you belong on the stock exchange."3

Between 1919 and 1923 many playwrights persisted with the Cohan-Bennison model. Such a comic business protagonist appears as the character Nat Alden in John Booth's *Like a King* (1921). This penurious hero, who gives up on failed "high financial adventures" in New York, returns to his Massachusetts hometown pretending to have struck it rich in the city. In league with his old war buddy Dan, a former chauffeur, he "appropriates" a Rolls Royce for his triumphant entry into town and easily fools his credulous old neighbors, who put him in charge of modernizing the community. At the climax, a genuinely wealthy outsider is struck by Nat's plans and saves the day by offering a fifty-thousand-dollar check, an action that veils the conclusion with a "rose tint of prosperity," a typical finale for such plays. Significantly, Nat is not penalized for his subterfuge but viewed by both the townspeople and reviewers as a "conquering hero."4

Not all business plays of the early twenties celebrated commercialism, however. One of the best and most popular satirical treatments of the business world appeared in 1921, when Marc Connelly collaborated with George S. Kaufman to create the widely admired *Dulcy*. The first of eight cooperative projects by Kaufman and Connelly, *Dulcy* is a portrait of officious, trendy, cliché-ridden Dulcinea Smith, who ignorantly but well-meaningly meddles with her wealthy husband Gordon's business deal in artificial pearls. Several scenes satirize the rich, boring businessman, C. Roger Forbes, who is exasperated by everything Dulcy says, as well as Tom Sterret, Forbes's pushy "advertising engineer." Sterret ingenuously considers his commercial achievements to be as momentous as those of an accomplished artist. "Mozart was composing at fifteen; William Cullen Bryant wrote *Thanatopsis* when he was nineteen; Homer did part of the *Iliad* . . ." His encomium to commercialism is in keeping with much journalistic propaganda of the 1920s, which glorified business to the point of making it the world's most practical religion. Coolidge himself once said: "The man who builds a factory builds a temple; the man who works there worships there." In *Dulcy*, young Angela, Forbes's impulsive but sometimes sensible daughter, attacks Sterret, who is in love with her but will never win her because his "idea of romance is to sit in the moonlight and talk about the income tax." While commercialism is clearly tweaked here, the heart of the comedy is eccentric characterization, misunderstanding, and matchmaking.[5]

More biting satire and an expressionistic vision were used to attack the commercial world in O'Neill's *Hairy Ape* (1922), as the brutish shipboard stoker Yank Smith begins to question his role in society. The Fifth Avenue scene, especially, features what O'Neill describes as "a background of magnificence cheapened and made grotesque by commercialism." Masked, wealthy Sunday strollers chatter about the necessity of purging the world of troublesome radicals "and the false doctrines that are being preached." Yank viciously attacks the "gaudy marionettes" who seem virtually unaware of his presence as he is literally repelled, as if an invisible force field separates him from the elite. The wealthy reduce him to submission without lifting a finger except to call for the police. Ultimately Yank decides that he belongs not in a world determined by such creatures but rather in the cage of a powerful ape—which crushes Yank as well. By contrast with this dark vision, most of the business plays before 1923 had been celebrations.[6]

As the decade commenced Arthur Hornblow wrote that "Wall Street dramas interest most men and a few women—those foolish enough to take chances in the stock market." Trends were shifting rapidly, however, and such chauvinistic assumptions came increasingly under attack. With expanding interest in women's rights during and just after the war, it is not surprising that the gender conflict in business came to the fore in a number of plays from 1922 to 1926. It is usually noted that the feminist movement peaked in 1920, with the ratification of women's suffrage. The younger generation of women were much less conservative socially and not as interested in social reform as their mothers had been. The flapper may have been sexually liberated, she may have smoked and imbibed more openly, but to her, "feminism seemed unfashionable." The new women were iconoclastic socially and sartorially— not politically. The movement, in its daughters at least, seemed to turn in on itself and celebrate individualism. Nonetheless, the theater was fascinated for awhile with the theme of women in business, and throughout the 1920s women made slow inroads into the business world.[7]

The most commercially successful play to explore gender roles in business celebrated the wife as the real power behind the successful businessman. *To the Ladies* (1922), by Kaufman and Connelly, sometimes cited as a companion piece to *Dulcy* in its reversal of roles for the female protagonist, introduces Leonard Beebe, an ambitious, confident clerk, who is short on intelligence and talent. His young wife, Elsie, makes all the important decisions while convincing Leonard that he is taking care of her. When Leonard's boss Kincaid invites the Beebes to his annual banquet, he expects Leonard to make a speech. The banquet scene, which Eleanor Flexner aptly called "a magnificent travesty of [paternalistic] American business," is an almost farcical satire, full of political and commercial "smugness and pomposities." Leonard cribs a speech from *Five Hundred Speeches for All Occasions* and is horrified to hear the speaker who precedes him deliver the very text he has memorized. Paralyzed with fear, Leonard cannot function, but Elsie improvises an excellent speech about returning humanity, compassion, and fellowship to the business world that she pretends that Leonard has prepared but cannot give because of laryngitis. Enthusiastic applause greets her oration, inspiring Leonard, in characteristic fashion, to leap to his feet to acknowledge the approbation. When the play went on tour after its Broadway run, audiences reportedly did not understand the satire of the banquet scene and identified strongly with Leonard. Thus, what passed as commercial satire in New York was considered business realism on the road. This is not just a comment on the relative sophistication of the audiences, but verification of how widespread the business ethic—and its sexism—was.[8]

The final act of *To the Ladies* takes place six months after the banquet in "that most sacred of masculine institutions—the office." Leonard, who is now Kincaid's assistant, insufferably dictates sexist memos to his female stenographer. "Mr. Toohey now has twelve girls in the mailing department," Leonard intones, "but believes with me that men not only could do the work better but much more quickly than women.... As you know, we believe that as a general rule women are not so capable as men in business." At the play's conclusion, however, we discover that Kincaid's wife also makes all decisions of consequence for her husband. As Elsie puts it: "Nearly every man that ever got any place ... has been married, and that couldn't be just a coincidence." Elsie and Mrs. Kincaid become friends and obviously will continue to silently run the business while their husbands front for them.[9]

Even in praising the play, some critics missed or attempted to subvert the point of the comedy and managed to paint the characters in language that denigrated the intelligence of the women and exonerated the self-centered obtuseness of their husbands that is so clearly depicted in the play. For example, Hornblow described Leonard as "dreamily ambitious," while Elsie's intelligence and mettle are referred to as the "intuitive initiative of the weaker sex." Connelly himself later wrote of the play that it allowed him to have fun "with the stuffy smugness becoming more and more puncturable in American business" in the early 1920s.[10]

Musical comedy contributed to the subject of women in business as well, with the popular *The Clinging Vine* (1922), by Zelda Sears, with music by

Harold Levey. Sears created a successful, workaholic business heroine, Antoinette Allen, who runs a paint business in Omaha and shows herself "a marvel of scientific intelligence and mercantile efficiency." She is a neophyte, however, in affairs of the heart. Yet when visiting her grandmother in Connecticut, she learns to play the feminine social games expected "in the midst of fashionable sport and luxurious idleness." If she demonstrates her intelligence and learning she gets nowhere, but when she flatters the men and pretends empty-headedness and ineptitude (pretending to be what the playwright calls "shyness and innocence personified"), she manages to manipulate the New York cads who try to take advantage of her in love affairs as well as business.[11]

Along the way, various characters take stabs at the business world, yet successful business, so long as it avoids indisputable wickedness, is lionized. Nonetheless, Antoinette is not above playing duplicitous charades and fabricating misleading business information to defeat unscrupulous speculators. "If everybody weren't at heart a gambler, Wall Street would shut down tomorrow," observes Antoinette's love interest, Jimmy, in a passage that presages the real-life mania that overtook the financial district as hordes of small-time investors flooded the market with visions of easy riches.[12]

By act 2 the heroine is in love and by the third act she finds out that "it's very difficult to be business-like and lady-like at the same time." Ultimately, the heroine wins at both love and business, but it is perhaps the playwright in commenting on her work who provides more interesting observations on both the period and the business ethic in the Broadway marketplace. Sears wrote that if she were inspired in her work, the sources were not artistic: "The inspirations I receive are commissions from stars and managers to deliver a play to them by a certain date."[13]

A similar theme of the businesswoman's search for amorous experience was explored by social reformer Annie Nathan Meyer in *The Advertising of Kate* (1922), in which a woman is shown as the equal business partner of a man. Meyer herself later called this "the first play to suggest the delicate adjustment of the claims of sex to the work of the business woman." She is correct in that the play preceded *The Clinging Vine* by some seven months. Furthermore, her protagonist Kate, unlike Antoinette, is shown extensively in the workplace, and her amorous entanglements also occur in the office, creating a dilemma for her on the job. Antoinette, on the other hand, is in complete control while at work and oblivious to outside problems.[14]

The *Journal of Commerce* at the time verified that *The Advertising of Kate* was breaking new ground with its subject matter. "The idea of the beautiful—but brainy—woman immersing herself in 'trade' to the utter exclusion of all else, including affairs of the heart, is rapidly becoming commonplace, and it is therefore a natural development that it should reach the dramatization phase."[15]

The Advertising of Kate presents the vicissitudes of Kate, who has followed her father in his advertising business and succeeded not only as a business-woman, but in being treated by the men in this traditionally masculine world as an equal. Her success is underscored early in the play when she is closing a publicity deal with Thaddeus Knox, president of Transcontinental Railroad. She notes that she had vowed to "play the game just like a man; [sworn] that the element of sex [would] not enter into her efforts to succeed."[16]

Kate's problems arise when she discovers that she has fallen in love with her junior partner, Robert Kent, but his association with her remains strictly business. He even informs Kate that "he forgets she is a woman and admires only her business ability." When a young, empty-headed but beautiful social butterfly (one Diana Verulman, who does not live up to the chastity of her namesake) visits the office and draws Robert's interest, Kate begins advertising herself to gain his attention romantically.[17]

Meyer saw Kate as an honest businesswoman who was also truthful to herself, although the character "remained totally blind to her appeal as a woman of charm" until the love crisis precipitated by the advent of Diana. With this realization, Kate "descended to the wiles of a society woman," with every intention of attracting Robert and freeing him from Diana's enchantment. As she "discards the serge of the office for the chiffons of the drawing room" to arouse her business partner (a development that probably inspired Zelda Sears), Kate also inadvertently attracts her Transcontinental Railroad client, Thaddeus, a married man who "seizes Kate in his arms . . . and forcibly kisses her," or in Meyer's words, "makes brutal love to her." At this point, angry with both men, she abandons her society games and declares: "I'll return to the world where a woman is what she *is* and not what she *wears!*" Many reviewers were fond of quoting this line.[18]

In the final act, however, Meyer reconciles Kate and Robert, who decide to marry. This disturbed some reviewers, who found the resolution too predictable and conventional. Meyer may have intended to undercut, or at least qualify, a blissful ending; at play's end Kate was described as murmuring, "You men will never grow up emotionally" as she fell "into the arms of" what a female critic called "the emotionally retarded male."[19]

Alexander Woollcott realized that Kate was an "intelligent, mentally sharpened woman," although he complained that the play was too conventional in that it assumed "that women of affairs never have any." H. Z. Torres described the play as a charming romance of what he called "a business girl," despite the fact that Kate was a senior partner in a large advertising firm. (Both the New York business newspapers that reviewed the play referred to Kate as a "business girl.") Displaying wishful thinking, Alison Smith, the only woman to review the play, panned *The Advertising of Kate* as "belated propaganda" more appropriate for "a world of bicycles, ragtime and Gibson girls." She thought that Kate belonged "to the era when women were still exceedingly self-conscious at finding themselves installed as a business equal in a man's office." When we now compare the reviews of many of the male critics, with their obviously and subtly sexist commentary, however, Smith's assumptions about the progress of the cause of women in 1922 may strike us as over-optimistic.[20]

Beginning in 1923, often aided by the tenets of expressionism, heavy-handed satire was used to attack the American capitalist system and its exploitative methods. John Howard Lawson's *Roger Bloomer* was among the plays most consistently critical of business and commercialism. The play's eponymous young loner rejects the Midwestern business environment of his boyhood and flees to New York to "chase rainbows." In the city, he attempts to move into the business world to survive but is rejected. As a child, Roger had been overwhelmed by a capitalist father more at home in his office than with his family. "There's no poor in America," Mr. Bloomer is fond of saying; yet he asserts contradictorily: "Overpay the poor and you cheat the rich!"[21]

Everywhere Roger turns he confronts commercialism and greed. A Yale student tells him: "College is a business proposition . . . to make friends . . . you can use all your life. . . . Stick to the guys with money and an American name and you can't go wrong." In New York, Louise, the only person he loves, aptly tells him: "This town makes you think . . . Money! . . . . It's everyone for himself in this town." Since she works as a filing assistant for a Wall Street broker, Louise attempts to secure a position for Roger, but even as she extends the invitation she elucidates the deadly monotony and conformity of the commercial world: "You must come, get in the crowd, get in the subway, get in the procession. . . . It's a kind of dance of death." The word *procession* becomes emblematic of the dehumanized condition for Lawson, who repeats it and incorporates it into the title of his next play, *Processional*. O'Neill and Rice also borrow this image or usage of the word in *The Great God Brown* and *The Subway*. It is possible that Rice had formulated the image at the same time as Lawson, since *The Subway* existed in unproduced form in 1923. Of course, both may have taken it from Kaiser's *From Morn to Midnight*.[22]

When interviewing for a job in a sterile Wall Street office, where all the businessmen look like identically dressed automatons, Roger is dismissed by the broker on the basis of his "unreliable, nervous, careless appearance. . . . No place for you here, this is Wall Street, a gigantic exchange of energies." As Roger falls, so does Louise, who steals money and commits suicide. Suspected of killing Louise, Roger is put in jail, where he has an expressionistic nightmare that exorcises many of the demons of commercialism: greed, power, and corruption, as well as sexual confusion and a deathwish that plagues him throughout the play. Although the play ends with a new beginning for the protagonist, Lawson presents a depressing commercial world, whose major promise for people of sensitivity and creativity is a bleak one. It is not surprising that Lawson began work on this dark play while serving as an ambulance driver during the Great War.[23]

Rice's *Adding Machine* stridently depicts depersonalization in an industrial world, the anonymity of the little person. Mr. Zero, the unimaginative, middle-aged bookkeeper, burdened with a resentful wife and a repetitious life, is engulfed by numbers, enslaved for twenty-five years by the business world. Seen on the job in a pitiful scene of cross-talk and hopeless fantasy, Zero and his fellow bookkeeper Daisy read and check their host of figures "in a dreary and monotonous sing-song" (in the first production at least). When Zero is unceremoniously replaced by an adding machine at the recommendation of efficiency experts, he loses all self-control and kills the Boss, who never even knew Zero's name. "In an organization like this," the Boss intones, "efficiency must be the first consideration." Zero is of course tried and convicted, but in his trial he anecdotally bewails the inequities of the commercial world. Zero notes that the Boss "left fifty thousand dollars just for a rest-room for the girls in the store. . . . That's more'n twice as much as I'd have if I saved every nickel I ever made."[24]

After his execution and brief sojourns in the graveyard and Elysian Fields, Zero finds himself in "another office," working perpetually at an adding machine, whose paper tape fills the room. Though not in the written play, in the production directed by Philip Moeller and designed by Lee Simonson Zero was at work on a cosmic-sized adding machine that dwarfed him. Even in afterlife Zero cannot escape the mindless monotony and dehumanization of the labor force. This station, however, is just a recycling room, and Zero will have to return to life again to be abused and manipulated, just as he has been thousands of times before. "You're a failure, Zero, a failure," he is told by the officer in charge. "A waste product. A slave to a contraption of steel and iron. . . . The ready prey of the first jingo or demagogue or political adventurer who takes the trouble to play upon your ignorance and credulity and provincialism."[25]

For Zero there is no rest from his suffering, no reward for his drudgery. He is exploited by management, which comes under attack for its insensitivity to its labor force and its complete unawareness of how the workers survive. It is important to note, however, that Rice differs from many of his contemporary critics of the commercial world in satirizing the victims as well as the exploiters and the system itself. This kind of objectivity is also evident in his realistic works, like *Street Scene*.

In the same year that *Adding Machine* appeared, and in stark contrast to Rice's play, Guy Bolton produced his comedy *Polly Preferred*, in which an unemployed women's underwear salesman rises to the top of the film industry on the back of a would-be actress, Polly, whose faked socialite background is manufactured by the salesman, who uses false advertising to sell shares in her career. "What a wonderful line this is," the protagonist Bob exclaims, "selling girls. Every man you meet may not be a buyer, but they're all interested in your goods." Like so many inventive, fast-talking business heroes of the early 1920s (outside the world of expressionism), Bob gets exactly what he wants both economically and romantically.[26]

Although Edward Laska's *We've Got to Have Money* (1923) also revolves around deceptive business practice, it has a more farcical tone. The hero, Dave Farnum, is a gadabout Broadway sport who successfully pays his penniless roommate Tom Campbell, a bright chemistry student, to swap names, attend Columbia for him, and complete a B.S. degree. Dave intends to become a businessman, so he sees no need to pursue a college education, but in order to qualify for his inheritance he must have a degree—hence the elaborate subterfuge.

Apparently the playwright agrees with his hero about the value of higher education, for Laska catapults Dave to business success and riches by the use of his wits and a host of manipulative lies. Dave, who insists on starting at the top, enlists his newly graduated pals to go into business without their having the least notion of what they are selling or promoting. Dave decides that "there's too much competition in everything," so he will have to "invent a *new* business."[27] The team members pool their resources and open an office in the Woolworth Building, complete with secretarial staff who rehearse choreographed routines to imitate a teeming business when a visitor or prospective client arrives. Dave quickly hooks backers and products by deceitful methods, and no one seems to mind, not even when he defrauds one of his best friends to get financial backing. Of course, all his schemes pay off enormously for him and his investors, as he outwits experienced businessmen. He even solves a major labor dispute with a single, high-handed decision that would be laughed out of serious arbitration. (This play appeared in the midst of labor difficulties, which had become particularly volatile during the Red Scare a few years earlier.)

In the second half of the play, Laska cleverly introduces a foreign villain,

Levante, who plants a secretarial corporate spy with "a cigarette-fiend complexion," who almost succeeds in unseating Dave. The secretary is a man. Although the secretarial stereotype by mid-twentieth century was a woman, in the 1920s most women in business were typists and stenographers. "A secretarial position was hard-won, usually reserved for college graduates and at the upper echelons frequently reserved for men." This dynamic appears repeatedly in the business plays.[28]

Levante's corruption makes the young entrepreneur's deceptions look comparatively harmless, thus diverting the audience from condemning Dave's practice. Of course, by the play's end not only is Dave's business back on track but, like the salesman in *Polly Preferred,* Dave wins Olga, his beloved.

In 1924 the popularity of both pro- and antibusiness plays continued. In Samuel Shipman's *Cheaper to Marry,* for example, business is used as a means to demonstrate that marriage is more economical and safer than free love. The young businessman and woman in this play openly live together, only to find that it drains business and investments, leading the male protagonist to misappropriate business funds. It is telling that a reviewer found it incredible that the central character would openly introduce "his mistress to social and business friends."[29] Ultimately, a traditional way of life is enshrined through the business ethic and shown to be necessary to uphold the proper standards in the business world.

The most sensational business play of 1924, however, not only spoofed expressionism but demonstrated the serious conflict of art versus commercialism. According to Alexander Woollcott, George S. Kaufman and Marc Connelly offered *Beggar on Horseback* "as a relieving antidote to the worship of material prosperity. It is a play written in the distaste that can be inspired by the viewpoint, the complacency and the very idiom of Rotarian America."[30] The comedy satirizes American mass production carried to absurdity as well as the runaway commercialism that ensnares the creative artist.

Although he loves another woman, the struggling composer Neil McRae agrees to marry his only piano pupil, Gladys Cady, because her father is a millionaire. Mr. Cady, however, with his "bromide mentality and rubber-stamp platitudes," lives by materialistic values that are diametrically opposed to Neil's aspirations. Music, Cady says, is "just like any other business. . . . We've all got to please the public. . . . You sort of go in for—highbrow music. . . . Well, there's no money in it." If a song makes money, according to Cady, it is good music. His solution for Neil's problems is that he should join the ranks of Cady's manufacturing firm after he marries his daughter.[31]

In his expressionistic nightmare, which dominates most of the action, Neil finds himself marrying Gladys, who carries a wedding bouquet of bank notes.

His new father-in-law has a business telephone permanently attached to his chest (an absurdity realized by late twentieth-century business and technology). All the businessmen are identical, much like those of Roger Bloomer's interview. At every turn Neil is faced with endless requisitions and bureaucrats. Although he has no idea what the company is manufacturing, Neil soon finds himself in a top-level conference, a diversion that all the businessmen love because they are protected from real work. "They're great!" Cady explains of conferences. "You make speeches and decide things, and nobody can get in while they're going on."[32] Desperate because he can no longer write his music, Neil kills the entire Cady family.

As in *The Adding Machine,* we see Neil's murder trial, although his guilty verdict is based not on the crime but on the nature of his music, which is found to be too sophisticated. After awakening from his nightmare, and now properly warned about the business world, Neil breaks his engagement and unites with Cynthia, the penniless woman he loves. While the playwrights were obviously enjoying themselves with the often disjointed satire, "touching everything as it passes with the witches' fire of fancy," the play's attack on the insensitivity and deadening spirit of the business world was nowhere in the 1920s more forcefully presented.[33]

By the time of *Beggar on Horseback* millions of new investors were buying stock in a market that seemed only to rise. With a virtually unregulated stock market people were foolishly encouraged to buy stock on margin. Margin buying meant that by presenting only 10 or 20 percent of the purchase price of stocks, an investor could procure the stocks while the brokers borrowed the difference. Toward the end of the decade the amount of money borrowed against the floated stocks was enormous. When already grossly overpriced stock began to fall, the losses were catastrophic, for the borrowed money had to be repaid. For much of the decade, however, it appeared that everyone could have a free ride.

Continuing the serious line of melodramatic business plays, *Open House* (1925), by Samuel Golding, centers on a businessman who uses the sexual attraction of his beautiful wife to close business deals. He claims such exploitation is necessary because he works in "a bitterly competitive age."[34] The wife, however, gets her revenge by pretending to have an affair, which leads her husband to self-reproach and conversion. Outside of expressionism, all pro-business plays of the 1920s that include villains provide a comeuppance for the scoundrels, who often repent . Evil manipulators as well as gullible dupes are contrasted with responsible business people. Until 1926 such plays were frequently staged, and most were melodramas.

However, 1925 also offered Lawson's *Processional,* subtitled a "jazz symphony of American life," a musical, satirical vaudeville. Dramatizing a West Virginia coal miners' strike, Lawson graphically displays the antics of conscienceless big business that result in industrial slavery of the workers. A musical band of miners plays "the jazz today for the glory of the working class" in the midst of martial law. Army troops have been called in to take over the mines, and the result is "industrial warfare." The ignorant sheriff is corrupt and on the side of insensitive but cowardly management, which appears to give in to the workers but is sandbagging because the strike has drawn so much publicity. Big business intends to get the upper hand in secret. "Make a list of the marked men and we'll get them in their beds tonight," management's anonymous Silk Hat instructs the Sheriff, then "turning suavely to" the miners, he says: "My friends, we have each other's confidence." For the critic Richard Dana Skinner the play dramatized the "struggle of man to free himself from materialism . . . and the discovery that this attainment comes only through suffering and torture."[35]

Marc Connelly's gentle comedy *The Wisdom Tooth* (1926) likewise castigated the insensitivity of the business world, but without the strident broadsides typical of Lawson and Rice. Connelly made use of a dream device in the often-sentimental story of Charley Bemis, the senior clerk of a large New York firm who cannot bring himself to appreciate Calvin Coolidge. Bemis and the other clerks are disturbed that their boss, Porter, has fired a new stenographer. Bemis claims that he will confront Porter, but when given the opportunity, he remains silent. What is seen in action is what Brooks Atkinson called "civil expediency, the dominant trait of commercial life." None of the clerks is willing to take chances that could jeopardize their jobs.[36]

In several scenes outside the dream sequence, Connelly satirizes the unimaginative, self-protecting talk of businessmen. All their conversation, even in a social situation, is dominated by money:

SPARROW: I guess the whole country's lookin' up, for that matter. The president of our company was telling me the other day that our business had practically tripled in the last year.

FRY: I was down in Washington a couple of weeks ago and a Congressman . . . said that as soon as the tax problems get settled we're in for the biggest expansion in twenty-five years.[37]

Bemis, because of his lack of will, is accused of having "no convictions about anything."[38] When he realizes that the woman he loves shares this view of him, his distress—and a bad toothache—lead him to hallucinate about his lack of backbone. Bolstered by the vision of himself as a brave little boy, Bemis in his dream resigns and stands up to Porter and the injustice of the business world. Impressed, the dream Porter hires him back and promotes him. After awakening, Bemis is inspired to confront Porter in reality, only to be summarily fired. Although the comedy ends happily, the business satire is strong.

By contrast, O'Neill's *The Great God Brown* pits an organized but unimaginative businessman who wishes to be an artist against a dissolute, failed artist. In this play Dion Anthony sounds like a John Howard Lawson hero as he chants of the dehumanization of the never-ending commercial parade: "Time to get up! Time to exist! . . . Learn to lie! Learn to keep step! Join the procession!"[39] The failed artistry on the part of the talented artist who is victim of his own sensitivity results in his destruction. The successful identity borrowing by Brown, the aspirant artist and naive businessman, likewise lead to his destruction. Dion self-consciously fashions himself as a mirror for Brown, a reflection that Brown not only tries to emulate but that he wholly enters as if he were some latterday Alice. He not only enters the looking glass, however, but becomes one with the reflection—quite literally, thanks to the stylization of the play. Here we see a businessman who is not content with his easy success; he recognizes and despises his ineptitude and lack of creativity so vehemently that he reaches for an identity and attempts to assume the personality of another—a personality for which he is unsuited. The consequence is annihilation.

After 1925 it is difficult to find a pro-business play on the Broadway stage. Nearly all treatments of the commercial world consider it a place of shark-infested waters, where the casualties are catastrophic. *Wall Street* (1927), for example, by James Rosenberg, himself a Wall Street lawyer, follows the ascent of stockbroker John Perry, who succeeds by out-crooking the crooks but who cannot sustain any personal relationships. In his obsession with money and power, he loses two wives and alienates his son, who turns out to resemble his father in his greed and who is far worse in his predatory villainy, which almost topples his father's financial empire. The son commits suicide, and Perry remains alone at play's end, a physical invalid, the controller of a fortune but with no one to love, no legacy to bestow.

Spread Eagle, also 1927, testified to the business corruption that went publicly unpunished. It is the first business play to link warfare with the business world. Like *International,* of 1928, *Spread Eagle* is not actually a play about World War I, despite its overtones. Both plays create a new war. Subtitled "a drama and a fiction for patriots," and written by moonlighting journalists George S. Brooks and Walter B. Lister, *Spread Eagle* presents Martin Henderson, a business tycoon who is manipulating international events and public opinion to cause war between the United States and Mexico in order to protect his business interests south of the Rio Grande.

Opening in Henderson's office, "furnished luxuriously . . . in the less ornate and more expensive fashion that came to Wall Street with the profits from the War Babies," *Spread Eagle* concerns a coldly efficient conglomerate that corresponds internally in coded messages and performs as strongly in the political arena as in the commercial one. Henderson, who has huge mining investments in Mexico, is so alarmed by the threatened confiscation of his land by the Mexican government that he secretly finances a military coup, headed by a corrupt, Pancho Villa-esque general. "The only kind of Mexican leader that's worth a damn," according to Henderson, "is one so bad he causes American intervention." Henderson wants a war, but insists on another label: "It wouldn't be war. We wouldn't send in an army, but an armed constabulary."[40]

Henderson hires Charles Parkman, the son of a former U.S. president, to be the fall guy in Mexico and insure American outrage if he is killed in the coup. When the coup comes, several Henderson employees at the Spread Eagle Mines are reported executed, Parkman among them. This catastrophe sparks the American government to mobilize the Army and carry out a police action to protect American lives and property in Mexico—exactly the intervention Henderson anticipated. "Although Charlie Parkman had to be martyred to make us realize it," a radio announcer intones, "we're going to make Mexico safe for every American citizen." The language echoes the rhetoric of Woodrow Wilson during World War I, and a mobilization order is read to the audience from the stage, much to the confusion of some military personnel there, who automatically rose to answer the call. Ironically, Henderson is appointed by the president to chair the National Defense Council, which will assist the military forces in their campaign. Henderson magnanimously accepts the job at the salary of only a dollar a year (another procedure popular during the Great War). In critic John Anderson's words, the play shows "how war may be bought over the diplomatic counter, and how, with proper jingo bait, people may be deluded to toss themselves away on the theories of heroic patriotism."[41]

In the final act, amid the "turbulent swirl of militarism," Henderson, operating from a private railway car alongside the troops, always the business politician, tries to distance himself from the Parkman connection. But then Parkman emerges, wounded but alive, armed with the truth. Although Parkman attempts to reveal Henderson's corruption, the magnate is saved by his assistant Joe Cobb, who epitomizes, according to Atkinson, "the cynicism and disillusion now commonly suspected of the war generation." Cobb demonstrates how he and the newspapers will effectively distort Parkman's story to turn him into a poltroon. "There were two of you left at the mine," Cobb reminds Parkman, "you and a woman—and here you are. There were two of you down there and you let the woman face the firing squad. There were two of you, and when the bandits came, where were you? Saddling up a horse to come north—alone. . . . I'll make it look as if Mr. Henderson and I were trying to cover up your cowardice."[42]

Broken by the threats, Parkman yields to the businessmen, but in the play's only contrived plotting, Henderson's daughter Lois engages herself to Parkman; Henderson must now play out an endless charade with a son-in-law he attempted to kill out of avarice. And the war goes on. Many men will die erroneously thinking that they are protecting honor, the flag, and American lives, and the public and government will never know the truth.

Although the play is a highly theatrical, sensational melodrama, it is also a satirical attack on the dark, selfish forces that maneuver an easily swayed public to underwrite the greed of the powerful in the name of patriotism. John Mason Brown observed that the irreverent play was "written . . . with such high spirits, such zestful and taunting scorn, that it fortunately avoids the sermonizing of most plays of its ilk."[43] Furthermore, the symbolism of the play's title suggests not only the growing interventionist nature of American politics and militarism but also the awkward, vulnerable position in which the government could find itself if it relied too heavily on an unregulated business community.

Another play of 1927, Paul Sifton's *The Belt*, addressed not only the business ethic but the continuing labor unrest that punctuated American city life throughout the 1920s. The assembly-line workers in the play are always too exhausted to function at home or to take pleasure from anything. The assembly line moves steadily across the stage in several scenes as "men and boys work monotonously" amid cacophonous noise. The belt grinds on relentlessly, twenty-four hours a day, "steady as the fires of hell," destroying and dehumanizing the workers, usually within a couple of years. Jim Thompson, called the iron man because he has lasted ten years, exudes acute "weariness . . . in every line of his body. . . . His eyes have a vacant gaze, almost as if he were in a trance." The management perpetually accelerates production rates, forcing the workers to compete against sister plants in other cities, with sinister consequences for the losers. When writing of this play, Ira Levine called the assembly line "the key symbol of capitalist industrialization, and . . . dramatic image for the psychosocial malaise of the working man."[44]

The Old Man of the company (a satirical portrait of Henry Ford) is talked about as if he were a god, the universal benefactor of the workers; but he has become a symbol, a folksy front man for a slick, exploitative management that drains the workers and periodically closes the plant without warning. The protagonist, Bill Vance, rails against the "murder factory," spurring on a workers' rebellion against the inhuman conditions. He also reveals that the Old Man is once again shutting down the plant—this time for nine months. The Old Man attempts to stop the demonstration and explain his position. When threatened by the workers, however, his persona alters from gentle casualness to "imperiousness like a father shooing bad children into the house." He attempts to defend mass production: "What's made America prosperous? The Belt—Straight Line Production—High Wages, Efficiency, Speed, Low Production Cost, Low Prices, High Purchasing Power." Failing to move the mob with his commercial litany he admits lamely that he and his management have misjudged the American consumers and have grossly overproduced. "The country's crazy! They don't know what they want! . . . Now the whole market's gone to smash. . . . Too many cars." He has seen himself as the workers' benefactor but when cornered he offers no assistance. He can only advise them to look for other work. As police are summoned to quell the demonstration, Vance is arrested, promising both the mob and the theater audience, "I'll be back!" His prophecy was fulfilled in the next decade by the rush of labor plays, but unlike the 1930s variety, *The Belt* presents a serious problem without offering a smug solution.[45]

Michael Gold's *Hoboken Blues* (1928) is set in both 1900 and 1927 to demonstrate the ballooning of the commercial zeal that drove white society at the turn of the century, then enveloped Harlem in the 1920s. The play satirizes the work ethic primarily through a dream sequence in the second act. The satire is set up in act 1, however, when black characters with heavy dialects explain why they have no intention of working. "De great Negro race . . . has never believed in work. Work is the ruination of the white race. . . . It's jest a disease. It's brutalizin."[46]

The dream vision of protagonist Sam Pickens is described as "a battle of jungle and modern industrialism." Various white characters alternate between persecuting Sam and delivering a musical paean to commercialism. The Mayor, for example, chants: "Chamber of Commerce Man am I, / "Business, business is my cry." The corrupt white Judge finds Sam guilty of being poor; in consequence, the black man is sentenced "to life imprisonment in a factory," where the "factory slaves" move in lockstep and work like machines in cages (an image reminiscent of *Beggar on Horseback*). By the last act Harlem is fully industrialized and cutthroat business has been literalized. When Sam, who has been asleep for some twenty-five years, fails to join the commercial parade, he is asked, "Ain't you been Americanized yet? Don't you believe in money?" Black values now imitate white, and all sing and dance to the acquisitive tune, symbolizing the ideological triumph of white over black America.[47]

In 1928, another expressionistic journey play presented the business world as a great deadener. Sophie Treadwell's *Machinal* reveals in its first episode ("To Business") an office scene containing stylized repetition of duties and vocalization by office workers. The stage directions say this could be "any day" at "any business." Relying on stream-of-consciousness delivery and cross-talk, the workers meld job anxiety with romantic pressures. They project machine-like personalities, yet all the workers realize that their environment is unnatural. When the Adding Clerk exclaims that the Young Woman "doesn't belong in an office," the Telephone Girl replies, "Who does?" The Young Woman, in the middle of this office cacophony, expresses "the confusion of her own inner thoughts, emotions, desires, dreams[, which cut] her off from any actual adjustment to the routine of work." This "tragedy of submission . . . [holds] an individual character against the hard surface of a mechanical age. . . . [It shows] frailty in the midst of a heedless world." Most of all, however, Treadwell demonstrates the particular incarnations of dehumanizing effects on a sensitive Everywoman.[48]

In a less devastating but more satirical and humorous examination of gluttonous Babbitts, *Marco Millions* (1928), Eugene O'Neill created a Marco Polo who is a crass capitalist: self-important and insensitive to beauty and the feelings of others. Although he has risen to commercial and political heights in both the European and Asian worlds, his emotional life is all but extinct, and he is incapable of comprehending anything other than the next business deal. Reacting to Marco's obtuseness and excesses, Kublai Kaan expresses what many playwrights observing the commercial skyrocket of the 1920s feared: "We have everything to lose by contact with [the West's] greedy hypocrisy. . . . Let the West devour itself."[49]

John Howard Lawson, combining singing and dancing choruses with the modern music of "broken rhythms, machine noises and chanting blues," opens his anticapitalist satirical tragedy *The International* on a global scene. Filthy rich Wall Street financiers wish to take over newly discovered oil fields in Tibet, but if successful they are likely to launch another world war. They persist, nonetheless, because "prosperity must be served," and the result is not only warfare but worldwide rebellion of the working classes. Protagonist David Fitch challenges his powerful father because he wants to "join" the working class to try to understand the world. This family and generational struggle personalizes the collective greed, chauvinism, and social struggle which are the true subjects of the play. When David asks: "How big will this war get?" he is told: "That depends on how much there is to be got out of it." David recognizes the real power of his father: "Your thoughts are stock market rumors, your whims are armies marching."[50]

The senior Fitch and his business partner Spunk manipulate not only the stock market but governments. Their economic decisions are political choices; commerce is synonymous with public policy. When European powers like France must be approached for military support and alliance in the Tibetan debacle, it is the financiers, not political leaders, who negotiate with the French Army. When General Fouchard assures Fitch and Spunk that "the heart of France beats with yours, our gold will supply armies to assist you," Spunk wishes to know what gold France, still smarting economically from World War I, could possibly have. "The gold which you are about to lend us," the general glibly replies.[51]

Once the workers' rebellion begins, martial law is declared, and eventually the streets of New York become a civil-war zone. The Red labor forces, which include David, are ultimately gunned down and crushed by the U.S. military in league with the fascist Italian Air Force. The action ends on the barricades, with the triumph of capitalism and the destruction of organized labor and socialist ideology. Fitch wins but loses his son in doing so.

Lawson was risking alienating much of his potential audience with such a volatile subject, especially when the United States was doing so well financially. Therefore, rather than provide a left-wing triumph of socialism, which he would have preferred ideologically, he demonstrated the victory of the forces that much of his audience would have supported but emphasized the sizable cost to humanity of that victory. Also by focusing so much of his action on a personal story, he was able to humanize the struggle and structure the play as both a personal and societal tragedy.

In a review of another play, *Spread Eagle*, Atkinson offered some comments on the still-painful Great War and its influence on the drama that apply to *The International* as well. "Only ten years after an epochal declaration of warfare," he wrote, "it is too sore a point to be ignored as pure theatrical fireworks."[52] The edge of both plays was startling for audiences, and the fears of further cataclysm, especially at the hands of the enormously powerful rulers of Wall Street, growing indomitable through the decade, were no longer absurd.

With such obvious attacks on commercialism appearing regularly in New York theaters, it is not surprising that subtler jibes at the business world were almost overlooked. Philip Barry, in *Holiday* (1928), the only comedy of manners in this study, satirically questioned the reigning business ethic while crafting stylish, delightful banter in an upper-class setting. The protagonist Johnny Case, a young lawyer who dreams of escaping Wall Street and retiring at age thirty, is engaged to Julia Seton, who admires the business world: "There's no such thrill in the world as making money." Not surprisingly,

Johnny becomes entangled with her free-spirited sister, Linda, the play's principal anti-commercial mouthpiece. The satire is somewhat disguised, however, by placing the comic and dramatic focus on Barry's unusual heroine, Linda, the most dynamic and delightful character in the play. The Seton patriarch, Edward, whom Linda calls "Big Business," cannot fathom Johnny's motivation. "I consider his whole attitude deliberately un-American," he opines. As things then stood among the upwardly mobile in the United States, Edward seemed quite correct.[53]

Barry satirized the spiritual emptiness of avarice in what outsiders saw as a "solidly affluent life." Some critics, however, had difficulty reconciling the serious subject matter's "half-tragic undertone" with the glib patter, finding the business satire too pointed to fit the manners comedy. Conversely, others claimed that because of Barry's accomplished wit and style, his "audience neither feels any resentment at his rebellion against traditional nonsense, nor a dogmatic preachment for reformation." Johnny's attitude and insistence on quitting are made a bit too easy, since he has already made money in the stock market, but at least he does not take excessive pleasure in wealth. It can be argued, nevertheless, that Barry has seriously undercut his use of satire because his hero can be independent of the stifling big-business atmosphere only by having first exploited it.[54]

The last two years of the decade also brought a wave of serious plays depicting big business as a killer. Most featured leading characters who suffered from Napoleonism. Writing of this frequent fixation in the 1920s business world, S. N. Behrman identified Napoleon as "the god of all the arrivistes . . . of all the high-powered executives who, when their destinies were running high, saw in their accidental and inflated careers replicas of him."[55]

Myron C. Fagan's melodrama *The Great Power* (1928) pits a big-businessman, John Power, who envisions himself as "the Divine Ruler of the universe," against his children, who emerge as his sole equals. The play was a response to scandals about corruption (especially in oil) that were becoming public in the late 1920s. A twentieth-century Richard III of the business world, Power manipulates the stock market with impunity, ruins the careers of congressmen— or anyone else who gets in his way—and corrupts legislators, judges, ministers, and whoever can render him some service. He is so wicked, in fact, that one reviewer quipped: "This kind of thing could not go unpunished after 11 o'clock."[56]

Although *Airways, Inc.* (1928), by John Dos Passos, presents no Napoleons, the play effectively demonstrates greed and the commercial spirit, which it aligns with corrupt police and government, and demonstrates the destruction of a Communist labor organizer, who is falsely accused and convicted of murder. Although one of the commercial leaders promises that a new air-transport industry, All-American Airways, Inc., will "fulfill a great scientific and patriotic duty," it soon becomes clear that the corporate heads have no interest in the airline except as a source of income. Their business meeting is ironically juxtaposed with a labor strike going on outside the building. The audience sees both activities simultaneously with the auditory focus shifting back and forth. Ultimately the strike is broken, and its leader arrested and killed, while the new corporation becomes rich.[57]

Elmer Rice's *The Subway* should be mentioned even though it did not receive a Broadway production. Although written in 1923, just after *The Adding Machine,* it was not produced until 1929, in Greenwich Village, some months after *Machinal,* which probably made *The Subway* seem derivative, for it also focused on a sensitive young woman overwhelmed and dehumanized by the commercial world and modern, mechanized, insensitive people. Like Tread-well's Young Woman, Rice's protagonist also feels that she is suffocating. The opening scene, especially, a business tour, underscores even more graphically than *The Adding Machine* the commercial spirit and business philosophy of industry: "The gods of commerce serve most generously those who make best use of their finest tools," the boss tells a journalist. The sterile, windowless filing room in which the protagonist, Sophie Smith, works is described with pride by the boss: "It never varies: day and night, summer and winter, rain or shine, it is always the same; unvarying in its brightness and efficiency. We have improved upon nature, gentlemen." In the end, Sophie throws herself under a subway train.[58]

The most trenchant of the late anti-commercial plays, *Meteor* (1929), by S. N. Behrman, follows the early career of Raphael Lord, a bright, energetic but condescending young man, who thinks everyone should yield to his vision. "I'm one of the few people in the world who's practically omniscient," he claims without a trace of facetiousness. True to his belief, he becomes a multi-millionaire in five years. Like so many other magnates mentioned in this study, he reveals insensitivity to the emotional needs of others, grows obsessed with accumulating wealth, ignores personal losses, including that of his wife, Ann, and ultimately suffers in loneliness. Eleanor Flexner calls him "the febrile incarnation of American enterprise and irresponsible individualism."[59]

Much of Lord's attention is devoted to gargantuan oil fields in South America, over which he is fighting to gain control. Not unlike those of Henderson in *Spread Eagle,* Lord's efforts involve political manipulation and military interference. His friend Avery tries to warn him: "The more you stir things up, the greater the chance of bloodshed—bloodshed leads to reprisal. First thing you know, you're identifying dividends with national honor." He is aware of his enemies, even those in his own employ, yet he allows them to betray him because it makes the power game more interesting. He arrogantly overestimates his mastery of events, however, and jeopardizes his entire fortune. Ann is pleased with his defeat and hopes that he will now abandon his obsessions, but the play ends with Lord's unwillingness to change, even as Ann is deserting him. Power is all, and the consequence is a loveless life. Lord not only loses Ann but also alienates all those who care for him. As Ann tells him: "You prate of remote Utopias that will pay dividends, but those near you you kill."[60]

"In the late boom in America," Behrman wrote, "the business Napoleon reached his apotheosis. . . . It is difficult to imagine, although it is only four years ago, how these colossi swaggered and what willing and sycophantic obeisance the world made to them."[61] Behrman wrote those words during the Great Depression years. For us in the late twentieth century it is no longer so difficult to imagine.

As the decade progressed farther away from the war, business plays revealed growing suspicion and alarm with typical business practice. Of all the plays produced commercially between 1919 and 1929 (extant or reconstructable) that are business-oriented in primary character, action, and conflict (not just set in the business world), 44 percent enshrine or support big business while 56 percent attack it. Certainly, there was considerable dramatic support on both sides. Pro-business plays appeared in every season from 1919 to 1926, with more produced in 1922 than any other year. After 1926 no play with business as its subject glorifies business. Antibusiness plays do not appear until 1921, but they show up every year thereafter. The peak year for these plays was 1928.[62]

It is possible that some of the earliest satirical swats in 1921 and 1922 may not have been intended as serious criticism of capitalism and business practice at all but only as humorous caricatures of recognizable business types—the comic responses are elicited from recognition of the familiar. By 1923, however, some playwrights are unmistakably attacking the business ethic and the damage it was doing to the working classes.

Although dramatic responses to both business ethics and World War I appear throughout the 1920s, they tended to be separate, overlapping only in *The International* and *Spread Eagle*. Perhaps Arthur Hornblow, with whom I usually disagree, was right when he compared *Dulcy* (a business play) and *Clarence* (a war play) early in the decade. He was fond of both these light comedies, which went on to score as great commercial successes. "'Dulcy,'" he wrote, "is as good as 'Clarence,' and that is high praise. These two plays, to my mind, are really reflexes of our American spirit and deserve permanent places in the repertoire of the native drama."[63] These comedies, effective as they were, did not survive the test of time, but they demonstrated, early in the development of the postwar business play and war play, that for most dramatists the two occupied separate spheres. Yet each was shaped in part as a response to the cataclysm and recovery which ensnared, mobilized, and to some degree liberated the nation after 1914.

Many simple statements of fact published before the crash and intended as positive endorsements of practice, when read afterward, signal the impending disaster. The *Wall Street Journal*, for example, following Hoover's election in November 1928, stated: "The job of the Coolidge administration has been to clear the track of obstacles and obstructions which threatened to block the progress of the business engine." The commercial machine had roared since the early twenties, but the first warnings of financial panic appeared as early as two months after Hoover's inauguration, and in less than a year following his landslide election, the unregulated market was in irreparable disarray. The theater was an immediate casualty, with Broadway business slumping within two weeks of Black Tuesday. Although the general theatrical decline—fewer Broadway openings and more theater closings—was gradual, the quantitative figures of the last two full seasons before the crash were never matched or even approached. The 1927–28 season, for example, opened 264 productions in 76 theaters. After 1938 Broadway never reached 100 productions, and by 1940 the numbers were reduced to 69 productions in 32 theaters. The boom was over.[64]

8

Red Dawn to Red Rust:
The Russian Revolution and Visions of Shifting
Political Power in Postwar Drama

*That's the trouble with a lot of people nowadays—as soon as they're down and out,
they become socialists and reformers.*
—Edward Laska, *We've Got to Have Money*

We ain't going to stand any of that Bolshevickeyism.
—Aaron Hoffman, *Give and Take*

Owing in large measure to the vicissitudes and distractions of the Great War
and the subsequent influenza epidemic, American theatrical responses to the
Russian Revolution were delayed until 1919. This was the year the attorney
general of the United States, A. Mitchell Palmer, assisted by Labor Secretary
William B. Wilson, launched an infamous Red Scare, which resulted in sum-
mary deportations, incarcerations, property seizure and destruction, beatings,
castrations, lynchings, and murders of foreign nationals and such suspected
troublemakers as known Communists, socialist organizers, union leaders, and
real or imagined anarchists. The most famous case, of course, was that of
Sacco and Vanzetti, which was treated dramatically in *Gods of the Lightning*

(1928), by Maxwell Anderson and Harold Hickerson. Hearings were held by Congress in 1919 to identify and characterize radical activity, and the results were predictably reactionary. The Russians were reported to be "killing everyone who wears a white collar or who is educated and who is not a Bolshevik."[1] In addition, it was asserted that the Russians were promoting global revolution, and their favored agents in the United States were the leaders of organized labor. Hence, labor strikes were usually labeled Red, anarchist, or Bolshevik activity. Much of the paranoia crystallized in September 1920, when the bomb of an alleged anarchist exploded on Wall Street, killing thirty-four people and injuring hundreds more. Meanwhile, many angry mob scenes (often bolstered by military and former military personnel), like copycat crimes, recurred throughout 1919 and 1920, as many left-wing or labor organizations were destroyed and looted, the members or employees beaten, persecuted, and sometimes murdered; these groups received no protection by police or help from the authorities. The spirit of the times, which encouraged anti-foreign and anti-Communist furor, also gave rise to urban race riots. A revitalized Ku Klux Klan radically expanded the membership in its "invisible empire" and become very conspicuous in the early 1920s.

In large measure because of both the war and the horrors of the Red Scare, many writers have referred to 1919 as the year in which the United States lost its innocence. This curious, overworked banality (as if it were possible for a nation to have an "innocence" to lose), seems to appear in the aftermath of every major catastrophe in the history of the United States. The Civil War, World War I, the Great Depression, World War II, and Vietnam have each raped the country's virgin sensibilities, it would seem, as if the country were some perpetual, lumbering adolescent. It is certainly true, however, that each debacle created a severe shift in social and political climate and invited drastic cultural change.

With two exceptions, the U.S. playwrights and American-produced foreign dramatists who addressed issues related to Communism, the Russian Revolution, and the Red Scare between 1919 and 1923 fed the fires of xenophobia with either serious or comic depictions of revolutionaries who wished to spread their doctrine to the United States by inciting rebellion among the American proletariat. After the Red Scare had subsided in the early twenties and the Moscow Art Theatre had visited the United States in 1923, Russian characters, often Bolsheviks, continued to grace the stage, but usually for comic purposes. Throughout the middle years of the decade, playwrights who referred to the revolution usually did so to poke fun at the Soviet regime, rather than to make propagandistic fodder of paranoid notions of subversion from within or invasion from without.

Toward the end of the twenties, however, despite the fact that the United States was successful financially and the Communist Party of America, though active, was deemed passé, a growing sympathy for socialist themes, oppressed labor forces, and Soviet ideology, as well as an increased disgust for exploitative capitalists, was evident in the work of a number of playwrights. This shift was apparent in more than the band of self-styled, radical reformers who led a contradictory exercise in left-wing commercialism called the New Playwrights' Theatre. The crash of 1929 and the Great Depression triggered a considerable outpouring of political theater, much of which took to the streets and factories, an era which has garnered considerable historical and critical examination. The preceding decade of activity, however, which frequently offered political and social statements, either overtly or implied, is not so easily categorized. Plays contained ambivalent messages, and playwrights had ambivalent feelings about the easy money and commercial exploitation available after 1923.[2]

Beyond their obvious linkage of political conservatism with economic prosperity and conspicuous materialism, what are the social and political implications of American theatrical responses to the Russian Revolution? Most of the anti-Communist plays also glorify commercialism; conversely, once the country entered an economic depression, prosocialist and Communist plays appeared everywhere. In 1919 there was a resurgence of a vocal socialist movement, which was identified with Bolshevism and Communism, the very idea of which terrified Americans. By mid-1919, most Americans were aware of the February and October revolutions, the dissolution of the Russian Assembly, the creation of the new Soviet government in Moscow, the execution of the Czar and his family, the Russian civil war and the Sparticist revolt in Germany. The fear, quickly promulgated by conservatives, was not only that such revolution might be possible anywhere but that the Soviets would try to force revolutions all over America—movements that would be bolstered by agitating, striking labor unions, and oppressed racial minorities. It was deemed prudent by many to preempt Red strikes by rooting out the dissenters and exposing "un-American" activity. The ubiquitousness of the fear and use of the revolution as a scapegoat is evident in a remark by Kenneth Macgowan in reviewing the Actors' Strike of 1919: "It is the only industrial conflict since November 11, 1918, in which newspapers or employers have not raised the cry of 'Bolshevism.'" The first American Communist parties (there were two), appeared in that year and Bolshevism quickly evolved as a whipping boy for the economic failures of the U.S. government to derail war-inspired inflation and the postwar recession with its accompanying widespread unemployment.[3]

What the Red Scare and its theatrical expression signaled in part was the steady cultural and ethnic fragmentation that had been quietly under way for some time. The discord was exacerbated by large population shifts to urban and away from rural regions, which were in the process of becoming the nation's minority environments. "There is evidence to show," wrote a critic reviewing *Processional* at mid-decade, "that the celebrated melting pot has not been doing much melting in the last thirty years." Many war-created organizations like the American Protective League and the newly formed American Legion, which was designed to foster "100% Americanism" in returning soldiers, instead of fading with the Armistice refocused themselves on the "enemy" at home and remobilized to ensure "national purity" and promote anti-unionism and scrutinize their neighbors for "disloyalty," anarchy, socialism, or Communism.[4]

The proponents of the Red Scare were also dedicated to perpetuating such views as if they were "traditional" American notions; they took a national, selective, mythic posture, one that has recurred at intervals throughout the twentieth century and that has contributed to cultural and racial division and oppression with catastrophic results. Michael Kammen, who astutely analyzes American tradition and mythmaking, writes: "Traditions are commonly relied upon by those who possess the power to achieve an illusion of social consensus. Such people invoke the legitimacy of an artificially constructed past in order to buttress presentist assumptions and the authority of a regime." Such militant inflexibility appeared at the time to dwell within a larger, ambivalent construct, one that also continues to affect American domestic and foreign policy, as well as cultural and artistic expression: "Opposed to [Americans'] sense of continental self-sufficiency and disposition to isolationism," Ralph Perry observed, "there is a missionary spirit which inclines to adventure abroad: a belief . . . that what is good for the United States is good for everybody, and should be extended to other peoples, whether they like it or not."[5]

For a few years, references to the revolution and Bolshevism seemed to appear everywhere. In Gilbert Emery's war play *The Hero* (1921), set in 1919, the word *Bolshevik* is used as a curse in a name-calling argument in which two angry brothers accuse each other of being cowardly and radical. In a review of Maxim Gorki's *Night Lodging* (*Lower Depths*), Arthur Hornblow complained that the Baron, "in a flaming crimson shirt, is made to mouth a generous supply of words which strangely resemble Bolshevik propaganda." Although discussing sexual themes on the stage in a 1919 article, actress Jane Cowl wrote: "There is, at times, a tendency in the theatre to exploit sex ideas that are in reality the ideas of sex anarchy. Such plays are the Bolsheviki propaganda of passion." Even Woodrow Wilson joined in when, on a 1919 stumping tour of

America intended to defend the proposed League of Nations, he called his senatorial opponents "jaundice-eyed bolsheviks of politics." Both Wilson and his successor, Harding, refused to recognize the new Russia or the Soviet Union formed in 1922.[6]

In spite of much popular and governmental disapproval of Communism and the Soviet Union, the U.S. government, in characteristically ambivalent style, deported hundreds and harassed thousands of alleged radicals, anarchist foreign nationals, and Russian sympathizers in 1919 and 1920 and then shipped tens of millions of dollars' worth of food to Russia for famine relief in 1921. Many reactionaries wailed that the bastion of democracy was "saving the Bolshevik regime."[7] And so, for whatever contradictory reasons, it was.

In the theatrical expression of the Red Scare, a number of undisguised anti-Communist, pro-capitalist plays were produced in New York between 1919 and 1922. These reactionary dramas ranged from plays that made passing Communist references or cracked Bolshevik jokes to melodramas set in revolutionary backgrounds to full-length efforts centering on socialist or Communist revolution in the workplace or government. Both imported and domestic fare made much of the revolutionary fervor to create mysterious or dangerous backgrounds for plays intended to thrill and entertain. *The Son-Daughter* (1919), by George Scarborough and David Belasco, set during a Chinese revolution, and Sacha Guitry's *The Grand Duke* (1921), demonstrating the Parisian vicissitudes of a Russian émigré nobleman, were popular examples. There was even an amateur, semi-biblical, allegorical extravaganza mounted by church groups at Madison Square Garden called *The Wayfarer,* written by the Reverend James Crowther of Seattle, where labor strife and a reactionary mayor had created a flash point for the Red Scare. The spectacle was intended to connect contemporary conflict with biblical stories and prophecy. One account of the production was entitled "Fighting Bolshevism with the Bible."[8]

Many of the professionally produced early plays reflect considerable fear of Bolshevik revolutions in the West and openly attack all socialist sensibilities, no matter how minor, while enshrining capitalism. This ideological line was most fully developed in such melodramas as *The Red Dawn, The Challenge, The Mask of Hamlet, Bavu,* and *The Drums of Jeopardy.* John J. Martin, reviewing for the *Dramatic Mirror,* characterized this new wave of plays with the warning, "the bolshevist menace has officially struck the drama." Likewise, Alexander Woollcott greeted the plays as "inevitable attempts to dramatize the social and political unrest with which the whole world is a-tremble." Paranoia and insistence on the American way were promulgated even in serious drama produced between 1919 and 1923. Those serious playwrights who may have felt differently but did not dare say so, remained quiet through the worst years.[9]

The Challenge (1919), by Eugene Walter (best known for *The Easiest Way*), demonstrates to a European-influenced and war-wounded young socialist that capitalism is the only system for a decent-thinking American to pursue; it asserts that electing a socialist governor is tantamount to opening a chamber of horrors. The common people, the play proposes, cannot be trusted to run the country responsibly because "radicalism and dirty collars [are] inevitable associates." The hero, Richard Putnam, "conscientiously but blindly" inspired by the terrors of his war experiences, organizes workers and a socialist party and convinces the workers to strike. Richard's desire to "dethrone the invisible masters of the world who had ordered the war," is an interpretation of events that is presented negatively here but is reactivated positively later in the decade. Although Richard contributes to the successful election of a socialist governor, he soon discovers that his political friends are frauds who have exploited him to gain power. The new socialist regime is on the take; it is presented as worse than the government Richard struggled to topple. Disillusioned, he at last converts to political conservatism and capitalism and, not incidentally, thereby wins Mary Winthrop, a good daughter of capitalism. Apparently, Walter's message was a warning that drawing on the untrained, uneducated working class for political leaders was a mistake, anathema to commerce as well as domestic and world order.[10]

Ario Flamma's oddly titled thriller *The Mask of Hamlet* (1921) tries to place blame for the Wall Street bombing on a network of Russian spies, who, using a seductive Russian woman, lure, brainwash, and demoralize an unsuspecting American man into setting the bomb and then dispose of him. Earl Carroll's *Bavu* (1922) actually sets its action in the Russian Revolution to demonstrate its corruption and danger at all levels, but the play simply follows formulaic expectations. As Woollcott wrote of it: "This is such a study of the revolution as might have been made from the vantage point of a Broadway hotel."[11] In the same year, adapting from his own novel, Harold McGrath collaborated with Howard Herrick on *The Drums of Jeopardy* (1922), a story of missing Russian jewels sought by villainous Bolsheviks. The melodramatic mystery seemed, with the added propagandistic, anti-Bolshevist subplot, to pursue the spirited thrills of Hopwood and Rinehart's highly successful *The Bat*, which opened in 1920 and was still running when *The Drums of Jeopardy* premiered. Such plays as these Red Scare melodramas were warning Americans that they must remain alert. The Great War was over, but the new enemy, it was emphasized, was perpetrating an insidious rebellion at home.

The most thoroughly reactionary in its plea for vigilance and call to arms was *The Red Dawn* (1919), subtitled *A Drama of Revolution,* by Thomas Dixon, the former clergyman whose novel *The Clansman* had inspired D. W. Griffith's *Birth of a Nation.* The play, which was produced in a short run at the Thirty-Ninth Street Theatre, fell victim to the Actors' Strike, but it has survived as an unpublished manuscript. *The Red Dawn* painted a scathing portrait of Soviets, who dreamed of conquering the world by counterfeiting 20 billion dollars to finance the revolution to be fought by hostile labor unions that they had organized and armed. The playwright, who had a special affinity for the exclamation mark, tried to bring his message home by creating a socialist colony on a California island that becomes a base of operations for Soviet infiltration. The revolutionary program is "stamp out first, every spark of opposition within—and seize power by force—level all intelligences, destroy all private property! Wipe out every distinction between human beings—and hold all things in common!" With no aversion to name-calling, Dixon attacked the IWW union as a center for Communist propaganda; he claimed that the union would be central in organizing a massive strike to paralyze the nation while the Russian organizers, numbering some four thousand, mobilized millions of social outlaws and malcontents as well as the racially oppressed to sweep down on the country, robbing banks, seizing the press, and usurping control of the government. "We will gather in one solid secret order," the Red Leader predicts, "this vast horde of discontent and arm them!"[12]

One of the Russians' chief aims, according to Dixon, was to enslave all American women to the Communists' depraved sexual appetites. This is a common propagandistic tactic used in war to create hatred for the enemy. After the Great War the image was transposed from the Germans to the Russians. Dixon had also used this tactic in *The Clansman,* identifying black men as sexually depraved and anxious to rape white women. The use of such propaganda on *all* sides of every war and cold war of the twentieth century is graphically described by Sam Keen as "apparitions of the hostile imagination" in archetypes like "the enemy as barbarian," hence a "threat to culture," or "the enemy as criminal," and "the enemy as rapist," using "women as bait and trophy."[13]

When Zorin, the Soviet operative in *The Red Dawn,* arrives from Moscow, he cross-examines the colony's leader, Richard Stanton, self-proclaimed "supreme dictator of the proletariat":

ZORIN: You trust your wife?
STANTON: As far as any woman can be trusted with our program.
ZORIN: And let me warn you that is—not at all.

Zorin and Stanton lay out their program for the slavery of women: "In the new moral world which we have established, the irrational names, husband, wife, parent, child—shall be heard no more—All children shall be controlled by the state and reared in public nurseries. And all women between the ages of 18 and 40 shall be the common property of the state." Of course, the evil Stanton even places his own wife in this pool so that he may sleep with any woman he wants. "Woman has no soul," he claims. "She is the mere matter on which the will of man acts!" In typical melodramatic fashion we then see Stanton begin the seduction and rape of an unwilling young woman, but at the crucial moment he is interrupted by gun shots which signal the beginning of a counterrevolution that defeats his wicked designs.[14]

All the revolutionaries in the play are unscrupulous thugs and ex-convicts (another wartime image of the enemy), but the playwright follows traditional melodramatic structure by providing a fully developed villain in Stanton to hate throughout the play. When the good people among the socialist inhabitants finally rise up to destroy Stanton and Zorin, their success is capped with a conversion and renunciation of the socialist experiment. "From today this colony is straight U.S.A. soil," the victors proudly announce.[15] This is a common refrain among right-wing patriotic groups during and after the Great War, and it is used satirically by Susan Glaspell in *The Inheritors*.

The perceived Soviet watchword espoused by this play is sounded by Zorin in the first act: "The Terror established in the East, must be the Red Dawn for the whole world." The genuine jingoistic message of the play, however, is stated by the socialist leader who converts and leads the counterrevolution: "I have come to realize fully for the first time, that my country—America—has a message for the new world—I see now, that our union of free democratic states is the *model for all*—the sublimist dream yet born in the soul of men!" (emphasis mine). This smug, unequivocal stance is also typical of both the chauvinistic political societies and the censorship leagues, which were sometimes the same group.[16]

Curiously, most of the seriously crafted melodramas like *The Red Dawn* were not received well critically or popularly, but comic plays like *Poldekin* (1920) and *Give and Take* (1923), which held a similar ideological point of view, were embraced by critics and audiences alike. Critics often reported that audiences of the reactionary melodramas tittered or laughed openly at some of the lines and events that were meant to be taken seriously. It was not the right-wing message that was rejected by popular audiences of the early postwar era, however, but the form in which it was sometimes cast. Standard melodrama was wildly popular when serving as a vehicle for escapist material, but serious or political subject matter needed to appear in tragedy, satirical comedy, or expressionistic trappings.

Written as a light, satiric comedy, Booth Tarkington's *Poldekin* (1920), which followed his war hit *Clarence,* was intended to laugh Communism out of existence. A comic rendering, he offered, was "more effective than to fall into a fury at mention of the word, as so many Americans are doing." The title character (played eccentrically by George Arliss) leads a group of Russian revolutionaries, who, seeing themselves as sociopolitical missionaries, intend to launch a rebellion in the United States by publishing propaganda and inspiring a class war. Referring to postwar upheaval, a professor among them intones: "We take advantage of the violent mood to produce *universal* war between the classes." The play is laced with hyperbolic statements backed by such specious reasoning as "All the wrongs in the world come from private ownership of property."[17]

Poldekin becomes obsessed with discovering the meaning of America. One of his comrades tries to explain to him that "America is capitalism and wage slavery," but Poldekin is not convinced. He travels to Long Island, Lexington, Massachusetts, and Washington, D.C., but finally naively discovers his answer and the beauty of American freedom at—of all things—a baseball game. "It is played on a green field," he explains, "all sparkling in the sunshine. There are the thousands and thousands of people all desiring constantly that something impossible should happen, and then suddenly they are bitterly disappointed . . . and then instantly again audible with the most radiant optimism. Down below, you see groups of athletes . . . all electric in action—like running Greeks—and the great masses of people rise and shout their wishes to the athletes. . . . There, with the sun shining on the people, you can see that everybody is an American—more than anywhere else."[18]

When the police and the Department of Justice raid the revolutionaries' apartment seeking seditious material (an act that in itself belies the ostensible American freedom that inspires Poldekin to convert; such raids were being conducted by Palmer, reactivating the Espionage and Sedition Acts and ignoring the First Amendment), Poldekin fools both authorities and his fellow Russians by printing six thousand copies of the U.S. Constitution and the Declaration of Independence. Tarkington also briefly satirizes the police by having them at first mistake these documents for Communist propaganda. Such mistakes were reported numerous times from all over America; demonstrators reading the Declaration of Independence in public were actually arrested. By his own account Upton Sinclair was arrested for reading the Constitution publicly in 1923 in Los Angeles. Although Tarkington originally had Poldekin shot and killed by one of his former comrades (a bit like killing off the fallen woman in nineteenth-century melodrama, even when she repents), in production the comic tone of the rest of the play was maintained by having the fatal bullet redirected to his arm in order to keep him alive and allow him to win the love of Maria, the heroine.[19]

Give and Take, by Aaron Hoffman, was not only a tribute to commercialism but also a farcical attack on socialism and Bolshevik-inspired industrial revolution. The seriousness of the issues at the time led some reviewers to declare the topic unsuitable for comedy, and my discussion of the play could make a reader believe that the play is actually a melodrama. It is nonetheless a farce, one that made much of the revolution to demonstrate the perceived pernicious effects of labor revolt and reorganization of capitalist factories.[20]

Hoffman depicts John Bauer's California canning factory; through the efforts of Bauer's socialist-minded son Jack, it is turned over to contentious and ignorant employees, who experiment with industrial democracy, or "Bolshevickyism," as the local bank president calls it. Jack himself, in his idealistic speeches, gives us the key to the play's title: "I'm going to establish harmony, the get together spirit between capital and labor, the principle of give and take." After demonstrating, not unlike *The Challenge,* that common workers are incapable of making responsible decisions or making a business successful, *Give and Take* brings the factory and its owner to the brink of disaster, which is escalated by the recalcitrant behavior of Drum, the bank president. "Ever since you put in this Industrial Democracy," he tells Bauer, "*we* have been out to get you. *We're* going to wreck your plant, put your men out of work and teach our own men a lesson." Although such threats should make Drum a villain, he is not so treated. The troubles of the business are brought about by the institution of the socialist system. It is also telling that throughout the action of the play Bauer is afraid of his own employees. At the point of crisis, Bauer thinks all is lost and that his workers may violently rise up against him; the factory is saved by the intervention of a peculiar but benevolent capitalist.[21]

The earliest plays in this reactionary collection reflect a distinctive set of social and political assumptions that elevate perceived American democratic principles to the exclusion of all else, exaggerate the tenets of Communism as immoral beliefs designed to reduce people (especially women) to slaves, and present the Russians as America's mortal enemies, whose primary purpose is not to settle the horrific social, economic, and political problems of their own new troubled country but to infiltrate and overwhelm the West within a matter of months. Not inconsequentially, all of these reactionary plays employ realistic form and style, following a conventional commercial approach to dramaturgy. When later playwrights chose experimental approaches to this subject matter, their aim was either to attack right-wing or Red Scare activity or to tolerate, exonerate, or glorify Communist or socialist ideology. Many so-called radical playwrights of the 1920s seemed to prefer experimental forms and styles, not only because they originated in Europe or signaled departure from the center of mainstream theater, but because realism was often identified by the left with emotionally based, nineteenth-century bourgeois art. Realism, however, especially late in the decade, was quite comfortable in left-wing drama as well.[22]

Standing virtually alone among these early plays is *The Inheritors* (1921), Susan Glaspell's "contribution to the literature of radicalism," as Woollcott had it, which attacked the kind of narrowness evident in the foregoing playwrights and the characters who served as their spokespersons. Glaspell, displaying "radical courage" in the face of pandemic reactionism, set the xenophobic action of her last three acts in a Midwestern American college in 1920, where open intellectual pursuits come under attack by provincial, political, racist, and capitalist forces during the height of the Red Scare. Her sympathetic characters are victimized by widespread paranoia. A state senator, for example, who is being courted by the college administration for financial support, is unwilling to lend assistance unless the school fires one of its prominent faculty members, Professor Holden, whom the politician perceives as radical because he stood up for conscientious objectors during World War I. "We can get scholars," he observes. "What we want is Americans. . . . You can pick [scholars] off every bush—pay them a little more than they're paid in some other cheap John college."[23]

The oppression extends to students as well, when two Indian Hindu students come under attack by the senator and Caucasian students because they are demonstrating for an India free of British control. A number of students dub the Hindus Reds and anarchists and proceed to rough them up, resulting in the arrest, not of the reactionary students but of the Indians. Even the college's chief administrator says: "This college is for Americans. I'm not going to have foreign revolutionists come here and block the things I've spent my life working for." Only Professor Holden and one intelligent student, Madeline Morton (the granddaughter of the school's founder), stand up to the reactionaries. As Holden tells the administration: "The day you dismiss [the Hindus], [you should] burn our high-sounding manifesto . . . and admit that Morton College now sells her soul to the—committee on appropriations!" Even Holden's moral courage yields to expediency, however, leaving Madeline to face the hostile field alone. The chauvinistic loyalty issue engaged many colleges and universities, just as it did during the era of McCarthyism. "The pressure brought to bear upon Professor Holden . . . epitomized a common situation in American institutions of learning."[24]

Madeline defends the Hindus for more personal reasons, and ultimately, unlike Holden, she risks her own life. "They're people from the other side of the world who came here believing in us," she argues, "drawn from the far side of the world by things we say about ourselves. Well, I'm going to pretend—just for fun—that the things we say about ourselves are true."[25]

In a play without a romantic love interest (highly unusual for American plays of the early twenties), young Madeline never becomes side-tracked from the political and social issues of the play. She leaves at the emotionally charged conclusion to face certain incarceration because she refuses to stop supporting those whose rights to free speech and dissent have been abolished. In a sweeping, often effective polemic, Glaspell had dramatized what Ludwig Lewisohn, alarmed by the conservative tenor of the country in 1921, called the "most burning problem of our national life . . . the tragic disintegration of American idealism."[26]

It is not surprising that this play was first produced by the Provincetown Players, who were outside the mainstream; nor is it unexpected that *The Inheritors* entered the mainstream in a 1927 revival by Eva Le Gallienne at the Civic Repertory, when its point of view was no longer unique. Le Gallienne suggested that the play should be required reading for all young Americans. Connecting the xenophobia of the play's reactionaries to America's love affair with commercialism (no doubt her primary reason for reviving *The Inheritors* when the stock market was peaking), she wrote that the play is "full of indignation against the results of a too rapid, too greedy prosperity, in which the material has become the ultimate goal in complete disregard of spiritual and ethical values." Unfortunately, many critics, while verifying the abuses dramatized or described in the play, considered the action outdated by 1927, probably because the Red Scare had receded, despite continuing, pervasive anti-Communist detraction in the media and the arts. Also, other plays sympathetic to dissent and socialist thought had appeared in intervening years. The play nonetheless remains, as John Mason Brown found it in revival, "a burning and compassionate study of retrogressive generations, of free speech and academic freedom."[27]

O'Neill in 1922 added a sympathetic if milder second to Glaspell's appeal. Although not the focus of the play, attacks on reactionaries and exoneration of the much-maligned IWW (the Wobblies), often associated with anarchism and Communism before and during the Red Scare, appear in *The Hairy Ape*. Yank's fellow stoker and political radical, Long, attempts to awaken the protagonist's class consciousness by taking him to Fifth Avenue in New York to see the upper classes (Long calls them "bleedin' swine") in action. Pointedly, as if to defuse popular reactionary descriptions of radicals, Long explains to Yank that violence "ain't our weapon. We must impress our demands through peaceful means." When the mechanistic socialites appear, coming from church, they report in verse, in a parody of patriot and purity leagues, on the sermon they have just heard "about the radicals . . . and the false doctrines that are being preached. / We must organize a hundred per cent American bazaar." The well-meaning Long flees the scene in horror when the bewildered Yank, who cannot comprehend either radical politics or upper-class behavior, begins to attack the socialites. No matter how violent and physical Yank becomes, the socialites are impervious to his attacks. His fury out of control, Yank "lets drive a terrific swing, his fist landing full on the fat gentleman's face. But the gentleman stands unmoved as if nothing had happened." The supremacy of social and legal control by the moneyed class is unshakable, and the police respond instantly to calls from the economic elite.[28]

In the IWW scene O'Neill asks for a completely ordinary room filled with commonplace activity in order to further undercut the popular depiction of this radical union as a pernicious fraternity of anarchists. Only Yank, in dealing with the union men, acts in a strange way, in response to the myths he has heard. The union Secretary insists, simply and honestly, that "we stand on our two feet in the open. We got no secrets." Once the union men realize that Yank wants to dynamite the industrial complex, however, they seize him, assuming that he is a police or federal spy intending to entrap them by inciting illegal activity. Of Yank's supposed governmental boss, the Secretary explains: "Tell him that all he'll ever get on us, or ever has got, is just his own sneaking plots that he's framed up to put us in jail. We are what our manifesto says we are, neither more or less." Yank, like so many others of his generation, never believes or understands their simple message. (The real IWW was destroyed by governmental and popular harassment and sabotage.) O'Neill rarely delivered social or political messages, and even here they were secondary to the depiction of the personal confusion, anguish, and destruction of Yank, the overwhelming power of which both play and production made clear.[29]

As the decade progressed (not coincidentally following the popular extended tour of the Moscow Art Theatre), the social and political values reflected in many plays are less easy to categorize. Shifts occurred not only in the political underpinning of the material but also in the genres used, the dramatic tone, and the quality of writing. Playwrights who chose to explore the subject did so with more verve, creativity, credibility, and dramatic experimentation. Although a few more right-wing plays attacking Communism, anarchists, and Russian spies appeared after 1923, notably *All Wet,* a farcical 1925 comedy about a Bolshevist revolution in Yonkers, and *The Yellow Sands,* a British import about labor unrest in 1927, most of the plays that ventured into political territory were of a different stamp.

It is probably not coincidental that as this shift was occurring, the Theatre Guild staged *Man and the Masses,* by German Communist and expressionist Ernst Toller. The choruses, especially, call for revolution and define the demarcations of working and privileged classes in broad, strident strokes:

Give orders to a group of comrades:
Dynamite in the machines!
Tomorrow factories will explode into the air.
. . . .
Down with the factories! Down with machinery!
. . . .
The masters live in palaces;
Our brothers rot in filthy trenches.[30]

The choral exchanges eventually shift, under pressure from more level-headed Communists, to a call for a strike rather than the destruction of the industries that give them work.

Some contemporary criticism, even while praising the play or production, argued that outside its European context, the play was not relevant. "*Man and the Masses* goes out of bounds," Macgowan wrote, "when it tries to give Americans a symbolic vision of proletarian sufferings and proletarian revolution."[31] Historical development proves Macgowan more or less correct in his assessment, but many contemporary American artists disagreed, as subsequent theatrical activity attests.

By the mid-1920s political shifts that later characterized the Great Depression were anticipated in the work of John Howard Lawson, who like Rice and O'Neill combined his radical subject matter with experimental form, most popularly in *Processional* (1925), produced by the Theatre Guild. As discussed earlier, this expressionistic extravaganza calls for social reform, out of sympathy for its striking West Virginia coal miners. When a worker is found to have a copy of the *Rubaiyat of Omar Khayyam,* the Sheriff assumes that he is "one of them Armenian Bolsheviks."[32]

With subsequent work of the 1920s, like the political farce *Loud Speaker* (1927), Lawson, along with others at the New Playwrights' Theatre, allied political and social drama with constructivism and to some degree futurism as his work became increasingly influenced by Russian theater—especially the experiments of Meyerhold. The written plays, however, while demanding theatrical stylization and generalized location, do not insist on strictly constructivist settings, nor were the plays mounted effectively. Although experimental, *Loud Speaker* only zanily and tangentially ventured into revolutionary politics; a mysterious, bearded "hypnotic stranger" with a "secret doctrine," for example, is taken by a conservative politician to be a "Russian Red" who should "go back where he came from."[33] The broadly drawn characters frequently dance during the confusing action, which is even more disjointed than in *Processional*.

More ominous, however, was Lawson's *The International*, which predicts that there will be a worldwide rebellion of the working classes when capitalist exploitation and greed start a second world war. Throughout the play the capitalists are terrified of the possible rise of Communism, which hits the streets of New York as a full-blown civil war. Lawson attacks jingoism of both American and European varieties, while demonstrating that the bottom line for the leaders of both continents is money rather than ideology. As the Red rebellion commences in the United States, a female Russian revolutionary describes the spirit of revolt: "Suddenly the ghosts of America's martyrs, Sacco and Vanzetti leading them, blacken the sky over New York." What really fills the sky, however, is the Italian Air Force, as the capitalist forces choose to unite with the fascists in order to defeat the Reds. Although the conservative forces are victorious, they are painted as monsters throughout the play. When business magnate Spunk, for example, brags that "we got our hands on the pulse of the world," David (a revolutionary convert) retorts, "You're sure it's not its throat?"[34]

Ultimately the power of oil swamps all ideologies and even civilization itself in scenes that seem to anticipate much later struggles in the Middle East. Russian Communists and Western capitalists both understand the need for control of the world's oil supply and are willing to sacrifice political vision to get it. "Dead men shall rise," proclaims Alise, the Russian activist, reflecting on and joining various important fluids in her images. "Blood and oil shall drive deep in the earth to waken you, dead soldiers sleeping in Asia." The Grand Lama even sees oil as a "precious liquid, a dynamic fluid," which not only "drives the great machines" but is both life giver and life sustainer as well as great destroyer: a "magic semen" that controls all and levels all.[35]

More important, with *The International* Lawson was still raising philosophical and sociopolitical questions without providing answers, for he had not yet completely converted to Communism. Gerald Rabkin aptly calls the play an expression of "Lawson's social ambivalence."[36] In consequence, the play is strident and disordered but more compelling than his drama of certitude in the next decade.

Likewise forecasting pessimism while invoking the memory of Sacco and Vanzetti during the Red Scare, Maxwell Anderson and Harold Hickerson's *Gods of the Lightning* (1928) sympathetically explored the debacle of the anarchists' trial and execution, which stood for years as a mighty symbol for left-wing thought concerning the injustices of the reigning system. As Edmund Wilson put it, the Sacco and Vanzetti case "raised almost every fundamental question of our political and social system." Sacco and Vanzetti were arrested for murder in 1920 during the Red Scare, convicted in 1921, and executed in 1927. The sensitivity and problematic nature of the play's subject matter (especially in Massachusetts, where the Sacco-Vanzetti trial took place) was underscored by the city of Boston's refusal to license the play for public performance.[37]

In the play, Capraro, a pacifist rebel who has been falsely arrested, convicted, and executed of robbery and murder (but who is really killed by a paranoid society for his anarchist beliefs), states his case in simplistic but understandable rhetoric, given the treatment he receives from the ruling parties: "When you take violence into your hands, you lower yourself to the level of government, which is the origin of crime and evil." Capraro, citing the typical anti-commercial line of the era, goes on to indict the motives behind the Great War as well. "It was a war for business," he explains, "a war for billions of dollars, murder of young men for billions."[38]

The real murderer, Suvorin, is known to the audience almost from the beginning, but the authorities are not interested in him because he is not a radical. In explaining why he chose a life of crime, Suvorin echoes the sentiments expressed by Glaspell in *The Inheritors* some six years earlier: "I came here from tyranny to find a free country, and this country set out to break me in its prisons because I believed in its liberty. . . . There are men with whips and there are whipped men!"[39]

Red Scare tactics are shown at work during the early years of the Harding administration, which the play characterizes as a "stupendous period of graft and prosperity." (The Red Scare actually began under the Wilson administration after the president's stroke.) Police raids on the unions are frequent and are usually instigated by a planted police spy trying to incite the men to violence, just as the IWW members think Yank is attempting in *The Hairy Ape*. The District Attorney and Judge are corrupt, witnesses are bullied into perjuring themselves, and the jury is "a hundred and forty proof Shriner and Chamber of Commerce." The play, of course is a polemic designed to indict xenophobia as well as the degraded legal system that allows or encourages the kind of miscarriages of justice that the playwrights and many other liberal or radical thinkers of the era believed took place in Massachusetts. Anderson returned to this material once again, with more popular success, in 1935, when he presented the more poetic and less literal play *Winterset,* considered by some critics his dramatic masterpiece.[40]

Gods of the Lightning also represents a return to realism for anti-reactionary drama. Although stylization would continue to be used throughout the 1920s for such work, a few of the most effective plays in this category opted for a conservative dramatic form. Robert Littell, reviewing the production with earnest enthusiasm, only regretted "that the authors were unable to deal with the impalpable monster of public opinion and had to accuse a few individuals instead."[41] To have accomplished this would have given the play more historical accuracy, but at the same time the task would have been nearly impossible for a play structured in realistic form. Perhaps an expressionistic chorus in the manner of Toller or Lawson could have served the purpose.

One year earlier Paul Sifton's *The Belt* proved to be more than an anti-commercial play in an expressionistic style. Brooks Atkinson identified it as "of the revolutionary color that flamed abroad in the works of Toller a few years ago."[42] Not only did Toller rage abroad, however, as we have seen. It is a curiosity that all the New Playwrights' anticapitalist, pro-socialist plays were partially subsidized by Otto Kahn, a rich capitalist who enjoyed supporting unusual arts projects, regardless of ideology.

The protagonist of *The Belt,* Bill Vance, who is viewed with suspicion by the workers because he attended college, is called a "trouble-maker" and "radical" by the conservative laborers when he attempts to mobilize them. Vance accepts these descriptions but not the label bestowed on him by Carlson, a management spy among the workers, who calls him "a damn bolshevik" (only characters representing management use this word), before raising the standard chauvinistic cry of the period: "We haven't got room here for anybody who ain't a hundred per cent our kind." Bill later turns the phrase on angry workers (now a mob), connecting it with their habitual self-delusion: "I'm one of those loony bozos that said you were workin' yourselves out of a job—just like all the other hundred per centers who believe in the right to work and starve to death." Just before the workers begin to riot and wreck the assembly line, the Old Man (a Henry Ford character) makes a last futile but characteristic appeal to stop them by invoking Red imagery again: "Don't act like a lot of fool Russians or savages! . . . God! . . . Are you Americans, or aren't you?"[43]

The years 1928 and 1929 were the busiest theatrically for exploration of Communist and socialist themes. In these two years, before the stock-market crash, at least ten major plays appeared, all of which made an appeal for tolerance and understanding or openly attacked the intolerant and bigoted. No one style or method predominated. Such plays were mounted either realistically or expressionistically; they were driven by compassion and intense anger as well as derisive, humorous cynicism. Some looked forward, like *The International,* others, like *Gods of the Lightning,* inspected the past.

In Michael Gold's *Hoboken Blues* the perceived foreign threat, as we have seen, is aligned with anti-labor practices and xenophobic behavior that connects hostility toward African Americans with hatred of all foreigners and alien ideas. Sam Pickens, the black protagonist, who in pursuit of his Hoboken dream is beaten and persecuted by white, racist policemen, is told to "Git outa town in ten minutes, or we'll give yuh a taste of real American law." Before being dragged before the white Judge to witness American justice, Sam is treated to a song and dance routine in which the white Mayor sings:

> Law and order must rule the day.
> America first, hip, hip, hooray!
> . . . .
> Down with the workers, down and out;
> Deport them all, that's my shout.[44]

Armed with a whip, the Judge reminds his court that "a case such as this brings again to the notice of every Nordic American that our immigration laws must be amended. Not only should no more foreigners be admitted, but every foreigner in the country should be kicked out! . . . All our problems would be solved . . . if we killed all the foreigners."[45]

Singing Jailbirds, by Upton Sinclair, author of *The Jungle* and distinguished by one critic as "our super-radical from California," was produced in New York in 1928, four years after it was written. The labor tragedy is based on a tumultuous 1923 strike in San Pedro and Los Angeles during which sympathizer Sinclair himself was arrested. Mixing styles, as does *The Belt,* and retracing real, catastrophic events in the manner of *Gods of the Lightning,* the play is a polemic that attacks a corrupt legal system, police brutality, abuse of Constitutional rights, and federal persecution of dissenters. Like *The Hairy Ape* Sinclair's play exonerates the IWW, but here this defense becomes the center of the tragedy. Most of the action, frequently punctuated by union songs, focuses on IWW leader Red Adams, who has been confined to prison solitary for his union activity in California. The central charge by which men are incarcerated and punished without trial or hearing was an extension of the Espionage and Sedition Acts. Charged with criminal syndicalism, the strikers are assumed to be attempting to gain economic control of industry and, by extension, the government. In the District Attorney's questioning of Red in the

opening scene, Sinclair demonstrates the reactionary's inability to comprehend the radical's motivation. The D.A., assuming that Red wants political and
material power, confers capitalist sensibilities on the proletariat.[46]

The play engages in much name-calling and slogans on both sides of the issue, but only the police commit acts of violence, pay perjurers, and plant spies
among the workers, much like government activity in *Gods of the Lightning*.
Here, however, the crimes are even crueler and more graphically presented.
In order to stop the prisoners from singing their labor songs (which keep up
their spirits), the guards suffocate them until they pass out. The audience
watches Red degenerate to near-madness and death, as the rats eat out his
eyes in the lightless, tiny dungeon.

In the most entertaining propagandistic passages (no doubt the most disturbing to some conservatives), the Dominie, a radical clergyman who supports the workers, preaches to the imprisoned Wobblies, calling Jesus Christ a
"working-class revolutionist, the rebel carpenter, the First Wobbly of the
World! . . . I prophesy and ordain the downfall of World Capitalism and the
Second Coming of the Saviour in the Social Revolution! . . . Like the best of
your glorious martyrs, He died in anguish, that mankind might be free from
the enslavement of Mammon!" Some of the criticism of this play engaged a
separate dialectic, arguing that the play truthfully reflected conditions of
"cruel punishment . . . not confined to California" or complaining that the
play's depiction of labor oppression "in this tenth year after the Great War in
these United States is . . . patently absurd."[47]

As some, like Sinclair, attacked the Red Scare and its political fallout in earnest, others, like Ben Hecht and Charles MacArthur in their wisecracking
comedy of newspaper reporters, *The Front Page* (1928), attempted to render
right-wing politics and public fear of Communism ludicrous. Their method,
though from the opposite point of view, was similar to Tarkington's in
Poldekin, but with much more popular and enduring dramatic results. The
playwrights here were not condoning Communism but attacking those people, especially politicians, who had exploited public xenophobia in order to
promote their own corruption and expand their eroding power base. In *The
Front Page* all was done, however, in the spirit of what reviewers were fond of
calling "hard boiled" comedy, which by act 3 shifts to rollicking farce. It is also
curious that the Red theme, so pervasive in the first two acts, virtually vanishes
in the third, which is dedicated to ridiculous complication, crisis, and the exposing of all the frauds.[48]

One of the two major lines of conflict in the play concerns the impending
execution of a condemned murderer, who is characterized as a Bolshevik.
Like Vance in *The Belt,* the prisoner Earl Williams will admit to being an anar-

chist, but he is insulted at being labeled a Bolshevik. The corrupt and ignorant Republican Sheriff and the Mayor, his smarter but duplicitous political crony, exploit the situation because election day is imminent. The politicians pretend that the hanging of Williams could bring about a Red uprising; yet they attempt to kill him even after receiving a reprieve from the governor. They insist on being characterized as iron men who refuse to be "intimidated by the Red menace." When speaking publicly, the Sheriff pontificates about liberal organizations, which he designates "a bunch of Bolsheviks," and declares that the execution of Williams signals a death warrant for these Bolsheviks, whom he equates with the heart of "the whole criminal element in [Chicago]." His motto in running for reelection is "Reform the Reds with a rope." It is telling that the Mayor (in private of course) tells the Sheriff, "There ain't any God damn Reds, and you know it."49

When Williams finally appears, after a supposed grand escape, he turns out to be "a poor little crazy fellow" who is both terrified and ostensibly harmless. The playwrights' disdain extends to nearly *all* the characters in the play, including the protagonist. As Robert Brustein wrote when reviewing a 1987 revival: "Nobody gives a damn about Earl Williams. . . . [He] has no value to anyone except as an opportunity for greed, ambition, vanity, or worse." Ultimately, the Red Scare theme is abandoned for the fun of the play's final series of reversals and cynical displays, but by this time xenophobic behavior in all its absurdity has been thoroughly debunked (a favorite term of the 1920s).50

Other dramatists, like Elmer Rice in the expressionistic *Adding Machine* but more importantly in the ensemble realism of *Street Scene* (1929), demonstrated the dehumanization of a capitalist bureaucracy and the insensitivity of anti-Communist sentiments. Rice wrote at the time of production that he had created *Street Scene* in part as a delayed response to Israel Zangwill's successful *The Melting Pot* (1909), a play that perpetuated the popular myth of easily blending cultures. Rice believed that New York (the America he knew) was no melting pot but a collection of cultures, races, religions, and political ideologies that were constantly at odds, jammed together in a mess of disparate ways of life, ethics, and social expectations. That his dramatic visions were violent and deadly is not surprising.51

With the decade's end it was not uncommon to see suggestions of Communist or socialist sympathies. *Great Scott* (1929), a comedy by Howard Koch, even openly presented socialism as a tonic for both business and society. Here the hero excites his fellow factory workers with the tenets of socialism, inspires a strike, and introduces profit sharing to the canning industry—almost as if the play were a delayed answer to *Give and Take* of 1923. Although presented with a light touch, *Great Scott* dared on a commercial stage to display socialism as a positive force. In this comedy Delancy Scott, a recent college graduate, comes home "full of handsome talk about the philosophy of Schopenhauer and industrial economics as they affect the laborer." Determined to put his new ideas to the test, he gets a job in a canning factory where his family works, fires up the other workers with his socialist ideas, starts a strike, and, after overcoming the obstacles intended to keep the action dramatic, helps to transform the working methods of the industry. He is especially successful in securing profit sharing and healthier environmental conditions for the laborers. Although Delancy finds his real calling in teaching rather than organized labor, he has helped to improve the local scene, for which he is rewarded with the leading lady—an interesting redistribution of the romantic rewards of *We've Got to Have Money*.[52]

Great Scott failed after playing only two weeks, although it is somewhat surprising that it was produced commercially at all. The critics in turn seemed mystified by it or dismissed it as a trifle. Even conservative critics identified it as a generational comedy rather than a threat to capitalism, calling it a "conflict between a cocky college graduate and his stand-pat father."[53]

John Dos Passos in *Airways, Inc.* (1929) dramatized labor strife and the corruption of commercialism in the middle-class urban community more trenchantly, sympathetically portraying Communist and socialist activities. The central character, Martha Turner, is primarily a sufferer, who functions as a lightning rod for the labor conflict waged around her. Walter Goldberg, the man she loves, is a young, attractive Communist labor organizer. He leads an eight-month strike that ends in his false arrest and electrocution for murder. The final scene is the vigil preceding his execution (similar to the conclusion of *Gods of the Lightning*). Throughout the play, however, many characters have either glorified the bravery of his activities or decried them, repeating the usual derogatory litany of the threat of Bolshevik uprisings and the Red menace (Dos Passos associates Red-baiting with the Chamber of Commerce and the American Legion). Martha's reactionary brother, for example, calls Walter "a long-haired anarchistic agitator," and Walter, in a reversal from earlier plays, denies being an anarchist but is clearly identified as a socialist and Communist.[54]

Like the D.A. in *Singing Jailbirds*, the conservatives assume that the Reds must be involved in the strike for what they can get out of it materially. One even suggests that "maybe they get [their money] from Russia." The police, again, like those in *Singing Jailbirds*, are characterized as puppets of industry; they are the only characters who commit acts of violence, including beating women. The image of the American melting pot is invoked in this play as well, when a conservative attributes the labor strike to "the melting pot boiling, that's all." Another, however, has a different but characteristic explanation for labor leaders: "They're all damn foreigners. They ought to be deported." Both assume that the disturbances will pass and all will be unified in the future. Conservatives did not like to think of America as permanently fragmented, unable to unite everyone under the same set of moral ideals, social values, and political assumptions.[55]

Airways, Inc., although written realistically, includes a tired old Hungarian radical called the Professor, who stalks through the play like a Red chorus, offering stories from his revolutionary past, which most of the other characters ignore but which serve as interesting counterpoint for the audience. He takes us back to the Great War years and the beginnings of the social rebellion that has culminated in the unrest of the late 1920s. "After the collapse of the shining socialist dream," he says, "I came to America. . . . I wanted to escape a war-shattered world without hope. I wanted to go far away. Nowhere is far any more. Distance has slapped back in my face like a broken elastic."[56] As the 1920s were about to end, the Great War was still very much alive (*All Quiet on the Western Front* was an American best-seller in 1929) and still the great cataclysm; it did not lose its potency until the economic debacle.

In the last year of the decade two Soviet plays, *The First Law* and *Red Rust*, appeared. *The First Law*, by Dmitry Scheglov, was a romantic intrigue melodrama of revolutionists versus capitalists in Siberia; it was billed as "the first play out of Soviet Russia." In outline, *The First Law*, as adapted for the New York stage, sounds like a reworking of American melodrama in the manner of the frontier play *Davy Crockett* (1872), by Frank Murdock, or David Belasco's *Girl of the Golden West* (1905).[57]

Red Rust, by V. Kirchon and A. Ouspensky, is a curiosity: a standard murder melodrama, complete with degenerate villain, emotionally distraught victim, and surprise discovery and comeuppance of the swaggering villain, it is set in Soviet Russia in 1926, and the discussion is about political theory and the extreme difficulties adjusting to postrevolutionary conditions. These include many complaints about the Communist bureaucracy, overcrowding, and shortages. Bolshevik jokes are also here, but now the jokes are self-referential, creating a mood entirely different from that found in American Red plays. One student, for example, defines a Communist as "a bolshevik who shaves and carries a portfolio." The paranoia and fear that "everybody is a self-styled Government spy" are prevalent as well. This corruption is what the title refers to as rust, already setting in, so few years after the revolution. Also, the good Communists who triumph at the end are worried that the corrupt ones "are like abscesses in a healthy body," who "indulge their lazy libertinism, and from *these* Communists [and here the play strikes home for those who defend or attack Communism in the West], the entire world judges us."[58]

The production of *Red Rust* not only depicted conditions in the current Soviet Union directly on the American stage, but it stands emblematically as a harbinger of the next decade, for it appeared just two months after the stock-market crash, was one of the last productions of the decade, and is often credited with launching the Group Theatre, although the production was actually a studio presentation under the Theatre Guild. The Group Theatre did not begin to produce plays for themselves until 1931, but many of the key actors and directors of the Group (including Harold Clurman, Cheryl Crawford, Lee Strasberg, Franchot Tone, and Stella Adler) were important contributors to the production of *Red Rust*.

If the political drama of the twenties is examined chronologically the commercial theater (with a few exceptions and aberrations) can be seen forcefully attacking the Russian Revolution initially but then shifting focus to Americans who are intolerant or terrified of Communism. Some drama by 1927 reflects toleration of, consideration for, or even an embrace of many socialist or Communist principles. Such shifts occurred well before the response to the crash, which is usually identified as the beginning of serious political comment and unrest on the modern American stage.

Many critics of political drama of the 1930s have all but dismissed the twenties, observing that while the playwrights dramatized social and political problems, their "social criticism was ill-defined because the[y] could not as yet offer a political alternative."[59] Such a position, however, condemns such playwrights as Ibsen, as well as many others, especially realists, who chose to heighten collective consciousness by making people aware of the social and political problems without taking the evangelistic or even arrogant or naive step of assuming that they had all the answers.

Many of the Marxist playwrights (or playwrights on the road to Marxism, "fellow travelers," or simply political radicals without a name for their ideology) opted fairly early in the 1920s for the experimental: they tried expressionism and obvious theatricality. With the early 1930s, they shifted to a kind of socialist realism or skitlike agit-prop, and few of their plays (the work of Clifford Odets excepted), even if dynamic historically, resonate today as works of artistic importance, unlike many plays of the mid- and late 1920s. Elmer Rice and John Howard Lawson, for example, produced much better work in the 1920s than in the later years.

Few playwrights actually endorsed Communism in the late 1920s, but many demonstrated the evils of conservative politics and reactionary ideology.

Ironically, and with traditionally American ambivalence, some playwrights and other theater artists capitalized economically on their attacks against capitalism throughout the mid- and late 1920s.

A call for the kind of political drama that appeared in the following decade seems to be sounded in *Street Scene,* when Kaplan, an aging radical Russian Jew, predicts a socialist revolution (I have anglicized here for clarity): "It is the fault of our economic system," he explains. "So long as the institution of private property exists, the workers will be at the mercy of the property-owning classes. . . . So long as the tools of industry are in the hands of the capitalist classes, we will have exploitation and slums. . . . Mister Morgan rides in his yacht and upstairs they turn a woman with two children in the street. . . . We must put the tools of industry in the hands of the working classes, and this can be accomplished only by a social revolution!"[60] Although his speech is rejected by the other characters ("we don't want no revolutions in this country"), Kaplan goes on at length, and Maurrant, the man who leads the group in its disapproval, is a villain: he kills his wife in the next act. Rice, however, makes Kaplan neither hero nor villain but a strong voice for the need for change. Yet exactly what that change should be was, for Rice and many other American playwrights between 1923 and 1929, a topic for further debate. Their explorations make the best of these plays worthy of examination—perhaps even theatrical revival—long after their composition.

Afterword

When I discussed American drama and the Red Scare at an academic conference a few years ago, I was asked whether I was making an appeal for realism.
That was certainly not my intent, especially because I believe that realism in
form and style is often ineffective in today's theater; with location shooting and
closeups, film can be so much more realistic, naturalistic, and—although I
hesitate to use the word—authentic. In a consideration of the 1920s, however,
we can reconsider realism's value and application in promoting propaganda or
its impact on social awareness, uses that Ibsen exploited effectively in his own
time. I am no celebrant of the wave of neorealistic American plays that has
flooded our contemporary stage in the 1980s and 1990s, but in an era like the
1920s, film, before it had reached its current level of sophistication and techni-
cal quality, may have threatened the stage, as we can see in *Birth of a Nation*,
but it had not yet rendered it negligible in this genre and style.

The most interesting and moving plays, political or otherwise, in the 1920s
were both realistic and expressionistic, and the best of the playwrights usually
attempted both. If we do not insist that playwrights dramatize a specific, pro-

grammed, ideology, we can celebrate expressionistic and other stylized plays, which, like the best in the realistic mode, heighten consciousness, instead of dictating policy. Although obviously anathema to popular Brechtian aesthetics, much of what Americans have really adopted and adapted from Brecht at the close of the twentieth century is not his surety of policy and thought but his methods for promulgating his political messages. We use not the metaphorical bombs but the delivery system.

Delivery systems in dramatic form, stage design, and directorial approach and authority are the models that resonate the most from the postwar–precrash period. It was a time that followed an extended era of isolationism, and Americans attempted to hide themselves politically and socially once again, but with less success, after the war. Perhaps it is this inclination, coupled with the European social and artistic invasion, that resulted in so much ambivalent artistic, political, and cultural activity. Isolationist claims and practice were at odds with the facts that Americans traveled extensively abroad and European artistic influence had come to America. Isolationism also subtended the escalating commercial buying and marketing frenzy that reached into the global arena. When the Great War began, many intelligent people thought that the war was too far away to touch them, yet European goods, art, and literature were everywhere to be found in America, and European immigration statistics were enormous.

Much of American postwar urban society basked in economic prosperity for most of a decade, yet many playwrights of both the right and the left responded to an extremely conservative political machine with either acute paranoia over the new enemy or increasing skepticism that the Calvin Coolidge–Henry Ford commercial dream could or should last. After 1927 political reactionism vanished for a while from the stage, yet the playwrights, who clearly intended to engage American audiences in political and social argument, to beg reconsideration of the purpose of government and business, were either cynical about the American system (at least as practiced by political and business leaders) or full of questions and doubts themselves. Many theater artists were nevertheless certain that America was in trouble and that its recurring ambivalence over unresolved issues was unlikely to solve the dilemma.

Although we now live in a post–Cold War society, many of the artistic challenges and predicaments facing American theatrical artists resemble those of the post–Great War era. Public ambivalence and contradictory values and behavior infuse social and cultural battles. Once again we have passed through an extended crisis in which the face of the enemy, once painted so emphatically, has vanished. Must it be replaced? It will be interesting—perhaps alarming—to see whether current ethnocultural and sociopolitical upheavals, to say nothing of post–Cold War recessionary economics, will yield parallel results. How will theatrical, cinematic, and television artists respond to lingering moral, economic, and political dilemmas that were created during the Cold War and that must be faced anew in its wake?

Appendix:
The Sex Farces That Appeared Between 1915
and 1921

Fair and Warmer, by Avery Hopwood: opened November 6, 1915, produced by Selwyn and Company, 377 performances.

Sadie Love, by Avery Hopwood: opened November 29, 1915, produced by Oliver Morosco, 80 performances.

His Bridal Night, by Lawrence Rising and Margaret Mayo: opened August 16, 1916, produced by A. H. Woods, 77 performances.

Our Little Wife, by Avery Hopwood: opened November 18, 1916, produced by Selwyn and Company, 41 performances.

What's Your Husband Doing? by George V. Hobart: opened November 12, 1917, produced by Hobart-Jordan Company, 40 performances.

Parlor, Bedroom and Bath, by C. W. Bell and Mark Swan: opened December 24, 1917, produced by A. H. Woods, 232 performances.

Double Exposure, by Avery Hopwood: opened August 27, 1918, produced by Selwyn and Company, 15 performances.

The Naughty Wife, by Fred Jackson: opened November 17, 1918, produced by Selwyn and Company, 72 performances.

Up in Mabel's Room, by Otto Harbach and Wilson Collison: opened January 15, 1919, produced by A. H. Woods, 227 performances.

A Sleepless Night, by Jack Larric and Gustav Blum: opened February 18, 1919, produced by the Shuberts, 71 performances.

Nightie Night, by Martha M. Stanley and Adelaide Matthews: opened September 9, 1919, produced by Adolph Klauber, 154 performances.

The Girl in the Limousine, by Wilson Collison and Avery Hopwood: opened October 6, 1919, produced by A. H. Woods, 137 performances.

No More Blondes, by Otto Harbach: opened January 7, 1920, produced by A. H. Woods, 29 performances.

An Innocent Idea, by Martin Brown: opened May 25, 1920, produced by Charles Cook, 7 performances.

Scrambled Wives, by Adelaide Matthews and Martha Stanley: opened August 5, 1920, produced by Adolph Klauber, 60 performances.

Ladies' Night, by Avery Hopwood and Charlton Andrews: opened August 9, 1920, produced by A. H. Woods, 360 performances.

The Girl with the Carmine Lips, by Wilson Collison: opened August 9, 1920, produced by the playwright, 16 performances.

Getting Gertie's Garter, by Avery Hopwood and Wilson Collison: opened August 1, 1921, produced by A. H. Woods, 120 performances.

A Bachelor's Night, by Wilson Collison: opened October 17, 1921, produced by John Cort, 8 performances.

The Demi-Virgin, by Avery Hopwood: opened October 18, 1921, produced by A. H. Woods, 268 performances.

Notes

CHAPTER 1: INTRODUCTION

Epigraph: Roger Rosenblatt, "How to End the Abortion War," *New York Times Magazine*, Jan. 19, 1992, p. 41. Although this line appears in an article on the abortion-rights controversy raging now, Rosenblatt's thesis is central to the subject of this book on American theater in the teens and twenties.

1 "New York Season," 131; Susman, *Culture as History*, xxiii.
2 Kammen, *Mystic Chords of Memory*, 299–300.
3 Fussell, *Great War and Modern Memory*, 21.
4 Susman, *Culture as History*, 107.
5 Although the 1927–28 season had the most openings, the total number of "theater weeks" (one theater week equals one production occupying one theater for one week), peaked in the season of 1925–26, suggesting that this earlier season was more successful economically. Poggi, *Theater in America*, 47, 49–50.
6 Downer, *Fifty Years of American Drama*, 22.

CHAPTER 2: DRAMA IN THE TRENCHES FROM *WAR BRIDES* TO *WHAT PRICE GLORY*

Epigraph: Downer, *Fifty Years of American Drama*, 40.
1 Tuchman, *Proud Tower*, 463.

2 *What Price Glory* is often cited with a question mark in the title, but it was originally produced and published without one. When the words appear in the text of
the play, however, the interrogative is used. *What Price Glory,* like O'Neill's *Desire
Under the Elms* and *They Knew What They Wanted,* by Sidney Howard, also produced in 1924, was threatened by the police, but producer-director Arthur Hopkins instructed the actors to cut the most offensive profanity on the night the police
brought a stenographer into the theater. *What Price Glory* was never formally
charged, but the other two plays had to face citizen play juries. See Shivers, *Life of
Maxwell Anderson,* 99; Wainscott, *Staging O'Neill,* 158.

3 Miller and Frazer, *American Drama Between the Wars,* viii–ix.

4 "Second Thoughts on First Nights," *New York Times,* Aug. 15, 1915, p. 2; Crane,
"Theatre in War Time," 119.

5 I have altered the order of phrases in this quotation from a review. "'Out There'
Proves Most Appealing," *New York Times,* p. 11. J. Hartley Manners is best known
for his long-running *Peg o' My Heart* (1912), also written for his wife Laurette Taylor, whose most memorable work remained *Peg* until she created the original
Amanda in Tennessee Williams' *The Glass Menagerie* (1945).

6 Wilson, *Twenties,* 362; Woods, "Why I Produce Bedroom Farces," 352; Brackett,
"Dance, Little Dancing Girls," 303.

7 To be fair, there were many reasons for the Senate's rejection of the League. Isolationism and political partisanship were only part of the story, yet the Senate's rebuff
of Wilson's dream is often viewed as strictly reactionary. See, e.g., Shannon, *Between the Wars,* 12–20.

8 Fussell, *Great War and Modern Memory,* 192.

9 Corbin, "Hyphen in Our Midst," *New York Times,* p. 6.

10 To be precise, O'Neill included war references in a few other early one-acts, but
only *In the Zone* and *Diff'rent* were professionally produced (the latter only in special matinees), and some of these plays were not produced at all. One could make
an argument for *Strange Interlude* (1928) being inspired by the war, but this psychological study uses the war simply to launch Nina Leeds's great loss, which sends
her into the arms of other men after her intended is shot down in Europe before
the action of the play begins.

11 *Across the Border,* a one-act, appeared at the Princess Theatre and featured the
nightmare of a delirious, wounded soldier in a field hospital, who upon awakening
tries to make an impassioned appeal for peace to which no one will listen. This was
found to be "a highly imaginative arraignment of the folly, cruelty and horror of
war." See the review "One-act Plays," *Theatre Magazine,* 44. *The Spoils of War,* by
Hilliard Booth, described as a "summons [to] womankind to a united rebellion
against war's inhumanity," probably owes something to *Agamemnon* because an invading general's wife turns against him and kills him when their daughter is mistaken by his men as an enemy civilian. See the review "Spoils of War," *New York
Times,* p. 15.

12 Wentworth, *War Brides,* 535, 531, 544.

13 G. F. P., "'Moloch': A Play About War," *Harper's Weekly,* 57; "First Nighter," *Dramatic Mirror,* Sept. 22, 1915, 8; Dix, "Moloch" [fragment], *Theatre Magazine,* 230–231; "Moloch," *Independent,* 18.

14 Corbin, "English Laughter," *New York Times,* p. 8. *Arms and the Girl* is a comedy by Grant Stewart and Robert Baker that manages to find humor among stranded Americans while Germany is invading defenseless Belgium. *Under Fire* is a sensational melodrama based on war news by Roi Cooper Megrue, who wrote a series of successful, topical, Broadway potboilers in 1914 and 1915. This play pits the heroic English against underhanded German spies and soldiers; it bears comparison to Bronson Howard's *Shenandoah* (1888) and William Gillette's *Secret Service* (1895), which glamorized the Civil War. One reviewer said of it: "President Wilson's appeals for strict neutrality were thrown to the winds. . . . It is a play full of thrills, hair-breadth escapes, thunder, blood and murder." "Under Fire," *Theatre Magazine,* 139.

15 When President Wilson drove to the Capitol to ask Congress to declare war, he had to be accompanied by the U.S. Cavalry because organized pacifists were attempting to block his entrance to the building.

16 Woollcott, "Out There," *New York Times,* p. 5.

17 Stevenson, *Babbitts and Bohemians,* 38; Sullivan, *Our Times,* 472; "Government Orders Play Closed," *Dramatic Mirror,* 4; "Sadie Love," *Theatre Magazine,* 10.

18 "Those Germans!" *Theatre Arts,* 166. The editor Sheldon Cheney wrote in the next issue, "We hold ourselves free to say what we believe about the art of any nation, whether enemy or ally." He went on to quote the contradictory statement suggestive of the blind patriotism espoused by many and issued to the local press by the chair of the Detroit Arts and Crafts Theatre Committee that controlled subsidy of *Theatre Arts:* "I am not a bigot. . . . But there are some things which I do not discuss. I cannot discuss them—I would not know how. One of them is my country." Cheney, "Why We Are Moving," *Theatre Arts,* 50.

19 See photographs of such tableaux in *Theatre Magazine,* July 1918, 35, and November 1918, 265.

20 This coinage is credited to the *New York Times* in September 1914. Sullivan, *Our Times,* 66.

21 Hornblow, "Friendly Enemies," *Theatre Magazine,* 143.

22 Shipman and Hoffman, *Friendly Enemies,* 52–53, 91–92.

23 Cohan at first gave the song to Nora Bayes in vaudeville. This song is emblematic of the popular patriotic fervor that excited so many in the first year of American mobilization. Some of the most stirring lyrics are: "Hoist the flag and let her fly, / Yankee Doodle do or die. / Pack your little kit, / Show your grit, do your bit. / Yankee Doodle fill the ranks, / From the towns and the tanks. / Make your mother proud of you. / And the old Red, White, and Blue. . . . So prepare, say a pray'r / Send the word, send the word to beware. / We'll be over, we're coming over, / And we won't come back till it's over / Over there." "Pack Up Your Troubles in Your Old Kit Bag," a popular English import that appeared in *Her Soldier Boy* (1916), in

later years lost its war edge and appeared to be a specimen of nostalgia. The Shubert brothers' romantic war musical by Rida Johnson Young, Sigmund Romberg, and Emmerich Kalman, climaxed in the surprise return of a soldier son believed killed in Belgium.

24 "New York Cheers 'Yip, Yip, Yaphank,'" *Theatre Magazine*, 222.

25 "First Nighter," *Dramatic Mirror*, July 1, 1916, 8; "New Attraction for New York Theatregoers," *Dramatic Mirror*, 7; "Winter Garden Takes to Cover," *New York Times*, p. 11; "'Over the Top' a Nine O'Clock Show," *New York Times*, p. 11.

26 The *Passing Show* was a series of end-of-season revues beginning in 1912 produced by J. J. Shubert that was intended to compete with the Ziegfeld Follies. Historian Brooks McNamara calls them "unabashedly girlie revues, full of low comedy and novelty effects, and produced with an eye to the budget and to the taste of the Tired Business Man." McNamara, *Shuberts of Broadway*, 96. As the Shuberts' other major chronicler relates, the *Passing Shows* were "filled with spectacle, girls, comedy, girls, fantasy, girls, music, and girls." Stagg, *Brothers Shubert*, 119. "'Passing Show' Is a Lively One," *New York Times*, p. 9; "First Nighter," *Dramatic Mirror*, July 1, 1916, 8; "Scenes in 'The Passing Show of 1916' at the Winter Garden," *Theatre Magazine*, 63.

27 "Submarine on Stage," *New York Times*, p. 11. A production photograph appears in McNamara, *Shuberts*, 98.

28 "'American Ace' Takes the Casino," *New York Times*, p. 11. *An American Ace* was actually pure spectacle with little music except for martial underscoring. It was filled with battle scenes on the ground and in the air featuring "American troops in action and mastering the Germans at every turn." "New Attractions for New York Theatregoers," *Dramatic Mirror*, Apr. 13, 1918, p. 509.

29 The original production was credited to Edmund Laurence Burke and Dorothy Donnelly, but the published play lists only Bennison as author. "Movie Life in New Play," *New York Times*, p. 9; Bennison, *Johnny Get Your Gun*.

30 Hornblow, "Watch Your Neighbor," *Theatre Magazine*, 210.

31 "'By Pigeon Post' Arrives," *New York Times*, p. 13; Corbin, "War Well Lost," *New York Times*, p. 6.

32 *Clarence* was not the first play to comically exploit the homecoming theme. This honor goes to *Civilian Clothes*, by Thompson Buchanan, which opened eight days earlier. But no other was so successful as *Clarence* in the season of 1919–20.

33 Woollcott, "Play," *New York Times*, Sept. 20, 1919, p. 14; Tarkington, *On Plays, Playwrights, and Playgoers*, 6.

34 Tarkington, *Clarence*, 18, 19; Shannon, *Between the Wars*, 134.

35 Tarkington, *Clarence*, 62, 17.

36 The critic is describing the soldiers in *What Price Glory* here, but the description is appropriate for Clarence as well. Krutch, *American Drama Since 1918*, 31.

37 Reid, "Dramatic Mirror," *Dramatic Mirror*, 2023; Hornblow, "Famous Mrs. Fair," *Theatre Magazine*, 98; Forbes, *Famous Mrs. Fair*, 206; Wilson, in Stevenson, *Babbitts*, 30.

38 Forbes, *Famous*, 217; Allen, *Big Change*, 13, 135; Perrett, *America in the Twenties*, 159.

39 Forbes, *Famous*, 242, 207.

40 Forbes, *Famous*, 210, 249–250.

41 Forbes, *Famous*, 225, 226–227, 230.

42 Schneider, *Into the Breach*, 31, 287–289.

43 Gilbert, "Soldier's Heart," *Behind the Lines*, 214.

44 Forbes, introduction to *Famous*, ix.

45 Since one reviewer reports Sylvia's age as seventeen, it is possible that the character's age was slightly lowered in the production. Hornblow, "Famous," 98.

46 Forbes, *Famous*, 262.

47 Hornblow, "He and She," *Theatre Magazine*, 270.

48 Forbes, *Famous*, 254.

49 Forbes, *Famous*, 260, 277, 273.

50 Shapiro, "Dreams Which Won't Come True," *Theatre Magazine*, 100.

51 "Hero," *New York Times*, Sept. 6, 1921, p. 13.

52 O'Neill, *Diff'rent*, 46–47.

53 Emery, *Hero*, 237, 226, 241.

54 Emery, *Hero*, 258, 245.

55 Emery, *Hero*, 233; Hornblow, "Hero," *Theatre Magazine*, 370; Emery, *Hero*, 245: variations on this quotation appear in much literature and journalism of the period, including *What Price Glory*.

56 The newspapers during the war were full of stories of "super slackers" and private citizens' reports that often led to their capture. The usual punishment was five years' imprisonment. A conscientious objector, however, who refused to serve in a noncombatant role for the military could be sentenced to ten years in prison. The mania for catching slackers was so severe that Florenz Ziegfeld felt obligated to inform his audiences for his 1918 *Follies* that none of the gentlemen in the chorus were slackers; all had genuine exemptions.

57 Emery, *Hero*, 268; Woollcott, "Play," *New York Times*, Mar. 15, 1921, p. 14.

58 Gilbert, "Soldier's Heart," 212; Emery, letter to Quinn, *Contemporary American Plays*, 221; Emery, *Hero*, 227, 229, 231.

59 Emery, *The Hero*, 255, 257, 287.

60 Quinn, *History of the American Drama*, vol. 2, 215.

61 Emery, *Hero*, 242; Macgowan, "Year's End," *Theatre Arts*, 7; Woollcott, "Play," *New York Times*, Mar. 15, 1921, p. 14.

62 Hoffman, *Twenties*, 57.

63 Although not produced on Broadway, the Provincetown Players production was very popular, appearing on three bills from 1919 to 1921; it was reviewed favorably by major critics, and revived by little theaters all over the country. The play premiered December 5, 1919, at the Playwrights Theatre in Greenwich Village. See Sarlos, *Jig Cook and the Provincetown Players*, 176–179.

64 Millay, *Aria da Capo*, 2, 31.

65 Woollcott, "Second Thoughts on First Nights," *New York Times*, Dec. 14, 1919, p. 2.

66 *The Inheritors* was first produced by the Provincetown Players March 21, 1921, but it had commercial revivals in both New York and London throughout the 1920s.

67 Glaspell, *Inheritors*, 13, 92.

68 Glaspell, *Inheritors*, 65, 73.

69 Susman, *Culture*, 113; Glaspell, *Inheritors*, 99.

70 *The Verge* opened in Greenwich Village on November 14, 1921, and moved to the Theatre Guild's Garrick Theatre on December 6 for a series of matinees.

71 Glaspell, *Verge*, 33, 61, 54.

72 Vollmer, *Sun-Up*, 992.

73 France, "Apropos of Women and the Folk Play," *Women in American Theatre*, 151.

74 Folk art and folk culture in general received enormous attention from the mid-1920s through the 1930s. The Broadway and off-Broadway response was significant; many dialect plays appeared, often dramatizing conditions and problems in the agrarian South or among repressed racial minorities. *Sun-Up* and *Hell-Bent fer Heaven*, along with Paul Green's *In Abraham's Bosom* and the Heywards' *Porgy* are among the most important. Theatrically, these plays represented, in addition to a burgeoning cultural movement across the country, a tension between "elite and popular culture," between "competing conceptions of cultural identity" that continues today in both artistic and political arenas. See Kammen, *Mystic Chords of Memory*, 407. Brenda Murphy argues that *Sun-Up* and the others are not folk plays at all but examples of regionalism, which at the time was grouped with the newly popular folk art and was most significant realistically in its evocation of milieu. She calls these dramas "commercial exploitations of regional eccentricities rather than serious studies of regional customs and mores." Murphy, *American Realism and American Drama*, 137.

75 Vollmer, *Sun-Up*, 1001. Before learning the identity of the deserter, the mother says, "I recken ye air [honest] if ye ain't done nothin' worse than run away from war" (1005).

76 *Hell-Bent* bears other similarities to *Sun-Up* as well, most notably in that both feature North Carolina family feuding, both have young major characters named Rufe (Hughes's is a villain, however), and in both the younger generation is brighter than the old and a trifle more savvy about contemporary problems and events. All the characters in both plays, however, are uneducated and backward without becoming the monstrosities of a play like Jack Kirkland's *Tobacco Road*. Hughes, *Hell-Bent fer Heaven*, 17, 15; Wilson, in Stevenson, *Babbitts*, 28.

77 Hughes, *Hell-Bent*, 106, 107. "As young men became increasingly alienated from their prewar selves . . . women seemed to become, as if by some uncanny swing of history's pendulum, ever more powerful. . . . The Great War at least temporarily dispossessed male citizens of the patriarchal primacy that had always been their birthright." Gilbert, "Soldier's Heart," 200.

78 Hughes, *Hell-Bent*, 45, 168; Hughes, "Hell-Bent fer Heaven," *Theatre Magazine*, July 1924, 26, 28, 48, 50; See also Quinn, *History*, vol. 2, 248.

79 Hughes, *Hell-Bent*, 114.

80 Anderson and Stallings, *What Price Glory*, 5; Fussell, *Great War*, 71.

81 Arthur Hopkins in Anderson, *What Price Glory*, 3.

82 Mantle, *Best Plays of 1924–25*, viii–ix; Corbin, "War Well Lost," *New York Times*, Dec. 8, 1918, p. 6. For more material on the war experiences of Stallings see Shivers, *Life of Maxwell Anderson*, 87, and Shivers, *Maxwell Anderson*, 49.

83 Krutch, *American*, 32, 40.

84 Hopkins' press agent did in fact use this statement in much of the publicity. Broun, "What Price Glory," *The World*, Sept. 6, 1924.

85 Hornblow, "What Price Glory," *Theatre Magazine*, November 1924, 15.

86 Anderson, *What Price Glory*, 12, 28, 20, 48.

87 Anderson, *What Price Glory*, 18–19.

88 New Jersey was the usual point of departure for troops sailing for France. Anderson, *What Price Glory*, 30–31.

89 Anderson, *What Price Glory*, 43; Fussell, *Great War*, 84; Anderson, *What Price Glory*, 48.

90 The trenches appeared frequently during the war years, but usually in romantic or fantastic incarnations in musical revues or martial spectacles that were parades of scenery and scantily clad women.

91 Anderson, *What Price Glory*, 52, 58, 59.

92 Anderson, *What Price Glory*, 52; Quinn, *History*, vol. 2, 234.

93 Anderson, *What Price Glory*, 64, 56.

94 Anderson, *What Price Glory*, 79, 84.

95 Anderson, *What Price Glory*, 88.

96 The final line is actually "Hey, Flagg, wait for baby!" but the quoted line, which precedes it, finalizes the play, like a Shakespearean couplet, which is often followed by an exit line to get the character offstage. Similarly, this final sentence is an exit line that imbues the final moment with action. Anderson, *What Price Glory*, 89.

97 Brooks and Lister, *Spread Eagle*, 17; Anderson, "Marching as to War," *Theatre Magazine*, 18; Corbin, "War Well Lost," *New York Times*, p. 6.

CHAPTER 3: THE AMERICAN THEATER VERSUS THE CONGRESS
OF THE UNITED STATES

Epigraph: Producer Marc Klaw in "Tax Bill Stops 71 New Shows, Say Managers," *New York Tribune*, Jan. 21, 1919, p. 14.

  1 My article "American Theatre Versus the Congress of the United States: The Theatre Tax Controversy and Public Rebellion of 1919," *Theatre Survey* 31 (May 1990): 5–22, was the first historical account of this event; that article is an early and briefer version of this chapter.

2 "Admission Tax up to 20 Per Cent," *Variety*, 7; "Kitchin Fights for Profits Taxes," *New York Times*, p. 5.

3 "Year in Legitimate," *Variety*, Dec. 27, 1918, p. 14.

4 See Marc Klaw, "Tax on Theatre Tickets," *Theatre Magazine*, 263, 310; "First Week of War Tax Shows Bad Effect upon Theater Business," *Dramatic Mirror*, 3–4.

5 "Increase Theater Tax," *Dramatic Mirror*, 7; "Managers to Fight Bill," *Dramatic Mirror*, 7; "Fight Theater Tax Bill," *Dramatic Mirror*, 7; "Theater Tax Bill Killed in Senate," *Dramatic Mirror*, 1.

6 H.R. 12863, "Act to Provide Revenue, and for Other Purposes," Bills and Reports of the U.S. Congress, Library of Congress, Dec. 6, 1918, 188–191; "Revenue Bill's Clauses," *Variety*, Jan. 3, 1919, p. 7; "Kitchin," *New York Times*, Jan. 17, 1919, p. 5.

7 *Congressional Record*, 65th Congress, Feb. 1919, 3015; Representative Moore, *Congressional Record*, 65th Congress, Feb. 1919, 3017; H.R. 12863 [Report No. 767], "Bill to Provide Revenue, and for Other Purposes," Bills and Reports of the U.S. Congress, Sept. 3, 1918, pp. 122–124.

8 "Specs Organize to Fight Constitutionality of Law," *Variety*, Jan. 10, 1919, p. 12.

9 "Managers Fight Increase of Tax," *Morning Telegraph*, Jan. 16, 1919, p. 1. The *Morning Telegraph* was an arm of the Shubert organization; therefore nearly every report on this crisis appeared on the front page. The content, however, while sometimes hyperbolic, was in line with the reports published in all the daily newspapers covering the story.

10 "Stage Interests Raise $200,000,000 for Nation," *Morning Telegraph*, Jan. 19, 1919, p. 5; "Theatre Men Object to Proposed Tax," *New York Evening Post*, Jan. 16, 1919, p. 4; "All-Comedy Week Invites War Tax at Current Rates," *Washington Post*, Jan. 19, 1919, p. 9.

11 "Theatre Men," *Evening Post*, Jan. 16, 1919, p. 4; "Managers," *Morning Telegraph*, Jan. 16, 1919, p. 1.

12 "Invoke President on Theatre Taxes," *New York Times*, Jan. 16, 1919, p. 11; "Theatre Men," *Evening Post*, Jan. 16, 1919, p. 4.

13 "Invoke," *New York Times*, Jan. 16, 1919, p. 11; "Theatre Men," *Evening Post*, Jan. 16, 1919, p. 4; "Managers," *Morning Telegraph*, Jan. 16, 1919, pp. 1–2; "Double Tax Their Doom," *New York Herald*, Jan. 16, 1919, p. 7.

14 "Tax on Theatregoers," *New York Herald*, Jan. 16, 1919, p. 10; "Theatre Tax," *Sun*, Jan. 18, 1919, p. 6.

15 "Tax," *New York Herald*, Jan. 16, 1919, p. 10; "Overtaxing the Theatre," *New York Globe*, Jan. 17, 1919, p. 14; "Double Tax on Theatre Tickets," *Brooklyn Daily Eagle*, Jan. 18, 1919, p. 6; Wolf, "Marc Klaw Rebukes Government for Additional Theatre Tax," *Morning Telegraph*, Jan. 16, 1919, p. 4; "Double," *New York Herald*, Jan. 16, 1919, p. 7; Churchill, *Great White Way*, 274.

16 "Thousands Sign Theatre Tax Plea," *New York Times*, Jan. 17, 1919, p. 11; "Invoke," *New York Times*, Jan. 16, 1919, p. 11.

17 "Theatre Managers Fight 20 Cent Tax," *Sun,* Jan. 17, 1919, p. 7; Macgowan, "Peace Departs from Broadway," *Theatre Arts,* 234.

18 "Theatres Fight War Tax Raise," *New York American,* Jan. 17, 1919, p. 10; "Thousands," *New York Times,* Jan. 17, 1919, p. 11; "Theatre Men Fight War Tax Increase," *World,* Jan. 17, 1919, p. 11.

19 "Start Fight on Increased Tax in 500 Theatres," *Morning Telegraph,* Jan. 17, 1919, p. 1; "Theatres Begin Fight on New Tax," *New York Evening Journal,* Jan. 17, 1919, p. 10; "Thousands," *New York Times,* Jan. 17, 1919, p. 11; "Start," *Morning Telegraph,* Jan. 17, 1919, p. 1.

20 "Theatres Fight," *New York American,* Jan. 17, 1919, p. 10; "Thousands," *New York Times,* Jan. 17, 1919, p. 11.

21 "Public Protest, Managerial Tact and the Newspapers Saved Theatres in Crisis," *New York Herald,* Jan. 26, 1919, p. 9; "Theatre Men," *World,* Jan. 17, 1919, p. 11; "Protests Flood Washington Killing 20% Tax Increase," *Variety,* Jan. 24, 1919, p. 6.

22 The descriptions of Kitchin and his point of view seem to anticipate a more recent North Carolina senator and his struggles with the National Endowment for the Arts. "Broadway and Mr. Kitchin," *World,* Jan. 17, 1919, p. 10; "Protests," *Variety,* Jan. 24, 1919, p. 18.

23 "Showmen Plan National Fight on Tax Boost," *New York Tribune,* Jan. 18, 1919, p. 16; "Theatre Men Cable Appeal to Wilson," *Evening Post,* Jan. 18, 1919, p. 9; "Showmen," *New York Tribune,* Jan. 18, 1919, p. 16; "Send Theatre Tax Appeal to Wilson," *New York Times,* Jan. 18, 1919, p. 9.

24 "Showmen," *New York Tribune,* Jan. 18, 1919, p. 16.

25 "Entire Nation Protests Theatre Tax Increase," *Morning Telegraph,* Jan. 18, 1919, p. 1; "Showmen," *New York Tribune,* Jan. 18, 1919, p. 16; "Conferees at Odds over Profits Taxes," *New York Times,* Jan. 18, 1919, p. 13.

26 "3,000,000 Protest High Theatre Tax," *New York Times,* Jan. 20, 1919, p. 13; "Protests Showed Theatres' Power," *Morning Telegraph,* Jan. 27, 1919, p. 1; "1,500,000 Sign Protest of Tax," *Morning Telegraph,* Jan. 19, 1919, p. 1; "Mr. Kitchin Chief Champion of the Double Theatre Tax," *New York Herald,* Jan. 19, 1919, p. 14.

27 "All-Comedy," *Washington Post,* Jan. 19, 1919, p. 9.

28 Broun, "Protest Against Law Which Threatens Drama," *New York Tribune,* Jan. 19, 1919, p. 2.

29 "Exacting a Pound of Flesh That Lies Very Near the Heart," *New York Tribune,* Jan. 19, 1919, p. 1.

30 "Stage World Sees Ruin in Proposed Tax," *New York Tribune,* Jan. 19, 1919, p. 6.

31 "Say Theatre Tax Will Take Work from 1,000,000," *New York Herald,* Jan. 20, 1919, p. 6; "3,000,000 Oppose Theatre Tax Jump," *Sun,* Jan. 20, 1919, p. 7; "60 Per Cent of Theatres Face Ruin, Says Gest," *New York Tribune,* Jan. 20, 1919, p. 14.

32 "3,000,000 Protest," *New York Times,* Jan. 20, 1919, p. 13; "250,000 Soldiers and Sailors Join in Tax Protest," *Morning Telegraph,* Jan. 20, 1919, p. 2; "3,000,000 Oppose Theatre Tax Jump," *Sun,* Jan. 20, 1919, p. 7.

33 "3,000,000 Oppose Theatre Tax Jump," *Sun,* Jan. 20, 1919, p. 7.

34 "Managers Halt New Show Plans," *Morning Telegraph,* Jan. 21, 1919, p. 1; "Tax Bill Stops 71 New Shows," *New York Tribune,* Jan. 21, 1919, p. 14; "May Drop 75 New Plays," *Sun,* Jan. 21, 1919, p. 7.

35 "Protest on Theatre Tax," *New York Times,* Jan. 21, 1919, p. 15.

36 The masculine nomenclature used in this paragraph and elsewhere was typical of business organizations of the period. "Managers Halt," *Morning Telegraph,* Jan. 21, 1919, p. 2.

37 "Managers Halt," *Morning Telegraph,* Jan. 21, 1919, p. 2.

38 "Canvass Shows Ticket Tax Will Not Be Raised," *Morning Telegraph,* Jan. 21, 1919, p. 1.

39 "Tax Bill," *New York Tribune,* Jan. 21, 1919, p. 14.

40 "Managers See Victory Ahead in Fight on Tax," *Morning Telegraph,* Jan. 22, 1919, p. 1; "Senator Jas. A. Reed Finds Theatre Tax Conditions Favorable," *New York American,* Jan. 22, 1919, p. 6.

41 "Managers See," *Morning Telegraph,* Jan. 22, 1919, pp. 1–2; "To Stop Theatre Tax Fight," *New York Times,* Jan. 22, 1919, p. 9; "Six Million in Theatre Tax Protest," *New York Evening Journal,* Jan. 22, 1919, p. 18.

42 "Theatres Win Fight Against Tax Increase," *New York Tribune,* Jan. 23, 1919, p. 1; "Drop Tax Increase on Theatres," *Brooklyn Daily Eagle,* Jan. 22, 1919, p. 1; "Congress Yields to Demand to Kill New Theatre Tax," *Morning Telegraph,* Jan. 23, 1919, p. 1; "Theatre Tax Not Raised," *New York Herald,* Jan. 23, 1919, p. 6; "Congress," *Morning Telegraph,* Jan. 23, 1919, p. 1; "Old Tax Restored on Show Tickets," *Washington Post,* Jan. 23, 1919, p. 3; *Congressional Record,* 65th Congress, Feb. 8, 1919, 3007; *Congressional Record,* 65th Congress, Feb. 25, 1919, 4245.

43 "Theater Managers Win Fight Against Tax of 20 Per Cent," *New York Call,* Jan. 23, 1919, p. 3; "Old Tax," *Washington Post,* Jan. 23, 1919, p. 3.

44 "Protests Flood," *Variety,* Jan. 24, 1919, 6; "Public Protest," *New York Herald,* Jan. 26, 1919, p. 9.

45 "Entire Nation," *Morning Telegraph,* Jan. 18, 1919, p. 2; "Moloch: A Play of Purposeful Horror," *Independent,* 18.

46 Isaacson, "Is Radio an Enemy of the Theatre?" *Theatre Magazine,* 15, 58.

CHAPTER 4: SHE WOULD BE EROTIC

1 One of the most successful examples of such musical comedy is James Montgomery's *Irene,* a Cinderella romance of a shop girl which ran for 670 performances from 1919 to 1921.

2 Corbin, "Tragedy Revised," *New York Times,* Sept. 9, 1923, p. 1.

3 Only two of the twenty plays discussed here have been published, but nine are preserved in manuscript by the Library of Congress and the Billy Rose Collection of the New York Public Library. When no manuscript has survived we can still draw on lengthy plot summaries, critical reviews, publicity materials, photographs, editorials, and occasional fragments of dialogue published in articles of the period.

4 "His Bridal Night," *Dramatic Mirror*, 8; Van Doren, "How to Write a Play," *Theatre Magazine*, 212; Toklas, *What Is Remembered*, 126.

5 "Fair and Warmer," *Dramatic Mirror*, 8; "'Fair and Warmer' Is Highly Diverting," *New York Times*, Nov. 8, 1915, p. 13.

6 "Sadie Love," *Theatre Magazine*, 10; "Sadie Love," *Dramatic Mirror*, 8; "Polyandrous Farce by Avery Hopwood," *New York Times*, Nov. 20, 1916, p. 10.

7 Otto Harbach was a former English teacher who was most successful writing lyrics and books for musicals with Jerome Kern, Rudolf Friml, Sigmund Romberg, George Gershwin, and others. His biggest musical hits were *Rose-Marie* (1924), *No, No, Nanette* (1925), and *Desert Song* (1926).

8 Note that the figures for money-making are much lower than today's minimums. Currently a Broadway show must run for years to return its investment. And in the teens and twenties most theaters closed down in the summer because of the heat and diminished audiences. Only hits would reopen in the fall. Therefore, a play opening in late spring was not usually expected by the producer to be a long-running production.

9 Sharrar, *Avery Hopwood*, 81.

10 Harbach and Collison, "Up in Mabel's Room," unpub. ms., title page.

11 Hopwood, "Fair and Warmer," unpub. ms., title page.

12 "'Nightie Night' Is Amusing," *New York Times*, Sept. 10, 1919, p. 16; Stanley and Matthews, *Nightie Night*, title page; advertisement for *Girl in the Limousine*, *New York Evening Journal*, Oct. 11, 1919, p. 11.

13 "'Girl in the Limousine' Gay Farce," *New York Evening Journal*, Oct. 9, 1919, p. 21; Gotthold, "Smartness in Stage Settings," *Theatre Magazine*, 83. A *Sleepless Night* also featured characters trapped beneath the bed; the victim was actress Carlotta Monterey, who later became the "other woman" and notorious third wife of Eugene O'Neill.

14 The play still bore this title while in its pre-Broadway run in Chicago. "'Gertie's Garter' Got at Republic," *Morning Telegraph*, Aug. 2, 1921, p. 14.

15 "Gertie's Garter Sought for in Vain," *New York Evening Journal*, Aug. 2, 1921, p. 8; "Parlor, Bedroom and Bath," *Dramatic Mirror*, 7; Bartlett, "Girl in the Limousine," *Dramatic Mirror*, 1610.

16 Hopwood, *Fair and Warmer*, act 2, p. 42; "Fair and Warmer," *Dramatic Mirror*, 8; De Foe, "Personal Triumphs of the Season," *Greenbook*, 691.

17 Collison, "Come up to the Haymow," unpub. ms., act 1, p. 2. This is the original version of *Getting Gertie's Garter*, before Hopwood's revisions. Hopwood, "The Demi-Virgin," unpub. ms., act 2, pp. 30–31.

18 Dale, "Cast in Farce at Republic Kept Busy Hiding," *New York American*, 7; Kaufman, "Getting Gertie's Garter," *Dramatic Mirror*, 193.

19 Only *Double Exposure* (1918), by Hopwood, centers on two men and relegates women to a secondary position. It was also the only play in this genre to dabble in the supernatural instead of grounding all its absurd vicissitudes in apparent reality. This wife-swapping, mind-exchanging farce, whose action in the final act proves to

be a dream, did not fare well at the box office. Hopwood's only sex-farce failure closed after fifteen performances.

20 Woollcott, "Second Thoughts on First Nights," *New York Times,* Oct. 12, 1919, p. 2; "His Bridal Night," *Dramatic Mirror,* 8.

21 Hopwood, "Demi-Virgin," act 1, pp. 2, 9; act 2, p. 18.

22 See Auerbach, *Woman and the Demon,* 18.

23 "Bedroom Farce to the Limit," *New York Times,* Oct. 7, 1919, p. 22; Hopwood in Van Doren, "How to Write a Play," *Theatre Magazine,* 276.

24 Harbach and Collison, "Up in Mabel's Room," act 1, p. 29; act 3, p. 25.

25 Stanley and Matthews, *Nightie Night,* 103.

26 Collison, "Come up to the Haymow," act 1, p. 22.

27 Doris Kenyon had been starring in movies with such titles as *The Ocean Waif* and *A Girl's Folly* since 1915; she subsequently starred opposite Rudolph Valentino in *Monsieur Beaucaire* in 1924 and worked frequently until 1939, having survived the transition to sound films. "Bedroom Farce to the Limit," *New York Times,* Oct. 7, 1919, p. 22; "Portrait of Claire Whitney," *Theatre Magazine,* 99; Broun, "Drama," *New York Tribune,* Jan. 16, 1919, p. 11.

28 Collison, "Come up to the Haymow," act 1, p. 34.

29 "Dolly Sisters in a Frisky Farce," *New York Times,* Aug. 17, 1916, p. 9; "His Bridal Night," *Dramatic Mirror,* 8; "His Bridal Night," *Theatre Magazine,* 140.

30 Castellun, "Stage," *New York Call,* Oct. 21, 1921, p. 4; Hammond, "New Play," *New York Tribune,* Oct. 19, 1921, p. 8; Wolf, "New Farce at the Eltinge Theatre," *Morning Telegraph,* Jan. 17, 1919, p. 9.

31 Marsh, "'Gertie's Garter' Got at Republic," *Morning Telegraph,* Aug. 3, 1921, p. 5.

32 Dawn, "Naughty Parts in Naughty Plays," *Theatre Magazine,* 278.

33 Dawn, "Naughty," 278. *The Pink Lady,* which opened in 1911 and ran for nearly a year (312 performances), propelled Dawn in her New York debut to stardom, which she exploited in the musical theater field until Woods cast her in the sex farces.

34 "Polyandrous Farce by Avery Hopwood," *New York Times,* Nov. 20, 1916, p. 10.

35 No longer well known, Rambeau was a popular Broadway actress who rose to New York stardom, a position she maintained from 1914 to the mid 1920s. She was enormously popular in Arthur Hopkins' production of *Daddy's Gone A-Hunting,* as well as in *The Eyes of Youth,* which ran for two seasons after *Sadie Love.*

36 "Extravagant Farce by Avery Hopwood," *New York Times,* Nov. 30, 1915, p. 13; "Sadie Love," *Dramatic Mirror,* 8.

37 Cumberland, "My Escape from the Bedroom Plays," *Theatre Magazine,* 9; Woollcott, "Second Thoughts on First Nights," *New York Times,* Oct. 12, 1919, p. 2; "Up in Mabel's Room," *New York Times,* Jan. 16, 1919, p. 11; Hornblow, "Up in Mabel's Room," *Theatre Magazine,* 142; Woollcott, "Scrambled Wives," *New York Times,* Aug. 6, 1920, p. 16; Stanley and Matthews, *Nightie Night,* 53.

38 Gordon, "Birth Control and Social Revolution," *Heritage of Her Own,* 446; "Right

to Regulate Objectionable Performances in Theaters," *American City,* 677; Forster, *Significant Sisters,* 244.

39 Stanley and Matthews, *Nightie Night,* 73.

40 Sanger in Forster, *Significant Sisters,* 273; Auerbach, *Women and the Demon,* 12.

41 "Stage," *New York Call,* Aug. 4, 1921, 4.

42 Sobel, "Ladies' Night," *Dramatic Mirror,* 283; Reid, "No More Blondes," *Dramatic Mirror,* 91; "'Getting Gertie's Garter' Has Few Novel Situations," *New York Herald,* Aug. 2, 1921, p. 7; Wolf, "New Farce at the Eltinge Theatre," *Morning Telegraph,* Jan. 17, 1919, p. 9.

43 Leamy, "Nice Clean Dirt," *Colliers,* 12.

44 "Music and Drama," *Sun,* Oct. 19, 1921, p. 16; See, for example, Castellun, "Stage," *New York Call,* Oct. 21, 1921, p. 4; "Intimate Farce, Oh, Very!" *New York Herald,* Jan. 16, 1919, p. 7; Dale, "'Demi-Virgin' Presented at Times Square," *New York American,* Oct. 19, 1921, p. 8.

45 "'A Bachelor's Night' Dull," *New York Times,* Oct. 18, 1921, p. 20; unsigned interview with Avery Hopwood, "Is the Undraped Drama Unmoral?" *Theatre Magazine,* 6.

46 Hawley is speaking generally here and not particularly of the sex farces or the theater. His observation is nonetheless apt. Hawley, *Great War and the Search for a Modern Order,* 14.

47 "New Risqué Farce Rapid and Noisy," *New York Times,* Aug. 2, 1919, p. 16; Broun, "Drama," *New York Tribune,* Jan. 16, 1919, p. 11; Dale, "'Demi-Virgin' Presented at Times Square," *New York American,* Oct. 19, 1921, p. 8; "'Fair and Warmer' Is Highly Diverting," *New York Times,* Nov. 8, 1915, p. 13.

48 Torres, "'Getting Gertie's Garter' a Scramble," *New York Commercial,* Aug. 2, 1921, p. 2; Torres, "'The Demi-Virgin' Needs the Censor," *New York Commercial,* Oct. 19, 1921, p. 2; Susman, *Culture as History,* xxvii.

49 Scott, "Bachelor's Night," *Dramatic Mirror,* 593; Hornblow, "Ladies' Night," *Theatre Magazine,* 186; "Dolly Sisters in a Frisky Farce," *New York Times,* Aug. 17, 1916, p. 9; "Theatre," *Sun,* Aug. 2, 1921, p. 10.

50 Elita, "Girl with the Carmine Lips," *Dramatic Mirror,* 277; "New Play," *Globe and Commercial Advertiser,* Jan. 16, 1919, p. 14; Sobel, "Ladies' Night," *Dramatic Mirror,* 283.

51 Towse, "Music and the Drama," *New York Evening Post,* Jan. 16, 1919, p. 9; Kaufman, "Getting Gertie's Garter," *Dramatic Mirror,* 193; Woollcott, "Second Thoughts," *New York Times,* Oct. 12, 1919, p. 2; "'Demi Virgin' Farce Is Usually Dull, Always Vulgar," *New York Herald,* Oct. 19, 1921, p. 9; "Extravagant Farce by Avery Hopwood," *New York Times,* Nov. 30, 1915, p. 13.

52 Macgowan, "New Play," *Globe and Commercial Advertising,* Aug. 2, 1921, p. 12; McAdoo, "Theater and the Law," *Saturday Evening Post,* 47; Hammond, "New Play," *New York Tribune,* Oct. 19, 1921, p. 8.

53 Leamy, "Nice Clean Dirt," *Colliers,* 12; "Shows in New York and Comment," *Variety,* Dec. 2, 1921, p. 14.

54 Cowl, "Sex on the Stage," *Theatre Magazine,* 210.

55 Leamy, "Nice Clean Dirt," *Colliers,* 12.

56 Broun, "New Woods' Farce Fails to Shock Anybody Much," *New York Tribune,* Aug. 2, 1921, p. 6.

CHAPTER 5: POPULAR CULTURE AT THE CROSSROADS

An earlier and shorter version of this chapter appeared as an article entitled "Attracting Censorship to the Popular Theatre: Al Woods Produces Avery Hopwood's *The Demi-Virgin,*" *Theatre History Studies* 10 (1990): 173–186.

1 Susman, *Culture as History,* 86, 90.

2 McAdoo, "Theater and the Law," *Saturday Evening Post,* 7; "Police Stop Two Plays," *Theatre Magazine,* 116; Dale, "Profanity on the Stage," *Theatre Magazine,* 279–282.

3 Niblo, "New O'Neill Play Sinks to Depths," *Morning Telegraph,* Nov. 13, 1924, p. 3; Wainscott, *Staging O'Neill,* 111, 147–148, 158.

4 Dale, "'Demi-Virgin' Presented at Times Square," *New York American,* Oct. 19, 1921, p. 8.

5 Churchill, *Great White Way,* 238; "A. H. Woods: Producer Was 81," *New York Times,* Apr. 25, 1951, p. 29.

6 Shapiro, "Dreams Which Won't Come True," *Theatre Magazine,* 100; Goff, "Owen Davis-Al Woods Melodrama Factory," *Educational Theatre Journal,* 200–207; "Producing Spine-Thrillers," *Literary Digest,* 222–223; Skolsky, *Times Square Tintypes,* 227–230; "Bedroom Farces Are Passé Declares Their Leading Producer," *Current Opinion,* 364; Woods, "Why I Believe in Deciding Things Quickly," *American Magazine,* 25–27, 71.

7 *The Bat,* a Long Island murder mystery, opened August 23, 1920, and ran for more than two seasons, mounting up 867 performances, the second–longest running Broadway show until 1925. Hopwood, "Gold Diggers," unpub. ms., act 1, p. 17.

8 "Avery Hopwood Dies in the Sea," *New York Times,* July 2, 1928, p. 19; Martin, *The Writer's Craft,* 2–3; Van Doren, "How to Write a Play," *Theatre Magazine,* 212; Churchill, *Great White Way,* 240.

9 Leamy, "Nice Clean Dirt," *Colliers,* 12; "Such Shocking Anticipations Excited Police Play Censor," *World,* Nov. 8, 1921, p. 12; "A. H. Woods in a Tender Mood Toward Theatre," *Morning Telegraph,* Aug. 14, 1921, p. 1.

10 "What News on the Rialto?" *New York Times,* Sept. 25, 1921, p. 1.

11 Hopwood, "Demi-Virgin," unpub. ms., act 1, p. 6.

12 Hopwood, "Demi-Virgin," act 2, p. 1; Castellun, "Stage," *New York Call,* Oct. 21, 1921, p. 4.

13 This line, which does not appear in the manuscript, was either added for the production or is an embellishment by the reviewer. Fred, "Demi-Virgin," *Variety,* Oct. 21, 1921, p. 17.

14 Castellun, "Stage," Oct. 21, 1921, p. 4; Hornblow, "Johnny Get Your Gun," *Theatre Magazine,* 216.

15 Leamy, "Nice Clean Dirt," *Colliers,* 12.

16 Hopwood, "Demi-Virgin," act 2, p. 65.

17 Hopwood, "Demi-Virgin," act 1, p. 20.

18 "700 New York Theaters Bar Arbuckle Films," *New York Tribune,* Sept. 14, 1921, p. 6; De Foe, "Drama," *World,* Oct. 20, 1921, p. 11.

19 Advertisement for *The Demi-Virgin, Pittsburgh Post,* Sept. 25, 1921, p. 6; "Next Week in the Theatres," *Pittsburgh Post,* Sept. 18, 1921, p. 7; "Pitt—'The Demi-Virgin,'" *Pittsburgh Dispatch,* Sept. 27, 1921, p. 15; "Pitt—'The Demi-Virgin,'" *The Pittsburgh Post,* Sept. 27, 1921, p. 9; "Pittsburgh," *Variety,* Oct. 7, 1921, p. 39; "Pitt Theater Closed by Police," *Pittsburgh Post,* Oct. 2, 1921, p. 2.

20 "Police Raid Stills in Cleanup Program Ordered in This City," *Pittsburgh Dispatch,* Oct. 2, 1921, p. 1.

21 "Pittsburgh," *Variety,* Oct. 7, 1921, p. 39.

22 "What News," *New York Times,* Sept. 25, 1921, p. 1; "Theatrical Notes," *New York Times,* Oct. 7, 1921, p. 20.

23 Torres, "'Demi-Virgin' Needs the Censor," *New York Commercial,* Oct. 19, 1921, p. 2; Towse, "Play," *New York Evening Post,* Oct. 19, 1921, p. 9.

24 "Music and Drama," *Sun,* Oct. 19, 1921, p. 16; De Foe, "Drama," Oct. 20, 1921, p. 11; Fred, "Demi-Virgin," 16; "'Demi-Virgin' Farce Is Usually Dull," *New York Herald,* Oct. 19, 1921, p. 9.

25 Dale, "Demi-Virgin," 8; "Demi-Virgin," *New York Times,* Oct. 19, 1921, p. 22; "'Demi-Virgin' Farce," *New York Herald,* 9.

26 Hammond, "New Play," *New York Tribune,* Oct. 19, 1921, p. 8; Fred, "Demi-Virgin," 16; Castellun, "Stage," Oct. 21, 1921, p. 4; Hammond, 8; "'Demi-Virgin' Farce," *New York Herald,* 9; Hammond, 8.

27 Macgowan, "New Play," *Globe and Commercial Advertiser,* Oct. 19, 1921, p. 16; Torres, "Demi-Virgin," 2.

28 "Shows in New York and Comment," *Variety,* Oct. 28, 1921, p. 14; "Hollywood Life Depicted in a Play," *New York Evening Journal,* Oct. 19, 1921, p. 16.

29 "Lowering Theatre Standards," *New York Herald,* Nov. 17, 1921, p. 10; Fred, "Demi-Virgin," 16–17.

30 "Complain of 'Demi-Virgin,'" *New York Times,* Nov. 3, 1921, p. 22; "'Demi-Virgin' Faces Trial," *New York Tribune,* Nov. 3, 1921, p. 10; "Complain," *New York Times,* 22; "'Demi-Virgin' Reprieved at Request of Counsel," *New York Tribune,* Nov. 4, 1921, p. 10; "'Demi-Virgin' Case Delayed," *New York Herald,* Nov. 4, 1921, p. 15; "Shows in New York and Comment," *Variety,* Nov. 4, 1921, p. 14.

31 Sumner, "Padlock Drama," *Theatre Magazine,* 12; "'Demi-Virgin' Semi-Naughty When Censor Stopped Looking," *New York Tribune,* Nov. 8, 1921, p. 9; "Such Shocking Anticipations Excited Police Play Censor," *World,* Nov. 8, 1921, p. 12.

32 "Such Shocking," 12; "Shows in New York and Comment," *Variety,* Nov. 11, 1921,

p. 14; advertisement for *The Demi-Virgin, New York American,* Nov. 13, 1921, p. CE-6.

33 "'Demi-Virgin' Bad," *World,* Nov. 15, 1921, p. 11; McAdoo, "Theater and the Law," *Saturday Evening Post,* 6.

34 "'Demi-Virgin' Storm Grows in Broadway," *New York Herald,* Nov. 15, 1921, p. 8; "Woods Defiant, Will Continue 'Demi-Virgin' Until Court Decides," *New York Daily News,* Nov. 25, 1921, p. 24; McAdoo, "Theater and the Law," 47.

35 "'Demi-Virgin' Storm," 8.

36 "Play Censor Soon," *Variety,* Nov. 18, 1921, p. 28; "Shows in New York and Comment," *Variety,* Nov. 18, 1921, p. 14; Nov. 25, 1921, p. 13; Dec. 2, 1921, p. 14; "'Demi-Virgin' Trial May Mean Prison Term," *New York Herald,* Nov. 18, 1921, p. 12; advertisement for *The Demi-Virgin, New York Herald,* Nov. 20, 1921, p. 9.

37 "A. H. Woods's Trial Delayed," *New York Herald,* Nov. 22, 1921, p. 15; "'Demi-Virgin' Must Be Closed To-Night," *New York Herald,* Nov. 24, 1921, p. 16; "'Demi-Virgin' Goes on Playing with Injunction," *New York Daily News,* Nov. 26, 1921, p. 17; "Court Gives 3 Days Life to 'Demi-Virgin,'" *New York Herald,* Nov. 26, 1921, p. 9.

38 "Woods Defies Ban on the 'Demi-Virgin,'" *New York Times,* Nov. 26, 1921, p. 18.

39 "Woods Wants Jury Trial for His 'Demi-Virgin,'" *New York Daily News,* Dec. 3, 1921, p. 15; "'Demi-Virgin' Case Goes Over," *New York Herald,* Dec. 3, 1921, p. 11; "Woods Tells Receipts in 'Demi-Virgin' Suit," *Sun,* Dec. 5, 1921, p. 2; "Jury to Try Al H. Woods," *New York Times,* Dec. 13, 1921, p. 24.

40 "Plays and Players," *New York Globe,* Nov. 29, 1921, p. 15; "Theatre Notes," *Daily News,* Dec. 15, 1921, p. 21; "A. H. Woods Resigns from Association," *Sun,* Dec. 8, 1921, p. 18; "Al Woods Follows George M. Cohan in Quitting P.M.A." *New York Herald,* Dec. 8, 1921, p. 12; "Woods to Stay in Managers Association," *New York Herald,* Dec. 14, 1921, p. 12; "Shows in New York and Comment," *Variety,* Dec. 16, 1921, p. 14.

41 "'Demi-Virgin' Case Dropped," *New York Tribune,* Dec. 24, 1921, p. 4; "Jury O.K.'s 'Demi-Virgin,'" *New York Herald,* Dec. 24, 1921, p. 8; advertisement for *The Demi-Virgin, New York Herald,* Dec. 25, 1921, p. 9.

42 Advertisements for *The Demi-Virgin, New York Times,* Dec. 24, 1921, p. 7; Mar. 19, 1922, p. 2; advertisement for *The Demi-Virgin, New York Herald,* Apr. 23, 1922, p. 10.

43 "'Demi-Virgin' Closing," *Morning Telegraph,* June 1, 1922, p. 4; "Notes of the Stage," *New York Herald,* June 1, 1922, p. 10; "To Be Continued," *New York Times,* May 21, 1922, p. 1; advertisement for *The Demi-Virgin, New York Times,* June 3, 1922, p. 8; "Naked Challenge," *Nation,* 229.

44 Woods, "Why I Produce," 352, 406.

45 "Housecleaning the Theater," *Literary Digest,* 27; "Heard on Broadway," *Theatre Magazine,* 174; Hornblow, "Red Lamp in the Theatre," *Theatre Magazine,* 142; "Stage and the Censor," *Nation,* 59–60; "Pussyfoot in the Theatre," *New Republic,* 32–33.

46 Sumner, "Padlock Drama," *Theatre Magazine,* 62; "Actors and Playwrights Unite to Battle Censor," *New York Daily News,* Dec. 26, 1921, p. 2; "Censorship from Within Proposed for Theaters," *New York Tribune,* Dec. 24, 1921, p. 4; "Housecleaning," *Literary Digest,* 27.

47 Sumner, "Padlock Drama," *Theatre Magazine,* 12; Howe in Susman, *Culture as History,* 89.

48 "A. H. Woods," *Morning Telegraph,* 3; Leamy, "Nice Clean Dirt," *Colliers,* 44.

CHAPTER 6: THE VOGUE OF EXPRESSIONISM IN POSTWAR AMERICA

Epigraphs: Kenneth Macgowan, "New Path of the Theatre," *Theatre Arts,* 84; Jacques Copeau, quoted in Saint-Denis, *Theatre,* 40.

1 See Budd, "Moments of *Caligari,*" 14–17, 59.

2 Written on the occasion of the Theatre Guild's presentation of Tolstoy's *The Power of Darkness.* Woollcott, "Play," *New York Times,* Jan. 22, 1920, p. 22.

3 Watkins, "Irish Players in America," *Craftsman,* 352; Jones, *Dramatic Imagination,* 75.

4 Craig, *On the Art of the Theatre,* 99. Although written for a theatrical periodical, much of this article seems appropriate for *Better Homes and Gardens:* "As a perfect example of modern furnishing, we have the exquisite bedroom in that most delightful of comedies, 'A Pair of Silk Stockings,' one of Mr. [Winthrop] Ames' particular triumphs. The walls are latticed in delicate grays, the furniture is enamelled in gray, with wicker panels and beautifully contrived roses modelled in the natural colorings. There are luxurious draperies of green silk with roses, and quantities of pillows." Gotthold, "Smartness in Stage Settings," *Theatre Magazine,* 82.

5 Craig, *Art,* illustrations facing pp. 136, 280.

6 Ironically, it is a Winthrop Ames production that is being described in note 4, above. With *Sumurun,* Ames as producer was working in conjunction with Lee Shubert, who subsequently booked the production in Boston and Chicago. McNamara, *Shuberts of Broadway,* 58; "Players," *Everybody's Magazine,* 534.

7 Stern's first name was later anglicized to Ernest. Stern, *My Life, My Stage,* 85; "Letters and Art," *Literary Digest,* 211.

8 Stagg, *Brothers Shubert,* 118.

9 Hamilton, "Decorative Drama," *Bookman,* 167.

10 Hartley, "Reinhardt Machine," *Max Reinhardt and His Theatre,* 89; "Reinhardt Play Is Seen at the Casino," *New York Times,* Jan. 17, 1912, p. 8.

11 Three such settings of Hume's are illustrated in Fuerst and Hume, *Twentieth-Century Stage Decoration,* vol. 2, plates 62–64, and five more in *Theatre Arts,* Nov. 1916, p. 34 and May 1917, pp. 121–124.

12 Macgowan, "America's First Exhibition of the New Stagecraft," *Theatre Magazine,* 28.

13 Jones spent most of his time abroad in Florence and Berlin; he was unsuccessful in

getting the attention of Gordon Craig. See Pendleton, *Theatre of Robert Edmond Jones*, 146.

14 "Second Thoughts on First Nights," *New York Times*, Feb. 7, 1915, p. 4; Gorelik, *New Theatres for Old*, 179. Two variations of Jones's design, representing the design as he first showed it to Granville-Barker and as it was ultimately mounted are reproduced in *Theatre of Robert Edmond Jones*, 31; and Salmon, *Granville Barker*, 245. A good photographic reproduction of the finished set appears in *Theatre Arts*, Feb. 1917, 56.

15 Rawls, *Wake Up, America!* 14–25.

16 Hackett, "Granville Barker in New York," *New Republic*, 25.

17 Since Jones was greatly influenced by Ernst Stern early in his career, having spent a year or so with him during his 1912 visit, it is appropriate that the critic compared Jones's design to that of *Sumurun* (which the reviewer also did not appreciate). "New Plays," *Theatre Magazine*, March 1915, 110.

18 Albert Rutherston is sometimes referred to as Rothenstein; he changed his name during the war. Granville-Barker was not always anti-illusionist; he was dedicated to giving a play its due. If a play was written realistically he staged it so, as he did with *The Doctor's Dilemma* (1915) in New York. Kennedy, *Granville Barker and the Dream of Theatre*, 172; Granville-Barker, *Exemplary Theatre*, 155.

19 Coward, "Barker's New Shakespearean Spectacles," *Theatre Magazine*, 198; "Midsummer Night's Dream," *New York Times*, Feb. 17, 1915, p. 11; Mazer, "Finders Keepers," *Nineteenth Century Theatre*, 40.

20 *Birth of a Nation*, Griffith Feature Films, 1915; Brady, "Motion Picture Competition Is Deadly," *Theatre Magazine*, 310.

21 Booth's action just before shooting Lincoln is described in a continuity compiled by Theodore Huff: "Stands up majestically—pulls out pistol—tosses head back—actor-like." This is reprinted in Fulton's excellent book, which analyzes this scene in terms of Griffith's editing skills. Fulton, *Motion Pictures*, 83.

22 It would be a bit absurd to attempt to exonerate Griffith of racism, as some historians and critics have done. See, e.g., Wagenknecht and Slide, *Films of D. W. Griffith*, 48. After all, Griffith's father was a Confederate cavalry officer and his mother sewed Klan costumes. In a 1930 film interview now packaged with the video of *Birth of a Nation*, Griffith told Walter Huston that "the Klan was necessary in those days." The NAACP published a pamphlet in 1915 that protested the film: "It is a deliberate attempt to humiliate ten million American citizens, and to portray them as nothing but beasts." "Fighting a Vicious Film," *Focus on D. W. Griffith*, 101. "Arrival of a New Stage in the Art of the Movies," *Current Opinion*, 251.

23 Klein wrote successful potboilers like *The Lion and the Mouse* and the *Potash and Perlmutter* series of comedies discussed in chapter 7. Forman, on his way to France as a war correspondent, wrote the successful *The Hyphen*, a war play mentioned in chapter 2.

24 "Charles Frohman Lost on the *Lusitania*," *Theatre Magazine*, 284.

25 "Play of Rare Charm Seen at the Hudson," *New York Times*, Jan. 22, 1913, p. 11; Klauber, "Plays for Children and Grown-Ups," *New York Times*, Jan. 26, 1913, p. 6.

26 Hopkins in Sayler, *Our American Theatre*, 60.

27 Hopkins, "Hearing a Play with My Eyes," *Harper's Weekly*, 13; "Foreign Lessons to American Playwrights," *Harper's Weekly*, 15; "Brain Plays in Germany," *Harper's Weekly*, 25. At the time of *On Trial* Rice was still known as Elmer Reizenstein.

28 Production photographs reproduced in *Theatre Arts*, Feb. 1917, 60; and *Theatre Magazine*, Feb. 1916, 68; Moderwell, "Art," *Theatre Arts*, 57, 60; Simonson, "Painter and the Stage," *Theatre Arts*, 3.

29 Langner, *Magic Curtain*, 90; Many full-color illustrations of Bakst's set and costume designs and some black-and-white production photographs are reproduced in Spencer, *Leon Bakst*, and *Bakst* (1977); Fuerst and Hume, *Twentieth-Century Stage Decoration*, vol. 1, p. 84. A color reproduction of one of his *Scheherazade* costumes appears in vol. 2, plate vii.

30 Throughout its history the publication underwent minor title changes, appearing often as a monthly, sometimes as a quarterly. Cheney wrote several books calling for or celebrating the little theater and the art theater in terms of what they were, and more significant, what they could become. See Cheney, *New Movement in the Theatre*, and *Art Theatre*; "Foreword," *Theatre Arts*, Nov. 1916, 1.

31 "Note on the Illustrations," *Theatre Arts*, Nov. 1916, 20.

32 The translation used in the Washington Square production was by Clarence L. Meader and Fred Newton Scott; Andreyeff [Andreyev], *Life of Man*, 68–69; "'Life of Man' Well Presented," *New York Times*, Jan. 15, 1917, p. 7; production photograph of final scene in *Theatre Magazine*, March 1917, 137.

33 Francis Hodge is not referring specifically to *The Life of Man*, but his words are apt. Hodge, "European Influences on American Theatre," *American Theatre*, 9.

34 See production photographs in Appelbaum, *New York Stage*, plates 25, 35, 36; "Chantecler," *New York Times*, Jan. 24, 1911, p. 9; "Lovely Fantasy on New Theatre Stage," *New York Times*, Oct. 2, 1910, p. 13.

35 See illustrations of the American version in *Theatre Arts*, Jul. 1921, 190; and *Theatre Magazine*, Dec. 1917, 342; Eliot, "Le Théâtre du Vieux Colombier," *Theatre Arts*, 25; "Third Bill at the Vieux Colombier," *New York Times*, Dec. 12, 1917, p. 13.

36 The tréteau nu is pictured and described in Rudlin, *Copeau*, 73–75.

37 Juliette Breffort-Blessing argues that Copeau's influence was enhanced by his joint project with Percy Mackaye, a champion of community theater, in his final season in New York. Breffort-Blessing, "Washington," 152. This is probably true, but perhaps more important is the fact that Copeau frequently lectured in little theaters and universities in the United States both before and during his New York seasons.

38 Hawley, *Great War and the Search for a Modern Order*, 14.

39 Pollock, "Redemption," *Green Book*, 236–237; Hopkins, *Reference Point*, 110.

40 The uncredited production translation was by Barrymore's wife Michael Strange; Tolstoy, *Redemption*, 720; Pendleton, *Theatre*, 33; "Tolstoi's 'Redemption' Told in

Pictures," *Theatre Magazine*, 359; Corbin, "New Stagecraft," *New York Times*, Oct. 20, 1918, p. 2.

41 Macgowan, "Repertory," 21; Macgowan, "Peace Comes to Broadway," 151.

42 See, e.g., Valgemae, *Accelerated Grimace*, 29–30.

43 O'Neill, "Playwright Explains," *New York Times*, Feb. 14, 1926, p. 2.

44 O'Neill, *Emperor Jones*, 1045–1046.

45 Hopkins, "Approaching 'Macbeth,'" *New York Times*, Feb. 6, 1921, p. 1.

46 Woollcott, "Second Thoughts on First Nights," *New York Times*, Feb. 27, 1921, p. 1; Photographs of the Macbeths in *Theatre Magazine*, Apr. 1921, 250–251; Hopkins, *To a Lonely Boy*, 224; Stark Young in Pendleton, *Theatre*, 5; Jones's designs are reproduced in *Theatre Arts*, Apr. 1921, 103–110; Pendleton, *Theatre*, 38–41; Jones, *Drawings*, plates 12–14.

47 Woollcott, "Play," *New York Times*, Feb. 18, 1921, p. 16; Hornblow, "Macbeth," *Theatre Magazine*, 298; Macgowan, "Centre of the Stage," *Theatre Arts*, 94.

48 Sayler, *Our American*, 209.

49 Hopkins, *To a Lonely Boy*, 224–225; Hopkins, "Approaching," 1.

50 Eaton, "American Producers," *Theatre Arts*, 234.

51 Miles, "Pump-and-Tub Drama," *Theatre Arts*, 216.

52 Rubenstein, "*Caligari* and the Rise of Expressionist Film," *Passion and Rebellion*, 370.

53 Wiene, *Cabinet of Dr. Caligari:* Gorelik, *New Theatres for Old*, 302; Budd, "Modernism and the Representation of Fantasy," *Forms of the Fantastic*, 18–19; Minden, "Politics and the Silent Cinema," *Visions and Blueprints*, 293; Budd, "Moments of *Caligari*," 17.

54 Sherwood, "Cabinet of Dr. Caligari," *American Film Criticism*, 123.

55 During and shortly after the war, the time lag between Continental European and American productions was usually quite long (a decade being typical), but the gap was considerably reduced as the interest in European plays escalated throughout the twenties. The twelve-year gap between European and American productions of *Liliom* was typical, yet Karel Capek's *R.U.R.* appeared a year after its debut.

56 Lewisohn, "Drama," *Nation*, 695; Martin, "Liliom," *Dramatic Mirror*, 733; Simonson, *Stage Is Set*, 97; Woollcott, "Second Thoughts on First Nights," *New York Times*, May 1, 1921, p. 1.

57 Brown, *Dramatis Personae*, 516; Six production photographs reproduced in Simonson, *Art of Scenic Design*, 120–122.

58 The translation used in the production was by Benjamin Glazer. Molnar, *Liliom*, 160, 171.

59 Although this production reached Broadway only briefly with a series of matinees at the Theatre Guild's Garrick Theatre in December, it had a professional cast, and the play's significance to the professional development of American expressionism is momentous. For performance schedule see Sarlos, *Jig Cook*, 179. O'Neill was specifically referring to Glaspell's *Chains of Dew*, which he sent to George C. Tyler

to consider for production. The play title is identified by Tyler's response. O'Neill unpub. letter to Tyler, Mar. 4, 1920; Tyler unpub. letter to O'Neill, Mar. 11, 1920, Princeton. Linda Ben-Zvi was apparently the first to suggest *The Verge* as an influence on *The Hairy Ape*. Ben-Zvi, "Susan Glaspell and Eugene O'Neill," *Eugene O'Neill Newsletter*, 28.

60 Sievers, *Freud On Broadway*, 70; Glaspell, *Verge*, 78; Gainor, "Stage of Her Own" *Journal of American Drama and Theatre*, 84. C. W. E. Bigsby aptly observes that Glaspell's "anthropomorphic flowers" suggest the chamber plays of Strindberg, but there is more of Strindberg than this in *The Verge*, despite Glaspell's feminism, which he doubtless would have abhorred. Her strident exploration of madness and psychosexual struggles also bear comparison to the Swedish progenitor of expressionism. Bigsby, *A Critical Introduction to Twentieth-Century American Drama*, vol. 1, p. 33. Glaspell, *Verge*, 21, 56.

61 Ozieblo goes on to say that "it is precisely [Claire's] determination to create a satisfactory life for herself that aroused the fervent admiration of the Greenwich Village feminists." Ozieblo, "Rebellion and Rejection," *Modern American Drama*, 72; Linda BEN-Zvi notes that it is typical in Glaspell's plays for all the men to be "incapable of understanding the women and, for the most part, resent their superiority." BEN-Zvi, "Susan Glaspell," 26; Woollcott, "Play," *New York Times*, Nov. 15, 1921, p. 23.

62 Sievers, *Freud*, 71.

63 Glaspell, *Verge*, 60; production photograph in *Theatre Arts*, Jan. 1922, p. 12; "Scene from *The Verge*," *Theatre Arts*, 12.

64 Woollcott, "Play," *New York Times*, Feb. 28, 1922, p. 17.

65 Production photographs reproduced in *Theatre Arts*, Jul. 1922, pp. 184–185; *Theatre Magazine*, May 1922, pp. 290–291; Appelbaum, *New York Stage*, plate 57; Simonson, *Art of Scenic Design*, 124–125.

66 Attributed to Wilson by Laurence Stallings and Maxwell Anderson in Stevenson, *Babbitts*, 35.

67 O'Neill, *Hairy Ape*, 71.

68 O'Neill, *Hairy Ape*, 1.

69 Macgowan and Jones, *Continental Stagecraft*, 17, 131, 138–139; Shakespeare, *Richard III*, 1.4.53.

70 This is the translation used by the Guild. Kaiser, *From Morn to Midnight*, 665, 666.

71 Eaton, *Theatre Guild*, 64.

72 Lewisohn, "Drama," *Nation*, 726.

73 Although we see brief portions of the Cashier's family and personal life, we learn in the final Salvation Army scene that many others have experiences, lives, and families identical to his. "'Morn to Midnight' at the Frazee," *New York Times*, June 27, 1922, p. 16.

74 John Corbin proclaimed *R.U.R.* "the first dramatic importation from our new world neighbor, Czechoslovakia." Corbin, "Play," *New York Times*, Oct. 10, 1922, p. 16.

75 Corbin, "Revolt Against Civilization,", *New York Times*, Oct. 15, 1922, p. 1. This

translation by Paul Selver and Nigel Playfair was used in the Guild production. Capek, *R.U.R.*, 423, 427.

76 Wechsler, "Karl Capek in America," *Cross Currents,* 176; Capek, *R.U.R.,* 432; Macgowan, "Diadems and Fagots on Broadway," *Theatre Arts,* 8; Hodge, "European," 13.

77 Designs reproduced in Jones, *Drawings,* plates 19–23; Pendleton, *Theatre,* 46–49; *Theatre Arts,* Jan. 1923, pp. 43–46; Macgowan, "And Again Repertory," *Theatre Arts,* 99.

78 Young, "Hamlet," *New Republic,* Dec. 6, 1922, p. 46; Macgowan, "And Again Repertory," 98.

79 Most of Svend Gade's career was spent in Germany, where he was particularly noted for his interpretations of Strindberg. The play's German title was *Die Wunderlichte Geschichten des Kapellmeister Kreisler* (The odd tale of Conductor Kreisler). "'Johannes Kreisler'—An Ingenious Nightmare in Forty-Two Scenes," *Theatre Magazine,* March 1923, 17.

80 Hornblow, "Johannes Kreisler," *Theatre Magazine,* Feb. 1923, p. 15; the staging methods are described and illustrated in "Six Stages in One," *Scientific American,* 154–155. See also Bauland, *Hooded Eagle,* 76.

81 Lewisohn, "Drama," *Nation,* Jan. 10, 1923, p. 48; "'Johannes Kreisler,' a Scenic Novelty," *New York Times,* Dec. 25, 1922, p. 20.

82 Lawson, *Roger Bloomer,* 105.

83 Susman, *Culture,* 277.

84 Photographs of all settings are reproduced in the first edition of the play. Rice, *Adding Machine,* plates; scene 5 of the play as published was omitted from production; Rice, *Adding Machine,* 30; "'Adding Machine' Replaces Poor Zero," *New York Times,* Mar. 20, 1923, p. 24; Macgowan, "Experiment on Broadway," *Theatre Arts,* 181; Moeller quoted by Simonson in Eaton, *Theatre Guild,* 198.

85 Arthur Hornblow, of course, would be expected to defend the commercial playwright, but he was probably correct. Hornblow, "Adding Machine," *Theatre Magazine,* 19.

86 "Scenes from *The Spook Sonata,*" *Theatre Arts,* 217; the quotations are from the translation used for the production. Strindberg, *Spook Sonata,* 132–133.

87 Corbin, "Play," *New York Times,* Jan. 7, 1924, p. 23. As written, the action of the play begins outside the house, but one can see into the Round and Hyacinth rooms. In scene 2 the action moves into the Round Room but one can see into the Hyacinth Room. When scene 3 moves into the Hyacinth Room, one can see back into the Round Room. At conclusion the Hyacinth Room opens onto the Isle of Death. In this production, although each location was given a representation, Strindberg's scheme of looking forward or backward to contiguous locations was abandoned.

88 Strindberg, *Spook Sonata,* 139.

89 The Mummy tells Hummel: "Crime and guilt and secrets bind us together, don't you know?" Strindberg, *Spook Sonata,* 128.

90 Apel's play is entitled *Hans Sonnenstossers Hollenfahrt* (1912). The impetus for this production apparently came from Winthrop Ames, who wanted a free-form, comic adaptation of the play, not a translation of the more serious German work. Goldstein, *George S. Kaufman*, 98–99.

91 Actually the play had a lot of music (jazz and ragtime especially) and a musical pantomime, all composed by Deems Taylor, who also wrote the incidental music for *The Adding Machine*. Macgowan, "From the Four Corners of American Art," *Theatre Arts*, 221.

92 Corbin, "Among the New Plays," *New York Times*, Feb. 17, 1924, p. 1; Kaufman and Connelly, *Beggar on Horseback*, 54; Mason, *Wise-Cracks*, 26.

93 Kaufman and Connelly, *Beggar on Horseback*, 118.

94 Although efficient and widely used for productions throughout the 1920s, Woodman Thompson was always overshadowed by Jones and Simonson, as well as by Cleon Throckmorton, Norman Bel Geddes, Jo Mielziner, and Mordecai Gorelik, of his own "generation." Although imaginative, he did not possess the artistry of these others. Macgowan, "From the Four Corners," *Theatre Arts*, 216. Production photographs and designs reproduced in Leitner, "Scene Designs of J. Woodman Thompson," 231, 233, 235; Appelbaum, *New York Stage*, plate 67.

95 Typically, successful burlesque or satire on forms marked the death of the form; for example, John Brougham's *Metamora; or The Last of the Pollywogs* and *Po-Ca-Han-Tas* finished off the previously popular romantic American Indian plays like John Augustus Stone's *Metamora*, a sensationally popular vehicle for Edwin Forrest.

96 Garten, *Modern German Drama*, 139.

97 Simonson, "New German Stage Craft," *New York Times*, Apr. 9, 1922, p. 7; Simonson, "Men as Stage Scenery Walking," *New York Times*, May 25, 1924, p. 15; Macgowan, "Crying the Bounds of Broadway," *Theatre Arts*, 359.

98 This is the translation by Louis Untermeyer used in Simonson's production. Toller, *Man and the Masses*, 455; "Scenes from *Man and the Masses*," *Theatre Arts*, Jun. 1924, p. 361.

99 Blackmur in Susman, *Culture*, 106; Littell, "Processional," *New Republic*, 261; Skinner, "Play," *Commonweal*, Feb. 4, 1925, p. 354; Littell, "Processional," 261.

100 Gorelik apprenticed under Robert Edmond Jones, assisting him on a number of productions. Production photographs and design reproduced in *Theatre Arts*, Mar. 1925, p. 148; Williams, *Stage Left*, 70–71; *New York Times*, Feb. 1, 1925, sec. 4, p. 18.

101 Lawson, *Processional*, 188–189.

102 Atkinson and Hirschfeld, *Lively Years*, 37.

103 Brock, "American Dance of Life Rhymed to Jazz," *New York Times*, Feb. 1, 1925, p. 18.

104 "Scene from *Beyond*," *Theatre Arts*, 149; Fuerst and Hume, *Twentieth-Century*, vol. 1, p. 57, vol. 2, plates 96, 97; Jones, *Drawings for the Theatre*, plate 18; Deutsch, *Provincetown*, 124; Young, "Play," *New York Times*, Jan. 27, 1925, p. 14.

105 Miles, "Pump-and-Tub Drama," *Theatre Arts*, 221.

106 Krutch, "Tragedy of Masks," *Nation*, 164.

107 Sievers, *Freud on Broadway*, 111; Mardi Valgemae calls the split character "an expressionistic objectification of a multiple personality." Valgemae, *Accelerated Grimace*, 37.

108 O'Neill, *Great God Brown*, 24, 51.

109 O'Neill, *Great God Brown*, 90, 98.

110 In the mid-1920s the constructivist productions of Meyerhold caught the attention of a few American artists fascinated by Russian experiments and socialism.

111 Sifton, *Belt;* Atkinson, "Troubles in the Crank Case," *New York Times*, Oct. 20, 1927, p. 33.

112 Lawson, *International*, 44; "International," *New York Times*, Jan. 16, 1928, p. 24.

113 Gold, *Hoboken Blues*.

114 Sinclair, *Singing Jailbirds*, 15; "'Singing Jail Birds' Called Propaganda," *New York Times*, Dec. 5, 1928, p. 34.

115 Reproductions of designs and photographs in Pendleton, *Theatre*, 68–69; *Theatre Arts*, Oct. 1928, p. 704; *Theatre Magazine*, Jan. 1929, pp. 32, 34, 58. The play is published as nine scenes but Hopkins produced it in ten. Atkinson, "Against the City Clatter," *New York Times*, Sept. 16, 1928, p. 1; "Scenes from *Machinal*," *Theatre Arts*, Oct. 1928, p. 704.

116 Ruth Snyder and her lover Judd Gray were tried and convicted of the murder of her husband in 1927 and executed in January 1928. Many events in that crime are included in *Machinal* but are given different weight and purpose. Ginger Strand notes that much of the play's language was borrowed from or suggests the newspaper coverage of the trial. Treadwell herself attended much of the trial. Strand, "Treadwell's Neologism," *Theatre Journal*, 165; Wynn, "Sophie Treadwell," *Journal of American Drama and Theatre*, 29.

117 Barbara Bywaters called the play a "piece of subversive drama, conveying the message that female insurrection can lead to 'one moment of freedom' [the Young Woman's description of the moment following the murder] before the patriarchal 'machinery' crushes the revolt." Bywaters, "Marriage, Madness, and Murder in Sophie Treadwell's *Machinal*," *Modern American Drama*, 97, 101. Treadwell, *Machinal*, 254, 246; Atkinson, "Play," *New York Times*, Sept. 8, 1928, p. 10.

CHAPTER 7: THE CALVIN COOLIDGE GRAND TOUR

1 American dramatic fascination with business had also occurred in the nineteenth century. Bronson Howard and Augustus Thomas were especially prominent: six of their plays "make the adjustments of big business the central subject of the drama, the major influence on character, and the basic cause of the dramatic conflict." Gottlieb, "Antibusiness Theme in Late Nineteenth Century American Drama," *Quarterly Journal of Speech*, 416.

2 Susman, *Culture as History*, xxiv; Stevenson, *Babbitts and Bohemians*, 11. Albert

Fall, of Teapot Dome fame, was the first presidential cabinet member to distinguish himself with a prison sentence.

3 Barry, *Paris Bound*, 90; Bennison, *Johnny Get Your Gun*, 109.

4 Hornblow, "Like a King," *Theatre Magazine*, 424; Woollcott, "Play," *New York Times*, Oct. 4, 1921, p. 10; Dwight, "Like a King," *Dramatic Mirror*, 520.

5 Her stridently etched role of Dulcy catapulted Lynn Fontanne to stardom. Kaufman and Connelly, *Dulcy*, 3, 36; Klingaman, *1929*, 9; *Dulcy*, 38.

6 O'Neill, *Hairy Ape*, 49, 54.

7 Hornblow, "Crooked Gamblers," *Theatre Magazine*, 187; Stricker, "Cookbooks and Law Books," *Heritage of Her Own*, 477, 492.

8 *To the Ladies* was written specifically to exploit the talents of Helen Hayes, an established young star managed by George C. Tyler, who also produced *Dulcy* and *Clarence*. Nolan, *Marc Connelly*, 37; Flexner, *American Playwrights*, 202; Woollcott, "Play," *New York Times*, Feb. 21, 1922, p. 20; Goldstein, *George S. Kaufman*, 77.

9 Kaufman and Connelly, *To the Ladies*, 355, 356, 373.

10 Hornblow, "To the Ladies," *Theatre Magazine*, 307; Connelly, *Voices Offstage*, 74.

11 Before turning to playwriting full time after 1920, Zelda Sears had been a successful character actress who appeared with considerable success as the puritanical blocking agent, Aunt Cicely, in the sex farce *The Girl in the Limousine* (discussed in chapter 4). Corbin, "Clinging Vine," *New York Times*, Dec. 31, 1922, p. 1; "Peggy Wood," *New York Times*, Dec. 25, 1922, p. 20. Peggy Wood played the role of Antoinette Allen. Sears, "Clinging Vine," unpub. ms., act 1, p. 33.

12 Sears, "Clinging Vine," act 1, p. 32.

13 Sears, "Clinging Vine," act 3, p. 2; Sears in Bettisworth, "Life and Career of Zelda Sears," 168.

14 Meyer, *It's Been Fun*, 3.

15 "'Advertising of Kate' Play of Business Girl," *Journal of Commerce and Commercial Bulletin*, 5.

16 Although the play seems not to have survived, the playwright's detailed account of it along with many reviews that provide additional details, which are helpfully consistent, allow a reasonable reconstruction. "New Comedy Seen at Ritz Theatre," *Morning Telegraph*, May 9, 1922, p. 14.

17 "'Advertisin of Kate' Full of Bright Lines," *New York Evening Journal*, May 9, 1922, p. 20.

18 Meyer, *It's Been Fun*, 245; Torres, "'Advertising of Kate' Succeeds," *New York Commercial*, May 10, 1922, p. 2; "'Advertising," *New York Evening Journal*, 20; Meyer, *It's Been Fun*, 245.

19 Smith, "New Play," *Globe and Commercial Advertiser*, May 9, 1922, p. 10.

20 Woollcott, "Play," *New York Times*, May 9, 1922, p. 22; Torres, "Advertising," 2; "Advertising," *Journal of Commerce*, 5; Smith, "New Play," 10.

21 Lawson, *Roger Bloomer*, 71, 5–6, 43–44.

22 Lawson, *Roger Bloomer*, 99, 102, 103.

23 Lawson, *Roger Bloomer*, 109; Valgemae, *Accelerated Grimace*, 74.
24 "'Adding Machine' Replaces Poor Zero," *New York Times*, Mar. 20, 1923, p. 24; Rice, *Adding Machine*, 29, 56.
25 Rice, *Adding Machine*, 138.
26 Although *Polly Preferred* was successful, Guy Bolton was better known as a librettist for musicals like *Anything Goes* with Cole Porter, *Girl Crazy* with the Gershwins, and *Sally* with Jerome Kern. Bolton's sensibilities are demonstrated in his memoir written with P. G. Wodehouse, the fittingly titled *Bring on the Girls!* Bolton, *Polly Preferred*, 39.
27 Laska, *We've Got to Have Money*, 62.
28 Laska, *We've Got to Have Money*, 85; Brown, *Setting a Course*, 96.
29 Corbin, "Play," *New York Times*, Apr. 16, 1924, p. 26.
30 Woollcott, preface to Kaufman and Connelly, *Beggar on Horseback*, 7.
31 Corbin, "Among the New Plays," *New York Times*, Feb. 17, 1924, p. 1; Kaufman and Connelly, *Beggar on Horseback*, 35–36.
32 Kaufman and Connelly, *Beggar on Horseback*, 72.
33 Corbin, "Jazzed Expressionism," *New York Times*, Feb. 13, 1924, p. 17.
34 "'Open House' a Naive Play," *New York Times*, Dec. 15, 1925, p. 28.
35 Lawson, *Processional*, 190, 198, 286; Skinner, "Play," *Commonweal*, Feb. 4, 1925, p. 354.
36 This was Connelly's first solo play after a long collaboration with George S. Kaufman; Atkinson, "Truth by Fantasy," *New York Times*, Feb. 28, 1926, p. 1.
37 Connelly, *Wisdom Tooth*, 88–89.
38 Connelly, *Wisdom Tooth*, 29.
39 O'Neill, *Great God Brown*, 482.
40 Brooks and Lister, *Spread Eagle*, 7, 40, 41.
41 Brooks and Lister, *Spread Eagle*, 102; Anderson, "Marching as to War," *Theatre Magazine*, 18.
42 Brooks Atkinson, "Play," *New York Times*, Apr. 5, 1927, p. 30; Brooks and Lister, *Spread Eagle*, 134–135. The escape and execution scene is staged earlier in the play. It was reported that in the production Aline MacMahon as the condemned woman "emits cries of such terrific anguish that they echo and rankle long after the final curtain." Brown, "Merry Month of May," *Theatre Arts*, 402.
43 Brown, "Merry," 401.
44 Sifton, *Belt*, 67, 72, 12; Levine, *Left-Wing Dramatic Theory in the American Theatre*, 59.
45 Sifton, *Belt*, 77, 179, 181, 183.
46 Gold, *Hoboken Blues*, 508.
47 Gold, *Hoboken Blues*, 584, 592, 599, 609.
48 Treadwell, *Machinal*, 250, 252, 250; Atkinson, "Tragedy of Submission," *New York Times*, Sept. 8, 1928, p. 10.
49 The play was published in 1927, before the first production in 1928. O'Neill, *Marco Millions*, 152.

50 Lawson, *International*, 7, 40, 179, 215.
51 Lawson, *International*, 163.
52 Atkinson, "Spreading the Eagle," *New York Times*, Apr. 10, 1927, p. 1.
53 Barry, *Holiday*, 241, 255.
54 "Holiday," *New York Times*, Nov. 27, 1928, p. 36; Littell, "Potpourri," *Theatre Arts*, 86; "Holiday," *Theatre Magazine*, 78.
55 Behrman, "Napoleonism: 1929," *Three Plays*, 111.
56 "Great Power," *New York Times*, Sept. 12, 1928, p. 25.
57 Dos Passos, *Airways, Inc.*, 88.
58 Rice, *Subway*, 15–16.
59 Behrman, *Meteor*, 163; Flexner, *American Playwrights*, 62.
60 Behrman, *Meteor*, 175, 213.
61 Behrman, "Napoleonism," 112.
62 The number of business plays available that meet these criteria is forty-three.
63 Hornblow, "Dulcy," *Theatre Magazine*, 234.
64 Klingaman, *1929*, 30; Poggi, *Theater in America*, 47–48.

CHAPTER 8: *RED DAWN TO RED RUST*

1 David Francis in Asinof, *1919: America's Loss of Innocence*, 141.
2 One could argue that the New Playwrights' Theatre had more internal argument and strife than leadership. This theater's brief life is chronicled in Knox and Stahl, *Dos Passos and "The Revolting Playwrights."*
3 Macgowan, "Peace Departs from Broadway," *Theatre Arts*, 231. The Communist Party and the Communist Labor Party both sprang from the Socialist Party of America, and in 1921 the two combined as the Communist Party of America. Because of ongoing harassment from government agencies the parties became somewhat secret organizations. Levine, *Left-Wing Dramatic Theory in the American Theatre*, 33–35.
4 Brock, "American Dance of Life Rhymed to Jazz," *New York Times*, Feb. 1, 1925, p. 18; Hawley, *The Great War and the Search for a Modern Order*, 29–30, 50.
5 Kammen, *Mystic Chords of Memory*, 4–5; Perry, "American Cast of Mind," *The Contrapuntal Civilization*, 104–105.
6 Emery, *Hero*, 268–269; Hornblow, "Night Lodging," *Theatre Magazine*, 100; Cowl, "Sex on the Stage," *Theatre Magazine*, 210; Woodrow Wilson in Sullivan, *Our Times*, vol. 5, 554.
7 Perrett, *America in the Twenties*, 128.
8 The pageant of *The Wayfarer* had been performed in Seattle before making its way to New York and other cities. "Fighting Bolshevism with the Bible," *Theatre Magazine*, 84, 136.
9 Martin, "Challenge," *Dramatic Mirror*, 1243; Woollcott, "Play," *New York Times*, Aug. 6, 1919, p. 7.

10 Woollcott, "Play," Aug. 6, 1919, p. 7; Martin, "Challenge," *Dramatic Mirror*, 1243.

11 Woollcott, "Play," *New York Times*, Feb. 27, 1922, p. 16.

12 Although they share a title and a right-wing ideology, as well as a paranoia about Soviet invasion of the United States, the 1919 play is not a discernible source for the 1984 action film *Red Dawn*. Dixon, "Red Dawn," unpub. ms., 1919, title page; act 1, p. 9; act 3, p. 19.

13 Keen, *Faces of the Enemy*, 15, 43, 50, 58.

14 Dixon, "Red Dawn," act 3, p. 5; act 1, p. 7; act 3, p. 22; act 3, p. 25.

15 Dixon, "Red Dawn," act 3, p. 40.

16 Dixon, "Red Dawn," act 1, p. 10; act 3, p. 21.

17 *Poldekin* was produced as another in the early postwar string of domestic comedies under the aegis of George C. Tyler, who produced *Clarence, Dulcy*, and *To the Ladies* (examined earlier). George Arliss was a remarkably successful, though now nearly forgotten, character actor, best known for *Disraeli* (1911), *The Green Goddess* (1923), and many years of playing opposite Minnie Maddern Fiske. Playing Pinsky, one of the revolutionaries, was Edward G. Robinson, who, ironically (since this was a right-wing play), would come under investigation by the House Un-American Activities Committee in the 1950s. Tarkington, "'Poldekin'—A Sunny Satire on Hearsay Bolshevism," *Current Opinion*, 481; Tarkington, *Poldekin*, 481, 482.

18 *Wage slave* is a socialist term used popularly and often sarcastically throughout the 1920s; it appears in many plays. Tarkington, *Poldekin*, 483, 486.

19 Sinclair, "Postscript," in *Singing Jailbirds*, 87.

20 "'Give and Take' Unreal," *New York Times*, Jan. 19, 1923, p. 13.

21 Hoffman, *Give and Take*, 6, 72.

22 Levine, *Left-Wing Dramatic Theory*, 29–33.

23 Woollcott, "Second Thoughts on First Nights," *New York Times*, Mar. 27, 1921, p. 1; Macgowan, "Broadway Bows to By-Ways," *Theatre Arts*, 183; Glaspell, *Inheritors*, 36.

24 Glaspell, *Inheritors*, 62, 65; Atkinson, "Play," *New York Times*, Mar. 8, 1927, p. 23; Atkinson, "Pioneer Traditions," *New York Times*, Mar. 20, 1927, p. 1.

25 Glaspell, *Inheritors*, 71–72.

26 Perrett, *America in the Twenties*, 51–55; Lewisohn, "Drama," *Nation*, Apr. 6, 1921, p. 515.

27 Le Gallienne, *At 33*, 205; Brown, "This Bad Showmanship," *Theatre Arts*, 328.

28 O'Neill, *Hairy Ape*, 53, 54, 57.

29 O'Neill, *Hairy Ape*, 75, 77.

30 Toller, *Man and the Masses*, 456.

31 Interestingly, Macgowan had seen and appreciated Fehling's famous German production of *Man and the Masses* in Berlin. Macgowan, "Crying the Bounds of Broadway," *Theatre Arts*, 356.

32 Lawson, *Processional*, 206.

33 Lawson, *Loud Speaker,* 128.
34 The play was published shortly before it was first produced. Lawson, *International,* 211, 26.
35 Lawson, *International,* 110, 91–92.
36 Rabkin, *Drama and Commitment,* 140.
37 Wilson, *Twenties,* 389; Shivers, *Maxwell Anderson,* 106.
38 Anderson and Hickerson, *Gods of the Lightning,* 26, 78–79.
39 Anderson and Hickerson, *Gods of the Lightning,* 34–35.
40 Anderson and Hickerson, *Gods of the Lightning,* 9, 41. Anderson was writing some seven years after the trial of Sacco and Vanzetti when he produced *Gods of the Lightning,* just as he had six years of distance from the Great War when creating *What Price Glory* with producer Stallings. There was much less objectivity in *Gods of the Lightning,* however, probably because only a year had passed since the executions. By contrast, the more controlled *Winterset* appeared seven years after the executions and fourteen after the trial.
41 Littell, "Where Are the New Playwrights?" *Theatre Arts,* 11.
42 Atkinson, "Troubles in the Crank Case," *New York Times,* Oct. 20, 1927, p. 33.
43 Sifton, *Belt,* 109–110, 128, 143, 187.
44 Gold, *Hoboken Blues,* 591, 592.
45 Gold, *Hoboken Blues,* 598.
46 Trask, "Upton Sinclair Abroad," *New York Times,* May 20, 1928, p. 2. The play was first produced in 1927 in Berlin, directed by Brecht's compatriot in epic theater, Erwin Piscator. There is so much music in the play that it could almost be categorized a musical. Between acts and scenes the audience is often encouraged to join in the singing of the most frequently reprised songs, some of which invoke the memory of Joe Hill.
47 Sinclair, *Singing Jailbirds,* 22; Littell, "Potpourri," *Theatre Arts,* 93; "'Singing Jail Birds' Called Propaganda," *New York Times,* Dec. 5, 1928, p. 34.
48 Robert Littell called *The Front Page* "concentrated essence of newspaperdom." "Front and Inside Pages," *Theatre Arts,* 702.
49 Hecht and MacArthur, *Front Page,* 18, 48, 50, 80.
50 Hecht and MacArthur, *Front Page,* 45; Brustein, *Reimagining American Theatre,* 132.
51 Rice, "New York: Raw Material for the Drama," *Theatre Magazine,* 82.
52 Howard Koch is more familiar as a screenwriter whose most famous work was *Casablanca* and the Orson Welles *War of the Worlds* radio broadcast. Given the subject of *Great Scott,* it should come as no surprise that he was blacklisted in the 1950s. "'Great Scott!' Proves a Baffling Comedy," *New York Times,* Sept. 3, 1929, p. 25.
53 "Great Scott," *Theatre Magazine,* 47.
54 Dos Passos, *Airways, Inc.,* 38.
55 Walter is also an easy target because he is Jewish. Dos Passos, *Airways, Inc.,* 119, 108, 92.

56 Dos Passos, *Airways, Inc.*, 31.
57 Atkinson, "Play," *New York Times*, May 7, 1929, p. 28.
58 Kirchon and Ouspensky, *Red Rust*, 5, 73, 134.
59 Rabkin, *Drama and Commitment*, 29.
60 Rice, *Street Scene*, 84–85.

Bibliography

UNPUBLISHED AND SPECIAL MATERIALS

Bettisworth, Denny L. "The Life and Career of Zelda Sears." Ph.D. diss., University of Georgia, 1974.

Bills and Reports of the U.S. Congress, 1918–1919. Law Library, Library of Congress.

Birth of a Nation, dir. D. W. Griffith, Griffith Feature Films, 1915.

Brackett, Parmlee. "Dance, Little Dancing Girls." *Theatre Magazine,* May 1918, p. 303.

The Cabinet of Dr. Caligari, dir. Robert Wiene, Film Renters, 1990.

Collison, Wilson. "Come up to the Haymow." Unpublished manuscript, 1919, Rare Book and Manuscript Collection, Library of Congress, Washington, D.C.

The Congressional Record, 65th Congress, January–February 1919. Law Library, Library of Congress.

Dixon, Thomas. "The Red Dawn." Unpublished manuscript, 1919, Rare Book and Manuscript Collection, Library of Congress, Washington, D.C.

"Exacting a Pound of Flesh That Lies Very Near the Heart." Political cartoon. *New York Tribune,* January 19, 1919, p. 1.

Harbach, Otto, and Wilson Collison. "Up in Mabel's Room." Unpublished manuscript, 1935, Rare Book and Manuscript Collection, Library of Congress, Washington, D.C.

Hopwood, Avery. "The Demi-Virgin." Unpublished manuscript, 1921, Rare Book and Manuscript Collection, Library of Congress, Washington, D.C.

———. "Fair and Warmer." Unpublished manuscript, 1915, Rare Book and Manuscript Collection, Library of Congress, Washington, D.C.

———. "The Gold Diggers." Unpublished manuscript, 1919, Rare Book and Manuscript Collection, Library of Congress, Washington, D.C.

Leitner, Paul E. "The Scene Designs of J. Woodman Thompson." Ph.D. diss., University of Nebraska, 1990.

O'Neill, Eugene. Letters to George C. Tyler [photocopies], 1920, William Seymour Theatre Collection, Department of Rare Books and Special Collections, Princeton University Libraries.

Sears, Zelda. "The Clinging Vine." Unpublished manuscript, 1922, Hargrett Rare Book and Manuscript Library, University of Georgia Libraries.

Tyler, George C. Letters to Eugene O'Neill [photocopies], 1920, William Seymour Theatre Collection, Department of Rare Books and Special Collections, Princeton University Libraries.

PUBLISHED PLAYS

Anderson, Maxwell, and Harold Hickerson. *Gods of the Lightning*. New York: Longmans, Green, 1928.

Anderson, Maxwell, and Laurence Stallings. *What Price Glory*. In *Three American Plays*. New York: Harcourt, Brace, 1926, pp. 5–89.

Andreyeff [Andreyev], Leonid. *The Life of Man*. In *Plays by Leonid Andreyeff*. New York: Charles Scribner's Sons, 1915, pp. 65–156.

Barry, Philip. *Holiday*. In *States of Grace*, ed. Brendan Gill. New York: Harcourt Brace Jovanovich, 1975, pp. 191–267.

———. *Paris Bound*. New York: Samuel French, 1929.

Behrman, S. N. *Meteor*. In *Three Plays*. New York: Farrar and Rinehart, 1934, pp. 115–236.

Benelli, Sem. *The Jest* [condensed version], trans. Edward Sheldon. In "'The Jest'—An Artistic Triumph." *Theatre Magazine*, June 1919, pp. 352–354.

Bennison, Louis. *Johnny Get Your Gun*. New York: Samuel French, 1927.

Bolton, Guy. *Polly Preferred*. New York: Samuel French, 1923.

Brooks, George S., and Walter B. Lister. *Spread Eagle*. New York: Charles Scribner's Sons, 1927.

Capek, Karl. *R.U.R.*, trans. Paul Selver and Nigel Playfair. In *A Treasury of the Theatre from Henrik Ibsen to Eugene Ionesco*, ed. John Gassner. New York: Simon and Schuster, 1963, pp. 411–433.

Connelly, Marc. *The Wisdom Tooth*. New York: Samuel French, n.d.

Crothers, Rachel. *He and She.* In *Representative American Plays,* ed. Arthur Hobson Quinn, 7th ed. New York: Appleton-Century-Crofts, 1953, pp. 896–928.

Dix, Beulah Marie. *Moloch* [fragment]. In *Theatre Magazine,* November 1915, pp. 230–231.

Dos Passos, John. *Airways, Inc.* New York: Macaulay, 1928.

Emery, Gilbert. *The Hero.* In *Contemporary American Plays,* ed. Arthur Hobson Quinn. New York: Charles Scribner's Sons, 1923, pp. 219–296.

Forbes, James. *The Famous Mrs. Fair.* In The Famous Mrs. Fair *and Other Plays.* New York: George H. Doran, 1920, pp. 203–290.

Glaspell, Susan. *The Inheritors.* London: Ernest Benn, 1924.

———. *The Verge.* Boston: Small, Maynard, 1922.

Gold, Michael. *Hoboken Blues.* In *The American Caravan,* ed. Van Wyck Brooks, Lewis Mumford, Alfred Kreymborg, Paul Rosenfeld. New York: Macaulay, 1927, pp. 548–626.

Hecht, Ben, and Charles MacArthur. *The Front Page.* London: Davis-Poynter, 1955.

Hoffman, Aaron. *Give and Take.* New York: Samuel French, 1926.

Hughes, Hatcher. *Hell-Bent fer Heaven.* New York: Harper and Brothers, 1924.

———. *Hell-Bent fer Heaven* [condensed, altered version]. In *Theatre Magazine,* July 1924, pp. 26, 28, 48, 50.

Kaiser, Georg. *From Morn to Midnight,* trans. Ashley Dukes. In *Twenty Best European Plays on the American Stage,* ed. John Gassner. New York: Crown, 1957, pp. 655–679.

Kaufman, George S., and Marc Connelly. *Beggar on Horseback.* London: Ernest Benn, 1925.

———. *Dulcy.* New York: Samuel French, 1923.

———. *To the Ladies!* In *Contemporary American Plays,* ed. Arthur Hobson Quinn. New York: Charles Scribner's Sons, 1923, pp. 297–376.

Kirchon, V., and A. Ouspensky. *Red Rust,* trans. Virginia Vernon and Frank Vernon. New York: Brentano's, 1930.

Laska, Edward. *We've Got to Have Money.* New York: Samuel French, 1926.

Lawson, John Howard. *The International.* New York: Macaulay, 1927.

———. *Loud Speaker.* New York: Macaulay, 1927.

———. *Processional.* In *Contemporary Drama: American Plays,* vol. 1, ed. E. Bradlee Watson and Benfield Pressey. New York: Charles Scribner's Sons, 1931, pp. 181–289.

———. *Roger Bloomer.* New York: Thomas Seltzer, 1923.

Millay, Edna St. Vincent. *Aria da Capo.* New York: Harper and Brothers, 1920.

Molnar, Ferenc. *Liliom,* trans. Benjamin Glazer. In *The Theatre Guild Anthology.* New York: Random House, 1936, pp. 115–172.

O'Neill, Eugene. *Desire Under the Elms.* New York: Boni and Liveright, 1925.

———. *Diff'rent.* In *Complete Plays, 1920–1931.* New York: Library of America, 1988, pp. 1–54.

———. *The Emperor Jones.* In *Complete Plays, 1913–1920.* New York: Library of America, 1988, pp. 1029–1061.

————. *The Great God Brown*. In The Great God Brown, The Fountain, The Moon of the Caribbees *and Other Plays*. New York: Boni and Liveright, 1926.

————. *The Hairy Ape*. In *The Hairy Ape, Anna Christie, The First Man*. New York: Boni and Liveright, 1922, pp. 1–87.

————. *In the Zone*. In *Complete Plays, 1913–1920*. New York: Library of America, 1988, pp. 469–488.

————. *Marco Millions*. New York: Boni and Liveright, 1927.

Pirandello, Luigi. *Six Characters in Search of an Author*, trans. Edward Storer. In *A Treasury of the Theatre [from Henrik Ibsen to Eugene Ionesco]*, ed. John Gassner. New York: Simon and Schuster, 1963, pp. 387–408.

Rice, Elmer. *The Adding Machine*. Garden City: Doubleday, Page, 1923.

————. *Street Scene*. In *Three Plays*. New York: Hill and Wang, 1965, pp. 63–157.

————. *The Subway*. New York: Samuel French, 1929.

Shipman, Samuel, and Aaron Hoffman. *Friendly Enemies*. New York: Samuel French, 1923.

Sifton, Paul. *The Belt*. New York: Macaulay, 1927.

Sinclair, Upton. *Singing Jailbirds*. Long Beach, Calif.: published by the author, 1924.

Stanley, Martha M., and Adelaide Matthews. *Nightie Night*. London: Samuel French, 1929.

Strindberg, August. *The Spook Sonata*. In *Plays by August Strindberg*, vol. 4, trans. Edwin Bjorkman. New York: Charles Scribner's Sons, 1916, pp. 101–148.

Synge, John Millington. *Riders to the Sea*. In *Contemporary Drama*, ed. E. Bradlee Watson and Benfield Pressey. New York: Charles Scribner's Sons, 1966, pp. 534–538.

Tarkington, Booth. *Clarence*. New York: Samuel French, 1921.

————. *Poldekin* [condensed version]. In "'Poldekin'—A Sunny Satire on Hearsay Bolshevism." *Current Opinion* 69 (October 1920): 481–488.

Toller, Ernst. *Man and the Masses*, trans. Louis Untermeyer. In *Contemporary Drama*, ed. E. Bradlee Watson and Benfield Pressey. New York: Charles Scribner's Sons, 1966, pp. 451–468.

Tolstoy, Leo. *The Power of Darkness*, trans. George Rapall Noyes and George Z. Patrick. In *Masterpieces of the Russian Drama*, vol. 2, ed. George Rapall Noyes. New York: Dover, 1961, pp. 547–623.

————. *Redemption*. In *Twenty Best European Plays on the American Stage*, ed. John Gassner. New York: Crown, 1957, pp. 708–733.

Treadwell, Sophie. *Machinal*. In *Plays by American Women: The Early Years*, ed. Judith E. Barlow. New York: Avon, 1981, pp. 243–328.

Vollmer, Lula. *Sun-Up*. In *Representative American Plays*, ed. Arthur Hobson Quinn, 7th ed. New York: Appleton-Century-Crofts, 1953, pp. 986–1009.

Wentworth, Marion Craig. *War Brides*. In *Century Magazine* 89 (February 1915): 527–544.

ARTICLES, REVIEWS, PUBLISHED INTERVIEWS

"Actors and Playwrights Unite to Battle Censor." *New York Daily News,* December 26, 1921, p. 2.

"'Adding Machine' Replaces Poor Zero." *New York Times,* March 20, 1923, p. 24.

"Admission Tax up to 20 Per Cent." *Variety,* January 17, 1919, p. 7.

"'Advertising of Kate' Full of Bright Lines." *New York Evening Journal,* May 9, 1922, p. 20.

"'Advertising of Kate' Play of Business Girl." *Journal of Commerce and Commercial Bulletin,* May 9, 1922, p. 5.

"After the Play" [*The Jest*]. *New Republic* 19 (May 10, 1919): 55.

"Again a Bedroom Farce" [*An Innocent Idea*]. *New York Times,* May 26, 1920, p. 9.

"A. H. Woods; Producer Was 81." *New York Times,* April 25, 1951, p. 29.

"A. H. Woods in a Tender Mood Toward Theatre." New York *Morning Telegraph,* August 14, 1921, sec. 4, pp. 1, 3.

"A. H. Woods Resigns from Association." New York *Sun,* December 8, 1921, p. 18.

"A. H. Woods's Trial Delayed." *New York Herald,* November 22, 1921, p. 15.

"All-Comedy Week Invites War Tax at Current Rates." *Washington Post,* January 19, 1919, sec. 2, p. 9.

"Al Woods Follows George M. Cohan in Quitting 'P.M.A.'" *New York Herald,* December 8, 1921, p. 12.

"'An American Ace' Takes the Casino." *New York Times,* April 3, 1918, p. 11.

Anderson, John. "Marching as to War," *Theatre Magazine,* March 1930, pp. 18–19, 64.

———. "Street Scene." *New York Evening Journal,* January 11, 1929. In *The Passionate Playgoer,* ed. George Oppenheimer, New York: Viking, 1958, pp. 564–567.

"Arbuckle Faces Probe in Death of an Actress." *New York American,* September 11, 1921, p. 1

"Arbuckle in Jail Accused of Murder." *New York Tribune,* September 12, 1921, p. 1.

"Arbuckle Is Held as Girl Guest Dies." *New York Tribune,* September 11, 1921, p. 1.

"Arbuckle Is Indicted for Girl's Death." *New York Tribune,* September 14, 1921, pp. 1, 6.

"Arrival of a New Stage in the Art of the Movies." *Current Opinion* 58 (April 1915): 251.

Asbury Bars Play by 'Demi-Virgin's' Author." *New York Herald,* December 2, 1921, p. 14.

"Asks for Jury Trial of 'Demi-Virgin' Case." *New York Herald,* December 6, 1921, p. 14.

Atkinson, J. Brooks. "Affairs of the West Side" [*Street Scene*]. *New York Times,* January 20, 1929, sec. 8, p. 1.

———. "Against the City Clatter" [*Machinal*]. *New York Times,* September 16, 1928, sec. 9, p. 1.

———. "Eva Le Gallienne as Hedda." *New York Times,* March 27, 1928, p. 30.

———. "Pioneer Traditions" [*The Inheritors*]. *New York Times,* March 20, 1927, sec. 8, p. 1.

————. "The Play" [*Carry On*]. *New York Times*, January 24, 1928, p. 26.

————. "The Play" [*The First Law*]. *New York Times*, May 7, 1929, p. 28.

————. "The Play" [*Head First*]. *New York Times*, January 7, 1926, p. 22.

————. "The Play" [*The Great God Brown*]. *New York Times*, January 30, 1926, p. 13.

————. "The Play" [*The Inheritors*]. *New York Times*, March 8, 1927, p. 23.

————. "The Play" [*Machinal*]. *New York Times*, September 8, 1928, p. 10.

————. "The Play" [*Spread Eagle*]. *New York Times*, April 5, 1927, p. 30.

————. "The Play" [*Three Sisters*]. *New York Times*, October 27, 1926, p. 24.

————. "Show-Folk Variously" [*Paris Bound*]. *New York Times*, January 8, 1928, sec. 8, p. 1.

————. "Spreading the Eagle" [*Spread Eagle*]. *New York Times*, April 10, 1927, sec. 8, p. 1.

————. "A Tragedy of Submission" [*Machinal*]. *New York Times*, September 8, 1928, p. 10.

————. "Troubles in the Crank Case" [*The Belt*]. *New York Times*, October 27, 1927, p. 33.

————. "Truth by Fantasy" [*Wisdom Tooth*]. *New York Times*, February 28, 1926, sec. 8, p. 1.

"Avery Hopwood Dies in the Sea." *New York Times*, July 2, 1928, p. 19.

"'A Bachelor's Night' Dull." *New York Times*, October 18, 1921, p. 20.

"Back to Methuselah." *New York Times*, March 7, 1922, p. 11.

"Barker's Season Happily Launched." *New York Times*, January 28, 1915, p. 9.

Bartlett. "The Girl in the Limousine." *Dramatic Mirror* 80 (October 16, 1919): 1610.

"Bedroom Farces Are Passé Declares Their Leading Producer." *Current Opinion* 73 (September 1922): 364.

"Bedroom Farce to the Limit" [*The Girl in the Limousine*]. *New York Times*, October 7, 1919, p. 22.

Behrman, S. N. "Napoleonism: 1929." *Three Plays*, New York: Farrar and Rinehart, 1934, pp. 111–113.

Bengels, Barbara. "'Read History': Dehumanization in Karel Capek's *R.U.R.*," *The Mechanical God: Machines in Science Fiction*, ed. Thomas P. Dunn and Richard D. Erlich, Westport, Conn.: Greenwood, 1982, pp. 13–17.

Ben-Zvi, Linda. "Susan Glaspell and Eugene O'Neill." *Eugene O'Neill Newsletter* (Summer–Fall 1982: 21–29.

"The Birth of a Nation." *Theatre Magazine*, April 1915, p. 212.

"Blind Guides." *The Freeman* 7 (May 2, 1923): 172.

Boleslawsky [Boleslavski], Richard. "The First Lesson in Acting: A Pseudo-Morality." *Theatre Arts* 7 (October 1923): 284–292.

————. "The Laboratory Theatre." *Theatre Arts* 7 (July 1923): 244–250.

Brady, William A. "Motion Picture Competition Is Deadly, Says Mr. Brady." *Theatre Magazine*, December 1915, pp. 310, 324.

"Brands 'Demi-Virgin' 'Coarsely Indecent.'" *New York Evening Post*, November 5, 1921, p. 9.

Breffort-Blessing, Juliette. "*Washington, Action Dramatique*: Jacques Copeau's Tribute to Franco-American Friendship," *Theatre Survey* 30 (May and November 1989): 147–153.

"Broad Humor in New Farce" [*Parlor, Bedroom and Bath*]. *New York Times*, December 25, 1917, p. 6.

"Broadway and Mr. Kitchin." *The World*, January 17, 1919, p. 10.

Brock, H. I. "American Dance of Life Rhymed to Jazz" [*Processional*]. *New York Times*, February 1, 1925, sec. 4, p. 18.

Broun, Heywood. "Drama" [*Up in Mabel's Room*]. *New York Tribune*, January 16, 1919, p. 11.

———. "New Woods' Farce Fails to Shock Anybody Much" [*Getting Gertie's Garter*]. *New York Tribune*, August 2, 1921, p. 6.

———. "Protest Against Law Which Threatens Drama." *New York Tribune*, January 19, 1919, sec. 5, p. 2.

———. "What Price Glory." *The World*, September 6, 1924.

Brown, John Mason. "Escapes from a Formula." *Theatre Arts* 11 (January 1927): 9–22.

———. "The Merry Month of May" [*Spread Eagle*]. *Theatre Arts* 11 (June 1927): 401–413.

———. "Sermons in Plays" [*The Belt*]. *Theatre Arts* 11 (December 1927): 893–908.

———. "This Bad Showmanship" [*The Inheritors*]. *Theatre Arts* 11 (May 1927): 325–335.

Budd, Mike. "Modernism and the Representation of Fantasy: Cubism and Expressionism in *The Cabinet of Dr. Caligari*." In *Forms of the Fantastic*. New York: Greenwood, 1986, pp. 15–21.

———. "The Moments of *Caligari*." In *The Cabinet of Dr. Caligari: Texts, Contexts, Histories*, ed. Mike Budd. New Brunswick: Rutgers University Press, 1990, pp. 7–120.

"'By Pigeon Post' Arrives." *New York Times*, November 26, 1918, p. 13.

Bywaters, Barbara L. "Marriage, Madness, and Murder in Sophie Treadwell's *Machinal*." In *Modern American Drama: The Female Canon*, ed. June Schlueter. Rutherford, N.J.: Fairleigh Dickinson University Press, 1990, pp. 97–110.

"Canvass Shows Ticket Tax Will Not Be Raised." *Morning Telegraph*, January 21, 1919, p. 1.

Castellun, Maida. "The Stage" [*The Demi-Virgin*]. *New York Call*, October 21, 1921, p. 4.

"Censorship from Within Proposed for Theaters." *New York Tribune*, December 24, 1921, p. 4.

"Chantecler." *New York Times*, January 24, 1911, p. 9.

"Charles Frohman Lost on the Lusitania." *Theatre Magazine*, June 1915, pp. 284–285.

Chase, Canon William Sheafe, and Channing Pollock. "Shall We Have a Censorship of the Theatre in America?" *Theatre Magazine*, July 1922, pp. 10–11, 58, 60.

Cheney, Sheldon. "Sam Hume's Adaptable Settings," *Theatre Arts* 1 (May 1917): 119–127.

———. "Why We Are Moving," *Theatre Arts* 2 (December 1917): 49–50.

"The Cherry Orchard." *New York Times*, October 16, 1928, p. 28.

"Comedy of Business Type" [*We've Got to Have Money*]. *New York Times*, August 21, 1923, p. 12.

"Complain of 'Demi-Virgin.'" *New York Times*, November 3, 1921, p. 22.

"Conferees at Odds over Profits Taxes." *New York Times*, January 18, 1919, p. 13.

"Congress Yields to Demand to Kill New Theatre Tax." *Morning Telegraph*, January 23, 1919, p. 1.

Corbin, John. "Among the New Plays" [*Beggar on Horseback*]. *New York Times*, February 17, 1924, sec. 7, p. 1.

———. "Clinging Vine." *New York Times*, December 31, 1922, sec. 7, p. 1.

———. "Drama" [*The Jest*]. *New York Times*, April 10, 1919, p. 9.

———. "Drama" [*A Sleepless Night*]. *New York Times*, February 25, 1919, p. 9.

———. "English Laughter." *New York Times*, January 6, 1918, sec. 4, p. 8.

———. "Hamlet Without the Play." *New York Times*, November 26, 1922, sec. 8, p. 1.

———. "The Hyphen in Our Midst." *New York Times*, August 11, 1918, sec. 3, p. 6.

———. "Jazzed Expressionism." *New York Times*, February 13, 1924, p. 17.

———. "The Jest." *New York Times*, April 27, 1919, sec. 4, p. 2.

———. "'The Miracle,' Fine Spectacle, Shown." *New York Times*, January 16, 1924, p. 17.

———. "Moscow and Broadway." *New York Times*, January 28, 1923, sec. 7, p. 1.

———. "The New Stagecraft." *New York Times*, October 20, 1918, sec. 4, p. 2.

———. "The Play" [*Cheaper to Marry*]. *New York Times*, April 16, 1924, p. 26.

———. "The Play" [*Hamlet*]. *New York Times*, November 17, 1922, p. 14.

———. "The Play" [*R.U.R.*]. *New York Times*, October 10, 1922, p. 16.

———. "The Play" [*Spook Sonata*]. *New York Times*, January 7, 1924, p. 23.

———. "The Play" [*You and I*]. *New York Times*, February 27, 1923, p. 14.

———. "The Revolt Against Civilization" [*R.U.R.*]. *New York Times*, October 15, 1922, sec. 8, p. 1.

———. "A Tragedy Revised." *New York Times*, September 9, 1923, sec. 7, p. 1.

———. "Tsar Fyodor Ivanovitch." *New York Times*, January 9, 1923, p. 26.

———. "The War Well Lost." *New York Times*, December 8, 1918, sec. 7, p. 6.

"Court Gives Three Days' Life to 'Demi-Virgin.'" *New York Herald*, November 26, 1921, p. 9.

"Court Holds Arbuckle as Girl's Slayer." *New York Tribune*, September 13, 1921, p. 1.

Coward, Edward Fales. "Barker's New Shakespearean Spectacles." *Theatre Magazine*, April 1915, pp. 196–198, 203.

Cowl, Jane. "Sex on the Stage." *Theatre Magazine*, April 1919, p. 210.

Crane, Frank. "The Theatre in War Time." *Theatre Magazine*, September 1917, p. 119.

Cumberland, John. "My Escape from the Bedroom Plays." *Theatre Magazine*, December 1926, pp. 9, 56.

Dale, Alan. "Cast in Farce at Republic Kept Busy Hiding" [*Getting Gertie's Garter*]. *New York American*, August 2, 1921, p. 7.

————. "'The Demi-Virgin' Presented at Times Square." *New York American,* October 19, 1921, p. 8.

————. "Profanity on the Stage." *Theatre Magazine,* May 1916, pp. 279–282.

Dawn, Hazel. "Naughty Parts in Naughty Plays." *Theatre Magazine,* May 1919, pp. 278, 280.

De Foe, Louis V. "Drama" [*The Demi-Virgin*]. New York *World,* October 20, 1921, p. 11.

————. "Personal Triumphs of the Season" [*His Bridal Night*]. *Green Book,* April 1916, p. 691.

"'The Demi-Virgin.' *Dramatic Mirror* 84 (October 22, 1921): 593.

"The Demi-Virgin." *New York Times,* October 19, 1921, p. 22.

"'Demi-Virgin' Bad, Is Ruling Holding Woods for Trial." New York *World,* November 15, 1921, p. 11.

"'Demi-Virgin' Case Delayed." *New York Herald,* November 4, 1921, p. 15.

"'Demi-Virgin' Case Dropped." *New York Tribune,* December 24, 1921, p. 4.

"'Demi-Virgin' Case Goes Over." *New York Herald,* December 3, 1921, p. 11.

"'Demi-Virgin' Closing." New York *Morning Telegraph,* June 1, 1922, p. 4.

"'Demi-Virgin' Dirty." *Variety,* November 4, 1921, p. 12.

"'Demi-Virgin' Faces Trial." *New York Tribune,* November 3, 1921, p. 10.

"'The Demi-Virgin' Farce Is Usually Dull, Always Vulgar." *New York Herald,* October 19, 1921, p. 9.

"'Demi-Virgin' Far from Virtuous; Woods Held for Trial." *New York Evening Journal,* November 15, 1921, p. 18.

"'Demi-Virgin' Gets Reprieve." *New York Times,* November 26, 1921, p. 18.

"'Demi-Virgin' Goes on Playing with Injunction." *New York Daily News,* November 26, 1921, p. 17.

"'Demi-Virgin' Is Too Risqué for Broadway." *New York Tribune,* November 15, 1921, p. 7.

"'Demi-Virgin' Must Be Closed To-Night." *New York Herald,* November 24, 1921, p. 16.

"'Demi-Virgin' Reprieved at Request of Counsel." *New York Tribune,* November 4, 1921, p. 10.

"'Demi-Virgin' Semi-Naughty When Censor Stopped Looking." *New York Tribune,* November 8, 1921, p. 9.

"'Demi-Virgin' Storm Grows in Broadway." *New York Herald,* November 15, 1921, p. 8.

"'Demi-Virgin' to Be Kept on to Test Law." *New York Herald,* November 25, 1921, p. 10.

"'Demi-Virgin' Too Naughty for Broadway, Court Rules." *New York Daily News,* November 15, 1921, p. 19.

"'Demi-Virgin' Trial May Mean Prison Term, Says Swann." *New York Herald,* November 18, 1921, p. 12.

"'Devil's Garden' a Sombre Drama." *New York Times,* December 29, 1915, p. 11.

Dickinson, Thomas H. "The Paradox of the Timely Play." *Theatre Arts* 8 (November 1924): 724.

Dietrich, Margaret. "Music and Dance in the Productions of Max Reinhardt." In *Total Theatre*, ed. E. T. Kirby. New York: E. P. Dutton, 1969, pp. 162–174.

"Divorce Theme in Farce" [*What's Your Husband Doing?*]. *New York Times*, November 13, 1917, p. 11.

"The Dolly Sisters in a Frisky Farce" [*His Bridal Night*]. *New York Times*, August 17, 1916, p. 9.

"The Double Tax on Theatre Tickets." *Brooklyn Daily Eagle*, January 18, 1919, p. 6.

"Double Tax Their Doom, Theatre Managers Assert." *New York Herald*, January 16, 1919, sec. 2, p. 7.

"Drama" [*The Jest*] *Nation* 108 (May 24, 1919): 843.

"Drop Tax Increase on Theatres." *Brooklyn Daily Eagle*, January 22, 1919, p. 1.

Dwight, Homer. "Like a King." *Dramatic Mirror* 84 (October 8, 1921): 520.

Dymkowski, Christine. "On the Edge: The Plays of Susan Glaspell." *Modern Drama* 31 (March 1988): 91–105.

Eaton, Walter Prichard. "American Producers: II. Arthur Hopkins." *Theatre Arts* 5 (July 1921): 230–236.

————. "Realistic Drama and the Experimental Theatre." *Theatre Arts* 2 (December 1917): 18–20.

Eliot, Samuel A., Jr. "Le Théâtre du Vieux Colombier." *Theatre Arts* 3 (January 1919): 25–30.

Elita. "The Girl with the Carmine Lips." *Dramatic Mirror* 82 (August 14, 1920): 277.

"Entire Nation Protests Theatre Tax Increase." *Morning Telegraph*, January 18, 1919, pp. 1–2.

"Extravagant Farce by Avery Hopwood" [*Sadie Love*]. *New York Times*, November 30, 1915, p. 13.

"Fair and Warmer." *Dramatic Mirror* 74 (November 13, 1915): 8.

"'Fair and Warmer' Is Highly Diverting." *New York Times*, November 8, 1915, p. 13.

"Fatty Arbuckle Dies in His Sleep." *New York Times*, June 30, 1933, p. 17.

"Fighting a Vicious Film: Protest Against *The Birth of a Nation*." In *Focus on D. W. Griffith*, ed. Harry M. Geduld. Englewood Cliffs, N.J.: Prentice-Hall, 1971, pp. 94–102.

"Fighting Bolshevism with the Bible." *Theatre Magazine*, February 1920, pp. 84, 136.

"Fight Theater Tax Bill." *Dramatic Mirror* 76 (July 29, 1916): 7.

"Film Comedian Is Locked up Without Bail; Will Not Talk." *New York American*, September 12, 1921, p. 1.

"The First Nighter" [*Moloch*]. *Dramatic Mirror* 74 (September 22, 1915): 8.

———— [*Passing Show of 1916*]. *Dramatic Mirror* 76 (July 1, 1916): 8.

"First Week of War Tax Shows Bad Effect upon Theater Business." *Dramatic Mirror*, November 17, 1917, pp. 3–4.

"Five More for Mr. Woods." *New York Times*, December 4, 1921, sec. 7, p. 1.

"Florence Moore All Evening." *New York Times*, February 4, 1920, p. 12.

"Foreword." *Theatre Arts* 1 (November 1916): 1.

"Les Fourberies de Scapin." *New York Times*, November 28, 1917, p. 11.

France, Rachel. "Apropos of Women and the Folk Play." In *Women in American Theatre*, ed. Helen Krich Chinoy and Linda Walsh Jenkins. New York: TCG, 1987, pp. 145–152.

Fred. "The Demi-Virgin." *Variety*, October 21, 1921, pp. 16–17.

"French in Emotional Play." *New York Times*, January 24, 1918, p. 7.

G. F. P. "Moloch: A Play About War." *Harper's Weekly*, July 17, 1915, p. 57.

Gainor, J. Ellen. "A Stage of Her Own: Susan Glaspell's *The Verge* and Women's Dramaturgy." *Journal of American Drama and Theatre* 1 (Spring 1989): 79–99.

"'Gertie's Garter' Got at Republic." *Morning Telegraph*, August 2, 1921, p. 14.

"Gertie's Garter Sought for in Vain." *New York Evening Journal*, August 2, 1921, p. 8.

"'Getting Gertie's Garter' Has Few Novel Situations." *New York Herald*, August 2, 1921, p. 7.

"'Getting Gertie's Garter' Presented by A. H. Woods." *The World*, August 2, 1921, p. 9.

Gilbert, Sandra M. "Soldier's Heart: Literary Men, Literary Women, and the Great War." In *Behind the Lines: Gender and the Two World Wars*, ed. Margaret Randolph Higonnet et al.. New Haven: Yale University Press, 1987, pp. 197–226.

"'Girl in the Limousine' Gay Farce." *New York Evening Journal*, October 9, 1919, p. 21.

"'Give and Take' Unreal." *New York Times*, January 19, 1923, p. 13.

Goff, Lewin. "The Owen Davis-Al Woods Melodrama Factory." *Educational Theatre Journal* 11 (October 1959): 200–207.

Gordon, Linda. "Birth Control and Social Revolution." In *A Heritage of Her Own*, ed. Nancy F. Cott and Elizabeth H. Pleck. New York: Simon and Schuster, 1979, pp. 445–475.

"Gossip on the Rialto." *New York Times*, November 13, 1921, sec. 6, p. 1.

Gotthold, Rozel. "Smartness in Stage Settings." *Theatre Magazine*, February 1916, pp. 82–83.

Gottlieb, Lois C. "The Antibusiness Theme in Late Nineteenth Century American Drama." *Quarterly Journal of Speech* 64 (1978): 415–426.

"Government Orders Play Closed." *Dramatic Mirror* 78 (April 6, 1918): 4.

Granville-Barker, Harley. "Two German Theatres," *Fortnightly Review* 89 (January 1911): 60–70.

"Granville Barker, the New Art of the Theatre and the New Drama." *American Review of Reviews*, April 1915, p. 498.

Gray, Paul. "Stanislavski and America: A Critical Chronology." *Tulane Drama Review* 9 (Winter 1964): 21–60.

"The Great Power." *New York Times*, September 12, 1928, p. 25.

"Great Scott." *Theatre Magazine*, November 1929, p. 47.

"'Great Scott!' Proves a Baffling Comedy." *New York Times*, September 3, 1929, p. 25.

Hackett, Francis [signed F. H.]. "After the Play" [*Out There*]. *New Republic* 10 (April 14, 1917): 325.

———. "Granville Barker in New York." *New Republic* 1 (January 30, 1915): 25.

Hamilton, Clayton. "The Decorative Drama" [*Sumurun*]. *Bookman,* April 1912, p. 167.

Hammond, Percy. "The New Play" [*The Demi-Virgin*]. *New York Tribune,* October 19, 1921, p. 8.

Hartley, Marsden. "The Reinhardt Machine." In *Max Reinhardt and His Theatre,* ed. Oliver M. Sayler. New York: Brentano's, 1924, pp. 89–97.

"Hazel Dawn's Start on the Stage at 17." *Pittsburgh Post,* September 25, 1921, p. 6.

"Heard on Broadway." *Theatre Magazine,* March 1922, p. 174.

Helburn, Theresa. "O'Neill: An Impression." *Saturday Review,* November 21, 1936, p. 10.

"The Hero." *New York Times,* September 6, 1921, p. 13.

"His Bridal Night." *Dramatic Mirror* 76 (August 26, 1916): 8.

———. *Theatre Magazine,* September 1916, p. 140.

Hodge, Francis. "European Influences on American Theatre: 1700–1969." In *The American Theatre: A Sum of Its Parts.* New York: Samuel French, 1971, pp. 3–22.

"Holiday." *New York Times,* November 27, 1928, p. 36.

———. *Theatre Magazine,* February 1929, p. 78.

"Hollywood Life Depicted in a Play" [*The Demi-Virgin*]. *New York Evening Journal,* October 19, 1921, p. 16.

Hopkins, Arthur. "The Approaching 'Macbeth.'" *New York Times,* February 6, 1921, sec. 6, p. 1.

———. "Brain Plays in Germany." *Harper's Weekly,* September 13, 1913, p. 25.

———. "Capturing the Audience." In *Directors on Directing,* ed. Toby Cole and Helen Krich Chinoy. Indianapolis: Bobbs-Merrill, 1963, pp. 205–213.

———. "Foreign Lessons to American Playwrights." *Harper's Weekly,* August 30, 1913, p. 15.

———. "Hearing a Play with My Eyes." *Harper's Weekly,* August 23, 1913, p. 13.

"Hopwood Writes a High Moral Farce" [*Double Exposure*]. *New York Times,* August 28, 1918, p. 5.

Hornblow, Arthur. "The Adding Machine." *Theatre Magazine,* May 1923, p. 19.

———. "Back to Methuselah." *Theatre Magazine,* May 1922, pp. 305–306.

———. "Crooked Gamblers." *Theatre Magazine,* October 1920, pp. 187–188.

———. "The Devil's Garden." *Theatre Magazine,* February 1916, p. 65.

———. "Dulcy." *Theatre Magazine,* October 1921, p. 234.

———. "The Famous Mrs. Fair." *Theatre Magazine,* February 1920, p. 98.

———. "Friendly Enemies." *Theatre Magazine,* September 1918, p. 143.

———. "Garden." *Theatre Magazine,* May 1917, p. 280.

———. "Hamlet." *Theatre Magazine,* January 1923, p. 21.

———. "He and She." *Theatre Magazine,* April 1920, p. 270.

———. "Helen of Troy, N.Y." *Theatre Magazine,* August 1923, p. 15.

———. "The Hero." *Theatre Magazine,* May 1921, p. 370.

———. "Her Soldier Boy." *Theatre Magazine,* January 1917, p. 24.

———. "Johannes Kreisler." *Theatre Magazine,* February 1923, pp. 15–16.

————. "Johnny Get Your Gun." *Theatre Magazine,* April 1917, p. 216.

————. "Ladies' Night." *Theatre Magazine,* October 1920, p. 186.

————. "The Life of Man." *Theatre Magazine,* March 1917, p. 149.

————. "Like a King." *Theatre Magazine,* December 1921, p. 424.

————. "Macbeth." *Theatre Magazine,* April 1921, p. 298.

————. "Man and the Masses." *Theatre Magazine,* June 1924, p. 15.

————. "The Moscow Art Theatre." *Theatre Magazine,* March 1923, pp. 15–16.

————. "Mr. Hornblow Goes to the Play." *Theatre Magazine,* October 1921, pp. 233–234.

————. "Night Lodging." *Theatre Magazine,* February 1920, pp. 100–101.

————. "La Nuit des rois." *Theatre Magazine,* February 1918, pp. 86–87.

————. "The Power of Darkness." *Theatre Magazine,* March 1920, p. 184.

————. "Redemption." *Theatre Magazine,* November 1918, p. 277.

————. "The Red Lamp in the Theatre." *Theatre Magazine,* March 1922, p. 142.

————. "Richard III." *Theatre Magazine,* April 1920, pp. 310, 312.

————. "Six Characters in Search of an Author." *Theatre Magazine,* January 1923, p. 23.

————. "Théâtre du Vieux Colombier." *Theatre Magazine,* January 1918, p. 21.

————. "To the Ladies." *Theatre Magazine,* May 1922, pp. 307–308.

————. "Up in Mabel's Room." *Theatre Magazine,* March 1919, p. 142.

————. "Watch Your Neighbor." *Theatre Magazine,* October 1918, p. 210.

————. "What Price Glory." *Theatre Magazine,* November 1924, p. 15.

"Housecleaning the Theater." *Literary Digest,* March 25, 1922, p. 27.

"Increase Theater Tax." *Dramatic Mirror* 76 (July 7, 1916): 7.

"Indictment for Manslaughter Is Handed in Against Actor." *New York American,* September 14, 1921, p. 1.

"Inside Stuff." *Variety,* October 21, 1921, p. 12.

"The International." *New York Times,* January 16, 1928, p. 24.

"Intimate Farce, Oh, Very! Is 'Up in Mabel's Room.'" *New York Herald,* January 16, 1919, sec. 2, p. 7.

"Invoke President on Theatre Taxes." *New York Times,* January 16, 1919, p. 11.

"The Irish Players in New York." *The Outlook,* December 2, 1911, p. 801.

"Irish Players in Sad Play." *New York Times,* December 5, 1911, p. 9.

Isaacson, Charles D. "Is Radio an Enemy of the Theatre?" *Theatre Magazine,* January 1923, pp. 15, 58.

"Is the Undraped Drama Unmoral?" *Theatre Magazine,* January 1921, p. 6.

"Jacques Copeau and His Theatre." *Theatre Magazine,* December 1917, p. 342.

"Jazzing up Shakespeare." *Current Opinion* 70 (April 1920): 499.

"'Johannes Kreisler'—An Ingenious Nightmare in Forty-Two Scenes." *Theatre Magazine,* March 1923, p. 17.

"'Johannes Kreisler,' a Scenic Novelty." *New York Times,* December 25, 1922, p. 20.

"John Barrymore in Tolstoy Tragedy." *New York Times,* October 4, 1918, p. 11.

"Jury O.K.'s 'Demi-Virgin.'" *New York Herald,* December 24, 1921, p. 8.

"Jury to Try Al H. Woods." *New York Times,* December 13, 1921, p. 24.

Kaufman, S. Jay. "Getting Gertie's Garter." Dramatic Mirror 84 (August 6, 1921): 193.

"Kitchin Fights for Profits Taxes." *New York Times,* January 17, 1919, p. 5.

Klauber, Adolph. "Plays for Children and Grown-ups" [*Poor Little Rich Girl*]. *New York Times,* January 26, 1913, sec. 7, p. 6.

Klaw, Marc. "The Tax on Theatre Tickets." *Theatre Magazine,* November 1917, pp. 263, 310.

Krutch, Joseph Wood. "The Tragedy of Masks" [*The Great God Brown*]. *Nation* 122 (February 10, 1926): 164.

———. "The Troupers of Fourteenth Street." *Theatre Magazine,* January 1930, pp. 28–29, 70.

Leamy, Hugh. "Nice Clean Dirt." *Colliers,* September 10, 1927, pp. 12, 44–45.

Le Gallienne, Eva. "My Adventures in Repertory." *Theatre Magazine,* April 1927, pp. 12, 52B.

"Letters and Art" [*Sumurun*]. *Literary Digest,* February 3, 1912, p. 211.

Lewisohn, Ludwig. "Drama" [*From Morn to Midnight*]. *Nation* 114 (June 14, 1922): 726.

———. "Drama" [*The Inheritors*]. *Nation* 112 (April 6, 1921): 515.

———. "Drama" [*Johannes Kreisler*]. *Nation* 116 (January 10, 1923): 48.

———. "Drama" [*Liliom*]. *Nation* 112 (May 11, 1921): 695.

———. "Drama" [*The Verge*]. *Nation* 113 (December 14, 1921): 708–709.

"'The Life of Man' Well Presented." *New York Times,* January 15, 1917, p. 7.

Littell, Robert. "Brighter Lights" [*Street Scene*]. *Theatre Arts* 13 (March 1929): 164–176.

———. "Chiefly About 'Machinal.'" *Theatre Arts* 12 (November 1928): 774–782.

———. "Front and Inside Pages" [*The Front Page*]. *Theatre Arts* 12 (October 1928): 701–708.

———. "Potpourri" [*Holiday*]. *Theatre Arts* 13 (February 1929): 84–96.

———. "Processional." *New Republic* 41 (January 28, 1925): 261.

———. "Where Are the New Playwrights?" [*Gods of the Lightning*]. *Theatre Arts* 13 (January 1929): 10–22.

Locke, Alain. "The Drama of Negro Life." *Theatre Arts* 10 (October 1926): 701–706.

———. "The Negro and the American Stage." *Theatre Arts* 10 (January 1926): 112–120.

"Lovely Fantasy on New Theatre Stage" [*The Blue Bird*]. *New York Times,* October 2, 1910, p. 13.

"Lowering Theatre Standards," *New York Herald,* November 17, 1921, p. 10.

Lynch, Gertrude. "Sumurun." *Theatre Magazine,* February 1912, p. 54.

McAdoo, William. "The Theater and the Law." *Saturday Evening Post,* January 28, 1922, pp. 6–7, 44, 47, 49, 51.

McElliott. "Farceurs Might Consult Blasé London Busman" [*Getting Gertie's Garter*]. *New York Daily News,* August 2, 1921, p. 15.

Macgowan, Kenneth. "America's Best Season in the Theatre." *Theatre Arts* 4 (April 1920): 91–104.

———. "America's First Exhibition of the New Stagecraft." *Theatre Magazine*, January 1915, p. 28.

———. "And Again Repertory" [*Hamlet*]. *Theatre Arts* 7 (April 1923): 89–104.

———. "Broadway at the Spring" [*The Hairy Ape*]. *Theatre Arts* 6 (July 1922): 179–183.

———. "Broadway Bows to By-Ways" [*The Inheritors*]. *Theatre Arts* 5 (July 1921): 175–183.

———. "The Centre of the Stage" [*Macbeth*]. *Theatre Arts* 5 (April 1921): 91–106.

———. "Crying the Bounds of Broadway" [*Man and the Masses*]. *Theatre Arts* 8 (June 1924): 355–362.

———. "Diadems and Fagots on Broadway" [*R.U.R.*]. *Theatre Arts* 7 (January 1923): 3–12.

———. "Experiment on Broadway" [*Adding Machine*]. *Theatre Arts* 7 (July 1923): 175–185.

———. "From the Four Corners of American Art" [*Beggar on Horseback*]. *Theatre Arts* 8 (April 1924): 215–228.

———. "A Mystical Month on Broadway" [*The Spook Sonata*]. *Theatre Arts* 8 (March 1924): 145–154.

———. "The New Path of the Theatre," *Theatre Arts* 3 (April 1919): 84–90.

———. "The New Play" [*A Bachelor's Night*]. *The Globe and Commercial Advertiser*, October 19, 1921, p. 16.

———. "The New Play" [*Getting Gertie's Garter*]. *The Globe and Commercial Advertiser*, August 2, 1921, p. 12.

———. "Peace Comes to Broadway." *Theatre Arts* 3 (July 1919): 151–159.

———. "Peace Departs from Broadway" [*Clarence*]. *Theatre Arts* 3 (October 1919): 231–238.

———. "The Portrait of a Season." *Theatre Arts* 6 (April 1922): 91–106.

———. "Repertory and the Broadway Season" [*Redemption*]. *Theatre Arts* 3 (January 1919): 19–21.

———. "Year's End" [*The Hero*]. *Theatre Arts* 6 (January 1922): 3–10.

"'Made in America' Shown." *New York Times*, October 15, 1925, p. 27.

"Managers Fight Increase of Tax." *Morning Telegraph*, January 16, 1919, pp. 1–2.

"Managers Halt New Show Plans; 60,000 Affected." *Morning Telegraph*, January 21, 1919, p. 1.

"Managers Move to Cleanse Stage and Avoid Censor." *New York Herald*, November 19, 1921, p. 10.

"Managers See Victory Ahead in Fight on Tax." *Morning Telegraph*, January 22, 1919, p. 1.

"Managers to Fight Bill." *Dramatic Mirror* 76 (July 15, 1916): 7.

Mantle, Burns. "Up in Mabel's Room." *Dramatic Mirror* 80 (February 8, 1919): 196.

Marsh, Leo A. "'Gertie's Garter' Got at Republic." *Morning Telegraph*, August 3, 1921, p. 5.

Martin, John J. "The Challenge." *Dramatic Mirror* 80 (August 14, 1919): 1243.

———. "Liliom." *Dramatic Mirror* 83 (April 30, 1921): 733.

———. "Opportunity." *Dramatic Mirror* 82 (August 7, 1920): 229.

———. "Scrambled Wives." *Dramatic Mirror* 82 (August 14, 1920): 277.

"May Drop 75 New Plays." *The Sun*, January 21, 1919, p. 7.

Mazer, Cary M. "Finders Keepers: Recent Scholarship on Granville Barker," *Nineteenth-Century Theatre* 15 (Summer 1987): 34–49.

Metcalfe, James. "Redemption." *Life*, October 17, 1918. In *Selected Theatre Criticism*. Volume 1: *1900–1919*, ed. Anthony Slide. Metuchen: Scarecrow, 1985, p. 235.

"A Midsummer Night's Dream." *New York Times*, February 17, 1915, p. 11.

Miles, Carlton. "Pump-and-Tub Drama" [*Beyond*]. *Theatre Arts* 9 (April 1925): 213–224.

"Mill Girl Heroine in New Dance Show." *New York Times*, June 20, 1923, p. 22.

Minden, Michael. "Politics and the Silent Cinema: *The Cabinet of Dr Caligari* and *Battleship Potemkin*." In *Visions and Blueprints*, ed. Edward Timms and Peter Collier. Manchester: Manchester University Press, 1988, pp. 287–306.

"Mme. Nazimova in 'War Brides.'" *Theatre Magazine*, March 1915, pp. 116–117, 147.

Moderwell, Hiram Kelly. "The Art of Robert Edmond Jones," *Theatre Arts* 1 (February 1917): 51–61.

"Moloch: A Play of Purposeful Horror." *Independent* 84 (October 4, 1915): 18.

"'Morn to Midnight' at the Frazee." *New York Times*, June 27, 1922, p. 16.

"Movie Life in New Play" [*Johnny Get Your Gun*]. *New York Times*, February 13, 1917, p. 9.

"Mr. Flamma's Fling" [*The Mask of Hamlet*]. *New York Times*, August 23, 1921, p. 10.

"Mr. Kitchin Chief Champion of the Double Theatre Tax." *New York Herald*, January 19, 1919, sec. 1, p. 14.

"Music and Drama" [*The Demi-Virgin*]. *The Sun*, October 19, 1921, p. 16.

"A Naked Challenge." *Nation* 117 (September 5, 1923): 229.

"New Arbuckle Case Sensation Hinted." *New York American*, November 2, 1921, p. 1.

"New Attractions for New York Theatregoers" [*An American Ace*]. *Dramatic Mirror* 77 (April 13, 1918): 509.

"New Comedy Seen at Ritz Theatre" [*The Advertising of Kate*]. *Morning Telegraph*, May 9, 1922, p. 14.

"New Farce Makes Audience Laugh" [*Up in Mabel's Room*]. *The Sun*, January 16, 1919, p. 7.

"The New Play" [*Up in Mabel's Room*]. *The Globe and Commercial Advertiser*, January 16, 1919, p. 14.

"The New Plays" [*The Man Who Married a Dumb Wife*]. *Theatre Magazine*, March 1915, pp. 110–111.

"New Risqué Farce Rapid and Noisy" [*Getting Gertie's Garter*]. *New York Times*, August 2, 1921, p. 16.

"News and Gossip of the Rialto." *New York Times*, October 2, 1921, sec. 7, p. 1.

"News in the Theatres." *New York Commercial,* January 16, 1919, p. 2.

"New War Drama Deeply Impressive" [*Moloch*]. *New York Times,* September 21, 1915, p. 11.

"New York Cheers 'Yip, Yip, Yaphank.'" *Theatre Magazine,* October 1918, p. 222.

"The New York Season," *Theatre Arts* 3 (April 1919): 131–134.

"New York Sees Diaghileff's Ballets Russes," *Theatre Magazine,* March 1916, pp. 128, 164.

"Next Week in the Theatres." *Pittsburgh Post,* September 18, 1921, sec. 6, p. 7.

Niblo, Fred. "New O'Neill Play Sinks to Depths" [*Desire Under the Elms*]. *Morning Telegraph,* November 13, 1924, p. 3.

"'Nightie Night' Is Amusing." *New York Times,* September 10, 1919, p. 16.

"Note on the Illustrations," *Theatre Arts* 1 (November 1916): 20.

"Notes of the Stage." *New York Herald,* June 1, 1922, p. 10.

"Old Tax Restored on Show Tickets." *Washington Post,* January 23, 1919, p. 3.

"One-Act Plays" [*Across the Border*]. *Theatre Magazine,* January 1915, p. 44.

O'Neill, Eugene. "Memoranda on Masks." In *O'Neill and His Plays,* ed. Oscar Cargill. New York: New York University Press, 1961, pp. 116–118.

————. "The Playwright Explains." *New York Times,* February 14, 1926, sec. 8, p. 2.

"1,500,000 Sign Protest of Tax; One State Acts." *Morning Telegraph,* January 19, 1919, p. 1.

"On the Pittsburgh Stage." *Pittsburgh Post,* September 27, 1921, p. 9.

"'Open House' a Naive Play." *New York Times,* December 15, 1925, p. 28.

"Our Little Wife." *Dramatic Mirror* 76 (November 25, 1916): 7.

"'Out There' Proves Most Appealing." *New York Times,* March 28, 1917, p. 11.

"Overtaxing the Theatre." *New York Globe,* January 17, 1919, p. 14.

"'Over the Top' a Nine O'Clock Show." *New York Times,* December 3, 1917, p. 11.

"'Over the Top' Opens New York's First Nine O'Clock Theatre." *Theatre Magazine,* February 1918, p. 89.

Ozieblo, Barbara. "Rebellion and Rejection: The Plays of Susan Glaspell." In *Modern American Drama: The Female Canon,* ed. June Schlueter. Rutherford, N.J.: Fairleigh Dickinson University Press, 1990, pp. 66–76.

Parker, Dorothy, "The Jest," *Vanity Fair,* June 1919. In *The Passionate Playgoer,* ed. George Oppenheimer. New York: Viking, 1958, pp. 550–553.

Parker, Robert Allerton. "Drama" [*Back to Methuselah*]. *Independent* 108 (March 25, 1922): 310.

"Parlor, Bedroom and Bath." *Dramatic Mirror* 78 (January 5, 1918): 5, 7.

"'The Passing Show' Is a Lively One." *New York Times,* June 23, 1916, p. 9.

"Peggy Wood." *New York Times,* December 25, 1922, p. 20.

Perry, Ralph Barton. "The American Cast of Mind." In *The Contrapuntal Civilization: Essays Toward a New Understanding of the American Experience,* ed. Michael Kammen. New York: Thomas Y. Crowell, 1971, pp. 91–106.

P. F. H. "The Play" [*Getting Gertie's Garter*]. *New York Evening Post,* August 2, 1921, p. 7.

"Pitt—'The Demi-Virgin.'" *Pittsburgh Dispatch,* September 27, 1921, p. 15.

"Pitt—'The Demi-Virgin.'" *Pittsburgh Post,* September 27, 1921, p. 9.

"Pittsburgh." *Variety,* October 7, 1921, p. 39.

"Pitt Theater Closed by Police; Show Held Vulgar by Alderdice." *Pittsburgh Post,* October 2, 1921, sec. 1, p. 2

"Play Censor Soon, Vice Crusader's Threat as Court Scores 'Demi-Virgin.'" *Variety,* November 18, 1921, pp. 12, 28.

"The Players" [*Sumurun*]. *Everybody's Magazine,* April 1912, p. 534.

"Play of Rare Charm Seen at the Hudson" [*Poor Little Rich Girl*]. *New York Times,* January 22, 1913, p. 11.

"Plays and Players." *New York Globe,* November 29, 1921, p. 15.

"Police Raid Stills in Cleanup Program Ordered in This City." *Pittsburgh Dispatch,* October 2, 1921, sec. 1, p. 1.

"Police Stop Two Plays." *Theatre Magazine,* October 1913, p. 116.

Pollock, Channing. "Redemption." *Green Book Magazine,* December 1918. In *Selected Theatre Criticism.* Volume 1: *1900–1919,* ed. Anthony Slide. Metuchen: Scarecrow, 1985, pp. 236–237.

———. "Sumurun." *Green Book Album,* April 1912. In *Selected Theatre Criticism.* Volume 1: *1900–1919,* ed. Anthony Slide. Metuchen: Scarecrow, 1985, pp. 266–270.

"Polyandrous Farce by Avery Hopwood" [*Our Little Wife*]. *New York Times,* November 20, 1916, p. 10.

"Portrait of Claire Whitney." *Theatre Magazine,* September 1920, p. 99.

"The Power to Close Theatres." *Variety,* November 11, 1921, p. 11.

"Producing Spine-Thrillers." *Literary Digest* 45 (August 10, 1912): 222–223.

"Protest on Theatre Tax." *New York Times,* January 21, 1919, p. 15.

"Protests Flood Washington Killing 20% Tax Increase." *Variety,* January 24, 1919, p. 6.

"Protests Showed Theatres' Power." *Morning Telegraph,* January 27, 1919, p. 1.

"Public Protest, Managerial Tact and the Newspapers Saved Theatres in Crisis." *New York Herald,* January 26, 1919, sec. 3, p. 9.

"Purity League Formed by Seniors of N.Y.U." *New York Herald,* December 2, 1921, p. 24.

"Pussyfoot in the Theatre." *New Republic* 29 (December 7, 1921): 32–33.

Reamer, Lawrence. "New York Theatres and Their Attractions." *New York Herald,* May 14, 1922, sec. 3, p. 9.

"'Red Rust' Is Given by Theatre Guild." *New York Times,* December 18, 1929, p. 31.

Reid, Louis R. "The Dramatic Mirror" [*The Famous Mrs. Fair*]. *Dramatic Mirror* 80 (January 1, 1920): 2023.

———. "First Is Last." *Dramatic Mirror* 80 (October 2, 1919): 1538.

———. "An Innocent Idea." *Dramatic Mirror* 81 (May 29, 1920): 1101.

———. "No More Blondes." *Dramatic Mirror* 81 (January 22, 1920): 91.

Reilly, Robert. "How Machines Become Human: Process and Attribute." In *The Mechanical God: Machines in Science Fiction,* ed. Thomas P. Dunn and Richard D. Erlich. Westport, Conn.: Greenwood, 1982, pp. 153–165.

"Reinhardt Play Is Seen at the Casino" [*Sumurun*]. *New York Times,* January 17, 1912, p. 8.

"Revenue Bill's Clauses." *Variety,* January 3, 1919, p. 7.

Rice, Elmer J. "New York: Raw Material for the Drama." *Theatre Magazine,* March 1929, pp. 26, 82.

———. "The Playwright as Director." *Theatre Arts* 13 (May 1929): 355–360.

"Right to Regulate Objectionable Performances in Theaters." *American City* 30 (June 1924): 677, 679.

"Riot in Theatre over an Irish Play." *New York Times,* November 28, 1911, p. 3.

Rohe, Alice. "Pirandello—The Theatre's Latest Genius." *Theatre Magazine,* February 1923, pp. 9, 58.

Rubenstein, Lenny. "*Caligari* and the Rise of the Expressionist Film." In *Passion and Rebellion: The Expressionist Heritage,* ed. Stephen Eric Bronner and Douglas Kellner. New York: Universe, 1983, pp. 363–373.

Ruhl, Arthur. "'Sumurun,' a New Kind of Stage Magic." *Colliers,* February 10, 1912, p. 33.

"Rules 'Demi-Virgin' Coarsely Indecent." *New York Times,* November 15, 1921, p. 9.

"Sadie Love." *Dramatic Mirror* 74 (December 4, 1915): 8.

———. *Theatre Magazine,* January 1916, p. 10.

"Say Theatre Tax Will Take Work from 1,000,000." *New York Herald,* January 20, 1919, sec. 2, p. 6.

"Scene and Characters in 'The Miracle' Soon to Be Seen in New York City." *Theatre Magazine,* September 1914, p. 109.

"Scene from *Beyond.*" *Theatre Arts* 9 (March 1925): 149.

"Scene from *The Verge.*" *Theatre Arts* 6 (January 1922): 12.

"Scenes from *Machinal.*" *Theatre Arts* 12 (October 1926): 704.

"Scenes from *Man and the Masses.*" *Theatre Arts* 8 (June 1924): 361.

"Scenes from *The Spook Sonata.*" *Theatre Arts* 8 (April 1924): 217.

"Scenes in 'The Devil's Garden' Recently Presented at the Harris." *Theatre Magazine,* February 1916, p. 68.

"Scenes in 'The Passing Show of 1916' at the Winter Garden." *Theatre Magazine,* August 1916, p. 63.

Scott. "A Bachelor's Night." *Dramatic Mirror* 84 (October 22, 1921): 593.

"Second Thoughts on First Nights" [*The Devil's Garden*]. *New York Times,* January 9, 1916, sec. 6, p. 2.

——— [*The Man Who Married a Dumb Wife*]. *New York Times,* February 7, 1915, sec. 7, p. 4.

——— [*Moloch*]. *New York Times,* September 26, 1915, sec. 4, p. 2.

——— [*Under Fire*]. *New York Times,* August 15, 1915, sec. 6, p. 2.

"Senator Jas. A. Reed Finds Theatre Tax Conditions Favorable." *New York American,* January 22, 1919, p. 6.

"Send Theatre Tax Appeal to Wilson." *New York Times,* January 18, 1919, p. 9.

"700 New York Theaters Bar Arbuckle Films." *New York Tribune,* September 14, 1921, p. 6.

Shapiro, Nathaniel S. "Dreams Which Won't Come True." *Theatre Magazine,* September 1920, p. 100.

Sherwood, Robert E. "The Cabinet of Dr. Caligari." In *American Film Criticism,* ed. Stanley Kauffmann and Bruce Henstell. New York: Liveright, 1972, pp. 121–125.

"Showmen Plan National Fight on Tax Boost." *New York Tribune,* January 18, 1919, p. 16.

"Shows in New York and Comment." *Variety,* October 21, 1921, p. 14.

———. *Variety,* October 28, 1921, p. 14.

———. *Variety,* November 4, 1921, p. 14.

———. *Variety,* November 11, 1921, p. 14.

———. *Variety,* November 18, 1921, p. 14.

———. *Variety,* November 25, 1921, p. 13.

———. *Variety,* December 2, 1921, p. 14.

———. *Variety,* December 9, 1921, p. 14.

———. *Variety,* December 16, 1921, p. 14.

———. *Variety,* January 6, 1922, p. 16.

Simonson, Lee. "Men as Stage Scenery Walking." *New York Times,* May 25, 1924, sec. 4, pp. 8, 15.

———. "The New German Stage Craft." *New York Times,* April 9, 1922, sec. 3, pp. 7, 25.

———. "The Painter and the Stage." *Theatre Arts* 2 (December 1917): 3–12.

Sinclair, Upton. Postscript to *Singing Jailbirds.* Long Beach, Calif.: published by the author, 1924, pp. 87–95.

"'Singing Jail Birds' Called Propaganda." *New York Times,* December 5, 1928, p. 34.

Sisk, Robert F. "The Guild Builds for Its Future." *Theatre Magazine,* February 1930, pp. 43, 60.

"Six Million in Theatre Tax Protest." *New York Evening Journal,* January 22, 1919, p. 18.

"The Six Orphans." *New York Times,* October 31, 1922, p. 11.

"Six Stages in One." *Scientific American,* March 1923, pp. 154–155.

"60 Per Cent of Theatres Face Ruin, Says Gest." *New York Tribune,* January 20, 1919, p. 14.

Skinner, Richard Dana. "The Play" [*Processional*]. *Commonweal* 1 (February 4, 1925): 354.

Smith, Alison. "The New Play" [*The Advertising of Kate*]. *The Globe and Commercial Advertiser,* May 9, 1922, p. 10.

Smyser, William Leon. "A Temporary Expatriate Again Views Broadway." *New York Times,* July 1, 1928, sec. 8, p. 1.

Sobel, Bernard. "Ladies' Night." *Dramatic Mirror* 82 (August 14, 1920): 283.

"Specs Organize to Fight Constitutionality of Law." *Variety,* January 10, 1919, p. 12.

"'The Spoils of War,' Another War Play Acted." *New York Times,* May 4, 1915, p. 15.

"A Sponge for the Stage." *Literary Digest,* December 22, 1923, pp. 29–30.

"Spotlights." *Theatre Magazine,* December 1927, p. 961.

"The Stage." *New York Call,* August 4, 1921, p. 4.

"The Stage and the Censor." *The Nation* 114 (January 18, 1922): 59–60.

"Stage Interests Raise $200,000,000 for Nation." *Morning Telegraph*, January 19, 1919, p. 5.

"Stage World Sees Ruin in Proposed Tax." *New York Tribune*, January 19, 1919, p. 6.

"Start Fight on Increased Tax in 500 Theatres." *Morning Telegraph*, January 17, 1919, p. 1.

Strand, Ginger. "Treadwell's Neologism." *Theatre Journal* 44 (May 1992): 163–175.

"Street Scene." *New York Times*, January 11, 1929, p. 20.

Stricker, Frank. "Cookbooks and Lawbooks." In *A Heritage of Her Own*, ed. Nancy F. Cott and Elizabeth H. Pleck. New York: Simon and Schuster, 1979, pp. 476–498.

"The Submarine on Stage" [*Show of Wonders*]. *New York Times*, February 13, 1917, p. 11.

"Such Shocking Anticipations Excited Police Play Censor." New York *World*, November 8, 1921, p. 12.

Sumner, John S. "Padlock Drama." *Theatre Magazine*, May 1928, pp. 11–12, 62.

Tarkington, Booth. "'Poldekin'—A Sunny Satire on Hearsay Bolshevism." *Current Opinion* 69 (October 1920): 481–488.

"Tax Bill Stops 71 New Shows, Say Managers." *New York Tribune*, January 21, 1919, p. 14.

"The Tax on Theatregoers." *New York Herald*, January 16, 1919, p. 10.

"Testing Licensing Power." *Variety*, December 2, 1921, pp. 1, 15.

"The Theatre" [*His Bridal Night*]. *The Sun*, August 2, 1921, p. 10.

"Theatre Managers Fight 20 Cent Tax." *The Sun*, January 17, 1919, p. 7.

"Theatre Managers Win Fight Against Tax of 20 Per Cent." *New York Call*, January 23, 1919, p. 3.

"Theatre Men Cable Appeal to Wilson." New York *Evening Post*, January 18, 1919, p. 9.

"Theatre Men Fight War Tax Increase." New York *World*, January 17, 1919, p. 11.

"Theatre Men Object to Proposed Tax." New York *Evening Post*, January 16, 1919, p. 4.

"Theatre Notes." *New York Daily News*, December 15, 1921, p. 21.

"Theatres Begin Fight on New Tax." *New York Evening Journal*, January 17, 1919, p. 10.

"Theatres Fight War Tax Raise." *New York American*, January 17, 1919, p. 10.

"Theatres Win Fight Against Tax Increase." *New York Tribune*, January 23, 1919, p. 1.

"The Theatre Tax." *The Sun*, January 18, 1919, p. 6.

"Theater Tax Bill Killed in Senate." *Dramatic Mirror* 76 (September 23, 1916): 1.

"Theatre Tax Not Raised." *New York Herald*, January 23, 1919, sec. 2, p. 6.

"Theatrical Notes." *New York Times*, October 7, 1921, p. 20.

———. *New York Times*, October 12, 1921, p. 18.

———. *New York Times*, October 14, 1921, p. 22.

"Third Bill at the Vieux Colombier." *New York Times*, December 12, 1917, p. 13.

"Those Germans!" *Theatre Arts* 1 (August 1917): 166.

"Thousands Sign Theatre Tax Plea." *New York Times,* January 17, 1919, p. 11.

"3,000,000 Oppose Theatre Tax Jump." *The Sun,* January 20, 1919, p. 7.

"3,000,000 Protest High Theatre Tax." *New York Times,* January 20, 1919, p. 13.

"To Be Continued." *New York Times,* May 21, 1922, sec. 6, p. 1.

"Tolstoi's 'Redemption' Told in Pictures." *Theatre Magazine,* December 1918, p. 359.

"Tomorrow at Theaters." *Pittsburgh Dispatch,* September 25, 1921, sec. 2, p. 6.

Torres, H. Z. " 'The Advertising of Kate' Succeeds." *New York Commercial,* May 10, 1922, p. 2.

——. " 'The Demi-Virgin' Needs the Censor." *New York Commercial,* October 19, 1921, p. 2.

——. " 'Getting Gertie's Garter' a Scramble." *New York Commercial,* August 2, 1921, p. 2.

"To Stop Theatre Tax Fight." *New York Times,* January 22, 1919, p. 9.

Towse, J. Ranken. "Music and the Drama" [*Up in Mabel's Room*]. *New York Evening Post,* January 16, 1919, p. 9.

——. "The Play" [*The Demi-Virgin*]. *New York Evening Post,* October 19, 1921, p. 9.

"250,000 Soldiers and Sailors Join in Tax Protest." *Morning Telegraph,* January 20, 1919, p. 2.

Trask, C. Hooper. "Upton Sinclair Abroad." *New York Times,* May 20, 1928, sec. 8, p. 2.

"Under Fire." *Theatre Magazine,* September 1915, p. 139.

"Up in Mabel's Room." *New York Times,* January 16, 1919, p. 11.

" 'Up in Mabel's Room' Opens at Eltinge Theatre." *New York American,* January 16, 1919, p. 6.

" 'Up in Mabel's Room' Proves Lively Farce." New York *World,* January 16, 1919, p. 11.

Van Doren, John. "How to Write a Play." *Theatre Magazine,* October 1921, pp. 212, 276.

Wagner, Richard. "Essence of Drama Is Knowing Through Feeling." In *Total Theatre,* ed. E. T. Kirby. New York: E. P. Dutton, 1969, pp. 5–8.

Wainscott, Ronald H. "American Theatre Versus the Congress of the United States: The Theatre Tax Controversy and Public Rebellion of 1919." *Theatre Survey* 31 (May 1990): 5–22.

——. "Attracting Censorship to the Popular Theatre: Al Woods Produces Avery Hopwood's *The Demi-Virgin*." *Theatre History Studies* 10 (1990): 127–140.

——. "Commercialism Glorified and Vilified: 1920s Theatre and the Business World." In *The American Stage: Social and Economic Issues from the Colonial Period to the Present,* ed. Ron Engle and Tice L. Miller. Cambridge: Cambridge University Press, 1993, pp. 175–189.

Washburn-Freund, Frank E. "The Evolution of Reinhardt." In *Max Reinhardt and His Theatre,* ed. Oliver Sayler. New York: Brentano's, 1924, pp. 44–56.

Watkins, Ann. "The Irish Players in America." *The Craftsman,* January 1912, p. 352.

Wechsler, Robert. "Karel Capek in America." *Cross Currents* 9 (1990): 173–186.

"The Week's Plays." *New York Times,* October 16, 1921, sec. 6, p. 1.

"What News on the Rialto?" *New York Times,* September 25, 1921, sec. 6, p. 1.

"What's Your Husband Doing?" *Dramatic Mirror* 77 (November 24, 1917): 5.

"What We Stand For," *Theatre Arts* 1 (August 1917): 149.

Whittaker, James. "'The Demi-Virgin' Recalls Two of Huck Finn's Pals." *New York Daily News*, October 19, 1921, p. 17.

———. "Public Taste as to Plays Seems to Have Improved." *New York Daily News*, December 4, 1921, p. 21.

Willis, Ronald A. "The American Lab Theatre." *Tulane Drama Review* 9 (Fall 1964): 112–116.

"Winter Garden Takes to Cover." *New York Times*, October 19, 1917, p. 11.

Wolf, Rennold. "Marc Klaw Rebukes Government for Additional Theatre Tax." *Morning Telegraph*, January 16, 1919, p. 4.

———. "New Farce at the Eltinge Theatre" [*Up in Mabel's Room*]. *Morning Telegraph*, January 17, 1919, p. 9.

Woods, A. H. "Why I Believe in Deciding Things Quickly." *American Magazine*, March 1918, pp. 25–26, 71–74, 76, 79.

———. "Why I Produce Bedroom Farces." *Theatre Magazine*, June 1922, pp. 352, 406.

"Woods Defiant, Will Continue 'Demi-Virgin' Until Court Decides." *New York Daily News*, November 25, 1921, p. 24.

"Woods Defies Ban on the 'Demi-Virgin.'" *New York Times*, November 26, 1921, p. 18.

"Woods Defies License Chief." *New York Tribune*, November 25, 1921.

"Woods' 'Demi-Virgin' Ordered Closed." *Variety*, November 25, 1921, p. 13.

"Woods Obtains Court Order." *New York Tribune*, November 26, 1921, p. 8.

"Woods Tells Receipts in 'Demi-Virgin' Suit." *New York Sun*, December 5, 1921, p. 2.

"Woods to Continue to Offer 'Demi-Virgin.'" *New York American*, November 25, 1921, p. 7.

"Woods to Stay in Managers Association." *New York Herald*, December 14, 1921, p. 12.

"Woods Wants Jury Trial for His 'Demi-Virgin.'" *New York Daily News*, December 3, 1921, p. 15.

Woollcott, Alexander. "At 'Richard III.'" *New York Times*, March 21, 1920, sec. 6, p. 6.

———. "The Author-Producer at Large." *New York Times*, August 11, 1920, p. 6.

———. "Ernest Truex in a Bedroom" [*No More Blondes*]. *New York Times*, January 8, 1920, p. 22.

———. "A Farce Plus Roland Young" [*Scrambled Wives*]. *New York Times*, August 6, 1920, p. 16.

———. "Out There." *New York Times*, April 8, 1917, sec. 8, p. 5.

———. "The Play" [*The Advertising of Kate*]. *New York Times*, May 9, 1922, p. 22.

———. "The Play" [*Back to Methuselah*]. *New York Times*, February 28, 1922, p. 17.

———. "The Play" [*Bavu*]. *New York Times*, February 27, 1922, p. 16.

———. "The Play" [*The Challenge*]. *New York Times*, August 6, 1919, p. 7.

———. "The Play" [*The Famous Mrs. Fair*]. *New York Times*, December 23, 1919, p. 12.

————. "The Play" [*The Hairy Ape*]. *New York Times,* March 14, 1922, p. 11.

————. "The Play" [*The Hero*]. *New York Times,* March 15, 1921, p. 14.

————. "The Play" [*The Jest*]. *New York Times,* September 20, 1919, p. 14.

————. "The Play" [*Like a King*]. *New York Times,* October 4, 1921, p. 10.

————. "The Play" [*Macbeth*]. *New York Times,* February 18, 1921, p. 16.

————. "The Play" [*Poldekin*]. *New York Times,* September 10, 1920, p. 12.

————. "The Play" [*The Power of Darkness*]. *New York Times,* January 22, 1920, p. 22.

————. "The Play" [*Richard III*]. *New York Times,* March 8, 1920, p. 7.

————. "The Play" [*To the Ladies*]. *New York Times,* February 21, 1922, p. 20.

————. "The Play" [*The Verge*]. *New York Times,* November 15, 1921, p. 23.

————. "Scrambled Wives." *New York Times,* August 6, 1920, p. 16.

————. "Second Thoughts on First Nights" [*Aria da Capo*]. *New York Times,* December 14, 1919, sec. 8, p. 2.

————. "Second Thoughts on First Nights" [*The Demi-Virgin*]. *New York Times,* October 23, 1921, sec. 6, p. 1.

————. "Second Thoughts on First Nights" [*The Girl in the Limousine*]. *New York Times,* October 12, 1919, sec. 4, p. 2.

————. "Second Thoughts on First Nights" [*The Inheritors*]. *New York Times,* March 27, 1921, sec. 7, p. 1.

————. "Second Thoughts on First Nights" [*Liliom*]. *New York Times,* May 1, 1921, sec. 7, p. 1.

————. "Second Thoughts on First Nights" [*Macbeth*]. *New York Times,* February 27, 1921, sec. 6, p. 1.

————. "Second Thoughts on First Nights" [*Three Plays for a Negro Theatre*]. *New York Times,* April 29, 1917, sec. 8, p. 7.

————. "Turkish Bath Humors" [*Ladies' Night*]. *New York Times,* August 10, 1920, p. 10.

Wynn, Nancy. "Sophie Treadwell: Author of *Machinal.*" *Journal of American Drama and Theatre* 3 (Winter 1991): 29–47.

"The Year in Legitimate." *Variety,* December 27, 1918, p. 14.

Young, Stark. "Hamlet." *New Republic* 33 (December 6, 1922): 45–46.

————. "The Play" [*Beyond*]. *New York Times,* January 27, 1925, p. 14.

————. "The Play" [*Processional*]. *New York Times,* January 13, 1925, p. 17.

BOOKS

Alexandre, Arsène. *The Decorative Art of Leon Bakst.* 1913. Rpt. New York: Benjamin Blom, 1970.

Allen, Frederick Lewis. *The Big Change.* New York: Harper, 1952.

Alpert, Hollis. *The Barrymores.* New York: Dial, 1964.

The American Theatre: A Sum of Its Parts. New York: Samuel French, 1971.

Appelbaum, Stanley. *The New York Stage: Famous Productions in Photographs.* New York: Dover, 1976.

Asinof, Eliot. *1919: America's Loss of Innocence*. New York: Donald I. Fine, 1990.

Atkinson, Brooks. *Broadway*. New York: Limelight, 1974.

Atkinson, Brooks, and Albert Hirschfeld. *The Lively Years*. New York: Association, 1973.

Auerbach, Nina. *Woman and the Demon: The Life of a Victorian Myth*. Cambridge: Harvard University Press, 1982.

Bakst. New York: Rizzoli, 1977.

Barnes, Eric Wollencott. *The Man Who Lived Twice*. New York: Charles Scribner's Sons, 1956.

Bauland, Peter. *The Hooded Eagle: Modern German Drama on the New York Stage*. Syracuse, N.Y.: Syracuse University Press, 1968.

Bel Geddes, Norman. *Miracle in the Evening*, ed. William Kelley. Garden City, N.Y.: Doubleday, 1960.

Bigsby, C. W. E. *A Critical Introduction to Twentieth Century American Drama*. Volume 1: *1900–1940*. Cambridge: Cambridge University Press, 1982.

Blum, Daniel. *Great Stars of the American Stage*. New York: Greenberg, 1952.

———. *A Pictorial History of American Theatre, 1860–1970*. New York: Crown, 1969.

Bogard, Travis. *Contour in Time: The Plays of Eugene O'Neill*. New York: Oxford University Press, 1988.

Bogard, Travis, Richard Moody, and Walter J. Meserve. *The Revels History of Drama in English*. Volume 8: *American Drama*. London: Methuen, 1977.

Boleslavski, Richard. *Acting: The First Six Lessons*. New York: Theatre Arts, 1933.

Brady, William A. *Showman*. New York: E. P. Dutton, 1937.

Bronner, Stephen Eric, and Douglas Kellner, eds. *Passion and Rebellion: The Expressionist Heritage*. New York: Universe, 1983.

Brown, Dorothy M. *Setting a Course: American Women in the 1920s*. Boston: Twayne, 1987.

Brown, John Mason. *Dramatis Personae*. New York: Viking, 1963.

———. *Two on the Aisle*. Port Washington, N.Y.: Kennikat, 1966.

Brustein, Robert. *Reimagining American Theatre*. New York: Hill and Wang, 1991.

Bryer, Jackson, ed. *"The Theatre We Worked For": The Letters of Eugene O'Neill to Kenneth Macgowan*. New Haven: Yale University Press, 1982.

Budd, Mike, ed. The Cabinet of Dr. Caligari: *Texts, Contexts, Histories*. New Brunswick, N.J.: Rutgers University Press, 1990.

Cargill, Oscar, ed. *O'Neill and His Plays*. New York: New York University Press, 1961.

Cheney, Sheldon. *The Art Theatre*. New York: Alfred A. Knopf, 1917.

———. *The New Movement in the Theatre*. New York: Mitchell Kennerley, 1914.

Chinoy, Helen Krich, and Linda Walsh Jenkins, eds. *Women in American Theatre*. New York: Theatre Communications Group, 1987.

Churchill, Allen. *The Great White Way*. New York: E. P. Dutton, 1962.

———. *The Theatrical Twenties*. New York: McGraw-Hill, 1975.

Clum, John M. *Ridgely Torrence*. New York: Twayne, 1972.

Clurman, Harold. *The Fervent Years*. New York: Hill and Wang, 1957.

————. *On Directing*. New York: Macmillan, 1972.

Cole, Toby, and Helen Krich Chinoy, eds. *Directors on Directing*. Indianapolis: Bobbs-Merrill, 1963.

Connelly, Marc. *Voices Offstage: A Book of Memoirs*. Chicago: Holt, Rinehart and Winston, 1968.

Cott, Nancy F., and Elizabeth H. Pleck, eds. *A Heritage of Her Own*. New York: Simon and Schuster, 1979.

Craig, Edward Gordon. *On the Art of the Theatre*. Chicago: Browne's Bookstore, 1911.

Deutsch, Helen, and Stella Hanau. *The Provincetown*. New York: Farrar and Rinehart, 1931.

Dickinson, Thomas H. *Playwrights of the New American Theater*. New York: Macmillan, 1925.

Downer, Alan S. *Fifty Years of American Drama, 1900–1950*. Chicago: Henry Regnery, 1951.

Dunn, Thomas P., and Richard D. Erlich. *The Mechanical God: Machines in Science Fiction*. Westport, Conn.: Greenwood, 1982.

Eaton, Walter Prichard. *The Theatre Guild: The First Ten Years*. New York: Brentano's, 1929.

Engel, Lehman. *The American Musical Theater*. New York: Collier, 1975.

Engel, Ron, and Tice L. Miller, eds. *The American Stage: Social and Economic Issues from the Colonial Period to the Present*. Cambridge: Cambridge University Press, 1993.

Flexner, Eleanor. *American Playwrights: 1918–1938*. New York: Simon and Schuster, 1938.

Forster, Margaret. *Significant Sisters: The Grassroots of Active Feminism, 1839–1939*. New York: Oxford University Press, 1984.

Fuerst, Walter René, and Samuel J. Hume. *Twentieth-Century Stage Decoration*, 2 vols. New York: Dover, 1967.

Fulton, A. R. *Motion Pictures: The Development of an Art*. Norman: University of Oklahoma Press, 1980.

Fussell, Paul. *The Great War and Modern Memory*. London: Oxford University Press, 1975.

Gagey, Edmond M. *Revolution in American Drama*. New York: Columbia University Press, 1947.

Garafola, Lynn. *Diaghilev's Ballets Russes*. New York: Oxford University Press, 1989.

Garten, H. F. *Modern German Drama*. New York: Grove, 1959.

Gassner, John. *Form and Idea in Modern Theatre*. New York: Dryden, 1958.

————. *Producing the Play*. San Francisco: Holt, Rinehart and Winston, 1953.

Gassner, John, and Ralph G. Allen. *Theatre and Drama in the Making*. Boston: Houghton Mifflin, 1964.

Geduld, Harry M. *Focus on D. W. Griffith*. Englewood Cliffs, N.J.: Prentice-Hall, 1971.

Gelb, Arthur, and Barbara Gelb. *O'Neill*. New York: Harper and Row, 1973.

Goldstein, Malcolm. *George S. Kaufman: His Life, His Theater*. New York: Oxford University Press, 1979.

———. *The Political Stage: American Drama and Theater of the Great Depression*. New York: Oxford University Press, 1974.

Gorelik, Mordecai. *New Theatres for Old*. New York: Samuel French, 1940.

Gottfried, Martin. *Broadway Musicals*. New York: Harry N. Abrams, 1979.

Granville-Barker, Harley. *The Exemplary Theatre*. Boston: Little, Brown, 1922.

———. *On Dramatic Method*. London: Sidgwick and Jackson, 1931.

Hawley, Ellis W. *The Great War and the Search for a Modern Order: A History of the American People and Their Institutions, 1917–1933*. New York: St. Martin's, 1979.

Hewitt, Barnard. *Theatre U.S.A.* New York: McGraw-Hill, 1959.

Higonnet, Margaret Randolph, et al, eds. *Behind the Lines: Gender and the Two World Wars*. New Haven: Yale University Press, 1987.

Hoffman, Frederick J. *The Twenties: American Writing in the Postwar Decade*. New York: Viking, 1955.

Hokenson, Jan, and Howard Pearce, eds. *Forms of the Fantastic*. New York: Greenwood, 1986.

Hopkins, Arthur. *Reference Point*. New York: Samuel French, 1948.

———. *To a Lonely Boy*. New York: Book League of America, 1937.

Jones, Robert Edmond. *The Dramatic Imagination*. New York: Theatre Arts, 1941.

———. *Drawings for the Theatre*. New York: Theatre Arts, 1925.

Kammen, Michael, ed. *The Contrapuntal Civilization: Essays Toward a New Understanding of the American Experience*. New York: Thomas Y. Crowell, 1971.

———. *Mystic Chords of Memory: The Transformation of Tradition in American Culture*. New York: Alfred A. Knopf, 1991.

Kauffmann, Stanley, and Bruce Henstell, eds. *American Film Criticism*. New York: Liveright, 1972.

Kavanagh, Peter. *The Story of the Abbey Theatre*. New York: Devin-Adair, 1950.

Keen, Sam. *Faces of the Enemy: Reflections of the Hostile Imagination*. San Francisco: Harper and Row, 1986.

Kennedy, Dennis. *Granville Barker and the Dream of Theatre*. Cambridge: Cambridge University Press, 1985.

Kirby, E. T. *Total Theatre*. New York: E. P. Dutton, 1969.

Klingaman, William K. *1919: The Year Our World Began*. New York: St. Martin's, 1987.

———. *1929: The Year of the Great Crash*. New York: Harper and Row, 1989.

Knox, George A., and Herbert Stahl. *Dos Passos and "The Revolting Playwrights."* Upsala, Sweden: Upsala University Press, 1964.

Kobler, John. *Damned in Paradise: The Life of John Barrymore*. New York: Atheneum, 1977.

Krutch, Joseph Wood. *The American Drama since 1918*. New York: Random House, 1939.

Langner, Lawrence. *The Magic Curtain*. New York: E. P. Dutton, 1951.

Laufe, Abe. *The Wicked Stage*. New York: Frederick Ungar, 1978.

Le Gallienne, Eva. *At 33*. New York: Longmans, Green, 1934.

————. *With a Quiet Heart*. New York: Viking, 1953.

Levine, Ira A. *Left-Wing Dramatic Theory in the American Theatre*. Ann Arbor: UMI Research Press, 1985.

Lewis, Emory. *Stages: The Fifty-Year Childhood of the American Theatre*. Englewood Cliffs, N.J.: Prentice-Hall, 1969.

Locke, Alain, and Montgomery Gregory, eds. *Plays of Negro Life*. New York: Harper, 1927.

Macgowan, Kenneth, and Robert Edmond Jones. *Continental Stagecraft*. London: Benn Brothers, 1922.

McNamara, Brooks. *The Shuberts of Broadway*. New York: Oxford University Press, 1990.

Mantle, Burns. *The Best Plays of 1919–1930; and The Year Book of the Drama in America*. 11 vols. Boston: Small, Maynard, 1920–1925; New York: Dodd, Mead, 1926–1930.

Mantle, Burns, and Garrison P. Sherwood. *The Best Plays of 1909–1919; and The Year Book of the Drama in America*. New York: Dodd, Mead, 1943.

Martin, Robert A., ed. *The Writer's Craft: Hopwood Lectures, 1965–81*. Ann Arbor: University of Michigan Press, 1982.

Mason, Jeffrey D. *Wise Cracks: The Farces of George S. Kaufman*. Ann Arbor: UMI Research Press, 1988.

Meserve, Walter J. *An Outline History of American Drama*. Totowa, N.J.: Littlefield, Adams, 1965.

Meyer, Annie Nathan. *It's Been Fun*. New York: Henry Schuman, 1951.

Morehouse, Ward. *Matinee Tomorrow*. New York: McGraw-Hill, 1949.

Miller, Jordan Y., and Winifred L. Frazer. *American Drama Between the Wars: A Critical History*. Boston: Twayne, 1991.

Murphy, Brenda. *American Realism and American Drama, 1880–1940*. Cambridge: Cambridge University Press, 1987.

Nannes, Casper H. *Politics in the American Drama*. Washington, D.C.: Catholic University of America Press, 1960.

Nathan, George Jean. *Comedians All*. New York: Alfred A. Knopf, 1919.

Nolan, Paul T. *Marc Connelly*. New York: Twayne, 1969.

Oppenheimer, George. *The Passionate Playgoer*. New York: Viking, 1958.

Pendleton, Ralph, ed. *The Theatre of Robert Edmond Jones*. Middletown, Conn.: Wesleyan University Press, 1958.

Perrett, Geoffrey. *America in the Twenties*. New York: Simon and Schuster, 1982.

Poggi, Jack. *Theater in America: The Impact of Economic Forces, 1870–1967*. Ithaca: Cornell University Press, 1968.

Purdom, C. B. *Harley Granville-Barker*. London: Rockcliffe, 1955.

Quinn, Arthur Hobson. *A History of the American Drama from the Civil War to the Present Day*, vol. 2. New York: Harper, 1927.

Rabkin, Gerald. *Drama and Commitment: Politics in the American Theatre of the Thirties*. Bloomington: Indiana University Press, 1964.

Rawls, Walton. *Wake up, America: World War I and the American Poster*. New York: Abbeville, 1988.

Roberts, J. W. *Richard Boleslavsky: His Life and Work in the Theatre*. Ann Arbor: UMI Research Press, 1981.

Robinson, Alice M., Vera Mowry Roberts, and Milly S. Barranger. *Notable Women in the American Theatre*. New York: Greenwood, 1989.

Rudlin, John. *Jacques Copeau*. Cambridge: Cambridge University Press, 1986.

Saint-Denis, Michel. *Theatre: The Rediscovery of Style*. London: Heinemann, 1960.

Salmon, Eric. *Granville Barker: A Secret Life*. Rutherford, N.J.: Fairleigh Dickinson University Press, 1983.

Sarlos, Robert Karoly. *Jig Cook and the Provincetown Players*. Amherst: University of Massachusetts Press, 1982.

Sayler, Oliver M., ed. *Max Reinhardt and His Theatre*. New York: Brentano's, 1924.

———. *Our American Theatre*. New York: Brentano's, 1923.

Schanke, Robert A. *Eva Le Gallienne: A Bio-Bibliography*. New York: Greenwood, 1989.

Schlueter, June, ed. *Modern American Drama: The Female Canon*. Rutherford, N.J.: Fairleigh Dickinson University Press, 1990.

Schneider, Dorothy, and Carl J. Schneider. *Into the Breach: American Women Overseas in World War I*. New York: Viking, 1991.

Shannon, David A. *Between the Wars: America, 1919–1941*. 2d ed. Boston: Houghton Mifflin, 1979.

Sharrar, Jack F. *Avery Hopwood: His Life and Plays*. Jefferson, N.C.: McFarland, 1989.

Sheaffer, Louis. *O'Neill: Son and Playwright*. Boston: Little, Brown, 1968.

Shivers, Alfred S. *The Life of Maxwell Anderson*. New York: Stein and Day, 1983.

———. *Maxwell Anderson*. Boston: Twayne, 1976.

Sievers, W. David. *Freud on Broadway*. New York: Hermitage House, 1955.

Simonson, Lee. *The Art of Scenic Design*. New York: Harper and Brothers, 1950.

———. *Part of a Lifetime*. New York: Duell, Sloan, and Pearce, 1943.

———. *The Stage Is Set*. New York: Dover, 1932.

Skolsky, Sidney. *Times Square Tintypes*. New York: Ives Washburn, 1930.

Slavick, William H. *Dubose Heyward*. Boston: Twayne, 1981.

Slide, Anthony, ed. *Selected Theatre Criticism*. Volume 1: *1900–1919*. Metuchen: Scarecrow, 1985.

Spencer, Charles. *Leon Bakst*. New York: Rizzoli, 1973.

Stagg, Jerry. *The Brothers Shubert*. New York: Random House, 1968.

Stern, Ernest. *My Life, My Stage*. London: Victor Gollancz, 1951.

Stevenson, Elizabeth. *Babbitts and Bohemians: The American 1920s*. New York: Macmillan, 1967.

Styan, J. L. *Max Reinhardt*. Cambridge: Cambridge University Press, 1982.

Sullivan, Mark. *Our Times: The United States, 1900–1925*, vol. 5. New York: Charles Scribner's Sons, 1933.

Susman, Warren I. *Culture as History: The Transformation of American Society in the Twentieth Century*. New York: Pantheon, 1984.

Tarkington, Booth, *On Plays, Playwrights, and Playgoers: Selections from the Letters of Booth Tarkington to George C. Tyler and John Peter Toohey, 1918–1925*, ed. Alan S. Downer. Princeton: Princeton University Press, 1959.

The Theatre Guild Anthology, New York: Random House, 1936.

Timms, Edward, and Peter Collier, eds. *Visions and Blueprints: Avant-Garde Culture and Radical Politics in Early Twentieth-Century Europe*. Manchester, Eng.: Manchester University Press, 1988.

Toklas, Alice B. *What Is Remembered*. New York: Holt, Rinehart, Winston, 1963.

Tuchman, Barbara W. *The Proud Tower*. New York: Macmillan, 1966.

Valgemae, Mardi. *Accelerated Grimace: Expressionism in the American Drama of the 1920s*. Carbondale: Southern Illinois University Press, 1972.

Vardac, A. Nicholas. *Stage to Screen: Theatrical Method from Garrick to Griffith*. Cambridge: Harvard University Press, 1949.

Wagenknecht, Edward, and Anthony Slide. *The Films of D. W. Griffith*. New York: Crown, 1975.

Wainscott, Ronald. *Staging O'Neill: The Experimental Years, 1920–1934*. New Haven: Yale University Press, 1988.

Waterman, Arthur E. *Susan Glaspell*. New York: Twayne, 1966.

Who Was Who in the Theatre: 1912–1976. 4 vols. Detroit: Gale Research Press, 1978.

Williams, Jay. *Stage Left*. New York: Charles Scribner's Sons, 1974.

Williams, Martin. *Griffith: First Artist of the Movies*. New York: Oxford University Press, 1980.

Wilson, Edmund. *The Twenties*, ed. Leon Edel. New York: Farrar, Straus, and Giroux, 1975.

Wodehouse, P. G., and Guy Bolton. *Bring on the Girls!* New York: Simon and Schuster, 1953.

Index

Across the Border, 11, 194
Adams, Maude, 105
Adding Machine, The, 114, 116, 120, 124–27, 130–31, 139, 149–50, 152, 161, 183
Advertising of Kate, The, 60, 146–48, 217
Agamemnon, 10, 194
Airways, Inc., 160–61, 184–85, 221
Alderdice, Robert, 81–82
All God's Chillun Got Wings, 76
All Wet, 177
American Ace, An, 9, 196
Ames, Winthrop, 94, 128–30, 209, 215
Ancient Mariner, The, 116
Anderson, John, 36, 155
Anderson, Maxwell, 3, 7, 11, 31–36, 73, 75–76, 165, 179–80, 221
Andrews, Charlton, 56, 67, 192
Andreyev, Leonid, 104, 211
Androcles and the Lion, 96–97

Anglin, Margaret, 44
Anna Christie, 121
Apel, Paul, 128, 215
Appia, Adolph, 105, 122
Arbuckle, Fatty, 77, 80–82
Aria da Capo, 25–26, 28, 31, 197
Arliss, George, 172, 220
Arms and the Girl, 12, 195
Arms and the Man, 12
Artists and Models, 73
Arts and Crafts Theatre, 13, 96, 195
Astaire, Adele and Fred, 15
Atkinson, Brooks, 132, 153, 155, 159, 180
Atteridge, Harold, 15

Bachelor's Night, A, 57, 68, 70, 192
Back to Methuselah, 115–16, 119, 125–26
Bacon, Frank, 40
Bakst, Leon, 103
Ballets Russes, 103

Barrie, James, 105
Barry, Philip, 142, 159–60
Barrymore, Ethel, 13, 44, 65
Barrymore, John, 40, 52, 106–07, 111, 118, 121–22
Barrymore, Lionel, 40, 109–11
Basshe, Em Jo, 137
Bat, The, 78, 169, 206
Bates, Blanche, 16
Bavu, 168–69
Beckett, Samuel, 108
Beggar on Horseback, 124, 128–30, 137, 151–52, 157, 215
Behrman, S. N., 141, 160–62
Belasco, David, 41, 78, 168, 185
Bel Geddes, Norman, 96
Bell, C. W., 56, 58, 191
Belt, The, 136, 156–57, 180–82
Benelli, Sem, 17, 107
Bennison, Louis, 16, 142–43, 196
Berlin, Irving, 15
Bernauer, Rudolph, 122
Bertha, the Sewing Machine Girl, 77
Beyond, 116, 133–34, 138
Beyond the Horizon, 46, 107
Birth of a Nation, 99–100, 170, 188
Blackmur, R. P., 131
Blue Bird, The, 105
Blum, Gustav, 56, 192
Bolton, Guy, 150, 218
Booth, Hilliard, 11, 194
Booth, John, 143
Booth, John Wilkes, 100, 210
Bowery After Dark, The, 77
Brackett, Parmlee, 9
Brady, William A., 41, 43, 99, 121
Breakfast in Bed, 54
Brecht, Bertolt, 98, 106, 189, 221
Brieux, Eugène, 14
Brooks, George S., 36, 154–56
Broun, Heywood, 32, 46, 63, 69, 73
Brown, John Mason, 156, 175
Brown, Martin, 56–57, 192
Brustein, Robert, 183

Cabinet of Dr. Caligari, The, 111–13, 125
Caliban by the Yellow Sands, 103

Capek, Karl, 120–21
Capra, Frank, 49
Carousel, 114
Carroll, Earl, 73, 169
Castellun, Maida, 83
Challenge, The, 168–69, 173
Chantecler, 105
Cheaper to Marry, 151
Cheney, Sheldon, 103–04, 131, 195, 211
Children's Hour, The, 77
Claire, Ina, 78
Clansman, The, 100, 170
Clarence, 17–18, 19, 22–23, 162, 172, 196
Clinging Vine, The, 145–46, 217
Cohan, George M., 15, 88, 142–43, 195
Collison, Wilson, 54–57, 61, 70, 191–92
Connelly, Marc, 128–30, 143–45, 151–54
Cook, George Cram, 96, 108, 115
Coolidge, Calvin, 142–43, 153, 163, 189
Copeau, Jacques, 91, 93, 99, 105–06, 113, 117, 122, 127, 133, 211
Copeland, Royal S., 86
Corbin, John, 11, 12, 32, 54, 107, 120
Cornell, Katharine, 78
Cowl, Jane, 72, 167
Craig, Gordon, 93–94, 96, 102, 105, 117
Crothers, Rachel, 20–21
Crowther, James, 168
Cumberland, John, 55, 65–66

Dale, Alan, 68–69, 76–77, 83
Daly, Arnold, 76
Davis, Owen, 77, 90
Davy Crockett, 185
Dawn, Hazel, 63–65, 68
De Foe, Louis, 81–83
Demi-Bride, The, 88–89
Demi-Virgin, The, 54, 56, 58–61, 64–65, 68–71, 75–90, 192
Desert Song, The, 15, 203
Desire Under the Elms, 76, 83, 89, 109, 133, 194
Devil's Garden, The, 102, 113
Diaghilev, Serge, 103
Diff'rent, 11, 22–23, 194
Dix, Beulah Marie, 11–12
Dixon, Thomas, 100, 170–71

Doing Our Bit, 9, 15
Dolly Sisters, 63
Dos Passos, John, 136, 160–61, 184–85
Double Exposure, 57, 191, 203–04
Dream Play, A, 128
Drums of Jeopardy, The, 168–69
Duchamp, Marcel, 98
Duffy, Albert, 85
Duke, Ashley, 118
Dulcy, 143–44, 162, 217, 220

Easiest Way, The, 169
Eaton, Walter Prichard, 111
Edna, the Poor Typewriter, 77
Edwards, Bruce, 42, 51
Ellis, Edith, 102
Emery, Gilbert, 22–25, 32, 167
Emperor Jones, The, 96, 107–10, 114–15, 135–36
Enemy, The, 36
Equus, 106
Erlanger, Abraham, 101
Essman, Manuel, 137
Exchange of Wives, 57
Experimental Theatre, Inc., 127, 133

Fagan, Myron C., 160
Fair and Warmer, 55–58, 62, 69, 191
Famous Mrs. Fair, The, 18–25, 29, 32
Faversham, William, 13, 44
Fehling, Jürgen, 118, 130, 220
Feydeau, Georges, 54, 60
Fight, The, 76
First Law, The, 185
Fiske, Minnie Maddern, 44, 220
Flamma, Ario, 169
Flexner, Eleanor, 145, 161
Fokine, Michel, 103
Forbes, James, 18–22, 25, 32
Ford, Henry, 156, 180, 189
Fordney, Joseph, 51
Forman, Justus Miles, 14, 100–101, 210
Fourberies de Scapin, 105–06
France, Anatole, 96
Freksa, Friedrich, 95
Friendly Enemies, 14–15
Frohman, Charles, 101, 105

From Morn to Midnight, 108, 116–19, 148
Front Page, The, 182–83, 221
Fussell, Paul, 3, 10, 34

Gade, Svend, 122–24, 214
Gainor, Ellen, 114
Gantillon, Simon, 76
Garden of Allah, The, 94
Gates, Eleanor, 101
George White's Scandals, 73
Gest, Morris, 47, 50
Get-Rich-Quick Wallingford, 142
Getting Gertie's Garter, 53, 56–59, 62–64, 69–71, 74, 77, 81, 192
Getting Together, 16
Ghosts, 86, 89
Gilbert, Sandra M., 20, 24
Gilchrist, John, 87
Girl in the Limousine, The, 54, 56–59, 63, 65, 71, 81, 192, 217
Girl of the Golden West, The, 185
Girl with the Carmine Lips, The, 56, 70, 192
Give and Take, 164, 171, 173, 183
Glaspell, Susan, 26–28, 73, 103, 114–15, 128, 139–40, 171, 174–75, 179, 213
Glass, Carter, 45
Glass Menagerie, The, 123, 194
Gods of the Lightning, 164–65, 179–82, 184, 221
Gold, Michael, 137, 157, 181
Gold Diggers, The, 78
Golden, John, 40–41, 47
Golding, Samuel, 152
Good Gracious Annabelle, 142
Gorelik, Mordecai, 94, 97, 112, 132–33
Gorki, Maxim, 106, 167
Grand Duke, The, 168
Granville-Barker, Harley, 93, 96–99, 105, 110, 122, 127, 133, 210
Great God Brown, The, 60, 108, 133–36, 148, 154
Great Power, The, 160
Great Scott, 183–84, 221
Green, Paul, 93
Green Hat, The, 78
Griffith, D. W., 99–100, 170, 210

Group Theatre, 186
Guitry, Sacha, 168

Hackett, Francis, 97
Hairy Ape, The, 76, 114, 116–18, 120, 125,
    127, 131, 137, 139, 144, 175–76, 179, 181
Hamilton, Clayton, 95
Hamlet, 52, 94, 111, 118, 121–22
Hammond, Percy, 63–64, 71, 83
Harbach, Otto, 56, 61, 67, 191–92, 203
Harding, Warren G., 18, 21, 77, 142, 168,
    179
Harris, Sam, 42, 51
Harrison, Bertram, 58, 78
Hartley, Marsden, 95
Hasenclever, Walter, 133–34
Hauptmann, Gerhart, 14, 101
Hawley, Ellis, 69, 106, 205
Hay, Ian, 16
Hayes, Helen, 17, 217
He and She, 20–21
Hecht, Ben, 182–83
Hell-Bent fer Heaven, 21, 29–31, 198
Hellman, Lillian, 77
Her Unborn Child, 73
Hero, The, 21, 22–25, 29, 31–32, 34, 167
Herrick, Howard, 169
Hickerson, Harold, 165, 179
His Bridal Night, 57–58, 63, 70, 191
Hobart, George, 56, 191
Hoboken Blues, 137, 157, 181
Hodge, Francis, 121
Hoffman, Aaron, 14, 164, 173
Hoffman, Frederick, 25
Holiday, 159–60
Hoover, Herbert, 163
Hopkins, Arthur, 32, 39, 99, 101–02,
    106–07, 109–11, 116–18, 121–22, 125,
    135, 138–40, 194, 204, 216
Hopper, DeWolf, 44
Hopwood, Avery, 54–57, 59, 61, 67, 69,
    73–90, 169, 191–92, 203–04
Hornblow, Arthur, 18, 32, 65, 69–70, 110,
    144–45, 162, 167
Howard, Sidney, 73, 76, 89, 194
Howe, Frederick C., 90
Hughes, Hatcher, 28, 29–31, 93

Hull, Shelley, 124
Hume, Sam, 96
Hyphen, The, 14, 210

Ibsen, Henrik, 79, 86, 89, 105, 186, 188
Illington, Margaret, 65
In the Zone, 11, 14, 194
Industrial Workers of the World, 116–17,
    170, 175–76, 179, 181–82
Inheritors, The, 26–28, 31, 114, 171,
    174–75, 179, 198
Innocent Idea, An, 57, 63, 192
Insect Comedy, The, 121
Inside the Lines, 14
International, The, 136–37, 141, 154,
    158–59, 162, 178, 181
Irene, 54
Irish Players, 93–94
It Pays to Advertise, 142

Jackson, Fred, 56, 191
Jessner, Leopold, 118, 121–22, 130–31
Jest, The, 17, 107
Johann, Zita, 138
Johannes Kreisler, 122–24, 130, 214
Johnny Get Your Gun, 16–17, 79–80,
    142–43
Jones, Robert Edmond, 93, 96–97, 102–03,
    106–07, 109–11, 113, 116–18, 121–22,
    127, 131, 133–36, 138–40, 209–10
Journey's End, 36
Jouvet, Louis, 105–06
Jungle, The, 181

Kahn, Otto, 180
Kaiser, Georg, 108, 118–19, 148
Kammen, Michael, 3, 167
Kaufman, George S., 128–30, 143–45,
    151–52, 218
Kaufman, S. Jay, 59
Keen, Sam, 170
Keene, Laura, 100
Kelly, George, 29
Kennedy, Madge, 55, 58
Kenyon, Doris, 57, 63, 204
Kirchon, V., 185–86
Kismet, 94

Kitchin, Claude, 39, 45, 47, 50–51, 201
Klaw, Marc, 42–43, 50, 101
Klein, Charles, 100, 210
Koch, Howard, 183, 221
Krutch, Joseph Wood, 18, 32, 134

Labiche, Eugene, 60
Ladies' Night, 56–58, 67, 69–70, 192
Lang, Fritz, 120
Larrie, Jack, 56, 192
Laska, Edward, 60, 150–51, 164
Lawson, John Howard, 73, 119, 123–24,
    128, 130–33, 136–37, 139, 141, 148–49,
    152–54, 158–59, 177, 180, 186
Leamy, Hugh, 90
Le Gallienne, Eva, 175
Leonard, Robert Z., 89
Levey, Harold, 146
Levine, Ira, 156
Lewisohn, Ludwig, 123–24, 175
Life of Man, The, 104–05, 127, 211
Light, James, 116–17, 127, 133–34
Lightnin', 40
Like a King, 143
Liliom, 113–15, 212
Lister, Walter, 36, 154–56
Littell, Robert, 132, 180
Little Belgian, The, 13
Loud Speaker, 177–78
Luck of the Navy, The, 9
Lunt, Alfred, 17
Lure, The, 76
Lusitania, 99–101
Luxemburg, Rosa, 38

McAdoo, William, 71, 84–88
MacArthur, Charles, 182–83
Macbeth, 94, 107, 109–11, 115, 121, 135
Macgowan, Kenneth, 43, 69, 71, 83, 91,
    107, 117, 122, 127, 131, 166, 177, 220
McGrath, Harold, 169
Machinal, 137–40, 158, 161, 216
MacKaye, Percy, 103, 211
Maeterlinck, Maurice, 105
Magical City, The, 103
Major Barbara, 12
Man and the Masses, 118, 130–31, 177

Man of Mode, The, 61
Man Who Married a Dumb Wife, The,
    96–97, 122, 210
Manners, J. Hartley, 9, 16, 194
Mantell, Robert, 44
Mantle, Burns, 32
Marco Millions, 158, 218
Markey, Enid, 63
Marriage on Approval, 73
Marsh, Leo, 64
Martin, John J., 168
Mask of Hamlet, The, 168–69
Mason, Jeffry, 129
Massey, Edward, 136
Matthews, Adelaide, 56–57, 192
Matthews, Brander, 79
Maya, 76
Mayo, Margaret, 55–56, 58, 191
Maytime, 15
Mazer, Cary, 98
Meinhard, Carl, 122
Melting Pot, The, 183
Merchant of Venice, The, 47
Meteor, 141, 161–162
Metropolis, 120
Meyer, Annie Nathan, 60, 146–48
Meyerhold, Vsevolod, 136–37, 177, 216
Midsummer Night's Dream, A, 98, 105
Millay, Edna St. Vincent, 26, 28
Minden, Michael, 112
Miracle, The, 95
Moeller, Philip, 104, 120, 125–26, 131–33,
    149
Molière, 105
Molnar, Ferenc, 113–14
Moloch, 11–12
Morrison, Frank, 45
Moscow Art Theatre, 117, 165, 176
Mother's Liberty Bond, 9
Mrs Warren's Profession, 76, 84, 89
Murdock, Frank, 185

Naughty Wife, The, 56, 191
Nazimova, Alla, 11, 13
Neighborhood Playhouse, 96–99, 103, 115
Nellie, the Beautiful Cloak Model, 77

New Playwrights' Theatre, 136–37, 166, 177, 180, 219
Night at an Inn, A, 103
Night Lodging, 106, 167
Night of January 16, The, 77–78
Nightie Night, 57, 62, 66, 192
Nijinsky, Vaslav, 103
No More Blondes, 56, 67, 89, 192

Odets, Clifford, 186
On Trial, 102, 125
O'Neill, Eugene, 3, 5, 11, 18, 22–23, 31, 46, 60–61, 69, 73–77, 83, 89, 93, 103, 107–09, 114, 116–19, 125, 127–28, 134–36, 139, 144, 148, 154, 158, 175–77
Open House, 152
Ordynski, Richard, 95
Our American Cousin, 99–100
Our Little Wife, 55–56, 65, 191
Ouspensky, A., 185–86
Out There, 9, 12
Over the Top, 9, 15–16
Ozieblo, Barbara, 114–15, 213

Palmer, A. Mitchell, 164, 172
Paris Bound, 142
Parlor, Bedroom and Bath, 57–58, 191
Passing Shows, The, 16, 95, 196
Perry, Ralph, 167
Peter Pan, 105
Pink Lady, The, 65, 204
Pirandello, Luigi, 134
Pirchan, Emil, 118
Pitoëff, Georges, 117–18
Platoon, 32
Poldekin, 171–73, 182, 220
Pollock, Channing, 107
Polly Preferred, 150–51, 218
Poor Little Rich Girl, The, 101, 109, 115
Processional, 120–21, 131–33, 148, 152–53, 167, 177–78
Proctor, Thomas, 50
Prohibition, 5, 38, 46, 50, 52, 58, 79, 82
Provincetown Players, 26, 28, 96, 99, 103, 107, 114, 116, 127, 175, 197–98
Puss in Boots, 128

Quinn, Arthur Hobson, 35

Rabkin, Gerald, 178
Rambeau, Marjorie, 65, 204
Rappe, Virginia, 80–81
Red Dawn, The, 100, 168, 170–71, 220
Red Rust, 185–86
Redemption, 39–40, 102, 106–07, 211
Reicher, Frank, 113, 118–19, 122–24
Reichman, Arthur, 13
Reid, Louis, 18
Reinhardt, Max, 93–99, 102, 117, 128, 130
Reisner, Christian, 50
Rice, Elmer, 73, 102, 114, 118–19, 124–26, 128, 139, 148–50, 153, 161, 177, 183, 186–87, 211
Richard III, 106–07, 118, 121, 130
Riders to the Sea, 93
Rinehart, Mary Roberts, 78, 169
Rising, Lawrence, 56, 58, 191
Roger Bloomer, 123–25, 130, 137, 148–49, 152
Romberg, Sigmund, 15–16, 196, 203
Roosevelt, Theodore, 10
Rosenberg, James, 154
Rostand, Edmond, 105
Rubenstein, Lenny, 111
Ruggles, Charles, 65–66
R.U.R., 120–21, 125, 213–14
Rutherston, Albert, 97, 210

Sacco and Vanzetti, 164–65, 178–79, 221
Sadie Love, 56, 65, 71, 191
Sanger, Margaret, 6, 66–67, 80
Sardou, Victorien, 60
Scarborough, George, 76, 168
Scheglov, Dmitry, 185
Scrambled Wives, 56, 60, 192
Sears, Zelda, 59, 145–47, 217
Selwyn and Company, 54, 65, 77, 191
Sex, 54
Shaffer, Peter, 106
Shaw, George Bernard, 12, 76, 96–97, 116
Shaw, Mary, 76, 89
Shearer, Norma, 89
Sheridan, Richard Brinsley, 60
Sherwood, Robert, 112

Shipman, Samuel, 14, 151
Show of Wonders, The, 16
Showboat, 54
Show-off, The, 29
Shubert brothers, 16, 42, 73, 95, 101, 192
Sievers, David, 114–15
Sifton, Paul, 136, 156–57, 180
Simmons, F. M., 40, 51
Simonson, Lee, 93–94, 96, 102, 113, 116, 118–20, 125–26, 130–31, 149
Sinclair, Upton, 137, 172, 181–82
Singing Jailbirds, 137, 181–82, 184, 221
Six Cylinder Love, 57
Skinner, Richard Dana, 131–32, 153
Sleepless Night, A, 57, 192, 203
Smith, Alison, 148
Sobel, Bernard, 67
Son-Daughter, The, 168
Spoils of War, The, 11, 194
Spook Sonata, The, 127–28, 214
Spread Eagle, 36, 154–56, 159, 161–62
Stallings, Laurence, 3, 7, 11, 32–36, 199
Stanley, Martha, 56–57, 192
Stern, Ernst, 95–96, 209–10
Steuer, Max D., 84, 87
Strange Interlude, 77, 194
Street Scene, 150, 183, 187
Strindberg, August, 22, 127–28, 213–14
Strohbach, Hans, 118
Subway, The, 126, 148, 161
Sumner, John S., 85, 88–90
Sumurun, 94–95, 97, 122, 128, 210
Sun-Up, 28–29, 198
Susman, Warren, 4, 70, 75, 142
Swan, Mark, 56, 58, 191
Synge, John Millington, 93

Tarkington, Booth, 17–18, 172–73, 182
Taylor, Laurette, 9, 194
Théâtre du Vieux Colombier, 105, 117
Theatre Guild, 113, 115, 118–22, 125–26, 130–31, 177, 186, 211
Theatrical Syndicate, 38, 101
They Knew What They Wanted, 76, 89, 121, 194
Thompson, Woodman, 94, 124, 129–30
Three Plays for a Negro Theatre, 93

Throckmorton, Cleon, 94, 108, 115, 127
Tieck, Ludwig, 128
To the Ladies, 144–45, 217, 220
Toklas, Alice B., 55
Toller, Ernst, 118, 130–31, 177, 180
Tolstoy, Leo, 102
Torrence, Ridgely, 93
Torres, H. Z., 69–70, 83–84, 147–48
Towse, J. Ranken, 82
Treadwell, Sophie, 73, 137–40, 158, 161
Trial of Mary Dugan, The, 77
Trilby, 61
Truex, Ernest, 65–66
Tuchman, Barbara, 7
Turgenev, Ivan, 125
Twin Beds, 55

Under Fire, 8, 12, 195
Up in Mabel's Room, 40, 54, 56, 61–65, 68–70, 191
Urban, Joseph, 103

Veiller, Bayard, 76
Verge, The, 28, 114–15, 139, 198, 211
Vienna Lusthaus, 123
Vollmer, Lula, 28–29, 93

Wales Padlock Law, 3, 76–77, 90
Walker, Stuart, 103
Wall Street, 154
Walter, Eugene, 169
War Brides, 11
Washington Square Players, 99, 103–04, 127
Watch Your Neighbor, 16–17
Waterloo Bridge, 36
Way of the World, The, 61
Wayfarer, The, 168, 219
Wedekind, Frank, 101
Welded, 128
Wentworth, Marion Craig, 11
West, Mae, 54
We've Got to Have Money, 60, 150–51, 164, 184
What Price Glory, 3, 7–9, 11, 31–36, 76
What's Your Husband Doing? 57, 191
White Feather, The, 14

Whitney, Claire, 63
Wiene, Robert, 111
Wilkinson, Norman, 97–98
Williams, Tennessee, 73, 123, 194
Wilson, Edmund, 9, 179
Wilson, Eileen, 67
Wilson, William B., 164
Wilson, Woodrow, 13, 19, 30, 38, 42–45,
    51, 116, 142, 155, 167–68, 179, 194–95
Wings over Europe, 36
Winterset, 180, 221
Wisdom Tooth, The, 153–54
Wolf, Rennold, 67
Wolheim, Louis, 117

Woman in Room 13, The, 40
Woods, Al, 9, 14, 41, 54, 63–65, 67–68, 71,
    73, 77–90, 141, 191–92, 204
Woollcott, Alexander, 12, 17, 24, 26, 71, 93,
    110, 113, 115, 147, 151, 168–69, 174

Yellow Sands, The, 177
Yip, Yip, Yaphank, 15
Young, Roland, 65–66
Young, Stark, 122, 133

Zangwill, Israel, 183
Ziegfeld, Florenz, 14, 41–42, 45, 61, 197
Ziegfeld Follies, 15, 42, 63, 73, 196, 197